The German-Jewish Experience Revisited

Perspectives on Jewish Texts and Contexts

Edited by
Vivian Liska

Volume 3

The German-Jewish Experience Revisited

Edited by
Steven E. Aschheim
Vivian Liska

In cooperation with the
Leo Baeck Institute Jerusalem

DE GRUYTER

Leo Baeck Institute Jerusalem
for the Study of German
and Central European Jewry

In cooperation with the Leo Baeck Institute Jerusalem.

ISBN 978-3-11-037293-9
e-ISBN (PDF) 978-3-11-036719-5
e-ISBN (EPUB) 978-3-11-039332-3
ISSN 2199-6962

Library of Congress Cataloging-in-Publication Data
A CIP catalog record for this book has been applied for at the Library of Congress.

Bibliographic information published by the Deutsche Nationalbibliothek
The Deutsche Nationalbibliothek lists this publication in the Deutsche Nationalbibliografie;
detailed bibliographic data are available on the Internet at http://dnb.dnb.de.

© 2015 Walter de Gruyter GmbH, Berlin/Boston
Cover image: bpk / Staatsbibliothek zu Berlin
Typesetting: PTP-Berlin, Protago-TEX-Production GmbH, Berlin
Printing and binding: CPI books GmbH, Leck
♾ Printed on acid-free paper
Printed in Germany

www.degruyter.com

MIX
Papier aus verantwor-
tungsvollen Quellen
FSC® C083411

Preface

The essays in this volume derive partially from the Robert Liberles International Summer Research Workshop of the Leo Baeck Institute Jerusalem, 11–25 July 2013. In addition to the papers presented at the workshop, we have included a few extra contributions that round out our reflections. The workshop and the present volume aim at revisiting interesting and important aspects of the German-Jewish experience and evaluating the present state of the field. Senior and junior scholars from Israel, Germany, and the United States all contributed to this work. We shall not summarize the arguments and theses of the essays in this collection. After all, what would be the point of reading them if one knows in advance what they are going to say? Readers will, no doubt, perceive some methodological, analytic, generational, and national divergences in these pieces but what emerges clearly is the ongoing vitality of this field, which in many ways is in transition. New paradigms, methods, and approaches co-exist with other more familiar and tried analyses. In the Postscript, we try to provide a retrospective account of the state of things as reflected in this volume.

We would like to acknowledge the generous support of the Leo Baeck Institute Jerusalem, particularly the encouragement and organizational help of Dr. Anja Siegemund. We are most grateful to Dr. Ulrike Krauss, our main contact person with our publisher de Gruyter for her commitment to the book series "Perspectives on Jewish texts and contexts" and for accompanying every stage of the production process of this volume. Above all, we want to thank Dr. Stefani Hoffman, who did much more for this book than her work as text editor would have required. With utmost professionalism and a fine sense for language, she painstakingly went through every line of the manuscript, suggested corrections and revisions at every level and contributed immensely to improving this book.

Contents

Ofri Ilany

The Jews as Educators of Humanity – a Christian-Philosemitic Grand Narrative of Jewish Modernity?

In a famous passage in his memoir *From Berlin to Jerusalem*, Gershom Scholem portrays the assimilated character of his parents' house. Scholem recalls how his father Arthur Scholem mocked the prohibition of smoking on the Sabbath and used the Sabbath candles to light a cigar. On the other hand, once or twice a year, the father "used to make a speech at the dinner table, praising the mission of the Jews. According to him, the mission was to proclaim to the world pure monotheism and a purely rational morality" (Scholem 1988, 11). In Scholem's description, the ideal of the "Jewish mission" was almost the only trace of Judaism left in his father's way of life. The renowned scholar, however, was far from enthusiastic about this ideal. Scholem cites this remark as an example of his father's typical shallow, bourgeois notion of Judaism.

Whether we accept Scholem's judgment or not, this paragraph distinctively depicts the role of this ideal within the worldview of educated German Jews by the turn of the nineteenth century. The notion of the Jewish people's universal mission is a most dominant theme in modern Jewish thought and culture from the time of the Haskalah, whose prevalence in the nineteenth and early twentieth century cannot be overestimated. The universal mission of the Jews is one of the grand narratives of modern Jewish culture.

The view of Jewish existence as an enterprise aimed at benefiting humanity played an important role in the formation of various modern Jewish identities. As Leila Gürkan (2009) shows, the modern age saw a shift in the Jewish understanding of the notion of chosenness from "holiness" to "mission." Whereas Orthodox Judaism could lean on traditional justifications for the Jews' chosenness, other post-Enlightenment streams needed this discourse in order to prove their worthiness as Jews in the face of antisemitism and conversion and to secure their symbolic place within European culture. In this context, the formulation of Judaism as a universal project functioned as an important axis of identity. As argued by Richard Cohen (2008, 12), the discourse of the Jews' contribution to civilization "significantly penetrated the sense of self of many Jews and sensitized others, consciously and subconsciously, to confront the question, time and again, of their sense of belonging to a particular society." A collection of texts dedicated to this theme could form a rich anthology, as many of the major modern Jewish thinkers attempted to define the essence of Israel's vocation.

Obviously, the "Jewish mission" is only a general conceptual framework whose actual components vary significantly among writers. One way to map this discourse is by distinguishing between conceptions of the religious role of Judaism in history on the one hand, and "secularized" visions of the Jewish people's quest on the other. The first variation, focusing on the role of *Judaism*, is an essential element in the writings of major Jewish scholars and rabbis of different religious streams. Typically, Samson Raphael Hirsch argues that Israel's mission is "to be the bearer of the Almighty's teachings regarding God and man's mission" and "to teach, by one's destiny and way of life, that there is a higher goal than wealth and pleasure, science and culture" (Hirsch 1995, 198).

Simultaneously, from the middle of the nineteenth century, socialist, liberal, nationalist and other intellectuals proposed many non-religious versions of the Jewish mission. In place of monotheism, these programs hail other features of Jewish existence and attribute universal significance to Jewish culture, the Jews as nation, and individual Jews. A few distinctive examples demonstrate the diversity of this discourse: Ludwig Philippson (1911), in his 1861 work *The Industrial Mission of the Jews* [Die industrielle Mission der Juden] argued that the Jew's mission in history was to bring the economic ideas of the East, particularly banking, to "sluggish medieval Europe." During World War I, Socialist leader Eduard Bernstein (1917) attributed the "universalist mission of world peace" to the Jews as the "born mediators between nations," and psychoanalyst Otto Rank (1981) saw the role of the Jews in spreading "primitive sexuality" – an antidote to the growing sexual repression in European society.

In this essay, I shall outline the genesis of the modern "Jewish mission" narrative. Actually, primitive theological views regarding the Jews' role among the nations have a long tradition within Judaism ever since the biblical idea of *or lagoyim* (a light unto the nations), and later in Tannaic literature, in the notion of "Torah for the entire world" [Torah lekol baei olam] (Hirshman 1999). Variations on these notions appeared in medieval Jewish philosophy and in the kabbalistic literature, or even earlier. I should like to follow a different path, or different historical continuity, however, in tracing the genealogy of this concept – a path that I consider more relevant to the German context. I argue that primarily Protestant writers of the *Aufklärung* conceived the view of the Jews as "teachers of humanity." Broadly sketching the traditional Christian view of Israel's chosenness, I shall present the transformation that this image underwent during the early modern age. I maintain that Gotthold Ephraim Lessing and other German Enlightenment theologians and philosophers forged the modern narrative of Israel's universal mission, mainly in order to defend the biblical tradition against rationalist and deist criticism. Finally, I shall demonstrate how nineteenth-century Jewish intellectuals adopted this image, using it for their own ends.

1 From *Verehrung Gottes* to *Weltweisheit*

As noted by Nils Roemer (2005, 16), until the end of the eighteenth century, Jewish history was regarded as the realm of God's action – for Jews and Christians alike. According to the traditional Christian concept of salvation history, the People of Israel were endowed with a definite, central role as God's chosen people and as the first "nation of believers." This view emphasized Abraham's universal role as "the father of believers" [*Vater der Gläubigen*], God's instrument for delivering the true faith to humanity, "that the blessing of Abraham might come on the Gentiles through Jesus Christ" (Galatians 3:14). According to this notion, God's covenant with Abraham inaugurated the third chapter in his relationship with humanity, following those with Adam and with Noah.

Many orthodox Christian theologians of the eighteenth century also adhered to this belief. For instance, the chronicle *Introduction to Universal History* [Einleitung zu der Universal-Historie], published by Pietist scholar Johann Friedrich Hochstetter (1698–?) in 1740, explains Abraham's appearance on the stage of history solely within the context of the history of faith: "From the moment humans began to disperse across the earth, they gradually forgot God and became more and more immersed in despicable idolatry; and that is what made God take Abraham, son of Terah, out of Chaldea, where his community had dwelt, and reestablish in his home the rite of the true god" (Hochstetter 1740, 7).

This narrative, which features in the many biblical chronicles written in the context of sacred history, attributes one basic meaning to the Israelites' origin: humanity's first shedding of idolatry and ignorance, which was to culminate with the arrival of Christ. Abraham's appearance on the historical scene signifies the transformation from an age of idolatry to an age of belief in the True God [*Verehrung des wahren Gottes*]. Many of these texts, therefore, include an extensive description of the expansion of idolatry in the stage preceding the Israelites' history.

Church historians generally held the view that the sons of Ham – especially the Egyptians and the Canaanites – spread idolatry in the world. Belief in the one true God remained intact only among the sons of Shem, even while idolatry spread among the rest of humankind. This account, therefore, deals with the transmission of tradition, religion, faith, or ancient divine knowledge. It accords Abraham and his progeny a special place at the center of world history for their sole function as bearers of the faith. The narrative presents Abraham as a link in a chain beginning with Adam and Noah and continuing through David and Jesus. Whether depicting a seamless transmission of knowledge from Noah to Abraham or describing the renewal of the True Faith following God's revelation to Abraham, this traditional description of the Patriarch answers the question of the sources and the roots of faith.

Changes in the storyline of human history in the early modern era undermined the Israelites' status as a nation of believers elected by God. The causal, naturalistic description of history demanded that writers stick to natural explanations, feeding into a rationalist theology that undermined the legitimacy of particular election. Tracts published in the Netherlands, France, and England as early as the first half of the seventeenth century rejected the Jewish people's special status in history (Mitchell 2012). Spinoza formulated the most resounding attack on the traditional concept of the Jews' election in *Tractatus Theologico-Politicus*, rejecting the assertion that God chose the Hebrews above all nations and claiming that this kind of choice would run contrary to God's nature. Spinoza (1989, 89) portrayed the Hebrews as a childish, vulgar people, contending that it was actually Moses who had chosen them, to bind them to his rules and convince them to uphold the covenant.

The German republic of letters, however, generally rejected Spinoza's ideas. As Ernst Cassirer demonstrated, the German Enlightenment traced its origins not to Spinoza but to the intellectual tradition of the Reformation. The aim of Enlightenment scholars, subsequently, was not to deconstruct the text and undermine its authority and supremacy but rather to distill its original meaning while dismantling the hermeneutic roadblocks barring access to it (Cassirer 1951, 187–194). Well into the 1770s, scholars in German universities were very careful not to topple fully the edifice of salvation history or the biblical Israelites' role in it.

Major essays of the period awarded the Israelites a new role – harbingers of the Enlightenment. This idea had many different manifestations of which some were closer to traditional Christian historical schemes while others were formulated on a "philosophical," i.e., rationality-based, conceptual system. The roots of these theories derive from the writings of Renaissance and Baroque-era Christian Kabbalists and Hebraists who wished to narrate the transmission of ancient knowledge or religion, of *prisca theologia* or *philosophia perennis* from Adam through to Abraham and Moses.[1]

One of the most prominent figures of the early German Enlightenment and of Classicism, Johann Christoph Gottsched (1700–1766), claimed in 1733 that Hebrew philosophy was the most ancient in existence – except for that of the Chaldeans. According to Gottsched, Abraham's family retained many of the inventions that had been known to humanity before the Deluge (and later subsequently lost), passing them down from father to son. Abraham brought this

---

1 See *Mulsow* (2005, 181–211).

wisdom, albeit "slightly imperfect" [*etwas unvollkommene*], over to Palestine. His family members developed additional ideas to ease mankind's life, especially in the realms of morality and the economy (Gottsched 1777, 18).

Gottsched's work replaces the Chosen People's religious calling with *Weltweisheit*, a term denoting a moral – but not a religious – philosophy.[2] In 1750, Friedrich Andreas Walther (1727–1769), who headed Göttingen's philosophy faculty, published an entire essay devoted to the wisdom of the Hebrews, "The History of the Ancient Hebrews' Wisdom" [Geschichte der Weltweisheit der alten Hebräer]. He describes Abraham as the first philosopher of the era following the Deluge:

> If we opt not to reduce the meaning of the word philosopher [...] it could include Abraham, as well. Scripture describes him as a man endowed with exceptional wisdom and intelligence [...]. In ancient times just as in new, it could not have escaped people's attention that Abraham must be regarded as one of the great philosophers, as well as the man responsible for bringing all wisdoms to the Orient at large (Walther 1750, 18).

In the same spirit, the Israelites as a whole are described as a nation of philosophers – the bearers of reason in the ignorance-stricken post-Diluvian world.

2 Lessing's "future educators"

This secularized version of sacred history, however, was difficult to reconcile with certain developments in the discipline of *Orientalistik*, which stressed the similarity between the Hebrews and other Oriental "nature peoples." The transformation of Orientalism into a distinct academic field of expertise in the eighteenth century led to the formation of the modern Orientalist worldview that rigidly associated the nature of the "Orientals" with sensuality, coarseness, and fanaticism. Once championed, "Oriental wisdom" [*Orientalische Weisheit*] was now ironically invoked to represent excess and fantasy.[3]

Simultaneously, in the mid-eighteenth century, a proliferation of iconoclastic attacks on the Bible and on the idea of the Chosen People appeared in different European countries. Voltaire's invective, published in 1765 in his *La philosophie de l'histoire* under the title "De Bram, Abram, Abraham" (1765, 106–108), was, perhaps, the most provocative. He claimed that Abraham was, in fact, an ancient Indian wise man whose name was connected to Brahma or the Brahmins. In Vol-

---

2 On the meaning of the term, see Carhart (2007, 200–201).
3 See Polaschegg (2005, 15–18); Toomer (1996, 309–313). See also Said (1978, 117–123).

taire's version, the Hebrews appropriated the figure of the Oriental wise man to add to their people's importance.

German Bible scholars were, overall, hesitant to join these attacks; they were busy striving for a historicizing of biblical description and its rational incorporation into contemporary anthropological models of their time and scheme of the natural development of humanity. Although they used similar methods and were influenced by the skeptical essays that attacked the Old Testament's authenticity, these scholars pursued an opposite goal: rather than undermine biblical description, they sought to establish the Patriarchs' narrative as historical past. As Carhart has stated (2007, 5–9), to fully explain the scholarly motivations of many of the eighteenth-century German scholars, we must differentiate between their ideas of criticism (*Kritik*) and skepticism (*Skeptizismus*). In many cases, they were attempting to guard traditional historical conceptions from the new skeptical stances that eschewed the credibility and authenticity of biblical description. The new Orientalist image of the Bible forced central scholars of the German Enlightenment to formulate new apologia of Revelation, the Bible, and the Hebrew people at its center.

Gotthold Ephraim Lessing (1729–1781) elaborated this developmental scheme of the Hebrew people's history in *The Education of the Human Race* (1957) [Die Erziehung des Menschengeschlechts], which was to become the canonical manifesto of German Protestant Rationalism. Lessing reinterpreted the idea of Revelation, describing it as the gradual development of the human mind from savagery to rationality and refinement. "What education [*Erziehung*] is to the individual, Revelation is to all humankind," he states in the essay's opening sentence. Lessing thus formulated a new philosophical version of salvation history in which the Israelites still play a major role. God chose this people as educators of humankind:

> He selected an individual People for His special education; and that exactly the most rude [*ungeschliffenste*] and the most unruly [*verwildertste*], in order to begin with it from the very commencement. This was the Hebrew People [...].But, it will be asked, to what purpose was this education of so rude a people, a people with whom God had to begin so entirely from the beginning? I reply, in order that in the process of time, He might employ particular members of this nation as the Teachers of other people. He was bringing up in them the future Teachers of the human race. It was the Jews who became their teachers, none but Jews; only men out of a people so brought up, could be their teachers (Lessing 1957, 82).[4]

As Jonathan Israel has stated (2011, 317–318), although opposed to Lutheran orthodoxy, Lessing was also at odds with the Deists in his desire to avoid direct

---

4 On Lessing's view of Judaism's role in history, see also Taubes (2009, 131–137).

confrontation with theology. Aiming at bridging the gap between the rationalist worldview and religious tradition, Lessing merges the revelation story of "God's people" with its modern description as a primitive people gradually refined. He defends the role of "The Israelite people" [*das Israelitische Volk*] in the process of Revelation, but stops short of defending the Hebrew people itself. In this version, God had chosen a people "still so fully in its infancy" [Noch so völlig in seiner Kindheit] to spread rationality in humanity and begin the process of universal education. The next step would be the Christian Revelation, which, in turn, would be replaced by a new religion to bring the process of education to its ultimate completion. Both the Old and the New Testament attain significance as essential steps on the way to the "Third Age." Each of them "contributes its own individual share" to humanity's perfection.[5]

As noted by Gerd Hillen (1986, 194), Lessing's celebrated ideal of religious tolerance is selective: He did not tolerate what he considered false. According to Lessing's historical scheme, the development of the human race from polytheism, through Judaism and Christianity, to an Enlightened Christian "Gospel of Reason" parallels the tortuous course of human development from birth through childhood to manhood. In this process, the Jewish people represent the childhood of humanity. Lessing continues: "He neither could nor would reveal Himself any more to each individual man; He selected an individual People for His special education; and that exactly the rudest and the most unruly, in order to begin with it from the very commencement" (Lessing 1957, § 8).

According to Lessing (1957, § 91), "It is not true that the shortest line is always the straight one." The Israelites were to become the Chosen People because they were "so crass and unfit for abstract thought" [so roh, so ungeschickt zu abgezogen Gedanken], i.e., at the very earliest stage of education (Lessing, 1957, § 18). In this view, Lessing (1957, § 11) seems to be following Spinoza, who also argued that God revealed Himself to the Hebrews at first as "only the God of their forebears," i.e., as Jehovah, the strongest of all other gods, out of consideration for their low level of abstract thought.

Lessing's essay, which touches on the philosophical meaning of almost every aspect of Enlightenment thought, illustrates the supreme importance accorded to ancient Israel in German Enlightenment's depiction of historical development; it also shows the complex stance of this philosophical milieu vis-à-vis the Jewish people.

Other writers interpreted the Hebrew's role as humanity's first educators differently. In an essay published in 1790 entitled "The Vocation of Moses" (*Die*

---

5 See also Hillen (1986, 186–197).

Sendung Moses),[6] Friedrich Schiller (1759–1805) contended that Moses' founding of the Jewish state [jüdischer Staat] was one of the most important events in history because of its implications for the whole world (Schiller 1802, 2). The Jews spread throughout the world the idea of the One True God, and thus not only is Moses's constitution the basis of the two religions reigning over most of the world, but also "we should thank it for a significant part of the Enlightenment [*Aufklärung*] we enjoy today" (Schiller 1802, 2). In light of this, Schiller formulates a representative image of the Hebrews' role in history:

> When examined from this standpoint, the Hebrew nation appears as an important people in world history. All of the ills traditionally associated with it, and all of the efforts of the wittiest of writers to disparage it, will not sway us from judging it fairly. The wretchedness and contemptuousness of this nation cannot undo the legislator's sublime calling, nor the great influence rightly attributed to this nation on world history. We must regard it as the conduit through which Divine Providence chose to transmit to us the dearest of values, the Truth. But Divine Providence broke this conduit after its calling was fulfilled (Schiller 1802, 3).

The Hebrew nation is, in this account, but a vessel entrusted with a precious treasure. The Hebrews thus have a decisive role in universal history, but not through any intrinsic virtues or skills of their own, rather *despite* their vile, coarse character. According to Schiller (1802, 3), that is the reason why God shattered this vessel after it had fulfilled its goal. The Hebrew nation itself is worthless and gains its meaning only within the context of historical development. The significance of the Hebrews rest solely upon their historical role in world history, while their specific characteristics are worthless.

Despite the differing worldviews and emphases, all of the descriptions quoted thus far posit the ancient Hebrews as a people entrusted with the universal task of educating humanity. Despite their limitations, the Hebrews were the ones who brought a gospel of universal rational religion transcending regional differences to point to humanity's oneness. The biblical story of the Israelites' origin, denuded of its timeless status as sacred history existing in absolute time and interpreted allegorically and typologically, is now awarded new meaning as one segment at the basis of civilization's natural development. It had become a source, an *Ursprung*, a loaded story from the dawn of humankind, thus testifying to the modern era's origins. German Enlightenment scholars placed the Hebrews within the history of reason, awarding them a newfound role in the history of Enlightenment itself.

---

6 On this text, see Hartwich (1997).

The Education of the Human Race is rarely listed among Lessing's philosemitic works, which include the play *The Jews* [Die Juden] and, of course, *Nathan the Wise* [Nathan der Weise]. Indeed, unlike those two works, which express a liberal, universalist idea of tolerance towards the Jews as humans, *The Education of the Human Race* is structured according to a particularistic notion. As part of his secularized history of redemption, Lessing presents the Jews as the people chosen by God to receive his "special education." He further contends that in the Jews, God was cultivating "the future Teachers of the human race," among them Moses, Jesus, and, perhaps implicitly, Spinoza.

The Christian narratives presented thus far point to the ancient Hebrews as key players in the universal process of educating humanity. The people of Israel, despite their limitations, bore the message of a rational universal religion that transcends local differences and paved the way to uniting the human race in its entirety. Appraised for their contribution to world education [*Weltaufklärung*], the Hebrews are hailed as the representatives of progress in the dark days of early history.

Another influential approach that emerged by the 1780s was Johann Gottfried Herder's *national* reading of Israel's history. Herder's book *Vom Geist der Ebraïschen Poesie* (Herder 1782) offers a novel perspective on the Hebrew people's function: he praises them not for their role as a disseminator of the universal religion but rather as a model for a *national* religion, a *national* culture. He considers their uniqueness and particularity, qualities so reviled by Enlightenment writers, as those that endow the Hebrew legacy with its universal power.

3 First revelation or "oriental jumble"?

Clearly, prominent German Enlightenment authors attributed special importance to the people of Israel's role in history. Gottsched, Lessing, Herder, Schiller, and many minor writers who were not mentioned here held that the Hebrews, despite their crass nature, played a pivotal role in universal history as educators of the human race: they were the ones who eventually delivered the gospel of a universal religion of reason to the world.

In order to contextualize the origin of the Jewish mission discourse, it is important to consider various opposing views regarding the Israelites' role. Several German anti-clerical writers, including Johann Christian Edelmann (1698–1767) and Hermann Samuel Reimarus (1694–1768), adopted the Deists' attacks on the Old Testament. Although those figures remained out of the German intellectual mainstream, they did have a noteworthy impact on the most important figure of the German Enlightenment, Immanuel Kant. In his 1770s lectures on anthropology, Kant (1928, 15: 345; Stangneth 2001, 27–29) argued that Oriental peoples are incapable of rational thinking, and he implicitly referred to the Old Testament as "oriental jumble" [*orientalischer Kram*]. He attacked the biblical legacy more explicitly in his *Religion within the Boundaries of Mere Reason* (1793). In this book, Kant celebrates a theological ideal of a "rational religion" [*Vernunftreligion*] that will be built upon the lower rungs of existing historical religions. In many aspects, Kant presents a more systematic phrasing of Lessing's *Education of the Human Race* unlike Lessing, however, Kant excludes Judaism from the religious progression. He describes the "Jewish faith" as a mere political constitution of a "specific tribe" [*besonderer Stamm*]:

> Strictly speaking, Judaism is not a religion at all but simply the union of a number of individuals who, since they belonged to a particular stock, established themselves into a community under purely political laws, hence not into a church [...]. Moreover, whereas no religion can be conceived without faith in a future life, Judaism as such, taken in its purity, entails absolutely no religious faith (Kant 1998, 130–131).

Kant does not merely contrast Judaism to his "true universal religion"; he also argues that Judaism has "no essential connection" to the development of the Christian faith, and, accordingly, to universal ethics. Members of the emerging Jewish *Bürgertum* found this claim, made by the most prominent representative of German philosophy, particularly offensive. As noted by Michael Graetz (1977, 4: 273–95), Jewish intellectuals were far from indifferent to this assessment of Judaism within the contemporary systems of *Geschichtsphilosophie*. This background explains why Lessing's evaluation of the Jews' contribution to the process of *Weltaufklärung* meant so much to Jewish thinkers around 1800. Even though Lessing's narrative locates the Jews at a primitive phase in the process of revelation/education, it nevertheless acknowledges their role in the salvation of humanity and integrates them into a continuum with Christianity and the imminent universal religion. Moreover, as the concept of *Bildung* played a major role in the self-perception of the Jewish middle class, the portrayal of the Jews as "educators" suited this ideal.[7]

The notion of the Jews' universal mission of education offered a solution to the fundamental tension that many educated Jews experienced between the pursuit of universalism and the insistence on a particular Jewish way of existence and a particular Jewish path in history. Accordingly, Jewish intellectuals sketched their own versions of universal history, endowing the Jews with a strategic role

---

7 See, for example, Mendes-Flohr (1999).

in the formation of civilization. An early example is *Leviathan* by Saul Ascher (1767–1822), published in 1792 (Ascher 1792, 104). This theological-political work was written under Kantian influence, but, unlike his mentor, the Jewish philosopher granted a crucial role to the Israelites, claiming that God gave Judaism to a certain group of people in order to teach them to live together socially or "grow accustomed to social life" [*zum gesellschaftlichen Leben*] after the devastation of the flood.

The second half of the nineteenth century saw several Jewish treatises formulated according to the "education" narrative, for instance, Moses Hess' early work *The Holy History of Mankind* (Hess 2004). Known as the first socialist revolutionary tract published in Germany, the treatise is an exceptional example of a Jewish attempt to relocate Jewish history within the general, i.e., Christian, history of humanity. Following Lessing, Hess' historical narrative consists of three parts: the period of the God the Father, beginning with Adam and continuing through the history of the Israelites; of the Son, beginning with the birth of Jesus and continuing through to the Middle Ages; and of the Holy Spirit, beginning with the birth of "our master Spinoza" and extending to the present. As shown by Jan Eike Dunkhase (2013, 47), Hess incorporates the Jewish philosopher as a crucial link in his eschatological process of history. Moses, Jesus, and Spinoza represent the three major leaps in human progress.

Hess' account of humanity's history seems like an odd combination of unorthodox philosophical naturalism and pious providential idealism. The narrative echoes the idea of the Jews as teachers of humanity, particularly in the very last paragraph of the book, according to which: "This nation has been summoned from the very beginning to conquer the world [...] through the inner virtue of its spirit" (Hess 2004, 95).

Hess' endeavor to invest the Jews with a crucial role in human history is manifest in his interpretation at the start of the book of the first chapters of Genesis. He reintegrates Hebrew history into universal history by presenting the biblical narrative as an allegory or prototype of greater social and political processes. Hess depicts God's revelation to Abraham as the first stage in humanity's redemption from political and social slavery. Abraham – traditionally considered the first monotheist – appears here as the first free man, a man whom God "had set apart from the great mass of idol worshipers and slaves" (Hess 2004, 9). Identifying the Mosaic Law as the next step in this process, Hess describes it as the first attempt, and the most daring one, to cope with the social inequality that had resulted from humankind's political fall after the flood. Hess thus originally structures humanity's history around the mission of the Jews, portraying the people of Israel as the main protagonist in the history of civilization. Second, he assigns the Jewish people a particular mission: the forbearers of social and political justice.

4 Conclusion: the modern Jew and the Judeo-centric tradition

I have demonstrated how the image of the people of Israel as the teacher of the human race was conceived, or at least molded, within the Christian *Aufklärung* discourse, as part of an attempt to defend the traditional sacred history against skepticism and against alternative profane histories of civilization.

Christian theology's influence on Jewish writers' self-perception is well known. In his essay on the beginnings of modern Jewish studies, Nahum N. Glatzer pointed out that nineteenth century Jewish thinkers were forced to explain Judaism in terms of world history: "World history had its own tradition: Christianity, which, reinterpreted, lived on in secular formulations. The Jew entered this domain without a tradition of his own [...]. He was a *homo novus* in search of a home in a world that was not yet ready to grant him this privilege" (Glatzer 1964, 200).

Further complicating Jewish scholars' inclusion in non-Jewish narratives of world history is the fact that Christian world history was indeed foreign, but far from unfamiliar. Jews are neither Indians nor Tasmanians, who were forced to adopt a completely strange symbolic order. The Jewish people play a major part in the Christian drama of world history, and the Christian philosophy of history was never indifferent towards them. The German Enlightenment's historical framework cast the Jews in a fundamental role in the past and future of human progress.

In the first decades of the nineteenth century, however, this conception was largely neglected. Consequently, Jewish writers gradually took over from their Christian counterparts the image of Jews as the educators of humanity.

In the generation after Lessing, non-Jewish historians and scholars' positioning of Biblical history changed significantly: increasingly, they excluded the history of the Israelites from the general, secular history of humanity. As we have seen, Kant's philosophy of history left the Jews out of the history of human progress – the continuing process of improvement from barbarity to civilization in the fields of society, politics, and technology. As shown by Helmut Zedelmaier (2006, 261), the history of the Jews was gradually reduced to the status of a mere "holy offshoot" [*heilige Nebenlinie*] within human history.

The emergence of the Indo-European hypothesis, which incorporated ancient India into the history of Western civilization, contributed to diverting the Jews from the main course of universal history. The supposed discovery of an ancient Brahmin tradition, older than the biblical one, induced scholars to revise the history of culture's origin. As concepts of race gained prominence, the distinction between the history of the Jews and the history of humanity became even more accentuated.

This shift posed a new challenge for Jewish intellectuals. While struggling to retain their place within the universal Christian view of history, now they also had to defend this entire Judeo-centric tradition against new theories such as the Indo-Aryan hypothesis that were much more hostile and exclusive in relation to the biblical legacy. This new symbolic order positioned Jews in a paradoxical position: on the one hand, the secularization of the political and cultural sphere opened new possibilities for Jews in the modern world; on the other hand, this very same secularization threatened to exclude the Jew – and his narrative – from its traditional, though unstable, place in European culture.

Bibliography

Ascher, Saul. *Leviathan, oder über Religion in Rücksicht des Judenthums*. Berlin: Franckesche Buchhandlung, 1792.

Bernstein, Eduard. *Die Aufgaben der Juden im Weltkrieg*. Berlin: [s.n.], 1917.

Carhart, Michael M. *The Science of Culture in Enlightenment Germany*. Cambridge, MA: Harvard University Press, 2007.

Cassirer, Ernst. *Die Philosophie der Aufklärung*. Princeton: Princeton University Press, 1951.

Cohen, Richard I. "Introduction." *The Jewish Contribution to Civilization: Reassessing an Idea*. Ed. Jeremy Cohen and Richard I. Cohen. Oxford: The Littman Library of Jewish Civilization, 2008.

Dunkhase, Jan Eike. *Spinoza der Hebräer*. Göttingen: Vandenhoeck & Ruprecht, 2013.

Glatzer, Nahum N. "The Beginnings of Modern Jewish Studies." *Studies in Nineteenth-Century Jewish Intellectual History*. Ed. Alexander Altmann. Cambridge, MA: Harvard University Press, 1964. 27–46.

Gottsched, Johann Christoph. *Erste Gründe der gesammten Weltweisheit*. Leipzig: Breitkopf, 1777 [1733].

Graetz, Michael. "'Die Erziehung des Menschengeschlechts' und jüdisches Selbstbewusstsein im 19. Jahrhundert." *Wolfenbütteler Studien zur Aufklärung* 4 (1977).

Gürkan, S. Leila. *The Jews as a Chosen People: Tradition and Transformation*. New York: Routledge, 2009.

Hartwich, Wolf-Daniel. *Die Sendung Moses: Von der Aufklärung bis Thomas Mann*. Munich: Fink, 997.

Hess, Moses. *The Holy History of Mankind and Other Writings*. Ed. Shlomo Avineri. Cambridge, UK: Cambridge University Press, 2004.

Herder, Johann Gottfried. *Vom Geist der Ebräischen Poesie*. Dessau: Buchhandlung der Gelehrten, 1782.

Hillen, Gerd. "Toleranz und Wahrheit. Absicht und Grenzen der Toleranz Lessings." *Lessing und Toleranz*. Ed. Peter Freimark et al. Detroit: Wayne State University Press, 1986.

Hirsch, Samson Raphael. *The Nineteen Letters*. Trans. Joseph Elias. Jerusalem: Feldheim, 1995.

Hirshman, Marc. *Torah for the Entire World: A Universalist Stream in Tannaitic Literature and Its Relation to Gentile Wisdom.* Tel Aviv: Hakibbutz hameuhad, 1999.

Hochstetter, Johann Friedrich. *Einleitung zu der Universal-History.* Tübingen: Schramm, 1740.

Israel, Jonathan. *Democratic Enlightenment: Philosophy, Revolution, and Human Rights 1750–1790.* Oxford: Oxford University Press, 2011.

Kant, Immanuel. "Reflexionen zur Anthropologie. " *Kants Gesammelte Schriften*, vol. 15. Ed. Preussische Akademie der Wissenschaften. Berlin/Leipzig: De Gruyter, 1928.

Kant, Immanuel. *Religion Within the Boundaries of Mere Reason: And Other Writings.* Trans. Allen Wood and George de Giovanni. Cambridge, UK: Cambridge University Press, 1998.

Lessing, Gotthold Ephraim. "The Education of the Human Race." *Lessing's Theological Writings.* Trans. Henry Chadwick. Stanford: Stanford University Press, 1957.

Mendes-Flohr, Paul. *German Jews: A Dual Identity.* New Haven: Yale University Press, 1999.

Mitchell, Harvey. *Voltaire's Jews and Modern Jewish Identity: Rethinking the Enlightenment*, vol. 7. New York: Routledge, 2012.

Mulsow, Martin. "Antiquarianism and Idolatry: The 'Historia' of Religions in the Seventeenth Century." *Historia: Empiricism and Erudition in Early Modern Europe.* Ed. Gianna Pomata and Nancy G. Siraisi. Cambridge, MA: MIT Press, 2005.

Philippson, Ludwig. "Die industrielle Mission der Juden." *Weltbewegende Fragen in Politik und Religion.* Leipzig: Fock, 1911. 378–392.

Polaschegg, Andrea. *Der andere Orientalismus: Regeln deutsch-morgenländischer Imagination im 19. Jahrhundert.* Berlin: De Gruyter, 2005.

Rank, Otto. "Das Wesen des Judentums." *Jewish Origins of the Psychoanalytical Movement.* Ed. Dennis Klein. New York: Praeger Publishers, 1981. 170–172.

Roemer, Nils. *Jewish Scholarship and Culture in Nineteenth-Century Germany: Between History and Faith.* Madison: University of Wisconsin Press, 2005.

Said, Edward W. *Orientalism.* New York: Vintage Books, 1978.

Schiller, Friedrich. "Die Sendung Moses" [1790]. *Kleinere prosaische Schriften.* Leipzig: Cursius, 1802.

Scholem, Gershom. *From Berlin to Jerusalem: Memories of my Youth.* Philadelphia: Paul Dry Books, 1988.

Spinoza, Benedict. *Tractatus Theologico–Politicus.* Trans. S. Shirley. Leiden: Brill, 1989.

Stangneth, Bettina. "Antisemitische und Antijudaistische Motive bei Immanuel Kant? Tatsachen, Meinungen, Ursachen." *Antisemitismus bei Kant und anderen Denkern der Aufklärung.* Ed. Barbara Neisser et al. Würzburg: Königshausen & Neumann, 2001.

Taubes, Jacob. *Occidental Eschatology.* Stanford: Stanford University Press, 2009.

Toomer, Gerald J. *Eastern Wisdom and Learning: The Study of Arabic in Seventeenth-Century England.* Oxford: Oxford University Press, 1996.

Voltaire. *La philosophie de l'histoire.* Geneva, 1765.

Walther, Friedrich Andreas. *Geschichte der Weltweisheit der alten Hebräer.* Göttingen: Victorinus Boßiegel, 1750.

Zedelmaier, Helmut. "Sintflut als Anfang der Geschichte." *Sintflut und Gedächtnis: Erinnern und Vergessen des Ursprungs.* Ed. Jan Assmann and Martin Mulsow Munich: Wilhelm Fink Verlag, 2006.

Moshe Idel

Transfers of Categories: the German-Jewish Experience and Beyond

1 Transfers of categories in Jewish culture

Contacts between cultures that coexist in the same geographical areas are natural and inevitable, even when they formally articulate some forms of mutual antagonism. This situation is more pronounced when minority cultures are interacting with majority cultures. In fact, acculturation is as natural as the reactions to it that attempt to obliterate or mitigate such phenomena of openness. Jewish culture as exemplified by rabbinic Judaism – Mishnaic, Talmudic and their extensions in the past and present – developed initially in areas of Greek, Hellenistic, Roman, and Iranian cultures, and their subsequent metamorphoses in the Middle Ages and modern times. The rabbinic elites attempted, however, to resist the basic approaches of Greek philosophies. Those philosophies included cosmological speculations that nourished a systematic vision of nature and man – as an individual and part of a polis; the rigorous universalist approach; and the refusal to subscribe to canonical texts as sources of paramount information. In fact, neither Greek nor Hellenistic thinkers embraced any single theory of the cosmos, anthropos, or polis, even less of the divinity, adopting instead a rather critical attitude toward the earlier forms of speculative thought. This approach permeated some aspects of Christian and Muslim philosophies or theologies. Some Jewish thinkers adopted and adapted them throughout the ages, from Philo of Alexandria in late antiquity, Shlomo ibn Gabirol, Abraham ibn Ezra and Maimonides, and their followers in the Middle Ages, Leone Ebreo in the Renaissance, Spinoza in the seventeenth century, and many brilliant thinkers in the eighteenth to twentieth centuries in Central Europe. All the medieval figures were of Sephardi extraction.

All enriched Judaism in very a significant manner by grafting it onto the various reverberations of the Greek speculative spirit in its diverse avatars; at the same time, however, they aroused sharp antagonism and even prolonged controversies. Rabbinic authorities relegated Philo of Alexandria to silence for a millennium and a half; critics censured the three medieval thinkers for the speculative innovations they introduced into Judaism. Ebreo's *Dialoghi d'Amore*, a best-seller in the Romance languages in sixteenth century Italy, was practically unknown even to Jewish elite figures. Spinoza was sharply criticized. Figures such as Moses Mendelssohn and Shlomo Maimon suffered similar treatment. This occurred despite the fact that those thinkers adopted, at least in some of their most important writings, some form of exegetical approach that offered new readings of classical texts. In nineteenth and early twentieth-century Germany, however, the so-called Science of Judaism [*Wissenschaft des Judentums*] devised a new approach to Judaism that opened the gates to a critical attitude toward Judaism along accepted European academic lines, especially the German one. As Ismar Schorsch (1994, 154–155) formulated it:

> One way of understanding *Wissenschaft des Judentums* is [as] a collective act of translation, a sustained effort to cast the history, literature, and institutions of Judaism in Western categories. Emancipated Jews quickly lost access to the language, wisdom, and symbols of their religion [...]. But, of course, I am not speaking of translation merely in the literal sense. The whole gigantic enterprise to impose a semblance of system on an untidy traditional Judaism [...] in terms comprehensible to the Western mind [ ] The effective translation of Judaism into Western categories, in turn, served to inculcate Jews with a sense of historical consciousness that at least partially offset the loss of communal constraints and personal piety.

The great contributions that this novel approach adduced to a reflective understanding of Judaism are well known. Scholarship has largely overlooked, however, the consequences of the discrepancies between the categories forged in Central Europe and the much earlier traditional culture to which they were applied. In this essay, I shall focus on the very specific type of interaction, limited to a very small, although intellectually very significant, part of the Jewish elite in Germany – some thinkers who attempted to interpret Judaism. I shall refer below to only a small part of this generally accepted Jewish-German scholarly tradition.[1] Nevertheless, one cannot propose simplistic generalizations because some of these intellectuals not only differ and polemicize with each other but they also express varying and even contradictory views on certain topics This applies particularly to Solomon Maimon, as he confesses in his autobiography, but also, obviously, to Martin Buber. Those caveats notwithstanding, I would mention four main ruptures with the past tradition that characterize the elite Jewish-German culture:

First, the linguistic one: In Germany, unlike most of the other Jewish communities, which did not adopt the vernacular as the main cultural language, the German language became the Jewish cultural elite's main medium of expression.

---

1 See, e.g., the various attempts to describe this tradition in Skinner (2002) as well as some of the other essays in this collection; Santner (2006, 12), or Niehoff (1993); Smith (1993), and Wiese and Urban (2012).

Second, the internal Jewish rupture, that is, the turn of the intellectual elite to the Sephardi Jewish culture, thus diminishing the local Ashkenazi forms of Jewish culture.

Third, the sharp decline of rabbinic creativity, especially with regard to Halakhah and Kabbalah.

Fourth, the conceptual rupture, the explicit or implicit adoption of modes of thinking deeply inspired by the majority German culture. Translation is sometimes also treason and thus a rupture. In my essay, I shall focus on this fourth variety of a rupture with the earlier forms of Jewish tradition.

Some of those ruptures were necessary for the emergence of a critical approach to Judaism that could generate serious academic research, and we stand on the shoulders of those giants.

2 The ideatic turn

As Harry A. Wolfson pointed out, applying the more critical Greek approach to study of the scriptures represents a contribution of Jewish thinkers that reverberated also in other cultures. Despite rejection by rabbinic Judaism with its particularistic propensities, the Jewish philosophers' syncretic approaches slowly entered into traditional Judaism via the exegetical strategies used to reinterpret canonical texts. I use the term "ideatic turn" to describe the innovations because they related mainly to theologies, cosmologies, and psychologies, and they rarely entailed specific instructions that modified rabbinic precepts.

This speculative-exegetical penchant in Jewish thought remained prominent up until the eighteenth century. From the nineteenth century onward, however, the interaction with other cultures occurred more at the level of interpreting Judaism rather than its canonical texts. This shifts the focus from textual exegesis to cultural or philosophical reinterpretations of a vast body of texts, variegated and even conflicting ideas, numerous rituals and customs, magic and superstitions embraced by different strata of Jewish people, a minority culture, in accordance with some sets of ideas found in the majority culture. In traditional cultures less concerned with systematic thought, and thus with systematic theology, the new approaches were sometimes grafted onto what had been conceived of as antecedents, such as Maimonides. We see this, for example, with the thought of Spinoza, Mendelssohn, and Solomon Maimon, who "translated" the views of the Great Eagle into new terminologies; they then improved and/or criticized them in line with the new rationalist ideas, especially those of the European Enlightenment. We shall see below an example of Maimonides' influence on three Jewish-German thinkers.

The innovations reduced a millennia-long variegated historical experience to some abstract contents that were conceived of as representative. Having internalized and accepted the ideals of the majority culture as absolute, followers of this ideatic attitude sublated the traditional exegetical relations to canonical texts and fixed rituals, thus offering a more palatable image of Judaism to the majority culture. The exegetical approaches had entailed inter-corporal exegesis, that is, interpreting one type of texts, the scriptures, against the conceptual background of another more systematic and abstract set of writings. The elite sometimes inserted their strong beliefs into the interpreted texts by means of what I call the medieval arcanization of Jewish scriptures. In premodern and modern times, however, this strategy has been strongly attenuated, and the insertion of new ideas has taken a much less exegetical turn.

Gershom G. Scholem's anecdote about his father, Arthur, is symptomatic of this approach: "Once or twice a year my father used to make a speech at the dinner table in praise of the mission of the Jews. According to him, that mission was to proclaim to the world pure monotheism and a purely rational morality" (Scholem 2012a, 11).[2]

Nota bene the resort to the past tense: he regarded the Jews' mission already as a matter of the past.[3] A page earlier, in the same context, Scholem (2012a, 10) depicted his father as "using the Sabbath candles to light a cigarette or cigar afterwards. Since the prohibition to smoke on Sabbath was one of the most widely known Jewish regulations, there was deliberate mockery in this act." To be sure, Scholem's attitude to what he describes in his home is sometimes sarcastic, especially because he did not subscribe to his father's rationalistic understanding of Judaism. Wanting to portray the plight of Judaism in Germany in his youth, he returns to this ridiculing presentation elsewhere in the same memoirs (Scholem 2012a, 10–11). Funny as these anecdotes are and representative of a spirit that was not antithetical to the speculative depths of the German-Jewish thinkers, they impart, in my opinion, something more profound regarding Arthur Scholem – not only about his naïve views but also about his son's thought and his contemporary intellectual Jews. The shift from the rabbinic praxis to "rational morality" and the emphasis on the missionary task of the alleged Jewish pure monotheism reflect the depth of the transformation of the image of the Jews in the first

---

2 We cannot discuss here whether "pure monotheism" reflects the impact of Maimonides.
3 Compare to the statement of Margarete Susman, cited in Scholem (1976b, 89): "The vocation of Israel as a people is not self-realization but self-surrender for the sake of a higher, transhistorical goal."

decades of twentieth-century Berlin. Given the intellectual capacities and the creativity of the thinkers I shall address, it is ridiculous to assume that they subscribed to some simple common denominators. We may, nevertheless, assume some selective affinities among them on certain issues and many important divergences on others. I would like to highlight those affinities, without reducing the independence of each of those Jewish-German thinkers. It is important to note, nevertheless, that Buber, Rosenzweig, and Scholem agreed on the centrality of three concepts in Jewish theology – creation, revelation, and redemption, while eschewing the centrality of the performance of commandments.[4] This strongly ideatic orientation – as opposed to the performative one of traditional forms of Judaism – touches upon not only the inner structure of Jewish theology (a precarious concept in Judaism in general) but also the academic approach to Jewish mysticism.[5]

First, I shall deal with a matter of principle that will inform, implicitly or explicitly, the following discussions. As mentioned earlier, the exposure to major developments in the surrounding cultures also enriched elite forms of Judaism. This enrichment was a rarer occurrence, however, among the vast majority of ordinary Jews and even a significant segment of the rabbinic elites. Most of those individuals who were instrumental in this conceptual enrichment were themselves rabbis or at least paid tribute to the rabbinic way of life, even if they were critical of some of its aspects. Maimonides' *Guide of the Perplexed* had been safeguarded from negative consequences of the sharp criticism because of Maimonides' earlier works, *Commentary on the Mishnah*, *Sefer hamitzvot*, and especially *Mishneh Torah*. This precarious balance was absent in the *Deutsch-Judentum*. None of the individuals we shall discuss below was a Halakhic figure. Modern Jewish-German figures accepted German cultural values as universal, and thus superior to the particularist Jewish traditional ones, especially the Ashkenazi traditional culture. At the same time as some figures adopted the idea of the universality and thus superiority of the German humanistic values, others targeted it as the main object of their polemics. Given the influence of these values after the fall of the Weimar republic on much larger elite audiences, it appeared that they gained universal recognition. This culture was so patently thin and feeble that, even in Germany, it did not stop the emergence and takeover of the worst European regime ever, just a few decades after the peak of the liberal period. A thin stratum of Jewish elite – no more than several dozen brilliant intellectuals writing in the interwar period in a language unfamiliar to the vast majority of the Jews – adopted a cultural

---

4 See Buber (1982, 5–6); Rosenzweig's *Star of Redemption* and Scholem (1976b, 261–289).
5 See Idel (2004).

structure that was unsuccessfully striving to be universalist. Using this structure to interpret Judaism, a much older and more diversified traditional culture,
and to educate the Jewish people in its light was doomed to failure from the very
beginning. A sublime elite ideology, philosophy, theology, or religiosity, – what I
call the ideatic dimension – shaped in a very specific cultural and social milieu,
cannot inspire larger segments of a population, whether German, Jewish, or
otherwise. Some ancient and medieval thinkers understood this fact, which Leo
Strauss and his followers reiterated in modern times in their writings, but it was
not understood in the twentieth century, and, I fear, it is still unacknowledged
today.

3 The historical turn

In addition to the influence of the elite's ideatic reduction, the German-Jewish
elite had been profoundly impacted by another influence that is related to its
conception of the history of the Jews as a central category defining the essence
of Judaism. More than just a matter of chronology, this attitude reflects a deeper
belief that a nation's history defines it, and, in the case of the Jews, history was
what has been done to them, or what has been encapsulated in the insightful title
of Ismar Schorsch's book: *From Text to Context: The Turn to History in Modern
Judaism* (1994, 149–344, especially 177–204). This explains the strong historical penchant that is evident from the writings of Heinrich Graetz to Gershom
Scholem and Yitzhak Baer. Let me start with the views of the latter,[6] perhaps the
most important Jewish historian at the Hebrew University from its inception:

> Our history is an evolutionary process of a great power, and it is necessary to define and
> demonstrate the nature of this evolution, even in those places and those ranks where
> this power, apparently coming from outside, is dispersed and increasingly degenerates to
> extreme baseness. We, who recognize ourselves as part of and messengers for this won-
> drous and occult power, we cannot escape this recognition [...] but by historical criticism
> we penetrate and fathom the secret of the existence of the historical phenomena, which are
> similar to personalities that develop according to their own laws,[7] which emerge, indeed,
> from the depths of their souls (Baer 1986, 1: 16).[8]

---

6 On the historical thought of Baer see, e.g., Myers (1995, passim); Yuval (1998); and Nirenberg
(2002).
7 The particularistic stand is obvious and is reinforced by many other statements dealing with an
organic vision of the Jewish communities and their history. See Yuval (1998).
8 (Baer 1986, 1: 16) The passage is part of an article printed originally in 1938.

I wonder to what extent the "great power" mentioned in this quote represents the same concept as the "power" elsewhere in Baer's opus. At the end of his book *Galut* [exile], he relates that the modern Jews who returned home had to come to grips with the "ancient Jewish consciousness of history" (Baer 1988, 119).[9] The immediately following passage explicates but also veils the meaning of the above statement:

> For us, perhaps, the final consequence of modern causal historical thinking coincides with the final consequence of the old Jewish conception of history, which comes to us from no alien tradition but has grown out of our own essential being: 'Our eyes saw it, and no stranger's: our ears heard it, and no others.' If we today can read each coming day's events in ancient and dusty chronological tables, as though history were the ceaseless unrolling of a process proclaimed once and for all in the Bible, then every Jew in every part of the Diaspora may recognize that there is a power that lifts the Jewish people out of the realm of all causal history (Baer 1988, 119–120).[10]

The phrase "Our eyes saw it, and no stranger's: our ears heard it, and no others" is not a biblical verse, but a short passage found in Maimonides's *Mishneh Torah*, *Sefer hamada* 8:1 describing the Sinaitic revelation. The "power" he speaks about here, and perhaps also in the previous passage, is thus the God of Israel. The history of the Jews differs, according to the end of Baer's passage, from that of the other nations.[11] This is a metaphysics of the nation, which, to put it mildly, is quite an exaggeration, but one connected to the nation's history.

Let us look at Martin Buber's portrayal of Judaism in his synthetic book on Hasidism:

> A unique event in world history is the phenomenon which appeared to us in the history of Judaism. The whole of the historical experience of a nation is there concentrated in one fateful problem of exile and redemption. Out of this common experience of exile and redemption the nation was born. On the memory of this historical event, which the spiritual leaders of Israel had declared time and again to be the work of God with the nation and a covenant between nation and God, is founded the connection between the past and the future which is living within the nation's consciousness in a way that is not to be found in any other nation (Buber 988, 202).

---

9 The book was originally written in 1936.

10 For an understanding of Baer's thought as circling around exile and redemption, see the introduction of Jacob Neusner to *Galut* (1988, unnumbered). See, however, the different reading and practice emphasizing the interaction between the Jews and their environment in Yuval (1998, 78).

11 See the Epilogue added ten years after the first publication of the book (Baer 1988, 123).

Buber locates the uniqueness of Judaism in the poles of exile and redemption. Presumably, the redemption mentioned here relates to the Jews' exodus from Egypt, whereas exile refers more generally to much later experiences related to the Diaspora. Moreover, this description underestimates the importance of the ritual, performed *de facto* for centuries, for defining the experience and the nature of the Jewish people. Buber takes for granted the historical veracity of the biblical story of redemption from Egypt, as an event experienced by the entire nation. Today, some historians doubt the historicity of this event. Neither, in my opinion, is exile a common or a homogenous experience.

In dealing with another major scholar, Gershom Scholem, who deals more with Jewish mysticism than with history, I shall address his attitude toward Judaism's historical aspects. He confessed that he arrived at an interest in Judaism through reading the historical account of Heinrich Graetz: "My first impetus for my Jewish consciousness was provided by my interest in history" (Scholem 2012a, 36). His interest in what he called, as Buber did in the passage quoted above, the "historical experience" strongly shaped his reading of Jewish mysticism: "The historical experience of the Jewish people merged indistinguishably with the mystical vision of a world in which the holy was locked in desperate struggle with the satanic. Everywhere and at every hour the simple and yet so infinitely profound fact of exile provided ground for lamentation, atonement, and asceticism" (Scholem 1969c, 146).

The affinities between this statement and Buber's earlier passage are obvious. Both scholars resort to the term "historical experience" and both view it in terms of exile and redemption. Scholem, however, assumes that historical experience radiated into the deep layers of the process that informed the Kabbalists' understanding of reality. In an additional statement that may serve also as a motto for the lachrymose history, he wrote: "In all the expanse of creation there is imperfection, flaw, *Galut*" (Scholem1972a, 46). In even sharper terms, he says: "All that befalls in the world is only an expression of this primal and fundamental Galut" (Scholem 1972, 45). This transformation of historical experience into a mystical vision of reality took place via a symbolic understanding of reality – "symbols of a very special kind, in which the spiritual experience of the mystics was almost inextricably intertwined with the historical experience of the Jewish people. It is this interweaving of two realms, which in most other religious mysticisms have remained separate, that gave Kabbalah its specific imprint" (Scholem 1969c, 2).

Scholem's 1944 essay also conveys the feeling that inspecting history may reveal a secret dimension of events. He recommended, as Baer did some years earlier, the praxis of "historical criticism" in the context of disclosing secrets of history: "Through its fruitful dialectic, through a radical breakthrough to its turning point on its way, which are the points of construction, historical criticism henceforth also serves as a productive decoding of the secret writing of the past, of the great symbols of our life within history" (Scholem 1997, 67; 1982, 399).

Resorting to the term "dialectic" reveals not merely a turn to history but to a Hegelian type of history. If historical definition of the nation reflects the more general impact of history's role in the emergence of German national consciousness, it is possible to detect also a more specific impact on the manner in which Scholem portrayed the history of mysticism. In the introduction to his *Major Trends*, Scholem enumerated three stages in the development of religion: the animistic or the mythical one; the institutional one, which is characterized by the belief in a deep gap between man and God; and, finally, the mystical one, that represents a synthesis between the two first stages, when the above gap is bridged at certain moments (Scholem 1969b, 7–9). Scholars have recognized the Hegelian structure of this scheme, which consists of a thesis, first stage; antithesis, the second one; and, finally, a synthesis.[12] Although this scheme is well known, its later reverberation escaped notice, and it requires some discussion. Scholem (1962, 162) wrote about the origin of Kabbalah in the Middle Ages: "It is difficult to say whether we should consider this process as the breakthrough of ancient, mythical images and 'archetypes' into a world where they had been mere metaphors or as a renewed historic contact with a gnostic tradition that had never ceased to make use of these images."

Two different explanations confront each other as alternatives in this passage. The latter is a historical one: Kabbalah emerged as the result of a contact with the "Gnostic tradition," which implies a certain rupture with rabbinic thought. In fact, Scholem explains the emergence of Kabbalah in the Middle Ages mainly in terms of this encounter (this is not the place to deal with the historical problems related to this explanation).[13] More interesting, however, is the first explanation, which assumes the revival of ancient "archetypes" in the Middle Ages. This 'breakthrough' should be understood mainly in psychological terms: themes and images from the past, suppressed for centuries, resurface at a certain moment and regain their freshness and lost valences. This is, to be sure, also an historical explanation, because it postulates three stages: the ancient, or the mythical one; the later one, when those myths turned into metaphors; and then the third, that of the return of the myths.

As mentioned earlier, Scholem already articulated this distinction in his *Major Trends*. In that work ([1941?] 1969b, 7), however, institutionalized religion constitutes the "breakthrough" as the second stage following the more animistic first stage, whereas in 1962, the "breakthrough" involves those elements that had

---

12 See Idel, (2009, 34–36, 127–128). See also Idel (1991).
13 See Idel (2009, 138–146).

been suppressed by the emergence of what he calls "religion."[14] In fact, in 1941, Scholem ([1941] 1969b, 8) expressly denied the need for the "breakthrough" that, in 1962, he saw as generating the third, mystical phase of religious development. The major difference between the schemes of 1941 and of 1962, however, is the appearance of the term "archetypes" in the latter. In my opinion, it reflects the influence of Scholem's participation in the Eranos conferences in Ascona, under the aegis of Carl G. Jung. He introduced the term in the first lecture he delivered at Eranos in 1949, when he stated: "Foreign mythical worlds are at work in the great archetypal images of the Kabbalists, even though they sprang from the depths of an authentic and productive Jewish religious feeling" (Scholem 1969c, 98). Here, too, the Jungian valence of the term "archetype" as referring to a psychological entity is obvious. It is, therefore, an overstatement to exonerate Scholem from any Jungian influence.[15]

The shift of the center of gravity from the ritual to the experience, to the idea or to history is paramount for understanding how a minority retold its culture in a new, rationalistic milieu. As personal convictions, those views are no better or worse than any others are, as all pertain to some forms of *imaginaire*. Problems arise, however, when someone presents personal views as an interpretation of his or her reading of history; regards them as representative of Judaism as a whole; or considers that they constitute the right interpretation of certain views found in traditional authors.

4 The symbolic turn: from meaninglessness to infinite meanings

Let me turn now to an aspect of modern research on Kabbalah where the impact of the German cultural tradition is even more pronounced: the claim of the overwhelmingly symbolic nature of the kabbalistic discourse. Gershom Scholem depicts the symbolic function in Kabbalah as part of a wider theosophical structure that assumes a transcendental stratum within the divine sphere, beyond human perception, and the intuition of the divine structure, or the divine inner life, by means of symbols. The apophatic approach is described by the term '*Ein Sof*, the Infinite, and the sefirotic realm that is symbolized by words and deeds belonging to Jewish religious life. In Scholem's views, the former is sometimes

---

14 See also the similar use of "breakthrough" elsewhere in the same book, *Origins of the Kabbalah* (original title *Ursprung und Anfänge der Kabbala*, 1962, 345).
15 See Dan (1991, 6, 8–9).

related to an inchoate sound but one that is infinitely pregnant with meaning. In a letter written in 1934 to Walter Benjamin, Scholem proposed the concept of "the Nothingness of revelation" – *Nichts der Offenbarung* – in order to advance a theory of the inchoate form of the original revelation of the Law; this implies that meaning subsequently emerged only through the development of an interpretive tradition.[16] In the same year, he wrote in a poem, "With a Copy of Kafka's *Trial*," which he also sent to Walter Benjamin:

> "This is the sole ray of revelation
> in an age that disavows you [namely, God],
> entitled only to experience you
> in the shape of your negation."[17]

The nexus between Franz Kafka and Scholem's propensity to negativity in the context of revelation is obvious. Fascinating as this nexus is for understanding Scholem the theologian, it is even more interesting for understanding Scholem the philologist. In the fifth of his unhistorical aphorisms, he speaks about the "Nothingness of God" as the first emanation from the Infinite.[18] This "nothingness" that is, nevertheless, replete with meaning, a paradox that is characteristic of Scholem's approach in contrast to his other contemporaries, Martin Buber and Franz Rosenzweig, is a translation of the kabbalistic term *'Ayin*. In Hebrew, the word means "nothing," but it stands for the first *sefirah, Keter,* and it refers to the ontological fullness, a *superesse*, as it contains all the emanations and creations that evolve from it, not a negation.[19] Scholem's understanding of Nothingness, which is correct semantically but wrong ontologically, reflects a Hegelian approach to the negation found within the divinity, whereas the intention of the

---

16 See, especially, his letter to Walter Benjamin from 1934 in Scholem (1980, 157, 166–68, 175); and his response to H. J. Schoeps (Scholem 1932, 243). For discussions of these views see Biale (1982, 129–131); Mosès (1992, 218–119, 222–223, 236–237, 243); Alter (1991, 108–110; and Handelman (1991, 50–51, 165).
17 Original in Scholem (2003, 100–101).
18 See Biale (1987, 110–111).
19 See Scholem (1963, 441–443). Compare also to Scholem's *Major Trends in Jewish Mysticism* (1969b, 12–13, and especially 217); his *Kabbalah* (1974, 94–95, 147, 149, 156, 404), and his *On the Kabbalah and its Symbolism* (1969c, 41, 102–103, 122, 125) (the "nothingness of the divine idea"), where he emphasizes the divine "nothingness" as part of the process of creation in Kabbalah. The French translation of Scholem's book seems to be the source of Nancy (2007, 70). See also Nancy (2002). See Franck (1843, 186–187), as well as my forthcoming *Primeval Evil: Totality, Perfection and Perfectibility* (ch. 1, section 10). On Hegel and Kabbalah, see also Franks (2010, 269–275); Kilcher (1998, 226, 229–230); Wolfson (2005, 100–104); and Drob (2001, 185–240).

Kabbalists is ontological plenitude even though they used the term *'Ayin*.[20] In this case, similar to one mentioned above, a category found in a certain type of mystical literature – Kabbalah and Hasidism – is applied to a larger phenomenon, the relationship between mysticism and authority in general (Scholem 1969c, 31).

What about an infinity of potential meanings? It may reflect another well-known kabbalistic concept, that the highest level within the divine world is the Infinite, *'Ein Sof*. The Kabbalists themselves, however, are much more interested in an infinity of meanings – not of the primordial inchoate, but in the various types of infinities of the written Torah text.[21] In his essay on "The Meaning of the Torah in Jewish Mysticism,"[22] Scholem speaks about "the principle of the infinite meaning of the divine world,"[23] but what he actually discusses refers to the written text of the Hebrew Bible (Scholem, 1969c, 64–65). His ambiguous formulation imposes the concept of the potential infinity of the oral experience upon kabbalistic discussions of an infinity of meanings that are related to the textual form of the Hebrew Bible. Those are two different issues whose divergent content the scholar overlooked. Moreover, the emphasis on an infinity of meanings by a traditional figure such as a Kabbalist habitually adhering to a ritualistic way of life has a very different connotation than when a scholar who is not concerned with it articulates this view.

The theory of the infinite potentiality that can nevertheless be grasped recalls Scholem's treatment of another interesting category – symbolism. Following the lead of Johannes Reuchlin, an early sixteenth-century humanist and a major Christian Kabbalist, Scholem perceived Kabbalah as a symbolic expression of the metaphysical realm, which he conceived to be inexpressible.[24] Viewing Kabbalah *in toto* as a symbolic tradition is another instance of introducing a category within which Jewish Kabbalists did not explicitly operate and reflects his incorporating a view that stems from the Neo-Pythagorean Christian Renaissance.[25] In this case, the appropriation of the Christian Kabbalist thinker's category of symbolism is a modification of a Renaissance view that was reinterpreted in philosophical terms

---

20 On the flirtation with negativity in Scholem, see also the incisive remarks of Harold Bloom (1987, 7, 13, 55, 57, 60–67); idem (1983, 83); idem (1984, 53ff). See also e.g., Mosès (1989, 209–224; or Wolosky (1995). Compare to my remarks in Idel (2002, 423–427).

21 See Idel (2002, 80–110).

22 It was first published a year before Scholem delivered the lecture that became his essay on "Mysticism and Authority."

23 Scholem (1969c, 37), originally printed in *Diogenes* 14 (Summer 1956) and (Fall 1956) and in Scholem (1976, 268–269). This view reflects the impact of Ahron Marcus, as we shall see below.

24 See Idel (2009, 83–108 and 2002, 274–276).

25 See Idel (1988b, 1–7).

by eighteenth and nineteenth-century German thinkers.[26] At least once, shortly before his death, Scholem (1981/82, 283–284) referred explicitly and positively to Reuchlin's view of Kabbalah as *receptio symbolica*. Symbolic discourse thus plays a fundamental role in Kabbalah according to the first scholar of Judaism in the Renaissance and up to the greatest scholar of Jewish mysticism in our times.[27] Scholem, indeed, asserted in a lecture in Germany that if he believed in metempsychosis, he would assume that he was Reuchlin *redivivus*, a transmigration of Reuchlin's soul.[28] This, the most explicit and clear statement as to the centrality of the German-Jewish symbiosis in Judaic scholarship, comes as a confession by the most outspoken denier of such a symbiosis.[29] Without always knowing it, modern scholarship on Kabbalah that deals with symbolism speaks, following Reuchlin, the language of the Christianized version of Pythagoreanism.

5 The experience of revelation versus its content: Buber, Rosenzweig, and Scholem

In classical forms of Judaism, the content of revelation was much more important than the associated experience. Although classical texts regarded the Sinaitic experience as overwhelming, they were most concerned with its precise contents. Equally important was the widespread assumption that those contents, conceived to be concrete, were transmittable to others as they concerned not just the individual but also the entire community. This propensity remained dominant in the Jewish communities that lived as compact groups though the Middle Ages and premodern periods. With the urbanization of some segments of Jewish communities from the end of the eighteenth century, individual rather than communal Jewish experience started to loom as more significant. Jewish individuals were now living not merely in an urban environment but also in closer coexistence with the gentile milieu: linguistic, economic, social and, more important, intellectual, especially university studies. The emerging existentialist philosophy privileged individual experience over the content of that experience. By moving

---

26 See my "Johannes Reuchlin: Kabbalah, Pythagorean Philosophy and Modern Scholarship" (2008).

27 On the reticence of attributing a seminal role to symbolism in Judaism, see Heschel (1996, 83–84). For more on Heschel and symbolism, see Kaplan (1996, 75–89). For my reservations concerning the exaggeration of the status of symbols in Kabbalah, see my detailed discussion in Idel (2002, 272–94).

28 See Scholem (1969a, 7).

29 See the essays in *Scholem* (1976b, 61–92).

from the content to experience, or from the shared communal life to personal feeling, traditional Judaism lost much of its stake in the new Jewish philosophies. Let me address how three leading Jewish-German thinkers reformulated the nature of the Sinaitic revelation, one of the cornerstones of rabbinic Judaism.

In *I and Thou*, Buber regards revelation in similar experiential terms: "Man receives, and what he receives is not a specific 'content' but a presence, a presence as strength" (Buber 1980, 158).[30] A year later, in an exchange of letters between Buber and Franz Rosenzweig, the former openly differentiated between man as the receiver of the law, on one hand, and God, who is not the giver of the law, on the other.[31] For him, revelation is not a specific moment in time, but something occurring somewhere in the middle between two fixed dates: creation and redemption, a view that weakens the importance of the Sinaitic experience (Buber 1982, 5–6).[32]

For his part, Rosenzweig declared in a letter to Buber a year later, in 1925: "Revelation is certainly not lawgiving. The only immediate content of revelation – is revelation; with *vayered* ([he came down] Exodus 19:20), it is essentially complete; with *vayeddaber* ([he spoke] Exodus 20:1) interpretation sets in, and all the more so with *anokhi*."[33] Rosenzweig perceives what the Hebrew Bible presents as the beginning of revelation, *Anokhi*, as the beginning of interpretation, which he tacitly identified with lawgiving. This means that revelation consisted solely of the feeling of the divine presence descending upon Mt. Sinai, in a manner reminiscent of Buber (Kraut 1972).[34] I emphasize the occurrence of the *Anokhi* here as the end of revelation and the beginning of interpretation because it recalls Scholem's later formulation of the theory.

Legitimate private views expressed in personal correspondence about the situation in hoary antiquity or about philosophical or poetic issues, however, later turned into a statement considered a scholarly assessment of the meaning of revelation and interpretation in Judaism. This occurred in an important essay entitled "Religious Authority and Mysticism" that Gershom Scholem presented at the Eranos encounters in 1957; a scholar who adopted in principle and in practice the historical-philological method conveyed his view as some form of general

---

30 See also (1980, 160) and Scholem's analysis (1976, 156–159) of Buber's treat of the issue.
31 Letter to Rosenzweig, on 3 July 1924. In another instance, however, Buber says something quite different: "There is no revelation without commandments." See Buber (1948, 209).
32 See Kepnes (1992, 124, 190–191 n. 26).
33 Rosenzweig (1979, 1040: "So ist Offenbarung sicher nicht Gesetzgebung; sie ist überhaupt nur – Offenbarung. Sie hat unmittelbar nur sich selbst zum Inhalt, mit va-yered ist sie eigentlich schon fertig, schon mit va-yedabber fängt die Interpretation an, geschweige denn mit *anochi*." See Rosenzweig (1955, 118).
34 See Sommer's important study (1999, esp. pp. 440–441); and Bielik-Robson (2007, 39–67).

phenomenological truth. Referring to the Sinaitic revelation, much of which was considered to have been unheard, he wrote at the conclusion of his essay:

> Once in history a mystical experience was imparted to a whole nation and formed a bond between that nation and God. But the truly divine element in this revelation, the immense *alef,* was not in itself sufficient to express the divine message, and in itself, it was more than the community could bear. Only the prophet [namely, Moses] was empowered to communicate the meaning of this inarticulate voice to the community. It is mystical experience which conceives and gives birth to authority (Scholem1969c, 31).

It is worthwhile to unpack the content of this theological statement. If the mystical experience matters insofar as authority is concerned, indeed an example of the apotheosis of the mystical experience,[35] then not only the prophet Moses experienced it, but the entire nation. What, then, is the difference that gave Moses authority? Did Moses, according to Scholem's theology, invent the content he revealed, or not? Moreover, Scholem's wording about the entire nation's enjoying the mystical experience suggests that he understood it as a unique historical event that had a mystical valence for a collective that was, nevertheless, incapable of bearing the experience. If we compare this view to the earlier-mentioned three stages of religion, it is difficult to understand how the mystical phase occurs at the very beginning of Judaism.

Scholem conveys this approach not as the view of the Hasidic Rabbi, R. Menahem Mendel Torum of Rymanov [see discussion below], who did not care about history and would not know the meaning of the term "mysticism," but as his own judgment. This is part of the transfer of categories. The first part of the passage conveys Scholem's understanding of Jewish history as informed by a collective mystical experience. Some lines earlier, he describes the *alef* mentioned here as follows: "To hear the *alef* is to hear next to nothing; it is the preparation for all audible language, but in itself it conveys no determinate, specific meaning. Thus, with his statement that the actual revelation to Israel consisted only of the *alef,* Rabbi Mendel transformed the revelation on Mount Sinai into a mystical revelation, pregnant with infinite meaning,[36] but without specific meaning" (Scholem 1969c, 30).[37]

---

35 Compare, however, Magid (1995, 245–269).

36 Scholem's source, Ahron Marcus, already made this claim of infinity in the context of the alef of *Anokhi*. See Marcus (1901, 239). It does not exist, however, in Hasidic sources.

37 The original German is: "Das *Alef* zu hören ist eigentlich so gut wie nichts, es stellt den Übergang zu aller vernehmbaren Sprache dar, und gewiß läßt sich nicht von ihm sagen, daß es in sich einen spezifischen Sinn klar umrissenen Charakters ermittelt. Mit seinem kühnen Satz über die eigentliche Offenbarung an Israel als die des *Alef* reduzierte also Rabbi Mendel diese Offen-

"To hear next to nothing" is therefore what Scholem assumes was the most important revelation according to rabbinic Judaism, and all the details found in the Pentateuch are just human interpretations. In this regard, Scholem does not differ from Buber and Rosenzweig, and, indeed, in a footnote, he refers to Rosenzweig's above-cited letter (Scholem 1969c, 30, n. 3).[38] In the last quote, however, Scholem not only expresses his own views but also claims to explicate a statement, allegedly found in the writings of R. Menahem Mendel of Rymanov, a late eighteenth century and early nineteenth century ultra-orthodox Hasidic authority. As I have already dealt in detail with the problems related to the interpretation of this statement (Idel 2009, 119–25), I shall not dwell on it here.

I shall, however, address another text of Scholem's on this issue that I did not discuss earlier because it was unavailable in print. Curiously enough, it is a transcript of a series of issues Scholem addressed after a lecture I delivered in May 1980, which dealt, inter alia, with the kabbalistic sources of Rosenzweig's thought (Idel 1988a).[39] Dr. Enrico Lucca kindly drew my attention to the recently printed transcription of the English remarks, to which Scholem added a few corrections in his handwriting. Lucca added his own introduction to the text, which he published from Scholem's archive (Lucca 2012; Scholem 2012). Below are Scholem's remarks related to revelation, without some of the editor's footnotes:

> My last remark will be only that I really think that the concept of the revelation about which you spoke in the second book of Rosenzweig's [*Star of Redemption*] defies all the statements about his reluctance [to speak] as a mystic. If anybody has ever produced a mystical theory of revelation, it is, in my opinion, Franz Rosenzweig in the second part of the *Star of Redemption*. And I think you quoted Ernst Simon[40] who [...], when I had published a paper where I said that one of the great mystics, namely Rabbi Mendel of Rymanov, had said that the only revelation which was revelation clear and simple was the Alef of Anochi.... Now, that's quite a statement, in Jewish thought, that the Alef of Anochi was the only thing which Israel at Mt. Sinai got directly without interpretation, without all oral Torah. Everything besides the Alef was an oral Torah.
>
> Simon showed me the letter of Rosenzweig to Buber where he said about revelation the same thing without ever having known the place where this was quoted in the name of Rabbi Mendel of Rymanov, which he certainly had not read. It is really, if any mystical concept of revelation has existed, it is this. And it comes down to this in Buber, it comes down to this in Rosenzweig, in two thinkers who, more or less, decided to say that they have

---

barung zu einer mystischen, das heißt zu einer Offenbarung, die in sich selber zwar unendlich sinnerfüllt, aber doch ohne spezifischen Sinn war."

38 There he mentions Ernst Simon, who drew his attention to Rosenzweig's similar view.

39 The article was republished with slight changes and few bibliographical updates in Idel (2009, 159–167). See also Harvey (1987).

40 In fact, in my lecture I did not mention Ernst Simon but R. Shime'on bar Yohai.

nothing to do with it.[41] The late Buber certainly said so very emphatically, and Rosenzweig gave the impression to many people (not to all) that he did not like the whole idea of mysticism. So which, I find [,] utterly cannot strike anybody who tries to understand the second part.[42] What kind of revelation is this? What kind of Jew can accept what he said about the meaning of revelation? It is a fantastically radical mystical theory of revelation, down to the end. So I think there is really something to say and that could be speculated and I think we will be able to say that Rosenzweig did not take something from real kabbalistic sources. He has never read a kabbalistic book in Hebrew, as he was not yet good enough for that (Scholem 2012b, 5–6).

The problem of Rosenzweig's kabbalistic sources for his thought, which I addressed in my paper, is not the issue here. Scholem's claim that Rosenzweig could not read "real" kabbalistic sources does not exclude his finding ideas in other books. By now, in my opinion, Rivka Horwitz's erudite study (2006), in particular, has settled the entire question.[43] The new element here is Scholem's added reference to Buber regarding the mystical tradition, to which he had already enlisted Rosenzweig. Evidently, Scholem was not acquainted with Buber's stance in 1934 or later on in 1957, when he lectured at Eranos. Ernst Simon informed him of Rosenzweig's letter sometime before 1960 (Scholem 1960, 265 n.27).[44] I learn from this comment that three leading figures in the Jewish-German understanding of Judaism had formulated a vision that elevated mystical experience over content, which was applied to the Sinaitic revelation. Scholem learned about Rosenzweig's view just before 1960 and about Buber's similar view somewhat later. He inserted them, however, into his own earlier reading of revelation as a mystical event, assessing in 1974: "Rosenzweig's and Buber's disquisitions on this point, though executed within the framework of a philosophy of the dialogue between man and God, fundamentally acknowledge only one kind of Revelation – the mystical one, even though they refuse to call it by that name" (Scholem 1976, 272–273).

Moreover, in this work, Scholem applied the same principle to another famous Hasidic author, R. Pinhas of Koretz, again resorting to the phrase "pregnant with infinite meaning" (Scholem 1969c, 112). In another study, Scholem used similar words to describe the view of a thirteenth century Kabbalist, R. Joseph Gikatilla: "The word of God [...] is in fact infinitely pregnant with meaning, but has no fixed interpretation" (1972b, 180). Revelation is conceived of as a potential

---

41 Namely, with mysticism.
42 Of the *Star of Redemption*.
43 See also, e.g., Galli (1993); Grözinger (1994).
44 The time when the original German version was printed. See Scholem (1960, 265, n.27 and 1969c, 30, n. 3).

realm, devoid of a concrete and specific message, more a manifestation than a proclamation, which can be interpreted in infinite directions. By introducing the concept of an infinity of meanings of revelation – not only of the canonical text, Scholem, and his contemporaries, attempted to relativize or even to circumvent one single specific meaning – the rabbinic, or institutional one. Unlike Buber and Rosenzweig, Scholem referred to post-Biblical sources. In my opinion, however, those sources do not really tell the same story. Apparently, R. Menahem Mendel of Rymanov was not a great mystic, as Scholem insists he was, but rather a magical saint and one of the most important forefathers of modern Jewish ultra-ortho-doxy in Eastern Europe (Salmon 2010, 2013).[45] Relative to other Hasidic masters, he delved deeply into Halakhic literature and was seen as the reincarnation of ha-Rif, R. Isaac Alfasi. Scholem transformed him into the exemplary case of a mystical tradition; this transformation found its expression not only in the misin-terpreted passage of this rabbi, but it also inspired both Buber and Rosenzweig. This theory was presented orally by Scholem as an alternative to my claim as to the existence of Kabbalistic sources for the theory of revelation in Rosenzweig's *Star of Redemption* (Idel 2009, 162–163). In my opinion, Rosenzweig could easily have read it in the German original of Ahron Marcus' book on Hasidism, printed in 1901, just as Scholem did.[46] Marcus, however, did not quote any text or give a precise reference; nor does Scholem, who simply comments on Marcus' con-jecture, quote such a text. In other words, the early twentieth century German Jew (Marcus 1901, 239),[47] played an exceptional role in forming Rosenzweig's and Scholem's "mystical" understanding of Sinai, but it was mediated by Marcus' unnecessary imposition of the Maimonidean theory of revelation upon the Hasidic statement.

Scholem did not merely express this view as his personal philosophy, in a melancholic poem, or in private correspondence; he also presented it as a critical academic understanding of the historical situation, and, as I shall show later, it was accepted as such. Revelation, considered mystical at its core, is understood

---

45 On his view of the Torah, see Idel (2010, 90–91). About his student, see Salmon (1996).

46 On Marcus, see Scholem (2009) and the update of Assaf in the same work (393–394). It is sur-prising that Scholem, who wrote this strongly negative description of Marcus' book in 1954, only three years before lecturing at Eranos, nevertheless decided to rely on his conjecture and then extrapolate from it about mysticism and authority.

47 Marcus mentions R. Ezekiel Panet's compilation of R. Menahem Mendel of Rymanov's tra-ditions entitled *Menahem Tzion*. The Hebrew translation of Marcus' book does not quote the Hasidic source nor give a precise reference. The situation is the same in the Hebrew translation of his book *Hahasidut* (1954, 385). See Scholem (1969c, 30) and the later and enlarged Hebrew version translated under his supervision, as *Pirkei yesod be-havanat hakabbalah usemaleyah*, [Elements of the Kabbalah and its symbolism] (1976a, 34–35).

as initially inchoate and structured religion as one of its possible actualizations in time and place (Scholem 1969c, 8).

Let me return now to the anecdote regarding Scholem's father, who mocked the Sabbath interdictions but believed that the Jews should fulfill a sublime theological mission. As in Buber and Rosenzweig, the performative dimension of the commandments is secondary, probably considered a human invention, whereas something higher, more abstract – the idea of monotheism – is the dominant element. This is a case of an ideatic turn. As Eric L. Santner suggested regarding one of Scholem's statements about the "nothingness of revelation" cited above, they may reflect the impact of a Paulinian approach (Santer 2006, 39–40). This may hold true, too, in the case of Buber and Rosenzweig's above-mentioned statements, although they also expressed other views on the same topics. Paul's denial of the religious relevance of biblical commandments derives from his personal vision of Jesus; the three Jewish-German thinkers, however, deny only the divine origin of the content extracted by interpretation, and thus of the details of the biblical commandments, which they depict, at least implicitly, as part of what they would call an oral Torah. The written Torah, namely the Hebrew Bible, is consequently relegated to the status of an oral one. In a way, this interpretation of the Sinaitic revelation subverts the traditional views of both the written and oral Torah.[48]

The three thinkers conceived of the oral dimension of the revelation experience as a superior aspect of religiosity, part of the retreat from the shared text and its institutionalized status. The oral revelation represents more a personal type of experience in the present rather than a collective revelation in the past. This emphasis on the oral dimension is well known also from the theoretical assumptions that guided Buber and Rosenzweig's translation of the Hebrew Bible. Whereas the rabbis attempted to validate their exegetical innovations by claiming that these innovations had already been promulgated at Sinai, Scholem claims that everything articulated in the Hebrew text and in rabbinic literature consists solely of human interpretations.

This specific interpretation of the relationship between authority and mysticism has a strong universalist valence. Jewish mysticism is thus but one mode of interpreting a larger phenomenon: the transition from the inchoate and meaningless, the "nothingness of revelation" – which includes, nevertheless, all possible meanings – to a specific language and tradition. The Pauline mode of explanation, however, works much better in the cases of Buber and Rosenzweig, and less so for Scholem. I assume that, despite the three Jewish-German thinkers' similar

---

48 See also Sommer (1999, 448).

phenomenological approach, they relied on different sources, although in two cases at least, Marcus appears to have been one source.

As mentioned above, Marcus, who supplied to Scholem the misinterpreted text of Menahem Mendel of Rymanov, and Scholem mentioned the contribution of Maimonides to the specific interpretation of the Hasidic master (Marcus [1901, 239]; Scholem [1969c, 31], Sommer [1999, 440, n. 40]; Idel [2010, 107 n. 172 and 2009, 122–124]). Although R. Menahem of Rymanov's thought does not show the influence of the Great Eagle, nevertheless, the latter's views affected the way in which two German Jews understood, mistakenly in my opinion, the Hasidic author. The *Guide to the Perplexed* distinguishes between the inchoate sound heard by the children of Israel, on the one hand, and Moses, who heard an articulated voice, on the other. Although Scholem duly acknowledges this (1969c, 30, n. 1),[49] he elaborates on the vague tradition in the name of the Rymanover Rebbe, as if no articulated voice was heard at all. Maimonides, whose view the Hasidic author vaguely invoked, is thus hardly relevant for Scholem's interpretation.

Strangely, the Pauline propensity and the Maimonidean share an assumption about the existence of a higher religious realm that transcends the specific religious orientation of a specific religion. In Paul's case, it is the belief in Jesus; in Maimonides, it is the act of intellection, which means some form of internalized religiosity, in a manner very reminiscent of Buber's religiosity. In both cases, the performative aspect of religion is secondary or marginal. In the case of the Great Eagle, he perceived revelation as initially speechless because it is some form of intellectual illumination; indeed, one of his followers, R. Abraham Abulafia, explicitly understood this as tantamount to the Sinaitic revelation.[50] Moreover, I would follow the insight of Benjamin Sommer (1999, 447) as to the Kantian overtones of the distinction between the unheard Torah as the noumenal one and the interpretation of the revelation as the phenomenal Torah.

6 The transfer of the transfer of categories

The Jewish intellectual elites' acculturation to Christian propensities was an obvious phenomenon in the twentieth century, just as their forebears throughout the centuries such as Philo or Maimonides acculturated to their respective major-

---

49 Whether this is indeed the esoteric stance of Maimonides or not is a question we cannot address here.

50 *Guide of the Perplexed* 2: 33. For Abulafia's views on this issue, see my "On the Secrets of the Torah in Abraham Abulafia" (Idel 2012, 1: 422–427).

ity cultures. My major point, however, relates to a new phenomenon: Jewish intellectuals were no longer merely exponents of Judaism, as they understood it; their propensity toward negativity infiltrated into an historical-oriented academic presentation of the various aspects of the past. Based on an analysis of a small number of specific texts, advocates of this new approach extrapolate to more comprehensive topics such as the affinities between mysticism and authority. Those interpretations are, in my opinion, dubious, with respect to more general phenomena of Judaism as a religion. Each Jewish intellectual – past or present – is entitled to his or her vision of Judaism. Presenting essentialist views of Judaism as if they are relevant for a historical phenomenon is, however, a totally different story, especially when the cloak of an academic position is involved.[51]

As pointed out, the richness of German culture indubitably enhanced the brilliance of the cultural contribution to new understandings of Judaism. Another factor was the relative openness of many Jews and some Germans to engage in an intellectual dialogue, modest as it might have been from the point of view of the majority culture. It was part of a specific historical and social constellation that changed in a very short time, dramatically and tragically, into the worst of nightmares for most of German Jewry and many Germans. The Jews descended from Enlightenment to apocalypse, to invert the title of a book on German intellectuals: Anson Rabinbach's *In the shadow of catastrophe: German intellectuals between apocalypse and enlightenment*. The developments between 1933 and 1945 annihilated much of the Jewish audience that produced and supported the German-Jewish intellectual dialogue. Some first-rate scholars such as Leo Strauss, Hans Jonas, Alexander Altmann, Walter Benjamin, Ernst Cassirer, Nachum Glatzer, the members of the Warburg Institute in Hamburg, and the Frankfurt Institute for Social Research left Germany, most of them forever. This obvious case of *translatio scientiae* brought the German-Jewish symbiosis to the West.

One of the first and most outspoken critics of this dialogue, Gershom Scholem, left Germany as early as 1923; other Jewish-German academicians such as Julius Guttmann, Yitzhak Baer, or much later, Martin Buber, followed, and they became his colleagues at the nascent Hebrew University in Jerusalem. Despite his leaving Germany as a matter of principle and repeatedly distancing himself from the perceived Jewish-German symbiosis, Scholem's so-called "Germanness" is amply evident (Geller 2011, 211–232). As noted above, Scholem suggested this in describing himself as a reincarnation of Reuchlin. On a personal note, after Scholem's death, his widow Fanya described Scholem to me as someone who remained a "Berliner boy."

---

51 See, e.g., my discussion of Steiner's approach in Idel (2009, 52–78).

The transfer of categories from the majority culture to the understanding of Judaism and to its portrayal in academic fields continued to inform Jewish theological and academic expositions. Both intellectual circles and academia accepted the findings in a complex field such as Kabbalah as evident truths rather than as merely the conclusions of a brilliant mind operating in specific cultural and historical circumstances. The above-mentioned scholars carried out the conceptual transfer of categories from Germany to the institutions where they worked, especially in the United States and in Israel.[52] In such places, a prevailing liberal attitude toward Jews, combined with an elite approach reminiscent of the Weimar Republic that prioritizes individual experiences over national issues, not only facilitates the reception of those views among the Jewish intelligentsia but more so in academic circles dealing with Judaica. In this approach, Judaism appears as a mandarin-like culture or religion that is disconnected from social reality. One can discern such a view not only in the thinkers mentioned above but also in George Steiner, for example.

Let me adduce some examples: Prof. Ismar Schorsch, while serving as the chancellor of the Jewish Theological Seminary in New York, delivered a sermon in 1994 on the first pericope of Leviticus dealing, inter alia, with the small letter *alef* in the first chapter of the book of Leviticus:

> Scholem then adds a comment rife with paradox, from an early Hasidic master, Rabbi Mendel of Rymanov, who died in 1814. "All that Israel heard at Sinai was the first letter of the first word of the first Commandment, that is, nothing more than the silent alef of *anokhi*, 'I am'" (Exodus 20: 2). "To hear the *alef*," comments Scholem, "is to hear next to nothing; it is the preparation for all audible language, but in itself conveys no determinate, specific meaning. Thus, with his daring statement that the actual revelation to Israel consisted only of the *alef*, Rabbi Mendel transformed the revelation on Mount Sinai into a mystical revelation, pregnant with infinite meaning, but without specific meaning." [...] In responding to God's voice, we cannot escape the need to interpret what we hear. Human beings are the filter through which revelation passes. In 1925, Franz Rosenzweig wrote to Martin Buber as follows: "The only immediate content of revelation [...] is revelation; with *vayered* (he came down, Exodus 19:20), it is essentially complete; with *vayeddaber* (he spoke Exodus 20:1), interpretation sets in and all the more so with *anokhi*."[53]

Born in Hamburg in 1935, Prof. Schorsch is a leading scholar in the field of modern Jewish history in the United States. This sermon exemplifies the statement in his

---

52 For the transfer to the Israeli center see Myers (1995, passim). This is the case also for the U.S. center.

53 Chancellor's Parashah Commentary, Parashat Vayikra 5754, Leviticus 1:1–5:26, 19 March 1994, 7 Nisan 5754. https://www.jtsa.edu/prebuilt/ParashahArchives/5754/vayikra.shtml. (last accessed 26.02.2015).

book: "Modern scholarship has permanently affected the way we think about Judaism" (Schorsch 1994, 156). Although he referred explicitly to Scholem and Rosenzweig, perhaps Buber is also involved here: The vision of the interpreter as filter is not found in Scholem or Rosenzweig, but it is reminiscent of Buber's claims during the polemics with Scholem on the nature of Hasidism that he was not a philologist or historian but only a filter. Another senior member of the Jewish Theological Seminary faculty adopted a similar approach toward revelation and interpretation in a study about Jewish theology.[54]

Elisabeth Weber's *Questions au judaïsme* contains another interesting example of the reverberation of Scholem's discussion. In a piece entitled *Devant la loi, après la loi*, Jean-François Lyotard answered a question posed by Weber, a professor at the University of California, Santa Barbara. Fascinatingly, in addressing Weber's question (Weber, 1996, 188–189), Lyotard contemplates the inaudible alef, which he views as "characteristic of the Jewish tradition, of its thought" (Weber 1996, 190).[55] A non-existent text thus became the representative type of thought. Whereas Lyotard mentioned Scholem explicitly, Gilles Bernheim, the former chief rabbi of France, appropriated his text without mentioning either the French philosopher or Scholem as his source in his *Quarante méditations juives* (2011, 128), an example of a plagiarism.[56] One can discern the influence of Scholem's interpretation not only on remarks by a Conservative Rabbi, Schorsch, and an Orthodox one, Bernheim, but also in comments of a Reform Rabbi, Lawrence Kushner.[57]

Nicholas Wolfson, an American law professor, also appropriated Scholem's interpretation of the Rymanover Rebbe in his book *Hate Speech, Sex Speech, Free Speech*. Alluding to Scholem's discussion of R. Menahem Mendel of Rymanov's nonexistent passage, Wolfson concludes: "*to hear the alef is to hear no meaning. The people of Israel heard nothing more than alef from God; everything thereafter was human interpretation and reinterpretation. There was no understandable, transcendental foundation for the religion revealed to the people of Israel*" (Wolfson 1997, 17. [Italics in the original]). In the same place, Wolfson also com-

---

54 See Gillman (2008, 132–133).

55 "Ce qui me paraît caractéristique de la tradition juive, de sa pensée." See also Peperstraten (2009, 31–32). See also above n. 30, in Buber's statement.

56 See Nehorai and Hamon (2013). Aware that the tradition quoted by Scholem and then by Lyotard does not stem directly from R. Menahem Mendel of Rymanov's book, the authors claimed that it was quoted in his name by R. Asher Isaiah Lipman and his master, R. Naftali Horowitz of Ropshitz. See Idel (2009, 122–124).

57 See, e.g., his *Dvar Torah* on the web: http://www.reformjudaism.org/print/1033. (last accessed 26.02.2015).

pares this view to Derrida's deconstruction on the one hand, and to John Dewey's pragmatism, on the other hand. Wolfson may represent the secular Jew.

As I see it, creative theologies, such as those of Buber and Rosenzweig, and to a certain extent also Scholem's, to some degree *reduce and distort significant parts of the Jewish tradition.* This simplification, by its nature inevitable, is evident also in the thought of the few Jewish theologians, whether Philo or Maimonides, indisputably very sophisticated thinkers. The first two modern thinkers, however, were more concerned with a framework for an experiential type of religiosity than with a historical picture. Scholem did not make that claim in his studies, especially in his sharp polemic against Buber's portrayal of Hasidism, on the one hand, and in his denial of writing as a theologian, on the other.[58] Nevertheless, he was definitely in search of an accurate historical picture. In my opinion, however, Scholem's picture and that of his followers who disagreed with Buber's rendering of Hasidism contains another type of distortion that I would term as otherworldly, Neoplatonically-oriented overemphasis.[59]

It is worth mentioning, however, that even a dubious scholarly interpretation of an earlier text can become a very creative and fruitful theological starting point. It is of outmost importance, however, to be aware of the clear distinction between the two stances. Was not such a separation one of the major goals of the *Wissenschaft des Judentums*?

As noted above, R. Menahem Mendel of Rymanov had a deep impact on the emergence of modern Hasidic ultra-orthodoxy, a particularistic linguo-centric approach from its very beginnings,[60] which rejects historically oriented academic studies. Modern thinkers, however, took the Hasidic master's apocryphal statement and reformulated it to support the opposite approach, the universalistic vision that affords broad scope for personal reinterpretations of an allegedly inchoate revelation. The rabbi's simile of God at the Sinaitic revelation actually dealt, in my opinion, with a teacher of small children who begin learning in the *heder* by reciting "*Kamats alef* – the most widespread experience of young Jewish children in Eastern Europe for centuries.[61] In the hands of critical scholars and twentieth-century rabbis, this became an expression of the alleged inaudible experience at Sinai, a claim having palpable anarchist overtones (Myers 1995, 173–174). Using categories from German thought, the same individuals interpret the

---

58 See Scholem's remark, cited in Myers (1995, 175).
59 See Idel (2014).
60 See Idel (2013 and 2014).
61 See Idel (2009, 122–124). Marcus speaks about hearing only the alef, but it is Scholem who added the assumption that there was no vowel associated with it.

naïve statements issued in East Europe concerning the plenitude of experience,[62] as if they deal with negativity. One form of *imaginaire* has been interpreted in accordance to another, totally different one. Well, that's how tradition works....

Bibliography

Alter, Robert. *Necessary Angels: Tradition and Modernity in Kafka, Benjamin, and Scholem.* Cambridge, MA: Harvard University Press, 1991.

Baer, Yitskhak. *Mekhkarim vemasot betoldot 'Am Yisrael* (Studies and essays in the history of Israel), vol. 1. Jerusalem: The Israeli Historical Society, 1986.

Baer, Yitskhak. *Galut.* Trans. Robert Washow. Lanham, MD: University Press of America, 1988.

Bernheim, Gilles. *Quarante méditations juives.* Paris: Stock, 2011.

Biale, David. *Gershom Scholem: Kabbalah and Counter-History*, 2d ed. Cambridge, MA.: Harvard University Press, 1982.

Biale, David. "Gershom Scholem's Ten Unhistorical Aphorisms." *Gershom Scholem.* Ed. H. Bloom. New York: Chelsea House Publishers, 1987.

Bielik-Robson, Agata. "Nihilism Through the Looking Glass: Nietzsche, Rosenzweig, and Scholem on the Condition of Modern Disenchantment." *Revista de Estudos da Religião* (September 2007): 39–67.

Bloom, Harold. *Agon, Toward a Theory of Revisionism.* Oxford: Oxford University Press, 1983.

Bloom, Harold. *Kabbalah and Criticism.* New York: Continuum, 1984.

Bloom, Harold. *The Strong Light of the Canonical.* New York: City College Papers, 1987.

Buber, Martin. "The God of the Nations and God." *Israel and the World: Essays in a Time of Crisis.* Trans. G. Hort, O. Marx, I. M. Lask. New York: Schocken Books, 1948.

Buber, Martin. *I and Thou.* Trans. W. Kaufmann. New York: Scribner, 1980.

Buber, Martin. "The Man of the Day and the Jewish Bible." *On the Bible.* Ed. Nahum Glatzer. New York: Schocken Books, 1982.

Buber, Martin. *The Origin and Meaning of Hasidism.* Trans. Maurice Friedman. Atlantic Highlands, NJ: Humanities Press International, 1988.

Dan, Joseph. "Foreword" to Gershom Scholem, *On the Mystical Shape of the Godhead.* Ed. J. Chipman. Trans. J. Neugroschel. New York: Schocken Books, 1991.

Drob, Sanford L. *Kabbalistic Metaphors: Jewish Mystical Themes in Ancient and Modern Thought.* Northvale, NJ: Jason Aronson, 2001.

Franck, Adolphe. *La Kabbale ou la philosophie religieuse des Hebreux.* Paris: Hachette, 1843.

Franks, Paul. "Inner Anti-Semitism or Kabbalistic Legacy? German Idealism's Relationship to Judaism." *Yearbook of German Idealism*, vol. 7, *Faith and Reason*. Ed. Fred Rush, Jürgen Stolzenberg, and Paul Franks. Berlin: De Gruyter, 2010. 269–275.

Galli, Barbara. "Rosenzweig Speaking of Meetings and Monotheism in Biblical Anthropo-morphisms." *The Journal of Jewish Thought and Philosophy* 2 (1993): 219–243.

---

[62] For another example of a similar misunderstanding in the interpretation of another Hasidic view as if antinomian, which also influenced modern thought, see Idel (2009, 236–247).

Geller, Jay Howard. "From Berlin and Jerusalem: On the Germanness of Gershom Scholem." *Journal of Religious History* 35.2 (2011): 211–232.

Gillman, Neil. *Doing Jewish Theology: God, Torah & Israel in Modern Judaism*. Woodstock, VT: Jewish Lights, 2008.

Grözinger, Karl E. "In Rosenzweigs Seele – die Kabbala." *Messianismus zwischen Mythos und Macht. Jüdisches Denken in der europäischen Geistesgeschichte*. Ed. E. Goodman-Thau and W. Schmied-Kowarzik. Berlin: Akademie Verlag, 1994. 127–139.

Handelman, Susan. *Fragments of Redemption*. Bloomington, IN: Indiana University Press, 1991.

Harvey, Warren Ze'ev. "How much Kabbalah in the *Star of Redemption?*" *Immanuel* 21 (1987): 128–134.

Heschel, Abraham J. *Moral Grandeur and Spiritual Audacity: Essays*. Ed. S. Heschel. New York: Farrar, Straus and Giroux, 1996.

Horwitz, Rivka. "From Hegelianism to a Revolutionary Understanding of Judaism: Franz Rosenzweig's Attitude toward Kabbala and Myth." *Modern Judaism* 26 (2006): 31–54.

Idel, Moshe. "Franz Rosenzweig and the Kabbalah." *The Philosophy of Franz Rosenzweig*. Ed. P. Mendes-Flohr. Hanover/London: New England University Press, 1988a. 162–171.

Idel, Moshe. *Kabbalah: New Perspectives*. New Haven: Yale University Press, 1988b.

Idel, Moshe. "Rabbinism versus Kabbalism; on G. Scholem's phenomenology of Judaism." *Modern Judaism* 1 (1991): 281–296.

Idel, Moshe. *Absorbing Perfections: Kabbalah and Interpretation*. New Haven: Yale University Press, 2002.

Idel, Moshe. "On the Theologization of Kabbalah in Modern Scholarship." *Religious Apologetics – Philosophical Argumentation*. Ed. Y. Schwartz, and V. Krech. Tübingen: Mohr Siebeck, 2004. 123–173.

Idel, Moshe. "Johannes Reuchlin: Kabbalah, Pythagorean Philosophy and Modern Scholarship." *Studia Judaica*. Ed. L. Gyemant. 16 (2008): 30–55.

Idel, Moshe. *Old Worlds, New Mirrors: On Jewish Mysticism and Twentieth-Century Thought*. Philadelphia: University of Pennsylvania Press, 2009.

Idel, Moshe. "*Torah Hadashah*: – Messiah and the New Torah in Jewish Mysticism and Modern Scholarship." *Kabbalah* 21 (2010): 90–91.

Idel, Moshe. "Al Sitrei Torah behaguto shel Avraham Abulafia." (On the Secrets of the Torah in the Thought of Abraham Abulafia.) *Religion and Politics in Jewish Thought, Essays in Honor of Aviezer Ravitzky*. Ed. B. Brown, M. Lorberbaum, A. Rosnak, and Y. Z. Stern. Jerusalem: The Israel Democracy Institute, Merkaz Z. Shazar, 2012.

Idel, Moshe. "Modes of Cleaving to the Letters in the Teachings of Israel Baal Shem Tov: A Sample Analysis." *Jewish History* 27 (2013): 299–317.

Idel, Moshe. "East European Hasidism: The Emergence of a Spiritual Movement." *Kabbalah* 32 (2014): 37–63.

Kaplan, Edward K. *Holiness in Words, Abraham Joshua Heschel's Poetics of Piety*. Albany, NY: SUNY Press, 1996.

Kepnes, Steven. *The Text as Thou, Martin Buber's Dialogical Hermeneutics and Narrative Theology*. Bloomington, IN: Indiana University Press, 1992.

Kilcher, Andreas. *Die Sprachtheorie der Kabbala als ästhetisches Paradigma. Die Konstruktion einer ästhetischen Kabbala seit der Frühen Neuzeit*. Stuttgart/Weimar: Metzler, 1998.

Kraut, Benny. "The Approach to Jewish Law of Martin Buber and Franz Rosenzweig." *Tradition* 12. 3/4 (1972): 49–71.

Lucca, Enrico. "Gershom Scholem on Franz Rosenzweig and the Kabbalah. Introduction to the text." *Naharaim* 6 (2012): 7–19.

Magid, Shaul. "Gershom Scholem's Ambivalence toward Mystical Experience and His Critique of Martin Buber in Light of Hans Jonas and Martin Heidegger." *The Journal of Jewish Thought and Philosophy* 4 (1995): 245–269.

Maimonides. *Guide of the Perplexed*. 2:33.

Marcus, Ahron. *Der Chassidismus*. Pletchen: Jeschurun, 1901.

Marcus, Ahron. *Hahasidut*. Trans. M. Shenfeld and Benei Brak: Netzah, 1954.

Mosès, Stéphane. "Patterns of Negativity in Paul Celan's 'The Trumpet Place.'" *Languages of the Unsayable: The Play of Negativity in Literature and Literary Theory*. Ed. S. Budick and W. Iser. New York: Columbia University Press, 1989. 209–224.

Mosès, Stéphane. *L'ange de l'histoire*. Paris: Le Seuil, 1992.

Myers, David. *Re-inventing the Jewish Past, European Jewish Intellectuals and the Zionist Return to History*. New York: Oxford University Press, 1995.

Nancy, Jean-Luc. *Hegel: The Restlessness of The Negative*. Trans. J. Smith and S. Miller. Minneapolis: University of Minnesota Press, 2002.

Nancy, Jean-Luc. *The Creation of the World or Globalization*. Trans. Fr. Raffoul and D. Pettigrew. Albany, NY: SUNY Press, 2007.

Nehorai, Jean and Benoit Hamon. "Gilles Bernheim, Plagiaire de Lyotard ? Du Nouveau dans l'affaire." *La Tribune*, 22 March 2013.

Niehoff, Maren Ruth. "The Buber-Rosenzweig Translation of the Bible within Jewish-German Tradition." *Journal of Jewish Studies* 44 (1993): 258–279.

Nirenberg, David. "The Rhineland Massacres of the Jews in the First Crusades: Memories Medieval and Modern." *Medieval Concepts of the Past: Ritual, Memory, Historiography*. Ed. Gerd Althoff, Johannes Fried, and Patrick Geary. Washington: The German Historical Institute, Cambridge University Press, 2002. 279–309.

Peperstraten, Frans van. "Displacement or composition? Lyotard and Nancy on the *trait d'union* between Judaism and Christianity." *International Journal for Philosophy and Religion*, 2009: 29–46.

Rosenzweig, Franz. *On Jewish Learning*. Ed. N. Glatzer. New York: Schocken Books, 1955.

Rosenzweig, Franz. *Star of Redemption*. Trans. William W. Hallo. New York: Holt, Rinehart and Winston, 1971.

Rosenzweig, Franz. *Der Mensch und sein Werk. Gesammelte Schriften 1. 2: Briefe und Tagebücher 1918–1929*. Haag: Martinus Nijhoff, 1979.

Salmon, Joseph. "R. Naphtali Zevi of Ropczyce ('the Ropshitser') as a Hasidic Leader." *Hasidism Reappraised*. Ed. Ada Rapoport-Albert. London: Littman Library, 1996. 321–342.

Salmon, Joseph. "Iggeret hakodesh be-Mareh Yehezkel, Teshuvah 104: lidemutam shel Rabbi Yehezkel Panet, Rabbi Menahem Mendel mi-Linsk ve-Rabbi Menahem Mendel mi-Rymanov." (*Iggeret hakodesh* in *Mareh Yehezkel*, Response no. 104: On the Image of R. Ezekiel Paneth, R. Menahem Mendel of Linsk, and R. Menahem Mendel of Rymanov). *Daat* 68–69 (2010): 277–297.

Salmon, Joseph. "Mevaserei ha-ultra-orthodoksiah be-Galitziah uve-Hungaria: R. Menahem Mendel mi-Rymanov vetalmidav" (The forerunners of ultra-orthodoxy in Galicia and Hungary: R. Menahem Mendel of Rymanov and his disciples). *Zehuyiot* 2 (2013): 25–54.

Santner, Eric L. *On Creaturely Life: Rilke, Benjamin, Sebald*. Chicago: Chicago University Press, 2006.

Scholem, Gershom. "Offener Brief an den Verfasser der Schrift 'Juedischer Glaube in dieser Zeit.'" *Bayerische Israelitische Gemeindezeitung*. (August 1932): 243.

Scholem, Gershom. *Zur Kabbala und Ihrer Symbolik*. Zurich: Rhein-Verlag, 1960.

Scholem, Gershom. *Ursprung und Anfänge der Kabbala*. Berlin: De Gruyter, 1962.

Scholem, Gershom. *Die Erforschung der Kabbalah von Reuchlin bis zur Gegenwart*. Pforzheim: Selbstverlag der Stadt, 1969a.

Scholem, Gershom. *Major Trends in Jewish Mysticism*. New York: Schocken Books, 1969b.

Scholem, Gershom. *On the Kabbalah and Its Symbolism*. Trans. R. Manheim. New York: Schocken Books, 1969c.

Scholem, Gershom. *The Messianic Idea in Judaism*. New York: Schocken Books, 1972a.

Scholem, Gershom. "The Name of God and the Linguistic of the Kabbalah." *Diogenes* 80 (1972b): 164–194.

Scholem, Gershom. *Kabbalah*. Jerusalem: Keter, 1974.

Scholem, Gershom. *Pirkei Yesod behavanat hakabbalah usemaleyah* (Elements of the Kabbalah and its symbolism). Trans. J. ben Shlomo. Jerusalem: Mossad Bialik, 1976a.

Scholem, Gershom. *On Jews and Judaism in Crisis, Selected Essays*. Ed. W. Dannhauser. New York: Schocken Books, 1976b.

Scholem, Gershom. "Die Stellung der Kabbala in der europäischen Geistesgeschichte." Jahrbuch des Wissenschaftskolleg zu Berlin (1981/1982): 281–289.

Scholem, Gershom. *Devarim bego* (Explications and Implications). Tel Aviv: Am oved, 1982.

Scholem, Gershom. *On the Possibility of Jewish Mysticism*. Philadelphia: JPS, 1997.

Scholem, Gershom. *The Fullness of Time*. Ed. Steven M. Wasserstrom. Trans. Richard Sieburth. Jerusalem: Ibis, 2003.

Scholem, Gershom. *Ha-Shalav haaharon* (The last phase: Essays on Hasidism by Gershom Scholem). Ed. D. Assaf and E. Liebes. Jerusalem: Am Oved and the Magnes Press, 2009. 384–392.

Scholem, Gershom. *From Berlin to Jerusalem*. Trans. H. Zohn. Philadelphia: Paul Dry Books, 2012a.

Scholem, Gershom. "On Franz Rosenzweig and his Familiarity with Kabbala Literature." *Naharaim* 6 (2012b): 1–6.

Scholem, Gershom, ed. *Walter Benjamin / Gershom Scholem, Briefwechsel*. Frankfurt on the Main: Suhrkamp, 1980.

Schorsch, Ismar. *From Text to Content: The Turn to History in Modern Judaism*. Hanover/London: Brandeis University Press, 1994.

Skinner, Anthony. "German-Jewish Identity and the Schocken Library." *Arche Noah: Die Idee der 'Kultur' im deutsch-jüdischen Diskurs*. Ed. B. Greiner and Ch. Schmidt. Freiburg: Rombach, 2002. 289–303.

Smith, Steven B. "Gershom Scholem and Leo Strauss: Notes Toward a German-Jewish Dialogue." *Modern Judaism* 13 (1993): 209–231.

Sommer, Benjamin D. "Revelation at Sinai in the Hebrew Bible and in Jewish Theology." *Journal of Religion* 79 (1999): 422–51.

Weber, Elisabeth. *Questions au judaïsme, Entretiens avec Elisabeth Weber*. Paris: Editions Desclée de Brouwer, 1996.

Wiese, Ch. and M. Urban, eds. *German-Jewish thought between religion and politics: Festschrift in honor of Paul Mendes-Flohr on the occasion of his seventieth birthday*. Berlin: Walter de Gruyter, 2012.

Wolfson, Elliot. *Language, Eros, Being*. New York: Fordham University Press, 2005.

Wolfson, Nicholas. *Hate Speech, Sex Speech, Free Speech*. Westport: Greenwood Publishing Group, 1997.

Wolosky, Shira. *Language and Mysticism: The Negative Way of Language in Eliot, Beckett, and Celan*. Stanford: Stanford University Press, 1995.

Yuval, Israel Jacob. "Yitzhak Baer and the Search of Authentic Judaism." *The Jewish Past Revisited: Reflections on Modern Jewish Historians*. Ed. D. N. Myers and D. B. Ruderman. New Haven: Yale University Press, 1998. 77–87.

Bernd Witte
German Classicism and Judaism

1 The three legitimating discourses in modernity

In the second half of the eighteenth century, during the period of the Enlightenment, new legitimizing discourses begin to dominate public opinion in Europe, relegating religion to the private realm of individual interests. Religion thus became separate from the social and political order and divorced from the structures governing it. At the outset of the century, a metaphysical discourse closely linked to religious concepts still dominated the public sphere in Europe. The deism of Anglo-Saxon provenance was prevalent in most Western European countries in the early period of the Enlightenment. The break with this cultural discourse, whose roots went back to antiquity, occurred in several spheres of thought in the second half of the eighteenth century. During the threshold of European transformation between 1770 and 1790, the predominance of metaphysical discourses waned, yielding to economics in England, politics in France, and art and literature in Germany. These new discourses established themselves as the primary intellectual positions shaping public opinion.

In England, the change of paradigm manifested itself in the area of economic endeavors. A canonical text transformed moral sense philosophy into the new leading discourse. The reference here is, of course, to Adam Smith's theory of liberal market economy in his treatise *An Inquiry into the Nature and Causes of the Wealth of Nations*, which appeared in 1776. Smith's fundamental notion of market economy optimism can be construed as a metaphor borrowed from religious discourse: he reasons that even when striving for personal gain, individuals acting on the basis of economic motives serve the welfare of society. "Man is in this, as in many other cases, led by an invisible hand to promote an end which was no part of his intention" (Smith 1994, 2:456). Modeling his theory on a rapidly industrializing, imperial England aspiring to world supremacy, Smith could base his theory on a belief in the absolute productivity of the economic subject. The metaphor of the invisible hand thus served as the watershed for the secularization of religiously circumscribed beliefs. On the strength of this analogy, capitalist economics attained a semi-religious dignity.

In France, a different change in public discourse took place within the context of its Great Revolution. Legislated by the National Convention on 26 August 1789, the *Declaration des Droits de l'Homme et du Citoyen* inaugurated a political system that converted a formerly metaphysical utopia into a modern society founded on secular values. From that time on, politics that availed itself of charismatic rhetoric, majority decisions, and acts of terror became an instrument for providing freedom, equality, and fraternity to all. This politicization of public discourse is an anthropological act with radical implications. Henceforth, the majority within the social framework and the measures it adopted to achieve its ends determined what is just. Any metaphysical grounding of the fundamental terms defining the social order thus seemed superfluous after 1789.

In Germany, in addition to the economic and political paradigms described above, fundamental change occurred in another sphere. Two years before the publication of Smith's *Wealth of Nations*, Johann Wolfgang Goethe wrote his novel *Die Leiden des jungen Werthers* [The sorrows of young Werther, 1774]. The novel's unprecedented European success rested not only on its introduction of the ideal of soulful love but also on the notion that literature is the medium in which fundamental existential issues are decided. It demonstrated that decisive stations in the life of an individual are no longer determined by metaphysical principles but by literary texts. The agitation that hit Europe after the novel appeared, inciting a number of young men to commit suicide, confirms the drastic effect that literature had on society. Goethe himself likened its development as a leading discourse to the young German generation's revolution against its fathers because it made poetry into a gospel, as the author suggests in *From my Life. Poetry and Truth* (1814, 426–427).

Comparing the books of Goethe and Smith reveals a subtle analogy that is characteristic for the developments shaping this phase of European social and cultural change. Both texts signal a radical anthropological turn that renders religion superfluous. At the end of the eighteenth century, all three new legitimizing discourses – economic, political, and literary – rested on a belief in the absolute productivity and sovereignty of man. Paradoxically, at this precise historical moment, Judaism leaves the cultural ghetto in which it had been locked in Western Europe for centuries and tries to enter into a dialogue with the enlightened culture of the West. In 1782, Moses Mendelssohn published his book *Jerusalem or Religious Power and Judaism*. For the first time, a Jewish intellectual who had been brought up in the traditional religious way of life challenged Kant and his contemporaries in their own field. He reintroduced a strict form of monotheism into the public discourse at the exact moment when the majority tried to abolish all links to traditional religion.

2 Homer – the new Bible

Around 1770, the young generation of German poets radically rejected the traditional religious beliefs, propagating in its place the new religion of the infinite productivity of man. Goethe publicly declared at an early stage that he was inaugurating a new socially legitimating discourse by giving literature a fundamental function in the life of each individual. He adopted Homer, the "father of occidental poetry," as the role model of the almighty genius and his boundless creativity. In his poem "Künstlers Morgenlied" [The artist's morning song], written in 1773 in Frankfurt and published three years later, he describes what the discovery of Homer and his epic songs meant to him.

In the first four verses of this poem, he programmatically replaces the Judeo-Christian tradition with the new concept of a religion of art, heralding a renewed Greek antiquity and the autonomy of the productive subject:

My dwelling is the Muses' home	Ich hab euch einen Tempel baut
What matters it how small?	Ihr hohen Musen all
And here, within my heart, is set	Und hier in meinem Herzen ist
The holiest place of all.	Das Allerheiligste.
When, wakened by the early sun,	Wenn Morgends mich die Sonne weckt
I rise from slumbers sound,	Warm froh ich schau umher
I see the ever-living forms	Steht rings ihr ewig lebenden
In radiance grouped around.	In heilgem Morgenglanz.
I pray, and songs of thanks and praise	Ich bet hinan und Lobgesang
Are more than half my prayer,	Ist lauter mein Gebet
With simple notes of music, tuned	Und Freudeklingend Saytenspiel
To some harmonious air.	Begleitet mein Gebet.
I bow before the altar then,	Und trete vor den Altar hier
And read, as well I may,	Und lese wie sich's ziemt
From noble Homer's masterwork,	Andacht liturgscher Lektion
The lesson for the day	Im heiligen Homer.
(Goethe 1901/02, 240).	(Goethe 2001, 60).

According to the German text of the poem, the poet, talking to the Muses, affirms in the first line: "I myself built a temple for you." Solomon's temple, one of the holiest places of the Jewish religion, is here replaced by the artist's subjective creation, as is Christ's claim to be able to restore the ruined temple within three days. The "Holy of Holies," that is, the part of the temple accessible only to the High Priest, is transferred into the "heart" of the artist. The Muses, the goddesses

Homer invokes to grant the poet memory and divine inspiration, rather than JHWH, are present in this temple.

In the second verse, the artist invokes the statues of the Greek gods that he has assembled around him in his studio as witnesses and objects of the new cult. The third verse continues the secularization of traditional religious metaphors. The joyful harp playing that the poet dedicates to the Muses replaces David's playing the harp, which the Jewish and Christian traditions regarded as the epitome of religious poetry. Finally, the fourth verse articulates explicitly the transformation of the religious tradition contained in the metaphors of the first three verses: "I approach the altar here / and read as is the custom / raptly the liturgical lecture / in holy Homer." It is revealing that the English translation of these lines tries to obscure the blasphemous directness of Goethe's confession. Instead of reading the Holy Scriptures, which constitute the weekly reading of the Jewish as well as of the Christian prayer service, the artist reads Homer's epic poetry as his sacred text. Would it be possible to express more clearly and with greater historical awareness the change of the cultural paradigm taking place in Germany around 1770? In the following period, the history of archaic wars and adventures, not the history of salvation, would prime the cultural memory and form the identity of the individual and his or her social group.

3 Schiller's "Juno Ludovisi"

In 1936 – a date with its own significance – an English historian, Elisabeth Butler, published a book under the title *The Tyranny of Greece over Germany* (Butler 1936). While precisely describing the influence of Greek art, philosophy, and literature in Germany in the nineteenth and the first half of the twentieth century, the title shows only one side of the coin. At the same time that Greek antiquity was becoming the canonical model for the developing classicist German culture, the admirers of this ancient art and literature continually rebuffed the awakening cultural self-confidence of Judaism.

Why this singular fascination with classical art works in Germany? Within the aesthetics of Weimar classicism, Homer's *Iliad* and *Odyssey* became the canonical paradigms of the literary work of genius. Moreover, the contemplation of Greek statues replaced the ritual of traditional religious services. It became the ultimate foundation and legitimation of the new anthropological discourse in Germany. The ideal of the human figure, the artistic representation of the human body now acquired a quasi-religious aura.

The classical aesthetics of German Idealism found its most influential expression in the *Letters on the Aesthetic Education of Man,* which Friedrich Schiller published in 1795 in the first volume of his periodical *Die Horen.* In his text, Schiller expressed the hope of supplanting the French political revolution in Germany with an aesthetic revolution that would bring about a new, peaceful society. In the exact middle of this manifesto, he summarizes his ideas in the description of an antique statue. The marble head of the so-called "Juno Ludovisi," three times larger than life, serves him as an example of the new function of classical art:

> It is neither charm nor is it dignity that speaks from the glorious face of the Juno Ludovisi; it is neither of these, for it is both at once. While the female God challenges our veneration, the godlike woman kindles our love. But while in ecstasy, we give ourselves up to the heavenly beauty, the heavenly self-repose awes us back. The whole form rests and dwells in itself – a fully complete creation in itself – as if she were outside of space, without giving way, without resistance. [...] Irresistibly carried away and attracted by her womanly charm, kept at a distance by her godly dignity, we also find ourselves at length in the state of greatest repose, and the result is a wonderful impression for which the understanding has no idea and language no name (Schiller 1795, 89).

As its religious terminology reveals, these sentences define the aesthetic experience as the new medium of human self-experience. The mise-en-scène of a soulful individuality achieved in pre-classical time through prayer is now expected to occur through the contemplation of the autonomous work of art. By means of his antithetical rhetoric, Schiller puts the antique statue in the place of a Christian image of God. Like the icon, it is outside of time and space. Likewise, it is surrounded by an aura that both brings it closer to the beholder and simultaneously distances it as far as possible from him. Schiller thus replaces the symbolic representation of the divine infinity by the image of an ideal human being created by man. In contemplating it, man is supposed to recognize himself as a human being elevated toward beauty.

It is worth noting how this statue acquired such a preeminent place in Schiller's aesthetics. Johann Joachim Winckelmann first pointed out its importance, calling the woman's head "sublime above others" [über andere erhaben] in his *History of Ancient Art* (Winckelmann 1764, 165). On a visit to Rome more than twenty years later, Johann Wolfgang Goethe discovered the city's antiquities, using Winckelmann's book as a guide. In January 1787, he wrote in a letter to Charlotte von Stein: "From yesterday, I own a colossal head of Juno [...]; it was my first love affair in Rome and now it is mine" (Goethe 1987c, 117). He had bought a plaster replica of the front of the head of "Juno Ludovisi." Upon his return to Weimar, Goethe left the enormous mask behind, giving it as a present to his friend, the painter Angelica Kaufmann. Beforehand, he had asked the art historian Johann Heinrich Meyer to make a drawing of it, which he then took with him to Germany. This is the object Schiller was viewing when he wrote the hymn about the presumably Greek marble in his *Letters on the Aesthetic Education of Man*.

Significantly, Schiller's description of the so-called "Juno Ludovisi" is based not on a vision of the statue itself or its three dimensional replica but on second-hand information that, moreover, is historically incorrect. The statue, in fact, was not of classical Greek origin but rather was sculpted in imperial Rome. Further-more, it does not represent Juno, the mother of all gods, as the eighteenth-century art historians believed. Archaeological research has determined that it is a por-trait of Antonia, the mother of the emperor Claudius, who, after her death in 37 C.E. was elevated to the rank of goddess (Soprintedenza Archeologica di Roma 2005, 140ff.). In other words, Schiller saw a pure projection of his own subjectivity in the "Juno Ludovisi." On the other hand, Wilhelm von Humboldt, when describ-ing the head in *Die Horen*, might have had the right intuition, calling it "womanli-ness in a new form" and "a pure imprint of humanity" (Humboldt 1795, 88). As these terms demonstrate, German classicism's rejuvenation of the polytheism of antiquity is antireligious, an expression of the fact that its aesthetic and moral values rested solely on a radically anthropological approach.

4 Judaism and the Christian Occident

Jewish monotheism first entered into the realm of modern occidental culture at the precise historical moment that the German cultural memory became obsessed with Greek antiquity. Moses Mendelssohn was the first European scholar to liber-ate himself from the Jewish ghetto and to seek and find an intellectual following in the Western European cultural milieu. At a time when religion had lost its influ-ence on the European public, civil society in England championed the ideology of free market liberalism and in France, the propagation of civic and human rights, and literature became the leading discourse in Germany, Judaism introduced a new element into the public discussion.

Moses Mendelssohn, educated in a traditional yeshiva and true to the tra-dition of his fathers, tried to turn the attention of the German-speaking public toward the other roots of occidental culture, the Jewish tradition, which had long been superseded by Christianity. To persuade his Christian readers of the worth of his religion, Mendelssohn quotes the commandment of love, commonly con-sidered as the epitome of the Christian religion, in its original Talmudic form. He paraphrases the haggadic tale told in treatise Shabbat 31a of the Babylonian

Talmud, casting the statement in a positive form: "A heathen said: 'Rabbi, teach me the entire law while I am standing on one foot!' He had previously approached Shamai with the same unreasonable request and had been dismissed contemptuously; Hillel, however, renowned for his imperturbable calm and gentleness, said: 'Son! Love thy neighbor as thyself. This is the text of the law; all the rest is commentary. Now go and study!'"(Mendelssohn 2001, 98).

Through his retelling, Mendelssohn points out that the commandment of love already played an important role in the Torah and that it pertains not only to your relationship to your own people, but to all men: "But the stranger that dwelleth with you shall be unto you as one born among you, and thou shalt love him as thyself; for ye were strangers in the land of Egypt: I am the Lord your God" (Leviticus 19: 34). By recalling the original wording, Mendelssohn wanted to refute the New Testament presentation in which Jesus admonished the scribes and thus accused the Jews of falseness or of forgetfulness. Mendelssohn hoped that the Christian majority could find common ground with the Jewish minority in the correlation between the commandment of love as related in the Talmudic tale, in the Torah, and in the Christian Gospel.

Mendelssohn's quotation also hints at the specificity of the Jewish tradition. In the admonition to the heathen: "Now go and study!" he addresses the reader who is not regularly reading the Torah and advises him to adopt the Jewish form of piety, study of the Holy Scriptures. He thus posits an additional commandment to the one of love that should be common to both religions. In referring to the Jewish tradition's view that the Holy Scriptures need commentary to render them understandable, Mendelssohn was upholding, not deprecating this approach. In Judaism, he believed, "the text of the Law," the canonical scripture, could guarantee the continuity of tradition and therefore the survival of religion only together with its commentary.

Mendelssohn formulates this correlation not only in theory but also in practice in his own text, quoting the dialogue between God and "his messenger, Moses." Condensing chapters 33 and 34 of the book of Exodus, in which after the sins of the Israelites, God renews the covenant with his people, he claims that "the doctrine of God's mercifulness" is the foundation of the human commandment of love. He bases this on the sentences in which God proclaims his pardon:

> With that, the appearance of God passed before Moses, and a voice was heard: 'The Lord is, was and will be the eternal being, all-powerful, all-merciful and all-gracious; long suffering, kind and true; he will preserve his loving kindness down to the thousandth generation; he forgives transgression, sin and rebellion, yet allows nothing to go unpunished.' What man's feelings are so hardened that he can read this with dry eyes? – Whose heart is so inhuman that after reading this he can still hate his brother and remain unreconciled with him? (Mendelssohn 2001, 120).

Mendelssohn breaks off the quotation of the biblical text, thus omitting the imprecation hurled at future generations in Exodus, which in the Christian tradition, for example in the German translation by Martin Luther, plays a major role. Whereas the Christian Occident represents JHWH as the furious avenger, Mendelssohn's version highlights his loving care for all generations to come. God's "envoy" Moses hands down his message to the "sages of his nation," whose wisdom is conserved in the Talmud and finally, in the present, reaches the people of Israel.

Evoking the Jewish tradition of JHWH's all-encompassing mercy, Mendelssohn refutes not only Christianity's one-sided image of the Jewish God. He also denounces the Western European elite's betrayal of the concept of a loving, fatherly God through its worship of Greek art and literature. The Jewish philosopher demonstrates his knowledge of the topic by distancing himself expressly from the idol of the new aesthetics and by professing his allegiance to the God of the Torah over the Olympian gods. "'The Athenians as well as the rest of the Greeks viewed all gods as so malevolent that they imagined any extraordinary or long-lasting good fortune would attract the ire and envy of the gods.'[1] [...] Even Homer, this spiritual, loving man, did not conceive the idea that the gods forgive out of love and that they would enjoy bliss in their celestial home without benevolence" (Mendelssohn 2001, 116ff.) Mendelssohn considered that the Olympian gods were guided by the lowliest human instincts and therefore not divine beings at all. He was directing his polemic, evidently, not only against ancient polytheism but also, especially, against the contemporary revival of antique idolatry.

5 Mendelssohn's theory of a "living scripture"

Mendelssohn's most important contribution to Western cultural memory consists of formulating the first notions about the interdependence of collective memory and its media. Above all, he helped introduce the concept of tradition into the legitimizing discourses of modernity. In his book *Jerusalem oder religiöse Macht und Judentum*, he refers to the religious ritual laws as "a living scriptural form" (Mendelssohn 2001, 98). He subsumes under these the rules governing the daily life of every practicing Jew. He also interprets these rules as having been derived from the "written book of laws." Although the Torah may appear immutable in comparison to historical advancements, Mendelssohn does not perceive the ritual

---

1 Mendelssohn quotes the first sentence from Christoph Meiners: *Geschichte des Ursprungs, Fortgangs und Verfalls der Wissenschaften in Griechenland und Rom*. 2 vol. 1781/82.

laws as bound solely to scriptural transmission. According to him, they continue to evolve through living example and find practical expression and interpretation in oral teaching. This implies that "they can keep in step with all changes in due time and under any condition." Mendelssohn thus transcends the traditional antagonism between oral and written tradition by upholding the notion that the ritual laws are "a meaningful form of scripture, which arouses heart and soul by generating new reflections on tradition and promoting opportunities for oral teaching" (Mendelssohn 2001, 98). Significantly, his interpretation of ritual law combines the advantages of both forms of language – the advantage of the written word to store memory in an unaltered form and the advantage of oral commentary to reflect cultural change and development.

Hence, he could exclaim: "We are *literati*, men of letters." He does not simply echo general criticisms regarding cultural pessimism and decay, although complaints about the increased desire to read as well as the excessive production of printed matter were common at the end of the eighteenth century. Rather, prompted by the meaning that the aggregate structures of language had for its content, Mendelssohn developed a general history of culture based on a theory of media that stemmed from the Jewish tradition. "I believe that the changes that affected the written signs in the various epochs of our cultural development exercised a decisive influence not only on the revolutions in human understanding and knowledge but also, more importantly, on the multitude of changes in opinions and terms regarding religious matters" (Mendelssohn 2001, 100). Mendelssohn's remarkable prognosis served to transform religion into a historical entity, refuting the approaches to history prevalent at the time. For the very first time in Western intellectual history, we see the conviction that the contents of cultural memory are dependent upon the media in which they manifest themselves. Moreover, Mendelssohn derived this media-based theory of Western cultural memory from fundamental insights into Judaic sources and traditions.

Basing his theory on Jewish religious sources as well as on Herder's treatise *On the Origin of Language*, Mendelssohn elaborates a typological history of scripture that also incorporates the distinction between oral and written language. Interestingly, today, we can view his concepts as a thought-provoking theory of signs or semiotics. According to Mendelssohn's theory, written signs and their objects of reference are identical at the point of scriptural origin. He remarks: "The first visual signs that mankind used to designate certain specific terms would most likely have been the things themselves. As every natural object reveals its own character, which distinguishes itself from all other objects, so is the impression that the object makes on our senses one that turns our attention towards the difference in signs. This serves to stimulate its ideal representation in us and helps constitute its correct signifier" (Mendelssohn 2001, 103). Mendelssohn outlines the development of the sign system constituting scripture, starting with the original convergence of sign and object in hieroglyphic writing, the emergence of scripture based on the alphabet, and, finally, from the development of the written word to the era of the printing press. In all of these developmental stages, however, meaning arises from the inherent differences of the written signs. This implies a separation of the sign from its referential object, a separation that has its prefiguration in the mystical concept of the Torah as a sign system comprised of letters that become meaningful only in their differentiality and are thus open to infinite exegesis. The mystical tradition thus enabled Mendelssohn to endorse the concept of a comprehensive sign system, on the basis of which he was also able to perceive a differentiated system of ritual laws as a form of scripture.

According to Mendelssohn, the different forms of scripture lead to different modes of knowledge and understanding: "Images and written imagery are the basis for superstition and idolatry, and our alphabetic writing causes mankind to be too speculative" (Mendelssohn 2001, 113). Accordingly, he rejects the systematic philosophy of German idealism, tracing its abstraction back to its medium of expression, that is, scripture based on the alphabet. On the contrary, he considers that Israel's superiority springs from its being the "priestly nation" to whom the ritual law was revealed. For him, this scriptural form unites the advantages of orality and literalness and at the same time promotes the "keenest understanding of sacred truths." The law revealed to Moses at Mount Sinai, read as scripture, guarantees the purity of the terms used to approach the eternal God by isolating the effects of nature and its mythical plurality. At the same time, the law enables Israel to develop as an ideal community by providing a scriptural medium for the cultural memory of a chosen people.

Mendelssohn's description could be viewed as the ideal model of a "mnemonic society." Societies in which cultural memory plays an important role keep tradition alive and transmit experience from one generation to the next, despite the finality of death. Tradition is also bound to the re-creation and repetition of ritual rules in conjunction with their continual exegesis, that is, the reliving of historical events and their significance for a living generation. Through reenactment, one experiences the past as a driving force behind the present, as in the Passover Seder, when the Jews commemorate their exodus from Egypt, their liberation from slavery, and the promise to return to the holy city of Jerusalem. The nineteenth-century philosophical and aesthetic discourse never accepted Mendelssohn's revolutionary insights into the functioning of oral and literal mnemonic societies. They did not find their way into Western public consciousness until the twentieth century. Once again, philosophers of Jewish origin, Maurice Halbwachs and Jacques Derrida, were instrumental in bringing this change about.

6 The Anti-Judaism of Goethe and Schiller

Mendelssohn's work situates Moses at the origin of religion and, therefore, at the source of Western civilization. In contrast, Weimar classicism regarded Homer's poetry as the canonical texts representing the ideal of a cultural memory based on literature and art. Schiller and Goethe no longer adhered to the Jewish and Christian view of Moses as a founding father of the Occident. They did not attack Christianity directly, but by attributing a new role to Moses, they eradicated the importance of monotheistic religion and opened the way for their Renaissance of Greek polytheism.

In 1738, the Scottish bishop William Warburton had already claimed in his book *The Divine Legation of Moses* that it was not divine revelation that had engendered monotheism; Moses, he contended, was an offspring of the Egyptian elite and as such had revealed the hitherto secret mysteries of the Egyptian religion to the Israelites. Schiller adopted this thesis in his lecture *Die Sendung Moses* (The Legation of Moses) published in 1790 in his periodical *Thalia*. The change in the title indicates that Schiller saw Moses in a very different light. He is no longer – as he was in Warburton's work – the founder of a new religion. Instead, he is the legislator who gives the Israelites a new constitution, trying to transform them from a savage group of shepherds into a civilized nation. Schiller, who never had a direct encounter with Jews, denigrates them as much as possible in order more strongly to accentuate Moses' political and legal merit. He thus speaks of their "unworthiness and depravity" (Schiller 1958, 784). Citing Greek historians, he asserts that during their 400-hundred year sojourn in Egypt, they were so "oppressed" that "the highest degree of uncleanliness and contagious diseases" became endemic with them: "This first set the stage for the misfortune that has been this Nation's downfall to the present time; back then, it ravaged them to a frightful extent. The most horrible epidemic in that latitude, leprosy, tore into them, and became the legacy of generations to come. The sources of life and procreation were gradually poisoned by it, and from a fortuitous ill, ultimately, a hereditary tribal constitution arose" (Schiller 1958, 785ff.).

Schiller extends his negative characterization up to the present, calling the Jews "the roughest, the most malicious and depraved people on earth" (Schiller 1958, 787). In his denigration of an entire nation, he clearly reproduced the antisemitic prejudices of his time. This attitude blinded the prophet of freedom and fraternity to the positive contribution of Judaism to the European cultural memory.

Goethe definitively destroyed the figure of Moses in a text written in 1797, but published only very late in 1819, under the title *Israel in the Desert* [Israel in der

Wüste], in the most improbable context of his *Notes to the West-Eastern Divan*.[2] Goethe seemingly adopts the most modern form of biblical criticism, arguing that under normal circumstances, the Israelites could not have spent forty years in the desert. His calculations suggest that they needed only two years for their journey. This seemingly objective analysis, however, is only the pretext for a very radical damnation of Moses and his people. Goethe calls him "a violent man." Lacking an education, Moses "presented himself as purely a man of nature" and committed a "patriotic assassination" (Goethe [1819], 1987b, 160). Fleeing from Egypt, Moses induced the Israelites to attack the Egyptians. This deed prompted a commentary revealing Goethe's most secret fears: "The stranger murders the native, the guest murders the host" (Goethe [1819], 1987b, 7: 163).

Goethe condemns not only the Israelites and Moses, their "commander and ruler," but he also criticizes the biblical text itself: "The books of Moses [2–5] are made utterly unpalatable by a deeply saddening, unintelligible mode of editing. We see the historical narrative obstructed everywhere by the interpolation of innumerable laws. [...] In such a vast campaign, inherently encumbered with so many obstacles, we cannot understand why anyone would try so deliberately and pedantically to pile up the religious baggage of rituals, making any progress immeasurably more difficult" (Goethe [1819], 1987b, 7: 156). One must understand this critique as a direct answer to Mendelssohn's praise of the "ritual laws" as a "living scripture." It shows that Goethe, although he knew many Jews and the traditional way of Jewish life personally, had no insight into the specificity of the Jewish religion and the importance of following the Torah's precepts. Furthermore, his text illustrates the clash between the culture of the majority and that of the Jewish minority. Judaism was unable to persuade even an enlightened German, as Goethe was, or to make him understand or at least tolerate its most important religious convictions.

Surprisingly, Goethe states in his interpretation of Exodus that Moses was murdered by his fellows. "Unfortunately, Moses had even less talent as a commander than as a ruler. [...] While these things were happening, Moses himself disappeared as Aaron had done. After tolerating the rule of a narrow-minded man for some years, Joshua and Caleb might well have deemed it proper to put an end to that regime and to send him out next, following the many unfortunate scouts he had delegated" (Goethe [1819], 7: 167, and 170). The Bible, of course, contains no trace of Moses' violent death. Goethe was the first to refer to it. Unlike Sigmund Freud, who a hundred years later interpreted the murder of Moses as the original traumatic experience guaranteeing the continuance of Jewish ethical rules,

---

2 Goethe intentionally concealed his attack on Moses among his notes, which are an explanation of his lyrics in the West-Eastern Divan.

Goethe used his invention for the ultimate damnatio memoriae of the witness to the revelation of monotheistic religion.

7 The cultural memory of Judaism versus the cultural memory of the Occident

At the end of the eighteenth century, the young Jewish elite, which was trying to transform its religious traditions in a way to make it compatible with Western culture, discovered in the classicist aesthetics of Weimar a cultural practice similar to its own traditional one. Having been educated as part of the "people of the book," this elite discovered in their German contemporaries people believing in the overwhelming power of the written word. In both cases, they considered that canonical figures and the scriptures presumably created by them laid the foundation for finding one's own cultural identity. For this reason, Jewish intellectuals on their way to emancipation greeted the new legitimating discourse in Germany with such enthusiasm. They believed that they had found another "people of the book" undergoing an experience similar to their own. Tragically, they did not realize that reading and rewriting the Homeric epos was a highly individual venture, not comparable to commenting on a text considered as God's revelation to his chosen people. Moreover, they rarely grasped that the classic aesthetics of Weimar were more than just another aesthetic theory, namely a new social and political discourse that was based on a specific opposition to the Jewish tradition. One might not call Schiller and Goethe's statements anti-Semitic, but they are anti-Judaic. They excluded the Jewish religion and the Jewish way of life at the very moment when Jews in Western Europe were trying to draw nearer to the civilization of modernity. They represented an attempt to eliminate monotheism from the European cultural memory by denigrating those who invented it.

Bibliography

Butler, Elisabeth. *The Tyranny of Greece over Germany*. Cambridge, UK: Cambridge University Press, 1936.

Goethe, Johann Wolfgang. *From my Life. Poetry and Truth* (1814) .*Goethes Werke. Weimarer Ausgabe* part 1, vol. 28. Munich: Deutscher Taschenbuch Verlag, 1987a.

Goethe, Johann Wolfgang. *Israel in der Wüste* (1819). *Goethes Werke. Weimarer Ausgabe*, part 1, vol. 7. Munich: Deutscher Taschenbuch Verlag, 1987b. 156–187.

Goethe, Johann Wolfgang. "Letters 1786–1788." *Goethes Werke. Weimarer Ausgabe*, part 4, vol. 8. Munich: Deutscher Taschenbuch Verlag, 1987c.

Goethe, Johann Wolfgang. "The Artist's Morning Song." *The Works of J. W. von Goethe*, vol. 9. Ed. Nathan Haskell Dole. London/Boston: F.A. Niccolls and company, 1901/1902.

Goethe, Johann Wolfgang. "Künstlers Morgenlied" (1773). *Johann Wolfgang Goethe: Gedichte*. Ed. Bernd Witte. Stuttgart: Reclam, 2001.

Humboldt, Wilhelm von. "Über die männliche und weibliche Form." *Die Horen* 1. 3. (1795).

Mendelssohn, Moses. *Jerusalem oder religiöse Macht und Judentum* (1783). Ed. David Martyn. Bielefeld: Aisthesis, 2001.

Schiller, Friedrich. *Die Sendung Moses* (1790). *Sämtliche Werke*, vol. 4. Ed. Herbert Göpfert et al. Munich: Hanser, 1958.

Schiller, Friedrich. "Briefe über die ästhetische Erziehung des Menschen." *Die Horen* 1. 2. (1795).

Smith, Adam. *An Inquiry into the Nature and Causes of the Wealth of Nations* (1776). *The Glasgow Edition of the Works and Correspondence*. Oxford: Oxford University Press, 1994.

Soprintedenza Archeologica di Roma: Museo Nazionale Romano. English Edition. Milano 2005. 140ff.

Winckelmann, Johann Heinrich. *Geschichte der Kunst des Alterthums*, part 1. Dresden: Walthersche Hofbuchhandlung, 1764.

Sander L. Gilman

Aliens vs. Predators: Cosmopolitan Jews vs. Jewish Nomads

The history of cosmopolitanism from the Enlightenment to the twentieth century focused on the double strand of a positive or a negative image of mobility.[1] The Jews were the litmus test for this in German-speaking Central Europe: were they "aliens," a beneficent or at least malleable population because they were mobile, or were they "predators," a threat to established or evolving national identity because of their mobility. This discourse, with all the ambiguities on both sides of the issue, finds expression in the idea of a cosmopolitan versus a nomadic people. The Jews, from the Old Testament to the present, figure as the exemplary cases for each position.

From the Baroque concept of the Jew as the original Gypsy to the Enlightenment discourse about the movement of peoples, and throughout the debates within Zionism in the nineteenth and twentieth centuries about the rootedness of the Jew, the antithetical idea of the movement of the Jews as an indicator of potential integration or isolation from the national state remains a factor in defining the cosmopolitan.

Cosmopolitanism and its sister concept nomadism repeatedly acquire different meanings when their referent is the Jews. Applying this litmus test reveals that both cosmopolitanism and nomadism are symbolic manifestations of the antisemitic stereotype that associates Jews with capital. This history of the term "cosmopolitan" points to the ambivalence of these concepts when applied in the present to specific categories of social and geographic mobility, whether in reference to the Jew, the asylum seeker, the migrant, or the undocumented immigrant. The marginal and excluded people of Enlightenment Germany may have transmuted into the global citizens of the twenty-first century in some instances, but the aura of the corrupt and corrupting, of the rootless and the transitory, of the foreign and the unhoused always remains beneath the surface and shapes what it means to be cosmopolitan and global. As such, it influences the self-image of those so defined.

The term "globalization" and its surrogate cosmopolitanism imply a universalist claim that all human beings share certain innate human rights, including the free movement of peoples across what are seen as the superficial boundaries of nation, class, race, caste, and, perhaps, even gender and sexuality (Brennan

---

1 See, for example, Beck and Sznaider (2006a and 2006b). Recently, David Nirenberg (2013) has raised the question of the projection of such spectral qualities onto the stereotype of the Jew.

1997). The tension between the universal and local meanings of cosmopolitanism, however, originally arose in the Enlightenment, as did the common use of the term itself. Standard etymologies in various European languages note that it is a Greek term, its modern use having been borrowed from the French into English as early as the sixteenth century by the necromancer John Dee to denote a person who is "A Citizen [...] of the [...] one Mysticall City Vniuersall" (Dee 1577, 54). It became common usage in English, however, only in the early nineteenth century. The German language introduced the term *Weltbürger* (world citizen) in the early sixteenth century to provide an alternative to the French *cosmopolitisme* and *cosmopolite*. The French Academy documents *cosmopolitisme* in its dictionary of 1762, but that is the first "official" recognition of a much older usage. The earlier German usages, similar to those in English, are sporadic. Erasmus, it seems, was the first to use it in the early sixteenth century in a letter to Zwingli, referring to Socrates who, when asked of what city he was a citizen, replied that he was a "Weltbürger (κοσμοπολίτην sive mundanum)" ("Mitteilungen: Weltbürger" 1926, 13). The term came into wider use in German during the Enlightenment, thus earlier than in English. Apparently, Jakob Friedrich Lamprecht popularized the term in German with his periodical entitled *Der Weltbürger* (1741–42). G. E. Lessing used the term cosmopolitan (rather than *Weltbürger*) in 1747, and a wide range of Enlightenment figures quickly followed suit. In all of these cases, the status of the Jews functioned as the litmus test for the cosmopolitan in the German Enlightenment.

Addressing the National Assembly during the French Revolution, one of the major Enlightenment thinkers, the Abbé Grégoire, attacked the facile use of a universal claim of cosmopolitanism:

> A writer of the last century (Fénelon) said: "I love my family better than myself: I love my country better than my family but I love mankind better than my country." Reason has criticized both those extravagant people who talked about a universal republic and those false people who made a profession out of loving people who lived at a distance of two thousand years or two thousand leagues in order to avoid being just and good towards their neighbors: systematic, de facto cosmopolitanism is nothing but moral or physical vagabondage (Lallement 1823, [1821] 15: 231).

Applying the idea locally, the Abbé was a powerful advocate for the universal emancipation of French Jewry as French citizens, a status that trumped their specifically Jewish identity (Berkovitz 2004, 152). For the Enlightenment, and it is with the Enlightenment that this tale begins, the Jews in Paris, not in the distant past nor in faraway Palestine, are the litmus test for true French cosmopolitanism. Anything else is merely "vagabondage," moral or physical nomadism. Attention to the immediate and the proximate defined true cosmopolitanism, a topic much debated at the time. It is immediately contrasted, however, with the merely nomadic.

The first major German literary advocate of cosmopolitanism was Christoph Martin Wieland, who devoted several essays to cosmopolitanism in the 1780s. In his most famous, "The Secret of Cosmopolitan Order," in 1788, he declared: "Cosmopolitans [...] regard all the peoples of the earth as so many branches of a single family, and the universe as a state, of which they, with innumerable other rational beings, are citizens, promoting together under the general laws of nature the perfection of the whole, while each in his own fashion is busy with his own well-being" (Wieland 1853–1858, 30: 422).

Wieland, similar to the *philosophes*, sees this as a transcendental category, trumping the local. He himself was paraphrasing Friedrich II's oft-cited note of June 1740 concerning Huguenot and Catholic toleration, but not emancipation: "Each should be blessed in their own manner" ("Jeder soll nach seiner Façon selig werden"), a tolerance grudgingly extended in 1750 to Prussian Jewry.[2] Wieland's own Enlightenment views on the Jews are clear: he mocks, in his *Private History of Pereginus Proteus* (1781), the pagan whose grandfather "had a boundless aversion for Jews and Judaism; his prejudices against them, were, perhaps, partly unjust, but they were incurable"; yet he equally detested Christians, who "[...] passed for a Jewish sect" (Wieland 1796, 2: 32). Enlightenment thought generally promoted a rooted cosmopolitanism, a universalist sensibility rooted in the nation. It rejected religious affiliation, particularly that of the Jews, because of its particularity. Wieland's cosmopolitanism thus contests the religious exclusivity of both Christians and Jews over the universal.

Jewish cosmopolitanism is negative when it is defined in terms of capital; when it is uncontested, any discussion of capital is avoided. Indeed, any discussion about some type of unitary definition of Jewish cosmopolitanism necessarily hangs on the very meaning associated with capital and its function within the new nation state. The stereotype of the Jews is that of a people or nation or race driven solely by their own economic motivation. It is Shylock's curse that the historian Derek Penslar (2001) so elegantly presents as a core reference for Jewish identity in modernity.

The Jews as an abstraction and as a social reality come to be the litmus test in the Enlightenment for analyzing these notions' potential and difficulties (Gilman 2006). Examining cosmopolitanism under this lens yields a double focus: first, the role that the abstraction "the Jews" played in formulating theories of the accept-

---

2 In fact, he wrote "Die Religionen Müsen alle Tolleriret werden und Mus der fiscal nuhr das auge darauf haben, das keine der andern abruch Tuhe, den hier mus ein jeder nach Seiner Fasson Selich werden!" Cited by Raab (1966, 194).

ability of, or dangers, in the movement of peoples beyond and across national boundaries and, second, the response of individual self-defined Jews to such attitudes and meanings. These contradictions are a forerunner of what the British scholar of geography, Ulrike Vieten (2012, 7), calls the "novel form of *regional cosmopolitanism* [that] is underway in Europe." Its historical roots, however, go deeper. As the meanings of these concepts (cosmopolitanism, boundary, Jews, and capital) shift and evolve, so, too, do the responses of those generating them and testing their applicability to the changing circumstances.

In order to examine the debates about the Jews as the touchstone of cosmopolitanism in the Enlightenment, and specifically within the German-language Enlightenment, we must distinguish between two conflicting definitions of the Jews. According to the first, the Jews are a people who ascribe to a particular religious belief and practice and who are, at least potentially, able freely to follow their beliefs in the new, enlightened world of the European nation-state. According to the second, the Jews are the concrete manifestation of the exploitative force of capital, whose rise parallels the very establishment of such states, at least in the eyes of these commentators.

J. G. Herder (1744–1803) is thus torn between these two poles. In his *Outlines of a Philosophy of the History of Man* (1784–91), he defines the nation as "a group of people having a common origin and common institutions, including language"; the nation-state represents the union of the individual with the national community; each people is unique; polyglot entities are "absurd monsters contrary to nature" (Herder 1800, 658). The Jews must join the body politic by integrating their linguistic practice into that of the naturally occurring nation-state, but can they? According to Herder: "The Jews of Moses are properly of Palestine, outside of Palestine there can be no Jew" (1800, 351). Yet "a time will come when no person in Europe will inquire whether a man be a Jew or a Christian. Jews will live according to European laws and contribute to the state" (1800, 486). Nevertheless, "each nation has its center of happiness in itself, like every sphere its center of gravity," he writes in *Also a History of Mankind* (1774). In his *Theological Letters* (1780–1), he, too, approvingly quotes the remark made by François de Salignac de La Mothe Fénelon, Archbishop of Cambrai, that the Abbé Gregoire (and virtually every other Enlightened commentator on cosmopolitanism) later evoked: "I love my family more than myself; more than my family my fatherland; more than my fatherland, humankind." Herder, however, considered that the status of the nation, of the fatherland, is at the core of all questions of individual identity and thus individual happiness.

The "nation" in question is not a racial entity but a linguistic and cultural one (indeed, in the *Ideas* and elsewhere, Herder rejects the very concept of a biologically defined race). Herder's views reflect those of the time, as expressed by Johann Georg Schlosser in the critical poem "Der Kosmopolit" (1777): "It is better to be proud of one's nation than to have none." Are the Jews a nation or merely wandering cosmopolitans? (Wirtz 2006). If a nation, can or should they become part of another nation? Or are they, as Johann Gottlieb Fichte notoriously stated in his 1793 pamphlet, "A Contribution to Correcting Judgments about the French Revolution," a threat: "In nearly all the nations of Europe, a powerful, hostile government is growing, and is at war with all the others, and sometimes oppresses the people in dreadful ways: It is Jewry!" The Jews are a "state within the state," incapable of any integration and thus damned to wander the world (Fichte 1845–1846, 3: 149). Truly vagabondage.

According to Herder, writing in the *Ideas for A Philosophy of the History of Mankind*, even if the Jews had stayed "in the land of their fathers, and in the midst of other nations, [...] they would have remained as they were; for and even when mixed with other people, they may be distinguished for some generations onward" (36). The "more secluded they live, nay frequently the more they were oppressed, the more their character was confirmed" (36). In fact, he suggests that, ideally, "if every one of these nations had remained in its place, the earth might have been considered as a garden, where in one spot one human national plant, in another, another, bloomed in its proper shape and nature" (36). The movement of peoples interferes with the natural function of language in defining people. The historical truth, however, is that almost every people on earth, as Herder points out, "has migrated at least once, sooner or later, to a greater distance, or less" (36). The impact of this migration is shaped by the "time when the migration took place, the circumstances that engendered it, the length of the way, the people's former level of civilization, the reception they encountered in their new country, and the like" (36).

Herder sees the very origin of "the coining of money" as one of the contributions of the "many little wandering hordes" in the Middle East, "according to the Hebrews" (317). As the Jews spread across Europe, "in the manner that they spread abroad as a people," they held its nations in thrall thanks to their command of money. They did not invent usury, Herder states, but "they brought it to perfection" (335). The Jews move among and across the nations like everyone else; yet, Herder seconds Kant's remark in his lectures on practical philosophy in seeing them as a unique case: "Every coward is a liar; Jews, for example, not only in business, but also in common life" (Mack 2003, 5). On this point, Herder and Kant agree.

An alternative Enlightenment manner of speaking about the Jews as a people, however, presents a different history of the concept of cosmopolitanism. For Christian Enlightenment thinkers, cosmopolitanism was the hallmark of the enlightened subject, rooted in a particularist universality. Jews, confined to their backward particularity, could not, by definition, achieve this status. In his *Ideas for A Philosophy of the History of Mankind*, Herder provided a rather standard Protestant reading of the Hebrew Bible (*Tanakh*) that presented the Jews as a nomadic people. Whether or not this was ever historically true, it is clear that the texts assembled into what came in Christianity to be called the Old Testament are the product of city-states, as Max Weber notes in my discussion below. Whether or not the Jews were just one of "many little wandering hordes" (51), as Herder describes them, is questionable, but the Old Testament, at least in Genesis, clearly projects a nostalgia for a simpler time and space that the Enlightenment defined as "nomadic." Herder lists all of the innovations of these nomads, which include the invention of "trade by weight and measure" and capitalism (52).

Herder considered that a nomadic nature characterized not only the earlier stages of Jewish development but also applied to Jewish existence in the present, in the form of a throwback to the earlier stage. This view is found in the overlapping histories of the Sinti and Roma and of the Jews. It should be noted that some early German commentators, such as W. E. Tentzel at the close of the seventeenth century, correctly argued that the 'Gypsies' had come from South Asia, even if their exact origins were uncertain (Tentzel's guess was Ceylon) (Tentzel 1689, 1: 833).

Theologians who focused on converting the Jews, however, looked closer to home. The Christian Hebraist Johann Christoph Wagenseil claimed in 1705 in his *Benachrichtigungen Wegen Einiger die Gemeine Jüdischheit Betreffenden Sachen* that the first Gypsies (*Zigeuner*) were, indeed, Jews who fled into the forests after having been accused in the fourteenth century of poisoning wells. Asserting that they had come from Egypt, they deceived the local peasants by claiming to be able to effect wondrous cures, tell the future, and prevent fires. Eventually, they returned to the cities, resumed a sedentary life, and declared themselves Jews. Vagabonds, thieves, and beggars had joined them, who continued their nomadic ways. As proof, Wagenseil contended that the Gypsies were unknown before the fourteenth century, the language of contemporary Gypsies was full of Hebrew words, and their amulets used kabbalistic formulas (Wagenseil 1705, 473–88). Johann Jakob Schudt's infamous *Jüdische Merckwürdigkeiten* (1714) contains a long chapter claiming that Wagenseil was wrong: the Jews were condemned to their wanderings in Egypt for having rejected Jesus and Mary on their flight to Egypt (Schudt 1714, 470–512). He follows this with a long digression on the Eternal Jew, the shoemaker Ahasverus, or Cartaphilus, condemned to wandering the world because of his rejection of Christ. Learning the language of each country he visits (502), the Eternal Jew must wander, as Christ condemned him to do, until the Second Coming. The Jews, according to Schudt, are, like the Turks, "sanctimonious cheats" because of their usury (504). In both cases, the economic role of the Jews as pseudo-nomads is integral to these contradictory images. Whether or not their views are accurate, the above authors portray the Jews as nomadic in the same way as the Sinti and Roma, even if they are not "Gypsies" *per se*.

The Enlightenment regarded nomads as not using their given space productively. As early as the mid-eighteenth century, in *Wilhelm Meister*, Goethe viewed the nomad through the colonist's lens in explaining why it is seductive for Germans to seek adventures abroad. The novel's protagonist Lenardo speaks of the enticement of "immeasurable spaces [that] lie open to action" and of "great stretches of country roamed by nomads."[3] In the present, nomads have no value and must be replaced by those who do, but, in Goethe's view, this is a false promise that may lead to the corrosion of the Europeans' national identity in such spaces.

According to this Enlightenment view, members of a national community ought to replace nomads because currently nomads add no value to the land. These same nomads, however, in the past, provided the impetus for the national state and for its most egregious exploitative feature, capital. Karl Marx in *Capital* wrote: "nomad races are the first to develop the money form, because all their worldly goods consist of moveable objects and are therefore directly alienable; and because their mode of life, by continually bringing them into contact with foreign communities, solicits the exchange of products" (Marx, 1976, 1/2: 182–3). Marx implicitly casts the nomad as the *Urcapitalist*, the Jew, whose drive in the modern world is shaped by his inheritance from the desert (this is also analogous to the explanation for the rise of monotheism among the Jews: the need for a portable God after the destruction of the Temple [Ezrahi 1988, 138–139]).

In contrast to Marx, George Simmel in the *Philosophy of Money* (1907) explains: "As a rule, nomadic peoples hold land as common property of the tribe and assign it only for the use of individual families; but livestock is always the private property of these families. As far as we know, the nomadic tribe has never been communistic with regard to cattle as property. In many other societies, too, movables were already private property while land remained common property for a long period thereafter" (Simmel 1978, 353). Not so much *Urcapitalists* as *Urcommunists*, perhaps?

Two decades earlier, the Russian Zionist Leon Pinsker had argued in his German-language pamphlet *Auto-Emancipation* (1882) that the Jew's statelessness in the age of nationalism condemns him to be a nomad. For the Jewish people:

---

3 All references are from Noyes (2006).

> [...] produces in accordance with its nature, vagrant nomads; so long as it cannot give a satisfactory account of whence it comes and whither it goes; so long as the Jews themselves prefer not to speak in Aryan society of their Semitic descent and prefer not to be reminded of it; so long as they are persecuted, tolerated, protected or emancipated, the stigma attached to this people, which forces it into an undesirable isolation from all nations, cannot be removed by any sort of legal emancipation.

Pinsker viewed them as nomads living as "Jew peddlers" because they refuse to acknowledge their own rootedness in the desert as true nomads.

The great Jewish Hungarian scholar of Islam, Ignaz Goldziher (1850–1921), suggests a link between two postulates – first, that the nation-state has its roots in a nomadic pre-capitalist world, and second, the cosmopolitan symbolically represents the dangers (and advantages) of capital. His detailed study of the formation of Jewish mythology (Goldziher 1876) adds a further nuance to the ambivalent image of the cosmopolitan wavering between advantage and danger. For Goldziher: "The national level [of Jewish mythopoeia] can be sorted out of the mix. Abraham, not yet rethinking these tales in national terms, was not yet a cosmopolitan figure but an individual [who formed these tales]" (my translation, 59). In Goldziher's portrayal of the Biblical Abraham, individuality – the particular – and cosmopolitanism – the universal – are portrayed as dichotomous features. Abraham is an individual, not a cosmopolitan, for he is part of "the nomadic stratum that was in its element in wandering incessantly from one grazing pasture to another, in continually changing its abode before it was historically grounded in completing the transition to agriculture" (64). Similar to the Arabs, whom Goldziher idealizes, the Jews (here he cites Philo) "glorify their nomadic life" (103). The Jews, he claims, detest artisan labor (*Handwerk*), no matter how intense "their desire for money," as below their status as nomads (105). Their storytelling thus differs inherently from that of the ancient Greeks and the Aryan inhabitants of South Asia:

> For the Hellenes and the Indians, the primary mythical figures are cosmopolitan in nature; Zeus and Indira have no specific national character, even though, occasionally, they are specifically local. The Hebrew mythical figures in this period become the national ancestors of the Hebrew people, where myth is elevated to become the national prehistory of the Hebrew people before its settlement in the land of Canaan (306).

In this case, the national and the cosmopolitan appear diametrically opposed. Jewish tales are restrictedly national and local, rather than cosmopolitan and global. They are the product of the nomadic world, at least as imagined from the viewpoint of the Biblical national Jewish state, which remained local, unlike the transcendental worlds of Greece and India.

The German economist Werner Sombart also pressed nomadism into service to explain the origin of the Jews' "natural" relationship to cosmopolitanism and to capital. In his classic response to Max Weber's *The Protestant Ethic and the Spirit of Capitalism* (1905), Sombart wrote in *The Jews and Modern Capitalism* (1911) of the "restless wandering Bedouins [who] were the Hebrews," who established in "this promised land" an "economic organization" in which "the powerful and mighty among them, after having conquered large tracts of land, instituted a sort of feudal society. They took part of the produce of the land for themselves, either by way of rent in kind, by farming it out to tax collectors, or by means of the credit nexus" (Sombart 1913, 325). In other words, proto-capitalists but of a particularly nasty kind – the origin of the stereotypical Jewish banker in the world of the nomad. Sombart regarded the contemporary Jew as an extension of the earlier nomad as far as the Jews' character and relationship to capital was concerned.

Max Weber argues against this view in *Ancient Judaism* (1920–1921) (Weber 1967). He accepts the existence of a narrative (but not historical) succession of "the stages of the three patriarchs from the 'nomad' Abraham to the 'peasant' Jacob" (438), but he refutes the idea that the nature of Jewish usury stems from any Biblical claims to divine approbation in Deuteronomy 28: 43–44:[4] "The medieval and modern money and pawn usury of the Jews, the caricature in which this promise was fulfilled, was certainly not intended by the holy promise." Instead, Weber reads this as symbolic of the triumph of city over countryside, "which prevailed in every typical polis throughout early Antiquity from Sumerian-Accadian times" (69). This particular quality, while typical of the Jews, was common to inhabitants of the cosmopolitan world of the ancient city with its myth of agrarian settlement.

Herder's reading of the Bible declares that the Jews are nomads, and according to this nineteenth-century pan-European antisemite, the essence of the Jew is captured by his nomadism in the present-day world. In *Foundations of the 19th Century*, the seminal antisemitic work of Richard Wagner's son-in-law Houston Stewart Chamberlain (1912), the history of the Jew in the distant past is also the history of the modern Jew: "Of all the histories of the ancient world, there is none that is more convincing, none more easily to be realized, than that of the wanderings of the patriarch Abraham. It is a story of four thousand years ago, it is a story of yesterday, it is a story of today." Chamberlain (1912, 369) argues, however, that it is the history of a degenerate people:

---

4 "The stranger that is within thee shall get up above thee very high; and thou shalt come down very low. He shall lend to thee, and thou shalt not lend to him: he shall be the head, and thou shalt be the tail."

Any change in the manner of living is said to have a very bad effect on the high qualities of the genuine and purely Semitic nomads. The learned [A.H.] Sayce, one of the greatest advocates of the Jews at the present day, writes: 'If the Bedouin of the desert chooses a settled life, he, as a rule, unites in himself all the vices of the nomad and of the peasant. Lazy, deceitful, cruel, greedy, cowardly, he is rightly regarded by all nations as the scum of mankind.'[5]

It is the history of an impure race as well: "As a matter of fact, the current opinion is that the Semite and even that purest Bedouin type are the most absolute mongrels imaginable, the product of a cross between negro and white man!" (Chamberlain 1912, 369). Because mixed races, Chamberlain suggests, have no space left for them, they simply wander.

As early as 1887, the Austrian-German Orientalist Adolf Wahrmund cast the Jew-as-nomad as the essential capitalist: "Thus we have the typical image of the private enterprise of the nomad, that continues until today, in the form of the wandering merchants and dealers who cross the land selling junk, stocks, and [...] thus rob our peasants and return on the Sabbath with their plunder home to wife and children [...]" (Wahrmund 1887, 91; [my translation]). The essential nature of the Jew and of capitalism itself is that of the "parasitic" nomad.

The Jews, however, are not very good nomads insofar as they violate one aspect of the Enlightenment's underlying assumptions concerning the claims of cosmopolitanism, namely the Greek concept of ξενία, *xenía*. As the German journalist Otto Gildemeister noted (1921, 15): "These nomads do not recognize even the highest law regarding the safety of the stranger (*Gastfreundschaft*). Thus, the Jewess Yael murders Sisera after he has been tempted into a tent and served milk. Trusting her, he goes to sleep. Then Yael drives a stake into his temple and mocks his mother when she comes to seek her son." From the Enlightenment onwards, critics often unfavorably contrasted the Jews to the ideal "true nomads."[6]

---

5 The Hittite scholar Archibald H. Sayce was indeed philo-Semitic. In his 1903 Gifford Lectures, he wrote: "It is usually the fashion to ascribe this concentration of religion upon the present world, with its repellent views of Hades and limitation of divine rewards and punishments to this life, to the inherent peculiarities of the Semitic mind. But for this, there is no justification. There is nothing in the Semitic mind that would necessitate such a theological system. It is true that the sun god was the central object of the Semitic Babylonian faith, and that to the nomads of Arabia, the satisfaction of their daily wants was the practical end of existence. But it is not among the nomads of Arabia that we find anything corresponding with the Babylonian idea of Hades and the conceptions associated with it. The idea was, in fact, of Babylonian origin. If the Hebrew Sheol resembles the Hades of Babylonia, or the Hebrew conception of rewards and punishments is like that of the Assyrians and Babylonians, it is because the Hebrew beliefs were derived from the civilisation of the Euphrates" (Sayce 1903, 295).
6 For an example, see the German philosopher Christoph Meiners (1793).

The ancient Jews violate the rules of many of the nomads described in the *Lebensraum* theorist Friedrich Ratzel's *History of Mankind* (1896, 83ff., 547ff.), which portrays the Jews as originally:

> [...] nomads like their kinsmen in Arabia and Syria [...]. Their oldest books know nothing of fixed altars and their sacrifices are always of cattle. They took to a settled life on conquering and dividing the land of Canaan. But the promised land was only an oasis [...]. The misfortunes of the national ruin, however, brought about a purification which in a race aesthetically deficient, but spiritually proud and austere, tended to strengthen the conception of a deity all-powerful and all-knowing, and at the same time jealous and severe.

It is only through "contact with the Greeks, fundamentally Aryan, yet touched by a Semitic spirit, who, independently of the Jews, had gone through a process of spiritual refinement in the direction of truth, knowledge, and beauty, [that] Christianity developed into a power capable of transforming races." The Jews' only value derives from qualities that were filtered through Greek sensibility and contributed to the creation of a modern consciousness. For Ratzel, the Jews' initial contribution to Western culture may have been a sort of primitive monotheism (as opposed to Christianity), but, in the long term, they affected "above all the economic life of other nations" (548).

The nineteenth-century philosopher Ernest Renan traced the survival of "nomadic instincts" and the "nomadic nomos" of the Jews into modern times; at the same time, René Guenon wrote about the "perverse nomadism of the Jews."[7] Renan and Guenon based their claim on the character of the Jews as nomads in the present day. In this context, it is worth quoting Felix Delitzsch, of *Babel und Bibel* infamy, who commented in 1920 concerning the Jews' ongoing nomadic nature from the Biblical period to the present: "It is obvious that such a people, which is deliberately landless or an international people, presents a great, a frightening danger for all other peoples of the earth" (Delitzsch 1920–1921, 1:105). In short, according to these writers, Jews had been aggressive nomads and remained that way.

According to others, the Jews are also terrible at being nomads because they are Jews. Adolf Hitler states this baldly in *Mein Kampf*, echoing his reading of Houston Stewart Chamberlain:

> Since the Jew never possessed a state with definite territorial limits and therefore never called a culture his own, the conception arose that this was a people that should be reckoned among the ranks of the nomads. This is a fallacy as great as it is dangerous. The nomad does possess a definitely limited living space; only he does not cultivate it like a sedentary

---

7 Cited by Rossman, *Russian Intellectual Antisemitism in the Post-Communist Era* (2002, 8).

peasant, but lives from the yield of his herds with which he wanders about in his territory. The outward reason for this is to be found in the small fertility of a soil that simply does not permit of settlement. The deeper cause, however, lies in the disparity between the technical culture of an age or people and the natural poverty of a living space (Hitler 1943, 300–311, 324–327).

These interpretations render the Jews as symbolic nomads in the modern world, with the pejorative implication that they exist, in the present world, as parasites living off settled, non-nomadic national peoples. Echoing Wagner's claim that the Jews lack the ability to create original art, the psychologist C. G. Jung stated in 1934 in a lecture in Hitler's Berlin:

The Jew, who is something of a nomad, has never yet created a cultural form of his own, and, as far as we can see, never will, since all his instincts and talents require a more or less civilized nation to act as a host for their development. Aside from certain creative individuals, the average Jew is already much too conscious and differentiated to be pregnant with the tensions of the unborn future. The Aryan unconscious has a higher potential than the Jewish; that is the advantage and the disadvantage of a youthfulness not yet fully estranged from barbarism (Jung 1977, 193).

This view emphasizes the role that identity plays in the world one inhabits: not what one does but who one is defines the nomad and defines the cosmopolitan.

Martin Heidegger said more or less the same thing in a lecture in 1937: "A Slavic people would experience the essence of our German space certainly differently than we do. Semitic NOMADS would most probably not experience it at all" (Heidegger 2009, 82). In his so-called *Black Notebooks*, he echoes the idea, writing: "The question of the role of World Jewry is not a racial but rather a metaphysical one about the type of human specificity, that in all cases can be extrapolated as a world-historical 'goal' from the ROOTLESSNESS of the Becoming from Being"[8] Such thinkers regarded Jewish nomadism as a permanent stain on Jewish character in contrast to the stability of the German (or even the Slav). Jewish thinkers about nomadism, on the other hand, saw it as a transitional phase to some further (and improved) state.

This image of the Jew affected the way Jews themselves viewed their function in the society they inhabited. Not surprisingly, Max Brod, writing in Buber's periodical *The Jew* in 1916, complained: "One should not inject us with [being] a centrifugal force [in society] and then marvel at the findings of 'nomadism' and

---

8 Heidegger (2014, 14:121). I am indebted to Peter Trawny, *Heidegger und der Mythos der jüdischen Weltverschwörung* (2014).

'critical destruction' in our corpse."[9] This internalization of the image of the cosmopolitan and the nomad has come to define the Jew in the post-Enlightenment world, indeed, even into the twenty-first century.

Modern Jewish historians, such as Jacob Neusner in *Self-Fulfilling Prophecy: Exile and Return in the History of Judaism* (1990; 1987), have argued for a material understanding of diaspora. For Neusner, it is the model of wilderness and land, the dialectic between tent and house, nomadism and agriculture, wilderness and Canaan, wandering and settlement, diaspora and state. The Welsh Congregationalist W. D. Davies maintained, in *The Territorial Dimension in Judaism* ([1982] 1991), that this dichotomy is well balanced in the Bible, that for every quotation praising wilderness as the decisive factor in Judaism, one could find a counterpart in praise of the Land of Zion.

Galut, on the other hand, is often understood as the experienced reality of being in exile, albeit structured, however, by the internalization of the textual notion of the diaspora and tempered by the daily experience (good or bad) of life in the world. The Jew experiences the daily life of exile through the mirror of the biblical model of expulsion, whether it be the expulsion from the Garden of Eden or freedom from slavery in Egypt. Galut has formed the Jewish self-understanding of exile. Yet, for some thinkers today, the involuntary dispersion of the Jews ("Galut" or "Golah") is articulated as being inherently different from the voluntary exile of the Jews ("Diaspora" or "tfutsot").[10] These two models exist simultaneously in Jewish history in the image of uprooted and powerless Jews on the one hand, and rooted and empowered Jews on the other. It is possible to have a firm, meaningful cultural experience as a Jew in the Galut or to feel alone and abandoned in the Diaspora (as well as vice-versa) – two people can live in the very same space and time and can experience that space and time in antithetical ways. Indeed, the same person can find his or her existence bounded conceptually by such models at different times and in different contexts.

German Jewry thus experienced their situation in complex and often contradictory ways. Jewish "mobility" was both a sign of modern cosmopolitanism or its contradiction. Nationalism was not seen as inherently oppositional to cos-

---

9 "Man soll uns nicht eine Zentifugalkraft einimpfen und hintenach wundern, 'Nomadentum' und 'kritische Zersetzung' an unserm Leichnam konstatiren!" (Brod 1916–1917, 1:35).

10 One current usage of the two terms, where *galut* refers to an involuntary – usually negative – exile, whereas diaspora (*tfutsot*) has a more positive, voluntary connotation is reflected by Steven Bowman on Jewish Diaspora in the Greek world in *Encyclopedia of Diasporas*: https://books.google.co.il/books?id=7QEjPVyd9YMC&pg=PA192&lpg=PA192&dq=%22diaspora+ versus+galut%22&source=bl&ots=uqsLVJlDPw&sig=_YsGBajmKxf_tpH-89sQe6Vgdfs&hl= en&sa=X&ei=TacOVd_UBYP8ywOjkoGYCQ&redir_esc=y#v=onepage&q=%22diaspora%20 versus%20galut%22&f=false (last accessed 21 March 2015).

mopolitanism unless, of course, it was seen as its contradiction. This tension marked and marks the status of Jews, alien cosmopolitans or Jewish nomads, from the Enlightenment to the present. In 2015, the Israeli Prime Minister, following attacks on Jewish institutions in Europe, stated: "to Jews, to our brothers and sisters, Israel is your home. We are preparing and calling for the absorption of mass immigration from Europe."[11] He does not conceive of his call as aimed at the ever-growing Israeli population of Jewish cosmopolitans (?) or nomads (?) in Europe. These contradictions still have their power.

Bibliography

Beck, Ulrich and Natan Sznaider. "Unpacking Cosmopolitanism for the Social Sciences: A Research Agenda." *British Journal of Sociology* 57 (2006a): 1–23.

Beck, Ulrich and Natan Sznaider. "A Literature on Cosmopolitanism: An Overview." *The British Journal of Sociology* 57 (2006b): 153–164.

Berkovitz, Jay R. *Rites and Passages: The Beginnings of Modern Jewish Culture in France, 1650–1860*. Philadelphia: University of Pennsylvania Press, 2004.

Brennan, Tim. *At Home in the World. Cosmopolitanism Today*. Cambridge, MA: Harvard University Press, 1997.

Brod, Max. "Erfahrungen im ostjüdischen Schulwerk." *Der Jude* 1 (1916–1917): 35.

Chamberlain, Houston Stewart. *The Foundations of the 19th Century*, 2nd ed. London: John Lane, The Bodley Head, 1912.

Davies, W. D. *The Territorial Dimension in Judaism* [1982]. Minneapolis: Fortress Press, 1991.

Dee, John. *General and Rare Memorials Pertayning to the Perfect Arte of Navigation*. London: John Daye, 1577.

Delitzsch, Felix. *Die große Täuschung. Kritische Betrachtungen zu den alttestamentlichen Berichten über Israels Eindringen in Kanaan*. Stuttgart: Deutsche Verlags-Anstalt, 1920–1921.

Ezrahi, Sidra DeKoven. "Considering the Apocalypse: Is the Writing on the Wall Only Grafitti?" *Writing and the Holocaust*. Ed. Berel Lang. New York: Holmes and Meier, 1988. 137–159.

Fichte, Johann Gottlieb. *Johann Gottlieb Fichtes sämmtliche Werke*. Ed. I.H. Fichte. Berlin: Veit und comp., 1845–1846.

Gildemeister, Otto. *Judas Werdegang in vier Jahrtausenden*. Leipzig: Weicher, 1921.

Gilman, Sander L. *Multiculturalism and the Jews*. New York: Routledge, 2006.

Goldziher, Ignaz. *Der Mythos bei den Hebraern: Und Seine Geschichtliche Entwickelung*. Leipzig: F.A. Brockhaus, 1876.

Heidegger, Martin. "Über Wesen und Begriff von Natur, Geschichte und Staat." Übung aus dem Wintersemester 1933/34. *Heidegger-Jahrbuch 4 – Heidegger und der Nationalsozialismus I. Dokumente*. Ed. Alfred Denker and Holger Zaborowski. Freiburg/Munich: Karl Alber Verlag, 2009.

---

11 http://www.reuters.com/article/2015/02/15/us-denmark-shooting-israel-idUSKBN-0LJOH620150215 (last acccessed 21 March 2015).

Heidegger, Martin. *Überlegungen,* vol. 12–14. *Gesamtausgabe.* Ed. Peter Trawny. Frankfurt am Main: Vittorio Klostermann, 2014.

Herder, Johann Gottfried. *Outlines of a Philosophy of the History of Man.* Trans. T. Churchill. London: 1800.

Hitler, Adolf. *Mein Kampf* (1927). Trans. Ralph Manheim. Boston: Houghton Mifflin, 1943.

Jung, Carl Gustav. *Interviews and Encounters.* Ed. William McGuire and R. F. C. Hull. Princeton: Princeton University Press, 1977.

Lallement, Guillaume N. *Choix de rapports, opinions et discours prononcés à la tribune nationale depuis 1789 jusqu'à ce jour* (1818–1823). Paris: Alexis Eymery, 1823.

Mack, Michael. *German Idealism and the Jew: The Inner Anti-Semitism of Philosophy and German Jewish Responses.* Chicago: University of Chicago Press, 2003.

Marx, Karl. *Capital.* Harmondsworth: Penguin, 1976.

Meiners, Christoph. "Kurze Geschichte der Hirtenvölker in den verschiedenen Theilen der Erde." *Neues Göttingisches historisches Magazin* 2 (1793): 654–685.

"Mitteilungen: Weltbürger," *Neuphilologische Mitteilungen* 27 (1926): 13.

Neusner, Jacob. *Self-Fulfilling Prophecy: Exile and Return in the History of Judaism.* Atlanta, GA: Scholars Press, 1990.

Nirenberg, David. *Anti-Judaism: The Western Tradition.* New York: W.W. Norton, 2013.

Noyes, John K. "Goethe on Cosmopolitanism and Colonialism: Bildung and the Dialectic of Critical Mobility." *Eighteenth-Century Studies* 39. 4 (Summer 2006): 443–462.

Penslar, Derek. *Shylock's Children: Economics and Jewish Identity in Modern Europe.* Berkeley: University of California Press, 2001.

Pinsker, Leon. *Auto-Emancipation* (1882). http://www.jewishvirtuallibrary.org/jsource/ Zionism/pinsker.html (last accessed 17 March 2015).

Raab, Heribert, ed. *Kirche und Staat: Von der Mitte des 15. Jahrhunderts bis zur Gegenwart.* Munich: Deutscher Taschenbuch Verlag, 1966.

Ratzel, Friedrich. *The History of Mankind.* London: MacMillan and Co., Ltd., 1896.

Rossman, Vadim Joseph. *Russian Intellectual Antisemitism in the Post-Communist Era.* Lincoln/ London: University of Nebraska Press, 2002.

Sayce, Archibald H. *The Religions of Ancient Egypt and Babylonia.* Edinburgh: Clark, 1903.

Schudt, Johann Jakob. *Jüdische Merckwürdigkeiten: vorstellende was sich Curieuses und denckwürdiges in den neuern Zeiten bey einigen Jahrhunderten mit denen in alle IV. Theile der Welt sonderlich durch Teutschland zerstreuten Juden zugetragen: sammt einer vollständigen Franckfurter Juden-Chronick Darinnen der zu Franckfurt am Mayn wohnenden Juden von einigen Jahr-hunderten biß auff unsere Zeiten merckwürdigste Begebenheiten enthalten: benebst einigen, zur Erläuterung beygefügten Kupffern und Figuren.* Frankfurt on the Main/Leipzig: [s.n.], 1714.

Simmel, George. *Philosophy of Money.* Trans. Tom Bottomore and David Frisby. London: Routledge and Kegan Paul, 1978.

Sombart, Werner. *The Jews and Modern Capitalism.* Trans. M. Epstein. New York: E. P. Dutton, 1913.

Tentzel, Wilhelm Ernst. *Monatliche Unterredungen Einiger Guten Freunde von Allerhand Büchern und andern annehmlichen Geschichten. Allen Liebhabern Der Curiositäten Zur Ergetzligkeit und Nachsinnen heraus gegeben,* vol 1. Leipzig: n.p., 1689.

Trawny, Peter. *Heidegger und der Mythos der jüdischen Weltverschwörung.* Frankfurt on the Main: Vittorio Klostermann, 2014.

Vieten, Ulrike M. *Gender and Cosmopolitanism in Europe: A Feminist Perspective*. Farnham: Ashgate, 2012.

Wagenseil, Johann Christof. *Benachrichtigung wegen einiger die gemeine Jüdischheit betreffenden wichtigen Sachen: worinnen-I. Die Hoffnung der Erlösung Israelis. II. Wiederlegung der Unwahrheit als ob die Jüden Christen-Blut brauchten. III. Anzeigung wie die Jüden von schinden und wuchern abzubringen. IV. Bericht von dem Jüdischen Gebeth Alenu. V. Denunciatio Christiana, wegen der Jüden Lästerungen. Diesen sind beygefügt – Rabbi Mose Stendels, in Jüdisch-Teutsche Reimen gebrachte Psalmen Davids*. Leipzig: Johann Heiniche Witwe, 1705.

Wahrmund, Adolf. *Das Gesetz des Nomadentums und die heutige Judenherrschaft*. Karlsruhe/Leipzig: H. Reuther, 1887.

Weber, Max. *Ancient Judaism*. Trans. Hans H. Gerth and Don Albert Martindale. New York, NY: Free Press / London: Collier Macmillan, 1967.

Wieland, Christoph Martin. *Private History of Peregrinus Proteus, the Philosopher*. Trans. from the German, vol. 2. London: J. Johnson, 1796.

Wieland, Christoph Martin. "Das Geheimnis des Kosmopolitenordens" (1788). *Sämmtliche Werke* 36 vol. Leipzig: G. J. Göschen'sche Verlagshandlung, 1853–1858.

Wirtz, Michaela. *Patriotismus und Weltbürgertum. Eine begriffsgeschichtliche Studie zur deutsch-jüdischen Literatur 1750–1850*. Tübingen: M. Niemeyer, 2006.

Stefan Vogt
Between Decay and Doom: Zionist Discourses of *"Untergang"* in Germany, 1890 to 1933

Around the turn of the twentieth century, the term "decay" – *Untergang* – permeated the intellectual debate of the German bourgeoisie. As was often the case, Friedrich Nietzsche, whose Zarathustra had proclaimed: "What is lovable in man is that he is transition and decay" (Nietzsche 1980a, 17), set the tone.[1] To be sure, Nietzsche was not the first to express his fascination with decay; for instance, romanticists of the early nineteenth century cultivated this concept, too. He was, however, certainly the most influential one. With or without direct reference to Nietzsche, the concept of decay – whether termed cultural decline, degeneration, or apocalypse – emerged in different guises and in various intellectual and political contexts. *Völkisch* thinkers such as Paul de Lagarde (1920a, 236–269), who considered that liberalism and, above all, the Jews, had destroyed German culture, and national liberals such as the young Max Weber (1988, 8), who warned that the "physically and intellectually primitive" Poles were about to overwhelm the German *Volk*, all alluded to the idea. Oswald Spengler's *Der Untergang des Abendlandes* (Spengler 1920–1922), written shortly before and published in the last year of World War I, probably presented the most elaborated version of this topos.

Decay was a multifaceted concept, but the dominant connotation was critical and pessimistic, in contrast to the optimistic, progress-oriented worldview of nineteenth-century liberalism. Although history was no longer conceived as a process that automatically led to the advancement of society and the refinement of culture, this did not necessarily imply a belief that there was no future. Decay was usually not a fatalistic, but a distinctly political concept that called for overcoming the decaying constellation and replacing it by something more fit and healthy. Detecting decay, therefore, could often stimulate a call for renewal. Those concerned about decay focused more on its effect on collectives, especially the national collective or the *Volk*, rather than on individuals.[2] The concept of decay always included cultural as well as bio-political connotations, alluding to the economic, social, and cultural deterioration and to the biological – which

---

1 All translations are mine.
2 Throughout the essay, I use the German term *"Volk"* as there is no fully adequate English translation.

often meant racial – decomposition or even extinction of the *Volk*. The notion of decay was thus particularly prominent in nationalist discourses.

Understandably, Zionist authors in Germany used this concept, too, in discussing the situation and prospects of German Jewry. In this essay, I shall examine these usages from the late nineteenth century up to the end of the Weimar Republic, presenting two arguments in this context. First, I want to show that the German Zionists' application of the concept of decay was informed and shaped by the general German discourse to a degree that we should even speak of a common or co-constituted discourse.[3] This implies that Zionist authors also participated in the highly problematic aspects of the German discourse of decay, especially its essentialism and its anti-liberalism. Second, I contend that precisely this ideological and problematic perception of German Jewry in terms of decay sometimes enabled the Zionists to perceive the impending dangers more clearly. Not a realistic analysis of antisemitic ideology but a certain affinity for some of its intellectual foundations, articulated from a specific position within this common discourse, allowed the Zionists to sense that another form of *Untergang* – not decay, but doom – was actually awaiting German Jews.

1 *Untergang* in Germany

In his seminal study *Die Apokalypse in Deutschland*, Klaus Vondung (1988, 153, 340–341; see also Fischer 1978; Petriconi 1958) showed that German nationalist thought from its onset at the end of the eighteenth century was replete with apocalyptic ideas and that by the end of the nineteenth century, the notion of *Untergang*, of an imminent end of the bourgeois world or of the German *Volk*, had become particularly pronounced within this apocalyptic mindscape, replacing the formerly prevalent optimistic outlook. At the fin de siècle, reflections on the decaying and degenerating condition of society and culture were, however, by no means confined to the German nationalist discourse. Rather, it was a transnational and European phenomenon to which authors such as Maurice Barrès in France, Cesare Lombroso in Italy, or Nikolai Berdiaev in Russia contributed as well.[4] Discourses of decay were not necessarily connected to a nationalist agenda, not even in Germany. They could focus, in an ostensibly apolitical manner, on the destiny of the individual, of humankind, or of culture as such, or they could

---

3 The concept of co-constitution was developed by Aschheim (1998).

4 On this European dimension, see Pick (1989); Chamberlin and Gilman (1985); and Greenslade (1994).

make a case for internationalism and social revolution. Although new research has shown that the intellectual climate of Wilhelmine society, including its bourgeois segment, was much more optimistic and self-assured than earlier studies had assumed, notions of degeneration and decay were widespread and influential throughout the intellectual and political culture of the *Kaiserreich*.

The concept of *Untergang* played a particularly prominent role, however, in contexts that were either directly nationalist or applicable to nationalist causes. References to Nietzsche abounded in the latter case.[5] Nationalist and *völkisch* authors widely embraced Nietzsche's thoughts on degeneration and decay despite his outspoken criticism of nationalism. Nietzsche totally rejected and denounced the liberal concept of progress. "Mankind," he wrote, "does not, in the way it is believed today, represent a development towards the better, stronger, or higher" (Nietzsche 1980b, 191). For Nietzsche, the liberal bourgeois society of the late nineteenth century was indeed hopelessly degenerate, completely lacking vitality and strength, and, therefore, liable to put an end to European culture as such: "Already for a while, and with a tortured tension that gets stronger every decade, our entire European culture has been moving towards a catastrophe: restlessly, violently, headlong, like a river that wants to reach the end" (Nietzsche 1980b, 189). For Nietzsche, it was clear that the elements that poisoned life and undermined its basis – the weak, decadent and unhealthy – had to be eliminated if humanity was to survive. Biological metaphors and bio-political connotations pervaded his writings on these issues. "Society," he claimed, "is a body of which no limb can be allowed to be sick. [...] A sick limb that is decaying must be amputated" (Nietzsche 1980b, 413). Nietzsche's *Übermensch*, who was conceived in equally biological and bio-political terms, would not prevent European culture from decaying, but could prove an alternative for selected individuals or, indeed, "*Völker*" (Nietzsche 1980b, 191).

A large number of German intellectuals at the end of the nineteenth century shared the conviction that European bourgeois culture was corrupted by liberalism, materialism, and rationalism and therefore marked for decay and that only a rejuvenated *Volk* could avert this destiny. Paul de Lagarde, for example, held the "Grey International" of liberalism responsible for what he considered society's "illness of putrefaction" and its "ineptitude to move into the future" (de Lagarde 1920b, 377, 344).[6] Julius Langbehn, too, considered "the contemporary spiritual life of the German *Volk* is in a state of slow decay; according to some, even of

---

5 The literature on Nietzsche is far too vast to be referenced here. On the various, including nationalist, appropriations of Nietzsche in Germany, see Aschheim (1992).
6 For Lagarde, the "Grey International" was, of course, essentially Jewish. On Lagarde, see Sieg (2007); Stern (1961, 1–94).

rapid decay" (Langbehn 1892, 1).[7] In his best-selling book *Rembrandt als Erzieher*, which opened with this statement, he claimed that the destruction of German culture by materialism and intellectualism could be halted only by a new kind of art that was anchored in the *Volk*. Another important proponent of this discourse was Arthur Moeller van den Bruck. For him, too, the materialist spirit of liberalism and the degenerate bourgeois culture prevented the German nation from assuming the leadership role for which it was predestined by race and its economic power. He described the "modern man of the nineteenth century" as "complicated and therefore unnatural, weak and sickly, if not totally foul" (Moeller van den Bruck 1906, 36–37; see also 1910, 243–318).[8]

Repeating many of these themes, Oswald Spengler painted the most colorful vision of decay. His work, which was an instant success, appealed to the audience with the catchword *Untergang* in its title. Incorporating the concept of decay into a comprehensive philosophy of history, Spengler clearly aimed his criticism at the achievements of modern bourgeois society, as exemplified above all in the big cities. Here, Spengler found "not a well-shaped, rooted *Volk*, but a new nomad, a parasite, the city dweller, the pure, ahistorical, shapeless realist, nonreligious, intelligent, unfertile, with a profound aversion to the peasantry, thus an enormous step towards the anorganic, the end" (Spengler 1920–1922, 1: 45).[9] Although decay was the destiny of Western civilization as a whole, Spengler was particularly concerned about Germany's being dragged down with it. Spengler's diagnosis of the *Untergang des Abendlands* was thus meant, und understood, as a call for a national revival.[10]

Even in discourses that were not explicitly nationalist, *Untergang* was often perceived as a threat to the existence of collectives, in most cases of the *Volk*. Ludwig Klages, for example, who was among the disciples of Stefan George and became an extremely popular author after World War I, lamented in his contribution to the *Freideutsche Jugendtag* in 1913 that "progress" was actually "an unprecedented orgy of destruction," which "under the pretext of 'benefit,' 'economic development,' and 'culture,' in reality aims at the destruction of life" (Klages 1913, 95, 98).[11] While the "decay of the soul" in principle affected all humanity,

---

7 On Langbehn, see Behrendt (1999); Stern (1961, 97–180).
8 On Moeller van den Bruck see Weiß (2012); Schlüter (2010); Stern (1961, 181–266).
9 On Spengler, see Felken (1988); Farrenkopf (2001); and Merlio (1981).
10 See, for instance, Spengler (1951, 63–79).
11 The text was not actually delivered as an address for the *Jugendtag* but included in the documentation. On Klages, see Leibovitz (2013).

Klages was particularly disturbed by the disappearance of rites and costumes "in which every Volk expresses its essence" (Klages 1913, 98–99).[12]

Thinking and writing about *Untergang* was popular not only in cultural and philosophical discourses; it also was particularly widespread in the fields of biology, anthropology, and medicine, which, too, considered decay as both an individual and a collective phenomenon. Many authors – scientists and others – discussed the potentially devastating consequences of the decline in the birthrate for the *Volk*, leading eventually to its extinction. They regarded the situation as all the more dire because other nations might fare better and thus occupy the vacated space. For instance, an article in the *Neue Deutsche Rundschau* stated: "A *Volk* that reproduces at a slower rate than its major competitors will inevitably fall behind, and there is nothing that could counterbalance it" (Friedlaender 1896, 236).[13] Both life scientists venturing into social, cultural, and political fields and cultural critics employing scientific concepts tended to apply biological and medical concepts to the "body" of the nation, thus turning it into a potential victim of disease and death. In the disciplines of anthropology and racial science, which began to thrive in Germany from the 1890s, scientists hotly debated the reasons for the growth and decline of races and *Völker*, without, however, seriously questioning the assumption that such processes did indeed occur. One of the very first works in this new discipline, a study by Wilhelm Schallmayer, was programmatically titled *Die drohende physische Entartung der Culturvölker* (The imminent physical degeneration of the cultured Völker) (Schallmayer 1891).[14] It pointed to modern urban living conditions as the cause for the decline. A disease that was very frequently diagnosed and thus considered a central component of the illness of bourgeois society was nervousness, or "neurasthenia," as it was often referred to by contemporaries. "Are we drifting towards an ever stronger and more widespread nervousness," asked Wilhelm Erb, a professor of medicine from Heidelberg, "and will this lead to the final decay of today's civilized *Völker*?" (Erb 1893, 25).

---

12 To be sure, Klages later turned toward an outspoken nationalist position.

13 On the discourses of demography and population policy, see Weipert (2006); Etzemüller (2007).

14 On German race science, see Weingart (1992); Weindling (1993); and Hoßfeld (2005).

2 Jewish bodies in decay

Given the common perception of decay as both a cultural and physical condition, it is not surprising that a trained physician, Max Nordau, played a crucial role in introducing the concept into the Zionist discourse. His book *Entartung* (Degeneration) (Nordau 1892–93), published several years before he turned to the Zionist movement, made him a household name in educated circles throughout Europe and a central reference point within the discourse of degeneration.[15] Nordau differed from most other thinkers involved in this discourse in vigorously defending liberalism and rationalism against what he considered the onslaught of the degenerates. In fact, *Entartung* was a thundering and highly knowledgeable diatribe against almost every form of modernist art and culture, which Nordau regarded as all but modern. He directed his scorn particularly at the representatives of the discourse of decay such as Friedrich Nietzsche and Richard Wagner. At the same time, Nordau participated in and even shaped this discourse with his own work. His descriptions of the state of European culture were no less bleak than those of other prophets of decay. The growth of the big cities, for example, spurs, according to Nordau, "the multiplication of degenerates of all kinds, of criminals, maniacs and 'elevated degenerates'" who play an increasingly important role in intellectual life, "striving to introduce more and more elements of madness into art and literature" (Nordau 1892–93, 1: 58). Liberally applying medical concepts on culture, Nordau not only used diseases as a metaphor to describe cultural developments but also considered these developments to be actual symptoms of physiological deformation, neurological disorder, or even mental illness. "In the mood of the fin de siècle," he wrote, "the physician recognizes [...] two specific medical conditions with which he is familiar, degeneration and hysteria, moderate versions of which are known as neurasthenia" (Nordau 1892–93, 1, 26)[16]. When Nordau later turned to Zionism, he also interpreted the Jewish condition in the Diaspora in pathological terms. The emancipated Jew, he claimed, is "crippled on the inside, artificial on the outside and, therefore, to every elevated and aesthetically minded man, ridiculous and disgusting like all false things" (Nordau 1898a, 17; see also 1898a, 20, 1900).[17] Nordau viewed Zionism as the cure for the degeneration of the Jewish *Volk* and thus its salvation from decay.

---

15 On Nordau see Schulte (1997); Zudrell (2003).

16 Tellingly, Nordau named various chapters of his book "Symptoms," "Diagnosis," "Etiology," "Prognosis," and "Therapy."

17 With this, Nordau argued primarily against antisemitic discrimination and against the antisemitic allegation that Jews were racially degenerate and thus beyond the possibility of recovery. This theme appeared already in his critique of degeneration in *Entartung*. See Söder (1991).

To this end, Nordau turned himself into the *"Turnvater Jahn* of Zionism," as Hans-Peter Söder (1991, 479) nicely put it.[18] Nordau not only played a key role in setting up the Zionist gymnastics movement but also provided its ideological foundation, most notably by formulating the concept of the *"Muskeljudentum"* (Nordau 1898b, 24).[19] According to Nordau, Zionism should create a "muscular Judaism," featuring physical strength, vitality, heroism, and self-assurance, which would replace the feeble and overly intellectual Jews of the time. Members of the Zionist gymnastics associations enthusiastically adopted this concept along with the underlying discourse about degeneration. The overwhelming majority of contributors to the *Jüdische Turnzeitung* were convinced that the Jewish *Volk* did suffer from symptoms of degeneration. Emanuel Edelstein (1900, 74), for example, detected such symptoms on the moral, mental, and physical levels. Jews, he claimed, cowardly defected from Judaism, increasingly suffered from nervousness and mental illness, and fell ill with tuberculosis and diabetes in a disproportionally large number.[20] Many articles held modern urban life and the Jews' inclination to intellectual occupations at least partly responsible for this development. Another author even dubbed the Zionist gymnastic associations the "defense associations against the one-sided, threatening accentuation of intellectualism in Jewish education" (Moses 1901, 17; see also the article "Was wir wollen!" 1900; Edelstein 1900; Burin 1910; Theilhaber 1911b). The Zionist athletes thus participated in the general tendency of the discourses of decay to connect degeneration to the modern city and to an alleged dominance of rationalism and intellectualism in modern bourgeois society.[21] When they pointed to the specific degeneration of the "assimilated" German Jews, these Zionists sometimes also echoed antisemitic allegations, which were rather prominent in these discourses.[22] They assigned an even more important role, however, to the influence of the Jews' environment, which imposed particularly unhealthy living conditions. "No cunning," wrote Hermann Jalowicz, "could more effectively bring about the degeneration and destruction of the body than the all-decomposing atmosphere of the ghetto, which undermines health, strength, and optimism" (Jalowicz 1901, 60).

---

18 On the Zionist gymnastics movement in Germany see Wildmann (2009); König (1999).

19 The concept of the *"Muskeljude"* owed quite a few of its characteristics to the Nietzschean model of the *Übermensch*. On this concept and its role in Zionist ideology and politics, see Presner (2007).

20 See also, among many other examples, Friedländer (1901); Nacht (1906); and (Wolff) 1907.

21 See, for example, Spengler (1920–1922, 2: 101–131). On the topic of anti-urbanism, see Bergmann (1970); Lees (2002). On the topic of anti-intellectualism, see Bering (1978).

22 See, for example, "Ein Nichtjude" (1902, 69), which approvingly quoted the journal *Kraft und Schönheit* that "the *Kulturjudentum*, having partially degenerated physically and nervously, should not overemphasize the dominant intellectual element of its character."

Zionist athletes thus regarded Jewish degeneration not as the result of a racial predisposition but rather as the effect of Diaspora conditions. "The fundamental physical condition must be distinguished from the actual," explained an anonymous author in the *Jüdische Turnzeitung*. "The fundamental condition of the Jewish body is still good. [...] The actual physical condition, however, is very bad" (H. 1905, 154; see also Besser 1909, 7–9; Jalowicz 1901; and Nacht 1906). In this sense, the appropriation of the discourse of decay served to counter antisemitic charges of the Jews' racial inferiority. In addition, gymnastics was considered a defense against antisemitism because it strengthened the Jews' self-confidence. Most importantly, however, it provided opportunities for recovery. Gymnastics, it was argued, was the best way to regain physical and mental strength. In its statement on the first page of the first issue of the *Jüdische Turnzeitung*, the Bar Kochba gymnastics association declared that its primary aim was to "restore to the limp Jewish body its lost resilience" ("Was wir wollen" 1900, 1; see also Jalowicz 1901). Physical and mental recovery was considered an essential part of the overall renaissance of the Jewish *Volk*, which was, of course, the goal of the Zionist movement.

The Zionist discourse of decay, in general, as in the Zionist gymnastics associations' debates in particular, argued for the necessity and possibility of resurrection.[23] In this respect, too, it did not differ from the general discourse: the decaying Volk was frequently portrayed as awaiting its rebirth. Both the Zionist and the general discourse expected redemption to come from the healing forces of nature and soil. "As long as we do not provide for a reliable and solid mass of farmers," wrote the *Jüdische Turnzeitung*, "who, having strengthened their bodies and refreshed their spirits through generations of soothing contact with mother earth, could compensate for the spent energy, we have not averted the danger of perpetual degeneration" (Nacht 1906, 120).

One of the founders of the Zionist gymnastics movement, a physician and a regular contributor to the *Jüdische Turnzeitung*, Felix Theilhaber gained wide recognition with a book that displayed "decay" most prominently in its title: *Der Untergang der deutschen Juden* (Theilhaber 1911a).[24] The book, which claimed to use the most up-to-date scientific methods and data, offered a detailed assessment of the demographic and eugenic status of German Jewry. Its conclusion was devastating: "German Jews," wrote Theilhaber, "are a *Volk* in decay. [...] Mixed

---

23 For lack of space, I shall not develop this line of argumentation here but concentrate on the aspect of decay. On the concepts of regeneration, renaissance and resurrection in Zionist thought, see, for example, Presner (2007); Wildmann (2009). See also Brenner (1996).

24 There is no comprehensive study on Theilhaber, but see Efron (1995, 141–153); Lipphardt (2008).

marriages, baptism, abandonment of the religious community, a declining birthrate, physical and mental defects, an increase of mental illness and suicide, all of this in alarmingly growing dimensions – and no relief in sight!" (Theilhaber 1911a, 154). He identified two interrelated processes that led to this decay: Jewish participation in modern civilization and Jewish assimilation. With regard to the first process, Theilhaber's arguments were completely consistent with those employed in the general discourse of the medical and racial sciences. The "harmful milieu" of the big cities, he declared, was a principal source of physical and moral decay, a second one being the industrial organization of work, and a third one changing sexual habits and morals, especially the "hedonism of the women who, for rather selfish reasons, want no or only a few children" (Theilhaber 1911a, 49, 69; see also Theilhaber 1913a). Richard von Krafft-Ebing, for example, made similar charges in his widely read study of "deviant sexuality," *Psychopathia Sexualis*, claiming that "the big cities are hotbeds of nervousness and degenerate sensuality" (Krafft-Ebing 1886, 7; see also Ploetz 1895, 186; Weismann 1886, 21).[25] According to Wilhelm Schallmayer, the dangers to the race caused by declining birth rates and "negative selection" were exacerbated by "the modern feminist movement which infuses many educated and sensible ladies with the ideal of independence and with the ambition to strive for the uninhibited development of their intellectual personality at the expense of their vocation as mothers" (Schallmayer 1907, 20).[26] The reasons why urban life, industrialization and more liberal sexuality were considered dangerous were similar. The most dangerous consequence of the Jews' exposure to modern civilization was, according to Theilhaber, the decline of the birthrate. In addition to an extensive treatment in *Der Untergang*, he devoted a whole article to this problem, which he published in the leading journal of race science, the *Archiv für Rassen- und Gesellschafts-Biologie*. Here, he concluded that "the decline in fertility among Berlin Jews is evident" and that it represented a "most severe danger in terms of racial hygiene" (Theilhaber 1913b, 91–92, see also 1911a, 133–135).[27] An important reference for Theilhaber was the leading German race scientist, Wilhelm Schallmayer, who adhered to the common beliefs that the declining birthrate was a major threat to the existence of the *Volk* and that population growth was "a matter of survival for the German nation" (Schallmayer 1914/15, 729; see also Grotjahn 1914, 183–198; Schallmayer 1903, 326–336).

---

25 On Krafft-Ebing, see Ammerer (2006).

26 On Schallmayer, see Weiss (1987); Weingart (1992); Becker (1988, 1–56).

27 On this journal, which was founded by Alfred Ploetz, see Weingart (1992, 188–216).

Conversely, non-Jewish racial scientists extensively discussed and positively received Theilhaber's work.[28]

Assimilation, the second process that Theilhaber considered as leading to decay, was, at first sight, a specifically Jewish problem. Concerned mainly with conversion and intermarriage, Theilhaber presented a series of statistics to prove that conversion rates were rising, especially in urban areas. He explained that the rates were much higher among academics than among merchants, and he thus claimed that conversion was the "strongest manifestation of assimilation" (Theilhaber 1911a, 91). Intermarriage was, according to Theilhaber, an even more severe problem, as it threatened the very existence of the Jewish race. "Inbreeding," he declared in bold letters, "ensures the only objective indicator for Jewishness, preserves the racial ["*das Rassige*"] of the Jew. [...] It is the last thing that effectively safeguards Jewish distinctiveness" (Theilhaber 1911a, 102; see also Sander 1904). He supplied extensive statistical material indicating that intermarriage was a widespread phenomenon, particularly in urban areas, and that it was directly connected to the declining birthrates among Jews. "German Jewry," concluded Theilhaber, "surrenders without a fight to intermixing and thus to its emasculation" (Theilhaber 1911a, 103).

Whereas conversion and intermarriage did, indeed, affect only Jews, the assumed background for these phenomena was much less specifically Jewish. According to Theilhaber, conversion and intermarriage occurred because of the weakening of the individual's bonds with the Jewish religion and community. As the influence of religious and national perceptions has waned, lamented Theilhaber, "rootedness and down-to-earthness has given way to a phantom with no trace of healthy national and religious views" (Theilhaber 1911a, 93). Non-Jewish discourses of decay also pointed to a weakening of bonds, in this case with the Christian religion and the German national community and they, too, related this process to modern, especially urban civilization.[29] Theilhaber's views on the devastating consequences of Jewish conversion and intermarriage were, in fact, a variation on a very popular theme in the general discourse of decay. His negative view on intermarriage also related more directly to a thread within the broader field of race science in which racial mixing was thought to corrupt the essence of the race. This idea became particularly popular in Germany with the publication of Eugen Fischer's study on the "*Rehoboter Bastards*" (Fischer 1913),

---

28 See Rüdin (1911); Wilser (1912/13). See also the review in *Deutsche Tageszeitung*, 27 November 1911.
29 See, for example, Spengler (1920–1922, 1: 46).

demonstrating the influence of colonialism on the German discourse of decay.[30] Theilhaber's position in this case ought to be considered one of the more radical among German race scientists.[31]

Theilhaber was not alone in diagnosing such severe threats to the existence of German Jewry. Other Zionist authors who discussed the social, anthropological, and racial status of the Jews, such as Arthur Ruppin or Ignaz Zollschan, came to the same conclusions.[32] Zollschan, whose main goal was to counter the antisemitic race scientists' allegations of Jewish inferiority on their own terms, and who, therefore, was more circumspect on the question of degeneration, nevertheless feared that the continuity of the Jewish race was endangered. For Zollschan, precisely because of the Jews' superior racial quality, it was "intolerable to let them just drown in the racial chaos around them" (Zollschan 1911a, 427).[33] Similarly to Theilhaber, he identified intermarriage and assimilation as the two main forces behind this threat. These "dissociating elements" would lead to the "annihilation of the race" (Zollschan 1911a, 429) if nothing was done to stop this process. If Zionism does not succeed in providing a territorial solution, "Judaism may continue to vegetate somewhere as an idea, but Jewry as a race will, because of its dispersion among racially alien *Völker*, [...] fall prey to brutish dissolution, [...] physical degeneration, and moral depravation" (Zollschan 1911a, 489).

Arthur Ruppin, who until 1907 was the head of the Bureau of Jewish Statistics and subsequently became the head of the Palestine Office of the Zionist Organization, adhered to very similar convictions. He, too, considered declining birth rates, conversion, and intermarriage to have destructive effects on "racial character" (Ruppin 1904, 159).[34] For Ruppin, the impact of modern civilization, urbanization, education, and secularization also had problematic consequences. "If the process of denationalization," he warned, "which everywhere in Western Europe has already quashed Jewish cultural distinctiveness, spreads to Eastern

---

30 On the problematics of racial mixing, see Weingart (1992, 91–103). On the role of colonialism in German anthropological scholarship, see Zimmerman (2001). For the relationship of Zionism and colonialism in Germany, see Penslar (1991); Vogt (2012).

31 As among non-Jewish racial scientists, the views among the Zionists were not uniform. Hugo Hoppe, for example, came to the different conclusion that endogamy was, along with the "impact of city life," a major cause of the proliferation of mental and physical illness among Jews and thus of degeneration. With this, however, he remained fully within the discourse of decay. See Hoppe (1903, 56).

32 As did, for example, Martin Engländer, Hugo Hoppe, Aron Sandler, and Leo Sofer. An important representative of this discourse from Eastern Europe was Max Mandelstamm.

33 On Zollschan, see Efron (1995, 153–165); Kiefer (1991); Weindling (2006); and Lipphardt (2008).

34 On Ruppin, see Bloom (2011); Hart (2000); and Morris-Reich (2006).

Europe – the beginning of this is already visible – then the existence of Jewry and of Jewish culture is finished for good." Zionism, Ruppin concluded, is thus "the Jews' desperate fight against the menace of destruction" (Ruppin 1904, 267–286).

3 The Jewish spirit in decay

Other Zionists identified a similar danger on a more spiritual level. Cultural Zionists such as Martin Buber revealed a sense of urgency and impending danger when they called for a "Jewish renaissance" to fight back the "inner enemies" of Jewry, "*Ghetto und Golus* [exile]" (Buber 1901, 9). In fact, the concept of renaissance made sense only if applied to a *Volk* that was seen as dead or in decay. "The chains of the Golus wounded, devastated our souls," he wrote in 1904. "Do not let ourselves be deceived: We are very sick" (Buber 1916b, 128–129; see also 1916a). While acknowledging the destructive influences of antisemitic discrimination and persecution, Buber considered the main reasons for this sickness to be the life style imposed on the Jews by modern civilization, the "unproductive money economy and the hollow-eyed homelessness" (Buber 1901, 9), or, simply, the "incoherence" (Buber 1916b, 131) of the Jewish *Volk*. Buber regarded these as symptoms not only of Jewish assimilation but also of the modern condition as such. In his article "Jüdische Renaissance," he demanded that "the fight against the pitiful episode 'assimilation' [...] be replaced by the fight against more profound and powerful forces of destruction" (Buber 1901, 9). The rebirth of the Jewish *Volk* was, therefore, also supposed to alleviate this general condition. Buber clearly indicated that his call for a Jewish renaissance was part of a broader appeal for spiritual development, and it was, in fact, part of the broader discourse on *völkisch* decay and national renaissance.

Buber's "Jüdische Renaissance" was published in the first issue of the journal *Ost und West*, which was one of the central platforms for cultural Zionism in Germany and a strong advocate of Eastern European Jewish culture.[35] *Ost und West* also featured harsh criticism of the "Western Jew," who was often depicted as a parvenu, a social climber who showed off his wealth in order to be accepted into non-Jewish society.[36] In short, he was decadent. Martin Buber, who published his books on Hasidism in 1906 and 1908, further developed the theme of the confrontation between the decadent Western Jew and the healthy

---

35 On the journal *Ost und West*, see Brenner (1998). On the role of the East European Jew in German Jewish thought, see Aschheim (1982).
36 See, for example, Brieger (1901); Salter (1905a, 1905b).

and authentic Eastern Jew, and other cultural Zionists enthusiastically followed it up.[37] Several years later, Buber contrasted the "Occidental" with the "Oriental" type and found the Occidental type's approach towards the world was deficient and less "fundamental" (Buber 1916c; see also Kohn 1913). The similarities with the critique of Western civilization that was popular in the general discourse of decay and that culminated in Spengler's prophecy of the "decline of the West" are clearly evident. Here, too, it was popular to praise the Orient as a positive antithesis to the West.[38]

In his works, Theodor Lessing also presented the Orient, or, in this case, "Asia," as the counterpart to the dying West. To him, Asia represented harmony and balance, as opposed to the fragmentation of the West, community, as opposed to a conflict-ridden society.[39] Lessing, who had studied medicine for a while before turning to philosophy, described the state of Western culture in medical terms, as a cultural disease.[40] Until the turn of the century, he was a friend of Ludwig Klages and close to the George Circle, whose ideas he shared about the antilife nature of modern civilization.[41] He regarded many aspects of European society and culture, from the destruction of nature, through industrialized mass production, to the horrors of World War I, as symptoms of the "*Untergang der Erde am Geist* (The decline of the earth through the intellect)," as the main title of his *Europa und Asien* (Lessing 1924) read, starting with the third edition. Lessing considered Jewish assimilation as just one aspect of this decay, yet a particularly problematic one. "The Jew," he claimed, "who is remarkable and significant as the representative of a community, immediately becomes insecure once he is detached from this community. Therefore, the Jews' individualization, liberation, and detachment eventually result in decay" (Lessing 1924, 275–276; see also 1930, 26; 1933, 29).[42] For Lessing, Jewish assimilation was problematic not only because of his own growing awareness of his Jewishness but also because the

---

37 See Buber (1906, 1908); Zweig (1920); and Gronemann (1924). See also Birnbaum (1910).
38 See, for example, Spengler (1920–1922, 2: 283–322). Spengler, for his part, paid tribute to Buber in that he referred positively to his work on Hasidism in the *Untergang des Abendlandes* (Spengler 1920–1922, 2: 397).
39 See Lessing (1923). A much shorter first edition was published in 1918 under the title *Europa und Asien*. On Lessing, see Hotam (2010); Kotowsky (2006); and Marwedel (1987).
40 See, for example, Lessing (1930, 27–29, 217).
41 The friendship broke up due to Klages' increasing antisemitism. On the relationship between Lessing and Klages, see Kotowsky (2000).
42 Similarly, Jakob Klatzkin, whose main Hebrew work was titled *Shekiat hahayim* (Decay of life, Klatzkin 1925), declared that "the process of de-nationalization has already disfigured and led to the degeneration of many essential parts of our *Volkskörper* and meanwhile produces decay" (Klatzkin 1918, 30–31).

Jews had originally been the most vigorous opponents of decay.[43] In his view, the Jews were both the antithesis to the *Untergang der Erde am Geist* and the *Volk* most affected by it.

In addition to using biological and medical metaphors to describe the state of modern culture or the condition of the Jewish *Volk*, the Zionist discourse on decay also drew heavily on the concepts of life philosophy, *Lebensphilosophie*. Zionist circles derived their reception of life philosophy primarily from Nietzsche but also from other eminent proponents of this school of thought such as Henri Bergson, Wilhelm Dilthey, or Rudolf Eucken.[44] It represented another important element that connected the Zionist discourse to general ones on decay. For Lessing, the development of modern civilization was a history of the replacement of life by intellectualism and rationalism, of the overpowering of the "*Erde*" by the "*Geist*." "In the era of Western philosophy," he wrote, "this horrible substitution of life by thought has become common practice" (Lessing 1923, 91). Whereas "life" signi-fied the ideal of an immediate relationship between man and the world, modern civilization was characterized by radical alienation. This also affected the exis-tence of *Völker*. Modern civilization not only alienated man from nature and earth, but it also detached the *Volk,* not least the Jewish *Volk,* from its origins and its essence. Lessing considered this the deeper reason for the decay of modern Jewry. In a similar vein, Martin Buber blamed the "degenerating destiny" of the modern Jew on his "lifeless, unbalanced, extra-organic intellectuality" (Buber 1963, 15; see also Weltsch 1913, 157–158). Buber, Lessing, and other Zionists thus alluded to life philosophy to substantiate their claim that the decay of the Jewish *Volk* was imminent if nothing was done to prevent it. Life philosophy not only had an inherent element of cultural pessimism that conceived of modern civilization in highly critical terms but it also provided a philosophical framework for cultural and bio-political understandings of decay.

This quality made life philosophy equally attractive to non-Jewish prophets of decay such as Ludwig Klages and Oswald Spengler. Already in his early writ-ings, but even more vigorously in his later work, Klages described the intellect as the enemy of life. The intellect, wrote Klages, strives "to detach the body from the soul, to detach the soul from the body, and eventually to kill all life it can possibly get hold of" (Klages 1929–1932, 1: 7, see also 1913, 104–105). For Oswald Spengler, the dominance of the intellect, which was opposed to creative and intuitive life, characterized civilization as the final and lethal stage of a culture. Civilization, he

---

43 See, for example, Lessing (1923, 298–332).
44 On Nietzsche's influence on German Zionist thought, see Aschheim (1992, 102–107); Golomb (2004, 21–64, 159–188); and Mendes-Flohr (1997). On the influence of life philosophy in general on German Zionism, see Hotam (2010, 117–237).

wrote, is a set of conditions that "replace making with that which has been made, replace life with death, replace development with ossification, replace landscape and inner childhood with spiritual senility and petrifying metropolis" (Spengler 1920–1922, 1: 44).

The popularity of philosophers such as Klages and Spengler derived partially from their attacks against rationalism and positivism, which echoed a widespread feeling of discomfort with the rule of instrumental reason as imposed on the Western world by the capitalist economy and bourgeois society. Life philosophy in principle thus had a critical dimension that addressed many problematic aspects of liberal politics and ideology. It could easily, however, turn into – and that frequently happened – a celebration of irrationalism and mysticism. In this context, contemporary European degenerate culture and society was often contrasted to either preceding or Eastern cultures, which were supposedly closer or still connected to life. Proponents of life philosophy thus gave prominence to the idea that forces of modernity that were hostile to life caused the deformation and degeneration of an essential and authentic *völkisch* identity and thus threatened it with decay. It was a concept to which both Zionists and German *völkisch* thinkers could relate affirmatively.

4 From decay to destruction

Ludwig Klages, however, regarded the assault of intellectualism and rationalism on life as inherently Jewish. Judaism, he wrote, "has either destroyed or enslaved each and every *Volk* on earth" (Klages 1929–1932, 3/1: 1240)[45] In the form that became dominant in Germany during the Weimar Republic, and of which Klages' *Der Geist als Widersacher der Seele* (The intellect as the adversary of the soul) was probably the most influential example, life philosophy lost whatever critical intention it originally had and became openly antisemitic.[46] It thus merged with an ever more widespread identification of Jewish presence and alleged influence in German society with decay. Responsibility for the downfall of the empire, for Germany's defeat in the war and the loss of national pride, and for the economic crisis that plagued the Weimar Republic through most of its existence was pinned on the Jews. Jews were, of course also blamed for the alleged cultural decay. Hans Blüher, for example, was convinced that "the Jewish spirit is the aspect of

---

45 Oswald Spengler's position was more ambivalent in this respect, but he, too, identified the "destructive" forces of modernity with modern Jewry. See Spengler (1920–1922, 395).
46 Theodor W. Adorno analyzed this ambivalence with regard to Spengler (1970).

Judaism that interferes with the history of other *Völker* and, with its typical twists, brings about destruction" (Blüher 1922, 37).

Identifying Jews with decay, however, was no invention of the Weimar period. Paul de Lagarde, for example, was convinced that "Jews and Liberals are allies" (Lagarde 1920b, 349) who were jointly responsible for the precarious condition of the German state and society. Friedrich Nietzsche, ambivalent as ever in this respect, also alluded to the Jews' affinity with the destructive forces of modernity, thus providing a reference point for many less sophisticated authors.[47] To be sure, discourses of decay at the fin de siècle were by no means necessarily antisemitic, and many non-Zionist Jews also participated in theses discourses. Yet within the antisemitic ideology that developed at that time, the theme of Jews' undermining and destroying German culture and the unity of the German *Volk* was practically omnipresent.[48]

Many anthropologists and race scientists also identified Jews as agents of decay. Even though most of the leading authorities such as Wilhelm Schallmayer or Alfred Ploetz refrained from expressing antisemitic convictions in public or in their publications, they were much less restrained in their private conversations.[49] More radical authors such as Karl Ludwig Schemann, Otto Ammon, or Ferdinand Hueppe openly declared that Jews were a degenerate and inferior race. Houston Stewart Chamberlain set forth the most outspoken and most influential version of this allegation. For him, the modern Jew had turned into "an open or hidden enemy of every other man, into a threat for every culture" (Chamberlain 1938, 1: 535).[50] In sum, antisemitism, although not a consistent feature of the German discourses of decay, was nevertheless an extremely common and often rather central element.

Antisemitism was also an issue within the Zionist discourses of decay, but in a quite different fashion. The Zionist versions of these discourses were often either direct or indirect responses to antisemitism. For Max Nordau, the degeneration that needed to be overcome through the creation of the muscular Jew was to a large degree caused by the hardships, the discrimination, and the persecution of the Jews in the Diaspora. "The others," he insisted in the *Jüdische Turnzeitung*, "have committed the act of disembodiment against us" (Nordau 1900, 10). Nordau's emphasis on the Jews' physical and moral degeneration thus, at the same time, represented an accusation against the antisemites. Moreover, the creation of the muscular Jew would refute the antisemitic allegation that the Jews were,

---

47 See, for example, Nietzsche (1980c, 266–270, 285–288).
48 See, for example, Marr (1879); Förster (1881); Ahlwardt (1890).
49 See Weindling (1993, esp. 106–154), with many references. See also Weingart (1992, 91–103).
50 On Chamberlain, see Field (1981).

by virtue of their race, inherently and irrevocably degenerate. Zionist athletes echoed these arguments. In its declaration of principles, the Bar Kochba gymnastics association listed the fight against antisemitism as one of its five main goals. Another one was the strengthening of Jewish self-confidence, which was also meant as a weapon against antisemitism.[51] Zionist writers regarded Jewish regeneration as the best means of opposing the antisemitism that led to Jewish degeneration.

Felix Theilhaber, too, blamed anti-Jewish attitudes, at least partly, for the *Untergang der deutschen Juden*. He noted, for instance, that in Germany conversion was often motivated by antisemitism, whereas in countries such as England, where antisemitism was marginal, there was virtually no stimulus for assimilation (Theilhaber 1911a, 93–94). The Jewish physician's warnings against the dissolution of the Jewish race implied, of course, that it was worth preserving. His comments, therefore, aimed at discounting theories about the Jews' racial inferiority on their own grounds, that is, the grounds of racial theory.

Similarly, and even more directly, Ignaz Zollschan confronted racial antisemites such as Chamberlain and insisted on the "cultural value of the Jewish race" (Zollschan 1911a, 299, see also 1911b).[52] The Zionist authors who conceived of decay in more spiritual terms also usually pointed to antisemitism as an important cause. For Theodor Lessing, antisemitism denoted the limits of the Enlightenment and, therefore, represented the main reason for the failure of emancipation and assimilation. Identifying antisemites such as Eugen Dühring as the true agents of decay, he claimed that the Jews were its victims rather than its perpetrators. "It was not the Jew," he wrote, "who drove mankind towards the intellect, but the path toward the intellect, which culture has to follow, has altered Jewry, too" (Lessing 1930, 23). Even Martin Buber, who declared that "antisemitism has nothing to do with our idea and our program" (Buber 1916b, 124), acknowledged that "the subjugation by the host *Volk*" (Buber 1901, 10) had contributed to the decay of the Jewish *Volk*.

In addressing the problem of antisemitism, all Zionist versions of the discourses of decay shared a common characteristic: they based the fight against antisemitism on an emphatic avowal of Jewish racial and cultural identity. This was a logical consequence of their specific understanding of antisemitism. In his article "Antisemitismus," published in 1915 under the pseudonym "Maarabi," Kurt Blumenfeld provided a definition that remained authoritative for the Zionist discourse throughout the Weimar years. Antisemitism, he argued, is the result of the constant confrontation of the Jews with other *Völker* in a single geographical

---

51 See "Was wir wollen!" (1900); Edelstein (1900, 74); and Meyer (1901, 48).
52 Efron (1995, 157) and Hart (2000, 87) make this point convincingly.

and cultural space. It is a consequence of the essential difference between the Jews and other *Völker*. "The reality of our Jewish particularity," he wrote, "is the true reason for antisemitism" (Blumenfeld 1915, 240). This essentialist concept of Jewry underlay the Zionists' view that Jewish life in the Diaspora had no future, at least not in terms of a Jewish-non-Jewish cultural symbiosis. Antisemitism was just another word for the irresolvable conflict between *Deutschtum* and *Judentum*. As long as German Jewry based its existence on the resolution of this irresolvable conflict, it was condemned to decay. The Zionist understanding of antisemitism implied agreement with some of the basic assumptions of antisemitic ideology such as the conviction of the incompatibility of German and Jewish identities, the rejection of assimilation, and a critical stance towards rationalist concepts of belonging. The Zionists, however, resolutely rejected certain antisemitic notions about the Jews and the "Jewish question." First, they undertook a radical revaluation of the image of the Jews, refuting any notions of inferiority, which sometimes even led to an inversion of the antisemitic degradation of the Jews. In most cases, however, the Zionists rejected the very idea of racial or cultural hierarchies. Second, the insistence on Jewish particularity was meant to bolster the Jews' self-confidence and armor them against anti-Jewish aggression. It was, therefore, a deliberate and well-conceived strategy against antisemitism.

These premises guided the Zionists in confronting antisemitism and later Nazism during the Weimar Republic. Instead of rejecting the antisemitic claim of an essential difference between Germans and Jews, the Zionists affirmed this difference but denied that any negative conclusion could be deduced from it. They asserted that Jewish self-respect should derive precisely from the difference from non-Jews – which could serve as a better basis to fight antisemitism – rather than from the insistence on equality. The goal of the fight against antisemitism, they argued, should not be integration but recognition, "*Anerkennung*."[53] Some Zionists thus expressed a measure of understanding for antisemitic ideas and believed in the possibility of an open and unprejudiced debate with moderate antisemites.[54] At the same time, however, the German Zionists confronted antisemitism during the Weimar Republic both on a practical and ideological level, and they did so much more intensively and consistently than most of the research to date

---

53 See, for example, Landauer (1931).
54 See, for example, the letter of Robert Weltsch to Hans Kohn, 6 November 1922, where he confessed: "I can understand antisemitism very well and have to admit that I feel close to it" (Weltsch 1922). See also the correspondence that Weltsch maintained with Wilhelm Stapel, which was partly published in Stapel's journal ("Liberalismus" [1932]).

has been prepared to acknowledge.[55] Especially in the first years of the Weimar Republic, when a wave of antisemitism swept over Germany, and in the last years, when the Nazi party rose to power, the Zionists published numerous articles in the *Jüdische Rundschau* and other journals, calling for the active defense of the Jews' rights, property, and life.[56]

Antisemitism was an equally important topic in meetings of the units of the German Zionist Association, which established special committees to coordinate the fight against antisemitism in 1923 and again in 1930.[57] The Zionists also collected material, published brochures, and held public meetings on the antisemitic threat.[58] During the Weimar Republic, the Zionist discourse thus increasingly linked the notion of a possible *Untergang* of German Jewry to the growing dangers of antisemitism. At the same time, the Zionists' treatment of antisemitic incidents and developments had an increasingly apocalyptic tone. After the pogroms and riots of 1923, the *Jüdische Rundschau* published an article entitled "The Hour of Destiny for German Jewry" (Schicksalsstunde 1923). The publication termed the success of the National Socialists in the *Reichstag* elections of 1930 "a terrible threat to German Jewry" ("6400000" 1930). The Zionists' agreement to establish a *Reichstagswahlausschuss*, a joint committee to confront antisemitism during the election campaign, together with their archenemies, the *Centralverein*

---

55 Despite their deep ideological differences, Jehuda Reinharz and Donald Niewyk, for example, agree on the inadequacy of the Zionist approach towards antisemitism. See Reinharz (1985); Niewyk (2001, 82–95).

56 See, for instance, Schäfer (1918); "Die antisemitische Welle," (1919); Löwenstein (1922); Krojanker (1919/20); Weltsch (1923); "Ausschreitungen im Berliner Westen" (1931); "Aus dem nationalsozialistischen Lager" (1932); "Zur Lage" (1932).

57 See, for example, "XIX. Der Delegiertentag. Tagesordnung," in: Jüdische Rundschau, no. 50, 22 June 1923, 309; "Protokoll der Sitzung des Landesvorstands," 8 November 1923, Schocken Archives, Jerusalem, 531/32 [this and all following protocols in this note are in the Schocken Archives, Jerusalem]; "Protokoll der 49. Sitzung des Geschäftsführenden Ausschusses," 28 November 1929; "Protokoll der 50. Sitzung des Geschäftsführenden Ausschusses," 13 December 1929; "Protokoll der 6. Sitzung des Geschäftsführenden Ausschusses," 19 February 1930, all in 531/61; "Protokoll der Sitzung des Landesvorstandes," 23 February 1930 "Protokoll der Sitzung des Landesvorstandes," 18 May 1931, all in 531/32. On the Zionist committees, see "Protokolle der Sitzungen der Arbeitskommission," 27 March 1924 and 3 April 1924, 531/32; "Protokoll der 6. Sitzung des Geschäftsführenden Ausschusses," 19 February 1930; "Rundschreiben an die Mitglieder des Landesvorstandes," 23 May 1930, in 531/31.

58 See Antisemitismus in Deutschland der Revolutionszeit und seine Bekämpfung (1919–1920); "Besprechung über allgemeine zionistische Propaganda," 9 October 1922, Schocken Archive, Jerusalem, 531/32; "Bericht der Zionistischen Vereinigung für Deutschland und den Delegiertentag in Breslau für die Zeit vom 1. Oktober 1926 bis 31. März 1928," Schocken Archives, Jerusalem, 531/4. Also, two important studies on antisemitism (Bernstein 1926; Zweig 1927) were published by Zionist authors.

deutscher Staatsbürger jüdischen Glaubens, illustrated the seriousness of this ter-minology.[59] At the Frankfurt *Delegiertentag* of the German Zionist Association in September 1932, its president, Kurt Blumenfeld, left no doubt when he described the antisemites' ideology: "The annihilation of Jewry is one of their main goals" (Blumenfeld 1932, 353).

Based on their belief in the Jews' particular ethnic identity, the Zionists real-ized that German antisemitism would not limit its attack on the Jews to under-mining their legal and social status. Assuming insurmountable differences between the two *Völker*, the Zionists recognized antisemitism as an all-out assault on the very existence of German Jewry. They were convinced that it was useless to insist on equality or affirm the Jews' national loyalty because anti-Semites did not care how "German" German Jews felt or presented themselves. The Zionists came to the conclusion that antisemitism was fundamentally independent of the Jews' actions and characteristics. No matter what the Jews' behavior, antisemites would still find their presence inacceptable. "It doesn't matter," wrote Fritz Bern-stein, for example, "what the Jews are like, what they do or do not do. [...] If they try to accommodate to their enemies' complaints, the latter will complain about any other conduct, too, because it is a Jewish conduct" (Bernstein 1926, 220; see also "Innere Sicherheit" 1933, 46; Rosenblüth 1913, 127).

This was also the central argument against the *Abwehr* strategy or the *Cen-tralverein*. "The usual methods," proclaimed the *Jüdische Rundschau* after the September 1930 elections, "of linking equal rights to a certain attitude, the per-petual assurance of national compliance, have failed" ("Was weiter" 1930; see also Landsberg 1924, 5–6). Zionists thus directly connected the reasons for Jewish decay that they had detected before World War I to the reasons for the current threat to the existence of German Jewry. The outburst of antisemitic violence, for instance, during the pogroms of 1923, proved to them that "the politics of assimi-lation, which is the politics of the systematic abandonment and decomposition of Jewry, has become totally bankrupt" (Schicksalsstunde 1923). The Zionists considered it obvious that the Jews' integration into German culture and their identification with it not only had not averted but also had strengthened and encouraged antisemitism. It had all but destroyed Jewish self-confidence and self-esteem, which were the only means of successfully withstanding antisemi-tism. Assimilation and antisemitism were thus two sides of the same coin: the decay of the Jewish *Volk*.

The Zionist awareness that antisemitism was directed not against any par-ticular characteristic, behavior, or action of specific Jews, but against Jewry as

---

59 See "Rundschreiben..." (1930) in note 57.

such was a highly accurate and extremely important insight, which very few, Jews or non-Jews, realized at the time. Nazi policy after they assumed power and later research on antisemitism have confirmed the validity of this perception. The Zionists also saw that antisemitism was not confined to a small radical minority but was widespread and that Nazism was "the strongest movement within the German *Volk*" ("Zur Lage" 1932). Even more importantly, perhaps, they had a foreboding of the historical significance of the Jews' experience during the Weimar years. The journal's regular coverage of antisemitic incidents, politics, and discourses repeatedly made the point that these were not the afterpains of a past era, but the harbingers of a new period that would be far more dangerous for the Jews.[60] From this perspective, the apocalyptic tone in these articles was not inappropriate. In all these points, the Zionists' perception of antisemitism and Nazism was closer to reality than the notions of most other German Jews.

The Zionists' perception, however, was not necessarily more realistic. Their assessment of the situation as serious and potentially destructive did not derive from a political or sociological analysis of Nazi antisemitism but from a specific perception of the state of German Jewry. The Zionists interpreted the threat that antisemitism posed to the Jews as another element of the decay of German Jewry. They saw this threat as a consequence of Jewish history's following the wrong path by denying the essential differences between Jews and non-Jews in the context of emancipation and assimilation. Their insistence on such an essential and immutable difference helped them understand, almost intuitively, the comprehensive and radical dimension of the antisemitic assault on the Jews. The assumption of an essential difference between Jews and non-Jews is, of course highly problematic because it originated in the contemporary discourses of *Volk*, race, and nation that also produced racial antisemitism. It is an ideological assumption, which, from a critical perspective, must be considered fallacious; yet, from a wrong assumption, the Zionists reached correct conclusions. It is too facile to explain this contradiction away by pointing to the irrational nature of antisemitism, which could be properly understood only from an irrational perspective. Rather, the Jews' specific status in German society should be taken into account. Postcolonial theories have shown that concepts and strategies of identity are highly dependent on the location from which they are developed and applied.[61] As a marginalized group, the Jews were able to understand and to employ a hegemonial discourse in an anti-hegemonial direction. This also applies to the Zionists' appropriation of the concept of physical and spiritual decay at the fin de siècle, and it distinguishes these appropriations from non-Jewish ones, despite

---

60 See, for example, Löwenstein (1919, 1922; m. w. 1928); "Hitler Reichskanzler" (1932, 305).
61 See, among others, Bhabha (1994); Hall (1990); and Chatterjee (1986).

being part of the same discourse. The anti-hegemonial dimension of the Zionist versions of this discourse is evident in the attempts to subvert racial hierarchies, the emphasis on environmental reasons for decay, the reference to the repressive aspects of assimilation, or the concept of gymnastics as mental self-defense. From this perspective, the insistence on difference could indeed be a way of confronting antisemitism. This does not, however, solve the contradiction, nor is it meant to do so. The Zionists' essentialist strategy remains problematic, as its price was accepting some of the very premises of racist and antisemitic ideology that they, in fact, opposed. In this sense, the Zionists are a paradigmatic example of both the potentials and the dangers of an anti-hegemonial strategy that is based on difference.

Bibliography

"6400000 nationalsozialistische Wähler. Niederlage der bürgerlichen Demokratie." *Jüdische Rundschau*, no. 73, 16 September 1930, 479.
Adorno, Theodor W. "Spengler nach dem Untergang. Zu Oswald Spenglers 70. Geburtstag." *Der Monat* 20 (1970): 115–128.
Ahlwardt, Hermann. *Der Verzweiflungskampf der arischen Völker mit dem Judentum*. Berlin: Grobhäuser, 1890.
Ammerer, Heinrich. *Krafft-Ebing, Freud und die Erfindung der Perversion*. Marburg: Tectum-Verlag, 2006.
Antisemitismus in Deutschland der Revolutionszeit und seine Bekämpfung, 1919–1920 (collection of newspaper clippings and leaflets). Central Zionist Archives, Jerusalem, F 4/22.
Aschheim, Steven E. *Brothers and Strangers: The East European Jew in Germany and German Jewish Consciousness, 1800–1923*. Madison: University of Wisconsin Press, 1982.
Aschheim, Steven E. *The Nietzsche Legacy in Germany: 1890–1990*. Berkeley: University of California Press, 1992.
Aschheim, Steven E. "German History and German Jewry. Boundaries, Junctions and Interdependence." *Leo Baeck Institute Yearbook* 43 (1998): 315–322.
"Aus dem nationalsozialistischen Lager." *Jüdische Rundschau*, no. 2, August 1932, 6.
"Ausschreitungen im Berliner Westen." *Jüdische Rundschau*, no. 72, 15 September 1931, 441.
Becker, Peter Emil. *Zur Geschichte der Rassenhygiene*. Stuttgart: Thieme, 1988.
Behrendt, Bernd. "August Julius Langbehn, der 'Rembrandtdeutsche.'" *Handbuch zur 'Völkischen Bewegung' 1871–1918*. Ed. Uwe Puschner, Walter Schmitz, and Justus H. Ulbricht. Munich: Saut, 1999. 94–113.
Bergmann, Klaus. *Agrarromantik und Großstadtfeindschaft*. Meisenheim am Glan: Hain, 1970.
Bering, Dietz. *Die Intellektuellen. Geschichte eines Schimpfwortes*. Stuttgart: Klett-Cotta, 1978.
Bernstein, Fritz. *Der Antisemitismus als Gruppenerscheinung. Versuch einer Soziologie des Judenhasses*. Berlin: Jüdischer Verlag, 1926.

Besser, Max. "Der Einfluß der ökonomischen Stellung der deutschen Juden auf ihre physische Beschaffenheit." *Körperliche Renaissance der Juden*. Ed. Ausschuss der Jüdischen Turnerschaft. Berlin: Jüdischer Verlag, 1909. 7–9.

Bhabha, Homi. *The Location of Culture*. London: Routledge, 1994.

Birnbaum, Nathan. "Etwas über Ost- und Westjuden." *Ausgewählte Schriften zur jüdischen Frage*. Czernowitz: Birnbaum & Kohut, 1910 (first published in 1905). 1: 276–282.

Bloom, Etan. *Arthur Ruppin and the Production of Pre-Israeli Culture*. Leiden: Brill, 2011.

Blüher, Hans. *Secessio Judaica*. Berlin: Weisse-Ritter-Verlag, 1922.

Blumenfeld, Kurt. "Antisemitismus." *Jüdische Rundschau*, no. 30, 23 July 1915, 239–240.

Blumenfeld, Kurt. "Die zionistische Aufgabe im heutigen Deutschland. Referat auf dem 24. Delegiertentag des ZVfD." *Jüdische Rundschau*, no. 73/74, 16 September 1932, 353–354.

Brenner, David A. *Marketing Identities: The Invention of Jewish Ethnicity in Ost und West*. Detroit: Wayne State University Press, 1998.

Brenner, Michael. *The Renaissance of Jewish Culture in Weimar Germany*. New Haven: Yale University Press, 1996.

Brieger Wasservogel, Lothar. "Das Alte Testament." *Ost und West* 1 (1901): 849–854.

Buber, Martin. "Jüdische Renaissance." *Ost und West* 1 (1901): 7–10.

Buber, Martin. *Die Geschichten des Rabbi Nachman. Ihm nacherzählt von Martin Buber*. Frankfurt on the Main: Rütten & Loening, 1906.

Buber, Martin. *Die Legende des Baal-Schem*. Frankfurt on the Main: Rütten & Loening, 1908.

Buber, Martin. "Die Schaffenden, das Volk und die Bewegung." *Die jüdische Bewegung. Aufsätze und Ansprachen 1900–1915*. Berlin: Jüdischer Verlag, 1916a (first published in 1902). 1: 68–77.

Buber, Martin. "Was ist zu tun?" *Die jüdische Bewegung. Aufsätze und Ansprachen 1900–1915*. Berlin: Jüdischer Verlag, 1916b (first published in 1904). 2: 122–137.

Buber, Martin. "Der Geist des Orients und das Judentum." *Vom Geist des Judentums. Reden und Geleitworte*. Leipzig: Kurt Wolff Verlag, 1916c (original lecture from 1912). 9–48.

Buber, Martin. "Das Judentum und die Juden." *Der Jude und sein Judentum. Gesammelte Aufsätze und Reden*. Cologne: Melzer, 1963 (original lecture from 1909). 9–18.

Burin, Erich. "Kaffeehausjudentum." *Jüdische Turnzeitung* 11.5–6 (1910): 74–75.

Chamberlain, Houston Stewart. *Die Grundlagen des neunzehnten Jahrhunderts*, 2 vols. 24th ed. Munich: Bruckmann, 1938 (first published in 1899).

Chamberlin, J. Edward and Sander L. Gilman, eds. *Degeneration. The Dark Side of Progress*. New York: Columbia University Press, 1985.

Chatterjee, Partha. *Nationalist Thought and the Colonial World: A Derivative Discourse?* London: Zed Books, 1986.

"Der XIX. Delegiertentag. Tagesordnung." *Jüdische Rundschau*, no. 50, 22 June 1923, 309.

"Die antisemitische Welle." *Jüdische Rundschau*, no. 47, 11 July 1919, 377.

"Die Schicksalsstunde des deutschen Judentums." *Jüdische Rundschau*, no. 96, 9 November 1923, 557.

Edelstein, Emanuel. "Die Aufgabe der jüdischen Turner." *Jüdische Turnzeitung* 1.7 (1900): 73–75.

Efron, John M. *Defenders of the Race: Jewish Doctors and Race Scientists in Fin de Siècle Europe*. New Haven: Yale University Press, 1995.

"Ein Nichtjude über die jüdische Turnerei." *Jüdische Turnzeitung* 3.4 (1902): 67–69.

Erb, Wilhelm Heinrich. *Über die wachsende Nervosität unserer Zeit*. Heidelberg: Hörning, 1893.

Etzemüller, Thomas. *Ein ewigwährender Untergang. Der apokalyptische Bevölkerungsdiskurs im 20. Jahrhundert.* Bielefeld: transcript, 2007.
Farrenkopf, John. *Prophet of Decline: Spengler on World History and Politics.* Baton Rouge: University of Louisiana Press, 2001.
Felken, Detlef. *Oswald Spengler. Konservativer Denker zwischen Kaiserreich und Diktatur.* Munich: Beck, 1988.
Field, Geoffrey G. *Evangelist of Race: The Germanic Vision of Houston Stewart Chamberlain.* New York: Columbia University Press, 1981.
Fischer, Eugen. *Die Rehoboter Bastards und das Bastardisierungsproblem beim Menschen. Anthropologische und ethnographische Studien am Rehoboter Bastardvolk in Deutsch-Südafrika.* Jena: Verlag Gustav Fischer, 1913.
Fischer, Jens Malte. *Fin de Siècle. Kommentar zu einer Epoche.* Munich: Winkler, 1978.
Förster, Bernhard. *Das Verhältnis des modernen Judenthums zur deutschen Kunst. Vortrag gehalten im Berliner Zweigverein des Bayreuther Patronats-Vereins.* Berlin: M. Schulze, 1881.
Friedlaender, Benedict. "Aphorismen ueber die Rassenfrage in der Völkergeschichte." *Neue Deutsche Rundschau* 7 (1896): 236.
Friedländer, M. "Warum wir nicht in der deutschen Turnerschaft turnen." *Jüdische Turnzeitung* 2.1 (1901): 2–5.
Golomb, Jacob. *Nietzsche and Zion.* Ithaca: Cornell University Press, 2004.
Greenslade, William. *Degeneration, Culture and the Novel, 1880–1940.* Cambridge, UK: Cambridge University Press, 1994.
Gronemann, Sammy. *Hawdoloh und Zapfenstreich. Erinnerungen an die ostjüdische Etappe 1916–1918.* Berlin: Jüdischer Verlag, 1924.
Grotjahn, Alfred. *Geburten-Rückgang und Geburten-Regelung. Im Lichte der individuellen und sozialen Hygiene.* Berlin: Marcus, 1914.
H., "Die körperliche Minderwertigkeit der Juden." *Jüdische Turnzeitung* 6.8 (1905): 152–155.
Hall, Stuart. "Cultural Identity and Diaspora." *Identity: Community, Culture, Difference.* Ed. Jonathan Rutherford. London: Lawrence & Wishart, 1990. 222–227.
Hart, Mitchell B. *Social Science and the Politics of Modern Jewish Identity.* Stanford: Stanford University Press, 2000.
"Hitler Reichskanzler?" *Jüdische Rundschau*, no. 64, 12 August 1932, 305–306.
Hoppe, Hugo. *Krankheiten und Sterblichkeit bei Juden und Nichtjuden. Mit besonderer Berücksichtigung der Alkoholfrage.* Berlin: Calvary, 1903.
Hoßfeld, Uwe. *Geschichte der biologischen Anthropologie in Deutschland. Von den Anfängen bis in die Nachkriegszeit.* Stuttgart: Steiner, 2005.
Hotam, Yotam. *Moderne Gnosis und Zionismus. Kulturkrise, Lebensphilosophie und nationaljüdisches Denken.* Göttingen: Vandenhoeck & Ruprecht, 2010.
"Innere Sicherheit." *Jüdische Rundschau*, no. 10, 3 February 1933, 45–46.
Jalowicz, Hermann. "Die körperliche Entartung der Juden, ihre Ursachen und ihre Bekämpfung." *Jüdische Turnzeitung* 2.5 (1901): 67–65.
Kiefer, Annegret. *Das Problem einer "jüdischen Rasse." Eine Diskussion zwischen Wissenschaft und Ideologie.* Frankfurt on the Main: Lang, 1991.
Klages, Ludwig. "Mensch und Erde." *Freideutsche Jugend. Zur Jahrhundertfeier auf dem Hohen Meißner 1913.* Jena: Diederichs, 1913. 89–107.
Klages, Ludwig. *Der Geist als Widersacher der Seele*, 3 vols. Leipzig: Bart, 1929–1932.
Klatzkin, Jakob. *Probleme des modernen Judentums.* Berlin: Jüdischer Verlag, 1918.

Klatzkin, Jakob. *Shekiat hahayim*. Berlin: Eshkol, 1925.

Kohn, Hans. "Der Geist des Orients." *Vom Judentum. Ein Sammelbuch*. Ed. Verein jüdischer Hochschüler Bar-Kochba in Prag. Leipzig: Kurt Wolff Verlag, 1913. 9–18.

König, Hans-Jürgen. *'Herr Jud' sollen Sie sagen! Körperertüchtigung am Anfang des Zionismus*. St. Augustin: Academia Verlag, 1999.

Kotowsky, Elke-Vera. *Feindliche Dioskuren. Theodor Lessing und Ludwig Klages. Das Scheitern einer Freundschaft*. Berlin: Jüdische Verlags-Anstalt, 2000.

Kotowsky, Elke-Vera, ed. *'Sinngebung des Sinnlosen.' Zum Leben und Werk des Kulturkritikers Theodor Lessing (1872–1933)*. Hildesheim: Olms, 2006.

Krojanker, Gustav. "Antisemitismus." *Der jüdische Wille* 2.4/5 (1919/20): 173–175.

Lagarde, Paul de. "Die Religion der Zukunft." *Deutsche Schriften. Gesamtausgabe letzter Hand*. 5th ed. Göttingen: Dieterich, 1920a (first published in 1878).

Lagarde, Paul de. "Die graue Internationale." *Deutsche Schriften*. 1920b.

Landauer, Georg. "Grundlinien des Referats der Antisemitismus-Kommission." Schocken Archives Jerusalem, 4 May 1931: 531/66.

Landsberg, Alfred. "Zionismus und Umwelt. Referat von Dr. Alfred Landsberg auf der Zentralkomitee-Sitzung vom 1. Januar 1924." *Jüdische Rundschau*, no. 1, 4 January 1924, 4–6.

Langbehn, Julius. *Rembrandt als Erzieher. Von einem Deutschen*. 40th ed. Leipzig: Hirschfeld, 1892 (first published in 1890).

Lees, Andrew. *Cities, Sin, and Social Reform in Imperial Germany*. Ann Arbor: University of Michigan Press, 2002.

Lessing, Theodor. *Europa und Asien oder Der Mensch und das Wandellose*. 2nd ed. Hanover: Adam, 1923.

Lessing, Theodor. *Der Untergang der Erde am Geist (Europa und Asien)*. 3rd ed. Hanover: Adam, 1924.

Lessing, Theodor. *Der jüdische Selbsthaß*. Berlin: Jüdischer Verlag, 1930.

Lessing, Theodor. *Deutschland und seine Juden*. Prague: Neumann, 1933.

"Liberalismus und Judentum. Ein Briefwechsel." *Deutsches Volkstum* 14.22 (1932): 944–946.

Lipphardt, Veronika. *Biologie der Juden. Jüdische Wissenschaftler über Rasse und Vererbung 1900–1935*. Göttingen: Vandenhoeck & Ruprecht, 2008.

Löwenstein, Fritz. "Antisemitismus." *Jüdische Rundschau*, no. 67, 19 September 1919, 513.

Löwenstein, Fritz. "Die antisemitische Gefahr." *Jüdische Rundschau*, no. 97, 8 December 1922, 95.

m. w. "Antisemitismus überall. Steine gegen Synagogen – 'Staatenlose' – 'Ritualmord' in Amerika." *Jüdische Rundschau*, no. 80/81, 12 October 1928, 565.

Marr, Wilhelm. *Der Sieg des Judenthums über das Germanenthum. Vom nicht confessionellen Standpunkt aus betrachtet*. Bern: Costenoble, 1879.

Marwedel, Rainer. *Theodor Lessing 1872–1933. Eine Biographie*. Darmstadt: Luchterhand, 1987.

Mendes-Flohr, Paul. "Zarathustra's Apostle: Martin Buber and the Jewish Renaissance." *Nietzsche and Jewish Culture*. Ed. Jacob Golomb. London: Routledge, 1997. 233–243.

Merlio, Gilbert. *Oswald Spengler. Témoin des son temps*. Stuttgart: Heinz, 1981.

Meyer, Felix. "Der hygienische Wert des Turnens." *Jüdische Turnzeitung* 2.4 (1901): 46–49.

Moeller van den Bruck, Arthur. *Die Zeitgenossen*. Minden: Bruns, 1906.

Moeller van den Bruck, Arthur. *Die Deutschen. Unsere Menschengeschichte*. vol. 7: *Scheiternde Deutsche*. 2nd ed. Minden: Bruns, 1910.

Morris-Reich, Amos. "Arthur Ruppin's Concept of Race." *Israel Studies* 11.3 (2006): 1–30.

Moses, Dr. "Jüdische Erziehungsprobleme." *Jüdische Turnzeitung* 2.2 (1901): 17–20.

Nacht, A. "Sind wir berechtigt, von einer Degeneration des jüdischen Volkes zu sprechen?" *Jüdische Turnzeitung* 7.5 (1906): 79–81 and 7.7: 110–120.

Nietzsche, Friedrich. *Also sprach Zarathustra. Kritische Studienausgabe.* Ed. Giorgio Colli and Mazzino Montinari, vol. 4. Munich: Deutscher Taschenbuch Verlag, 1980a.

Nietzsche, Friedrich. *Nachgelassene Fragmente 1887–1889. Kritische Studienausgabe*, vol. 13. 1980b.

Nietzsche, Friedrich. *Zur Genealogie der Moral. Eine Streitschrift. Kritische Studienausgabe*, vol. 5. Munich: Deutscher Taschenbuch Verlag, 1980c.

Niewyk, Donald L. *The Jews in Weimar Germany*. 2nd ed. New Brunswick: Transaction Publishers, 2001.

Nordau, Max. *Entartung*. 2 vols. Berlin: Duncker, 1892–93.

Nordau, Max. "Speech at the First Zionist Congress." *Zionisten-Congress in Basel (29., 30. und 31. August 1897). Officielles Protokoll.* Vienna: Verlag des Vereins Erez Israel, 1898a. 9–20.

Nordau, Max. "Speech at the Second Zionist Congress in 1898." *Stenographisches Protokoll der Verhandlungen des II. Zionisten-Congresses gehalten zu Basel vom 28. bis 31. August 1898.* Vienna: Verlag des Vereins Erez Israel, 1898b. 14–27.

Nordau, Max. "Muskeljudentum." *Jüdische Turnzeitung* 1.2 (1900): 10–11.

Penslar, Derek J. *Zionism and Technocracy: The Engineering of Jewish Settlement in Palestine, 1870–1918.* Bloomington: Indiana University Press, 1991.

Petriconi, Hellmuth. *Das Reich des Untergangs. Bemerkungen über ein mythologisches Thema.* Hamburg: Hoffmann & Campe, 1958.

Pick, Daniel. *Faces of Degeneration: A European Disorder, c. 1848 – c. 1918.* Cambridge, UK: Cambridge University Press, 1989.

Ploetz, Alfred. *Die Tüchtigkeit unserer Rasse und der Schutz der Schwachen. Ein Versuch über Rassenhygiene und ihr Verhältnis zu den humanen Idealen, besonders zum Sozialismus.* Berlin: S. Fischer, 1895.

Presner, Todd Samuel. *Muscular Judaism. The Jewish Body and the Politics of Regeneration.* New York: Routledge, 2007.

Reinharz, Jehuda. "The Zionist Response to Antisemitism in Germany." *Leo Baeck Institute Yearbook* 30 (1985): 105–140.

"Review of Felix A. Theilhaber, *Der Untergang der deutschen Juden*." *Deutsche Tageszeitung*, 27 November 1911.

Rosenblüth, Felix. "Nationaljudentum und Antisemitismus." *Jüdische Rundschau*, no. 13, 28 March 1913, 126–128.

Rüdin, Ernst. "Review of Felix A. Theilhaber *Der Untergang der deutschen Juden*." *Archiv für Rassen- und Gesellschafts-Biologie* 8 (1911): 674–682.

"Rundschreiben an die Mitglieder des Landesvorstandes und die Vorsitzenden der zionistischen Ortsgruppen." 19 August 1930. Schocken Archives, Jerusalem, 531/31.

Ruppin, Arthur. *Die Juden der Gegenwart. Eine sozialwissenschaftliche Studie*, Berlin: Calvary, 1904.

Salter, Siegbert. "Szene aus Berlin W." *Ost und West* 5 (1905a): 593–596.

Salter, Siegbert. "Das Glück des Hauses Löbenthal." *Ost und West* 5 (1905b): 797–802.

Sander, Aron. *Anthropologie und Zionismus. Ein popular-wissenschaftlicher Vortrag.* Brünn: Jüdischer Buch- und Kunstverlag, 1904.

Schäfer, Ernst. "Pogromagitation in Deutschland." *Jüdische Rundschau*, no. 52, 6 December 1918: 404–405.

Schallmayer, Wilhelm. *Die drohende physische Entartung der Culturvölker*. Berlin: Heuser, 1891.

Schallmayer, Wilhelm. *Vererbung und Auslese im Lebenslauf der Völker. Studie auf Grund der neueren Biologie*. Jena: Fischer, 1903.

Schallmayer, Wilhelm. *Vererbung und Auslese als Faktoren zu Tüchtigkeit und Entartung der Völker*. Brackwede: Breitenbach, 1907.

Schallmayer, Wilhelm. "Zur Bevölkerungspolitik gegenüber dem durch den Krieg verursachten Frauenüberschuss." *Archiv für Rassen- und Gesellschafts-Biologie* 11 (1914/15): 713–737.

"Schicksalsstunde des deutschen Judentums." *Jüdische Rundschau*, no. 96, 9 November 1923: 557.

Schlüter, André. *Moeller van den Bruck. Leben und Werk*. Cologne: Böhlau, 2010.

Schulte, Christoph. *Psychopathologie des Fin de siècle. Der Kulturkritiker, Arzt und Zionist Max Nordau*. Frankfurt on the Main: Fischer Taschenbuch Verlag, 1997.

Sieg, Ulrich. *Deutschlands Prophet. Paul de Lagarde und die Ursprünge des modernen Antisemitismus*. Munich: Hanser, 2007.

Söder, Hans-Peter. "Disease and Health as Contexts of Modernity: Max Nordau as Critic of Fin-de-Siècle Modernism." *German Studies Review* 14 (1991): 473–487.

Spengler, Oswald. *Der Untergang des Abendlandes. Umrisse einer Morphologie der Weltgeschichte*, 2 vols. 15th–20th ed. Munich: Beck, 1920–1922.

Spengler, Oswald. "Pessimismus." *Reden und Aufsätze*. 3rd ed. Munich: Beck, 1951 (first published in 1921). 63–79.

Stern, Fritz. *The Politics of Cultural Despair. A Study in the Rise of the Germanic Ideology*. Berkeley: University of California Press, 1961.

Theilhaber, Felix A. *Der Untergang der deutschen Juden. Eine volkswirtschaftliche Studie*. Munich: Reinhardt, 1911a.

Theilhaber, Felix A. "Jüdische Hygiene und jüdische Turnbewegung." *Jüdische Turnzeitung* 12.7 (1911b): 135–137 and 12.10: 188–191.

Theilhaber, Felix A. *Das sterile Berlin. Eine volkswirtschaftliche Studie*. Berlin: Marquardt, 1913a.

Theilhaber, Felix A. "Die Schädigung der Rasse durch soziales und wirtschaftliches Aufsteigen bewiesen an den Berliner Juden." *Archiv für Rassen- und Gesellschafts-Biologie* 10 (1913b): 67–92.

Vogt, Stefan. "Zionismus und Weltpolitik. Die Auseinandersetzung der deutschen Zionisten mit dem deutschen Imperialismus und Kolonialismus, 1890–1918." *Zeitschrift für Geschichtswissenschaft* 60 (2012): 596–617.

Krafft-Ebing, Richard von. *Psychopathia Sexualis. Mit besonderer Berücksichtigung der conträren Sexualempfindungen. Eine forensische Studie*. Stuttgart: Enke, 1886.

Vondung, Klaus. *Die Apokalypse in Deutschland*. Munich: Deutscher Taschenbuch Verlag, 1988.

"Was weiter?" *Jüdische Rundschau*, no. 74/75, 19 September 1930: 485.

"Was wir wollen!" *Jüdische Turnzeitung* 1.1 (1900): 1.

Weber, Max. "Der Nationalstaat und die Volkswirtschaftspolitik." *Gesammelte Politische Schriften*. Ed. Johannes Winckelmann. 5th ed. Tübingen: Mohr, 1988 (first published in 1895).

Weindling, Paul. *Health, Race and German Politics between National Unification and Nazism, 1870–1945*. Cambridge, UK: Cambridge University Press, 1993.

Weindling, Paul. "The Evolution of Jewish Identity: Ignaz Zollschan between Jewish and Aryan Race Theories, 1900–1945." *Jewish Tradition and the Challenge of Darwinism*. Ed. Geoffrey Cantor and Marc Swetlitz. Chicago: University of Chicago Press, 2006. 116–136.

Weingart, Peter, Jürgen Kroll, and Kurt Bayertz. *Rasse, Blut und Gene. Geschichte der Eugenik und Rassenhygiene in Deutschland*. Frankfurt on the Main: Suhrkamp, 1992.

Weipert, Matthias. *'Mehrung der Volkskraft'. Die Debatte über Bevölkerung, Modernisierung und Nation 1890–1933*. Paderborn: Schöningh, 2006.

Weismann, August. *Über den Rückschritt in der Natur*. Freiburg: Mohr, 1886.

Weiss, Sheila Faith. *Race Hygiene and National Efficiency. The Eugenics of Wilhelm Schallmayer*. Berkeley: University of California Press, 1987.

Weiß, Volker. *Moderne Antimoderne. Arthur Moeller van den Bruck und der Wandel des Konservatismus*. Paderborn: Schöningh, 2012.

Weltsch, Robert. "Theodor Herzl und wir." *Vom Judentum. Ein Sammelbuch*. Ed. Verein jüdischer Hochschüler Bar Kochba in Prag. Leipzig: Kurt Wolff Verlag, 1913. 155–165

Weltsch, Robert. Letter to Hans Kohn, 6 November 1922. Leo Baeck Institute New York. AR 6908/1/4b.

Weltsch, Robert. "Die judenfeindliche Welle in Deutschland." *Jüdische Rundschau*, no. 97, 20 November 1923: 561.

Wildmann, Daniel. *Der veränderbare Körper. Jüdische Turner, Männlichkeit und das Wiedergewinnen von Geschichte in Deutschland um 1900*. Tübingen: Mohr Siebeck, 2009.

Wilser, Ludwig. "Review of Felix A. Theilhaber, Der Untergang der deutschen Juden." *Politisch-Anthropologische Revue* 11 (1912/13): 335–336.

Wolff, Isidor. "Die Verbreitung des Turnens unter den Juden. Referat gehalten auf dem Dritten Jüdischen Turntag." *Jüdische Turnzeitung* 8.7 (1907): 117–133.

Zimmerman, Andrew. *Anthropology and Antihumanism in Imperial Germany*. Chicago: University of Chicago Press, 2001.

Zollschan, Ignaz. *Das Rassenproblem unter besonderer Berücksichtigung der theoretischen Grundlagen der jüdischen Rassenfrage*. 2nd ed. Vienna: Wilhelm Braumüller, 1911a (first published in 1910).

Zollschan, Ignaz. *Der Kulturwert der jüdischen Rasse. Vortrag, gehalten am 2. März 1911 im Verein jüdischer Hochschüler Bar Kochba in Prag*. Prague: Verlag der Selbstwehr, 1911b.

Zudrell, Petra. *Der Kulturkritiker und Schriftsteller Max Nordau. Zwischen Zionismus, Deutschtum und Judentum*. Würzburg: Königshausen und Neumann, 2003.

"Zur Lage in Deutschland." *Jüdische Rundschau*, no. 93, 22 November 1932: 451.

Zweig, Arnold. *Das ostjüdische Antlitz. Zu fünfzig Steinzeichnungen von Hermann Struck*. Berlin: Welt-Verlag, 1920.

Zweig, Arnold. *Caliban oder Politik und Leidenschaft. Versuch über die menschlichen Gruppenleidenschaften dargetan am Antisemitismus*. Potsdam: Kiepenheuer, 1927.

Peter Jelavich

Popular Entertainment and Mass Media: The Central Arenas of German-Jewish Cultural Engagement

"Roll over Beethoven and tell Tchaikovsky the news" (Chuck Berry).

This essay argues that accounts of German-Jewish cultural engagement in the modern era lack a central – indeed, *the* central – story. Scholarly attention has focused almost exclusively on *Bildungsbürger* – the educated elite of the bourgeoisie, who received their education at a *Gymnasium* (with heavy emphasis on Greek and Latin) and then a university. That caste, which comprised only a small minority of citizens, had a disproportionately high status and influence in German society. Because it required intellectual and cultural achievement, *Bildung* was a path for Jewish entry into the German bourgeoisie. Generations of scholars have studied *Bildungsbürger* to gauge the success of German-Jewish integration, assimilation, interaction, even "symbiosis." Without denying the importance of such studies and their fascinating (and sometimes wrenching) discoveries, this essay contends that, until recently, scholars have neglected a cultural arena in which Jews exerted much greater influence: popular entertainment and mass culture in the late imperial and Weimar eras. The impact of Jews on German "high" culture was minor compared to their contributions to popular music, revues, cabarets, operettas, and film. The immense Jewish contribution to popular culture in the United States has long been recognized; it is time to do the same for Germany.

The work of George Mosse is paradigmatic for privileging the *Bildungsbürgertum*, an approach favored by many in his émigré cohort that influenced later generations of academics. Mosse contended that Germany's cosmopolitan culture of the eighteenth and early nineteenth centuries – the culture of the Enlightenment and classicism – served as the vehicle whereby German Jews simultaneously emancipated themselves from Jewish traditions and integrated into the emerging bourgeoisie. According to Mosse, Germany's bourgeois Jews retained this cosmopolitan culture up to the 1930s, whereas the Gentile bourgeoisie abandoned it already by the middle of the nineteenth century: their notion of *Bildung* and *Kultur* was infused with romanticism and especially nationalism, defined in Christian and Germanic terms. In his later works, Mosse highlighted the role that traditional mores (*Sittlichkeit*) played in this worldview, producing a conformist attitude that repressed moral, religious, and sexual individuality and deviance. Some *Bildungsbürger* even adopted the racist worldview of the *völkisch* ideologues.

Scholars such as Shulamit Volkov have, to be sure, proposed significant modifications to Mosse's thesis. She contends that the Enlightenment/classical tradition acquired emotional and patriotic dimensions after 1800, a development that calls into question the decisive split postulated by Mosse. Moreover, Volkov argues that Jews took "an active part in the transformation of enlightened ideas and in the formation of Romanticism," as in "the salons of the famous Jewesses of Berlin" (Volkov 1996, 85). This attachment lasted well into the nineteenth century, inasmuch as "Jewish attraction to Richard Wagner [...] represents perhaps the peak of their romantic enthusiasm" (Volkov 1996, 87). Steven Aschheim proposed another modification to Mosse's thesis for a later historical era by highlighting how Weimar-era intellectuals such as Walter Benjamin, Ernst Bloch, Franz Rosen-zweig, and Gershom Scholem diverged from the rationalist tradition. He writes · "For all these men it was no longer the rational process of 'self-formation' and 'development' that would ultimately bring salvation but rather epiphanic events, flashing moments that by disrupting the flow of history would provide intima-tions of redemption" (Aschheim 1996, 37). He states further: "It is my contention that Weimar culture's most vital impulses were informed by an explicit suspicion, even outright rejection, of many of the essential postulates that made up the Bil-dungs tradition and that it was not only the increasingly brutalized nationalist camp that jettisoned the notion, as Mosse would have it" (Aschheim 1996, 33).

Despite their different emphases and interpretations, Mosse, Volkov, and Aschheim (along with others who have joined that debate) all focus exclusively on the Bildungsbürgertum, treating it as the primary sociocultural group by which to assess the success or failure of Gentile-Jewish cultural interchange in Germany. Without denying the importance of that scholarship, I want to emphasize a major problem: because Bildungsbürger constituted a small minority among German Jews (as they did among German Gentiles), these discussions neglect vast realms of popular and mass culture. Mosse, to be sure, dealt with popular culture, but in a very selective manner. In his examination of genres such as popular festi-vals and middlebrow novels, he argued that the nationalistic and later völkisch worldview of Gentile elites trickled down to the population at large, thus infus-ing Gentile culture (high and low) with an exclusivist nationalistic romanticism. Jewish Bildungsbürger remained the holdouts of Enlightenment and reason: "The Jews, unlike the masses, reached for Bildung in order to integrate themselves into German society. The Jews and the German masses entered German social and political life at roughly the same time, but the Jews were apt to reject the world of myth and symbol, the world of feeling rather than reason" (Mosse 1985, 8).

Mosse acknowledged that during the Weimar Republic, bildungsbürgerlich Jews attempted to influence the population at large and counteract the influence of romantic nationalism and völkisch ideology, but he noted only the efforts of two middlebrow bestselling authors – Emil Ludwig and Stefan Zweig. He wrote: "It is from the mountain of classical *Bildung* that these intellectuals descended to the people before and after World War I, hoping to find them ready for the message" (Mosse 1985, 20). This was a doomed effort, however, because (according to Mosse) the divide between elite and popular culture was unbridgeable: "Already isolated from the German masses, [Jews] were committed to the pursuit of a higher culture, making contact with the masses increasingly difficult" (Mosse 1985, 24). Mosse considered that the nationalistically-infected Gentile masses were resistant to change and any attempt to commune with them would have led to an adulteration of Enlightenment values: "Those who found consolation in *Nathan the Wise* were, after all, on firmer ground than those Jews who attempted to plunge into German popular culture – not to elevate it, but in order to swim with the tide" (Mosse 1985, 40). He concluded: "Ludwig and Zweig symbolized the alienation of the German-Jewish tradition from popular culture. They could not see past their own ideals to fathom the wishes and desires of the people" (Mosse 1985, 33).

Mosse delved no further into popular culture than middlebrow literature. Remaining outside of his purview – and that of many other scholars who focus on the Jewish *Bildungsbürgertum* – is the vast swath of entertainment and mass culture comprising popular music, performance (theater, cabaret, revues), and film. Indeed, far from being "isolated from the German masses," as Mosse contended, Jews were proportionately most active and influential in precisely these realms. Popular arts and media consciously differed from the culture of the *Bildungsbürger*, who in turn vociferously opposed the newer trends. In her discussion of the ambiguities and paradoxes of *Bildung*, Volkov notes that though it was in principle egalitarian and "open to all," in practice it had "elitist consequences" and "clearly played a divisive rather than an integrative social role": it resulted in "a systematic 'closing of the ranks,' the exclusion of the common from the elite" (Volkov 1996, 90). Barred from such circles, the vast majority of Gentiles as well as Jews turned to the popular arts and entertainment. Alfred Döblin clearly perceived this sociocultural division. Though he had impeccable *bildungsbürgerlich* credentials – he was a medical psychologist by training and profession – he lashed out mercilessly against what he called "das klassische Ensemble":

> For a long time, the tame classical ensemble remained completely outside my purview. It was alien to me. Slowly I made the connection between the classical ensemble, including schools and teachers, and the obtuse bourgeoisie. The same elements [...] that run the state politically also publish newspapers, collect paintings, build museums, go to concerts and theaters, look at actors' photographs – boring, despicable elements that can only be resisted. I saw that the same bourgeois strata are the ones who worship the classical ensemble (Döblin 1922, 41).

This perception induced Döblin to contribute to mass media such as radio and film and to incorporate themes and styles of the popular arts into his "high cultural" products such as *Berlin Alexanderplatz* (Jelavich 2006).

Similar to Döblin (whose wayward father had been a tailor), many of the Jews who were disproportionately active in crafting popular and mass culture – as writers, composers, filmmakers, and performers – did not come from the *Bildungsbürgertum*, but rather (like most Jews in imperial and Weimar Germany) from a commercial background. In 1895, a full 65 percent of German Jews were employed in trade and commerce, especially textiles; and 60 percent of these were self-employed (Richarz 1997, 37–38). Indeed, Jews involved in popular culture frequently stated in their autobiographical works that they regarded it as an escape from their fathers' "rag trade." In fact, the realm of popular and mass entertainment that the Jews entered was as commercial as the textile trade. It was, however, liberating as well, inasmuch as it was open to innovation and generally free from prejudice (*pace* Mosse's characterization of popular values). Most significantly, it was a new cultural sphere that Jews could shape to reflect their own concerns and aspirations, as well as those of Gentiles from comparable social classes – ones "lower" than and socially segregated from the "higher" reaches of the bourgeoisie. Film historian Heide Schlüppmann described those subordinate classes who flocked to early cinema: "Cinema and film production developed in Wilhelmine Germany largely independent of the *Bildungsbürgertum*. They were based on all of those middle-class elements that felt excluded from 'culture': the productive forces came from groups involved in technology, business, variety shows, and fairground displays, as well as actors, while the public consisted of women of diverse backgrounds, 'little people,' workers, and salaried employees" (Schlüppmann 1990, 13). Jews from commercial backgrounds – who were disproportionately represented among the "productive forces" – shared social proximity to these groups, which constituted the bulk of the audience for popular and mass culture.

Two factors contributed to the Jews' success in creating, sustaining, and innovating popular and mass culture in imperial Germany and the Weimar Republic: (1) these were spheres wherein Jews could present and elaborate issues that were important to their identity as Jews; and (2) Jews could simultaneously speak to the concerns of the Gentile lower middle and middle classes, which in many ways overlapped with their own. Socially middling Jews and Gentiles faced hurdles to professional success and social acceptance: Jews faced discrimination from Christian and Germanic-nationalist circles, whereas Gentiles (as well as Jews) of the lower-middle and middle classes – who possessed little *Bildung* and/or *Besitz* – suffered status and career denigration in a society dominated by bourgeois elites. Popular culture responded in a spirited manner: it directly challenged the worldview of the *Bildungsbürger,* who believed that film and other forms of mass entertainment undermined traditional values, social mores, good taste, and even mental and physical health (Jelavich 2004). At best, they considered the popular arts a waste of time because they provided no intellectual or moral uplift, as did (supposedly) elite *Kultur* – a relentlessly serious sphere that stressed stylistic and narrative coherence and privileged tragedy over comedy. Popular entertainment confronted that attitude by employing jokes, satire, and parody; it unmasked the hypocrisy of bourgeois society, whose pursuit of material gain and dogged defense of status privilege undercut its claim to moral sobriety and cultural high-mindedness. In particular, humorous plays and songs questioned traditional morality as they espoused freer sex, more openness to diversity, and a less restrictive attitude toward personal behavior. Moreover, they did so at venues such as variety shows, revues, cabarets, and nickelodeons, whose kaleidoscopic programs lacked aesthetic and narrative coherence. With a plethora of numbers lasting at most ten minutes, they expressed a diversity of moods (from humorous to sentimental) in a profusion of genres: variety shows and cabarets offered songs, dances, humorous monologues and dialogues, and pantomimes; early cinemas screened comic flicks, sentimental tales, absurdist slapstick, documentaries, shots of nature and landscapes, and travelogues (all accompanied by an improvised musical potpourri that mixed classical and popular music).

A subset of popular entertainment expressed the values and concerns of Jews in particular. One of the basic characteristics of popular and mass culture is its mobilization of stock figures, character types, and stereotypes. This is most obvious in genres such as commedia dell'arte, but it is true of many other forms of popular culture (and incidentally, of "high" culture as well, which on average is just as formulaic as "low" culture). One of those stock types was "the Jew." The image that had been coded in a clearly antisemitic fashion in Christian Europe during the medieval and early modern eras depicted "the Jew" as either a murderous demon (who had killed Christ or Christian babies) or an unscrupulous moneylender (most famously embodied in Shylock). By the nineteenth century, however, new stereotypes emerged – often at the initiative of Jews themselves – that presented "the Jew" more sympathetically. Although these new stock figures might not pass muster with anti-defamation leagues (an issue that will be addressed below), they were hardly expressions of "Jewish self-hatred," as some observers have claimed. Instead, Jewish entertainers portrayed comic (and sympathetic) Jewish characters in ways that resonated with Gentiles who lacked the privileges of *Bildung.* We shall examine three different examples that illustrate various new ways in which "the Jew" was deployed in popular culture and the mass media: two films – Ernst Lubitsch's *Schuhpalast Pinkus* and E.A. Dupont's *Das alte Gesetz* – and the revues staged by Berlin's Metropoltheater.

In Germany during the early decades of the twentieth century, film was the newest medium of mass entertainment in which Jews played a disproportionately large role, a phenomenon that has been examined in recent scholarship (Stratenwerth and Simon 2004; Prawer 2005; Ashkenazi 2102). The early (1914–1919) films of Ernst Lubitsch, which were immensely popular in their day, are replete with Jewish comic types. Like most people involved in the first decades of film, Lubitsch had no *bildungsbürgerlich* credentials: his father owned a women's clothing store in Berlin, and he too started out as an apprentice in the textile business before becoming an actor. After failing to make an impression in Max Reinhardt's famed Deutsches Theater, he switched to film, where he became wildly popular playing Jewish apprentices in the "rag trade" in *Die Firma heiratet* and *Der Stolz der Firma* (both 1914). He subsequently acted in and directed a series of films set in Jewish commercial milieus, most famously *Schuhpalast Pinkus* (Shoe palace Pinkus, 1916). These films draw upon a tradition of Jewish wit and joking (*Witz*) that had developed over the course of the nineteenth century. Jewish humor was commonly regarded as a response to the poverty and discrimination faced by the Jews of Central and Eastern Europe. Already in 1812, rabbi and poet Lippmann Moses Büschenthal asserted: "The fact that Jews in general are so witty [*witzig*] can be ascribed to the oppression they have suffered over the centuries." He proceeded to claim that "poverty and weakness [...] give birth to cunning [*List*], and cunning is the mother of wit [*Witz*], which is why wit is much more prevalent among the oppressed and impoverished rural Jews, than among the richer ones" (Büschenthal 1812, iv). Although some would consign the notion of Jewish "cunning" (especially in commercial and financial matters) to the antisemitic mindset, Büschenthal (as many commentators after him) considered *List* a "weapon of the weak." While viewing Lubitsch's early films, it is important to keep in mind this understanding of *List*, with its overtones of artfulness, guile, subterfuge, and trickery. Indeed, in jokes and humorous anecdotes, one can view Jews who live by their wits as avatars of the "trickster," a figure that plays a prominent role in global ethnography.

Schuhpalast Pinkus was immensely popular, and its success allows us to speculate on the reason for Jewish comedy's broad appeal. The story follows the young Sally Pinkus from his schooldays to commercial success as the owner of a "shoe palace." When we first see him as a schoolboy, he embodies a well-known figure in Jewish jokes of the day: *der kleine Moritz*. "Little Moritz" was an impudent, unconstrained, and uncontrollable boy – a consummate smart aleck – who was fixated on both sex and moneymaking; the humor of that stock character resided in imputing to someone so young (and sometimes he is very young) the supposed obsessions of Jewish adults. In Lubitsch's film, schoolboy Sally constantly flirts with girls his age, who return the attention by swarming around him, and in the process, he neglects his studies. Indeed, to succeed at all, he has to cheat in gymnastics as well as on tests, for which he is expelled from school. Because his poor grades prevent him from gaining employment at a respectable firm, he takes a job with a small-time cobbler and shoe salesman, who dismisses his poor report card with the comment: "I don't care about *Schulbildung*." Sally likewise questions the value of his education, remarking while sweeping the floor: "I had to learn Latin for this."

Sally soon loses this job for refusing to serve customers he finds disagreeable and for flirting with his boss's daughter. Thereafter, he matures from "little Moritz" to a "cunning" adult: he lands a sales job at Meyersohn's upscale shoe store by inflating his credentials and schmoozing with the boss (the intertitle reads: "*Sally schmust*"). Through his flirtatious behavior with female customers, Sally wins the affection of an elegant (and Gentile) dancer; Meyersohn also finds her attractive, but Sally sidelines him through a series of underhand ruses. The dancer loans him money to establish his own extravagant "shoe palace," which takes off when he highjacks one of her performances to advertise his wares. When he is successful enough to pay off the loan, he proposes marriage instead, so that the money can "stay in the family."

How do we account for the popularity of *Schuhpalast Pinkus* and similar works crafted by Jews that depict Jewish characters getting ahead by less than honest (though definitely not criminal) means? I suggest that such works appealed to the desires and aspirations of many audience members, both Jews and Gentiles, who came from the middling and lower classes represented by characters like Sally. What pupil in Germany's rigid schools had not dreamed of sleeping late, cutting classes, cheating, and simply calling it quits? What low-level shop employee had not thought of telling off offensive customers? Though young Sally's actions would have been wishful fantasies for most viewers, his means of getting ahead in the commercial world, though comically exaggerated, contained many nuggets of truth. *Schuhpalast Pinkus* and similar works implied that people who start at the lower or middling rungs of society must use their wits to succeed in a society stacked against them. Their occasional stretching of the bounds of *Sittlichkeit* and honesty is not coded as reprehensible because only people who already possess *Bildung* and *Besitz* can afford such virtues – and who knows how the well-to-do (or their forebears) acquired their status in the first place? To be sure, that attitude flew in the face of the dictum that hard, honest work would lead to social advancement: but manual and white-collar workers among cinemagoers knew that that Protestant precept was as fictitious as anything else on screen. *List* and *Witz* offered more hope for success than relentless hard work. General audiences watching a humorous film (or skit or play) about a commercially astute and eventually successful Jew probably did not laugh *at* him, but rather *with* him. The butt of the joke, after all, was not the up-and-coming Jewish protagonist but rather the better-off figures who stood in his way – the sort who blocked the advancement of both Jews and Gentiles on the lower and middling rungs of society. Lubitsch had ceased playing that Jewish stock character by the time he moved to Hollywood in 1922, but actors such as Curt Bois (*Der Jüngling aus der Konfektion*, 1926; *Der Schlemihl*, 1931) and Siegfried Arno (*Familientag im Hause Prellstein*, 1927; *Moritz macht sein Glück*, 1930; *Keine Feier ohne Meier*, 1931) adopted and updated it for Weimar audiences.

In addition to the popular trickster topos, the cinematic medium also presented images of Jews that were more respectable. E.A. Dupont's *Das alte Gesetz* (The ancient law, 1923), for example, enjoyed considerable commercial success. Dupont was one of the relatively few contributors to film who hailed from the *Bildungsbürgertum*: he graduated from a Gymnasium and studied for a while at a university, and his father was a journalist and long-time editor of the *Berliner Illustrierte Zeitung* (an example of one of the newest mass media, a weekly newspaper festooned with photographs). At the outset, *Das alte Gesetz* sympathetically depicts the rabbi's humble home and worshippers in the synagogue of a poor but respectable Galician *shtetl* in 1860. The plotline – whose incredible improbability was not unusual on screen then or now – follows Baruch, the rabbi's son, who gets bitten by the theatrical bug during Purim, runs off with a wandering troupe, and finally catches the romantic eye of a young Austrian archduchess, who secures him a position at the Burgtheater, Vienna's most prestigious stage. [NB: Turning characters as different as Sally and Baruch into cinematic girl magnets was a highly effective counter to antisemitic caricatures; in any case, it is worth taking more note of Jewish romantic leads – male and female, comic and serious – in German silent cinema.] Predictably, Baruch's trajectory initially leads to rejection by his father, who is bound by "*das alte Gesetz*" (as is the archduchess, who ends her attachment to Baruch by telling him that she too is bound by an "ancient law," which she calls "etiquette"). Baruch's father is reconciled, however, after witnessing his son perform the title role in Schiller's *Don Carlos*, a play that was second only to Lessing's *Nathan the Wise* in the canon of Jewish *Bildungsbürger*.

Although explicitly treating a Jewish theme, in a non-humorous vein to boot, *Das alte Gesetz* could and did speak to Gentile audiences. Not only Jews broke away from *shtetls* and religious orthodoxy as they moved to larger cities, but Gentiles likewise left behind the *Dorf* and the *Kleinstadt* along with traditional Christian practices and values. For both groups, the transition could be wrenching, as they faced conflicts of faith versus secularism and parental authority versus individual autonomy. Although moviegoers might have shed tears over such scenes, they most probably concurred with the message that traditional family life and worship, however sympathetically portrayed, were shackles on the path to individual success and happiness. Break-with-the-past films (in both Jewish and Gentile settings) evoked nostalgia only to lay it to rest.

Cinema – along with other forms of popular entertainment and mass culture – offered an enticing vision of commercial, social, and cultural modernity in place of the old. On his path to stardom, Baruch faces a crisis of conscience when he is cast in the title role of a new production of *Hamlet* at the Burgtheater, whose opening night falls on Yom Kippur. Needless to say, he goes on stage, as did Al Jolson (in the role of Jackie Rabinowitz) just four years later in *The Jazz Singer* (1927), a film that Lubitsch was originally supposed to have directed. For Jews in Weimar Germany, Jackie's assimilation through popular music was more the norm than Baruch's assimilation through classical theater. The 1920s witnessed a flood of Jewish talent in the popular arts: not just film, but also cabarets, revues, operettas, and popular music. Lubitsch's comic portrayal of the commercially successful Jew and Dupont's more somber account of sacrificing Jewish tradition for Gentile high culture each represented subgenres in the mass media. By far, however, the greatest theme promoted by Jewish writers, composers, and film-makers was the celebration of commercial and cultural modernity. It was a flag around which Jews and Gentiles lacking *bildungsbürgerlich* credentials could rally.

The annual revues staged in Berlin's Metropoltheater between 1903 and 1913 were paradigmatic (Jelavich 1993, 104–117; Otte 2006, 201–279). The Jewish crafters of most of these revues – scriptwriter Julius Freund and composer Viktor Hollaender – wrote peppy and highly successful skits and songs that touted the latest fads and fashions, particularly those of Berlin. The first revue – significantly entitled *Neuestes!! Allerneuestes!!* (Get the latest!! The very latest!!) – provided a tour of the newest sights of the metropolis such as the Wertheim department store and the elevated commuter train. It also celebrated recent inventions that affected everyday life such as coin-operated vending machines and Kodak handheld cameras. Skits parodied the latest productions on Berlin's highbrow stages – plays by Gerhart Hauptmann, Maurice Maeterlinck, Hermann Sudermann, and Frank Wedekind – and satirized politicians of all stripes. Fashion, however, represented the major theme of that and later revues, as the actors, singers, and chorus – particularly the women – paraded the latest styles. In imperial Berlin, the largest occupational sector after the civil service was the garment industry, in which Jewish enterprises played a disproportionate role. By displaying the latest fashions on stage, the revues promoted the commodity manufactured and retailed in the most "Jewish" sector of Berlin's economy. Not surprisingly, one of the Metropoltheater's largest investors was Hugo Baruch, a textile magnate specializing in theater and film costumes, whose Berlin-based enterprise had subsidiaries throughout Europe and in the United States. Even less surprisingly, he provided the outfits and décor for the Metropol revues.

Placement of "Jewish" products was not, however, the point of the revues. More generally, they promoted openness to the new – in fashion, consumer goods, and the arts. At the same time, they did not advocate uncritical acceptance of every novelty: their tone was one of lighthearted parody and satire. This receptivity toward modernity, tinged with a hint of caution, was an attitude that benefitted both Jews and Gentiles, especially those who had been excluded from traditional elite culture. Other popular genres and media during the imperial era – operettas, cabarets, popular songs – echoed the message of the Metropol revues, and it spread across additional fields of mass entertainment during the Weimar Republic. The works of Friedrich Hollaender (Viktor's son) were paradigmatic: he penned not only the music but also the lyrics for numerous songs in cabarets, revues, and eventually sound films (most famously, *The Blue Angel* of 1930). He was just one of many Jewish composers, such as Werner Richard Heymann, Rudolf Nelson, and Mischa Spoliansky, who crafted songs performed on stage, in bars, in dance halls, in cinemas, and broadcast on the air via the new medium of radio. Jewish writers such as Fritz Grünbaum, Fritz Löhner-Beda, Walter Mehring, Kurt Robitschek, and Kurt Tucholsky scripted the lyrics. These works simultaneously promoted and parodied the latest fads and fashions in consumer goods and the arts, in social behavior and sexual lifestyles.

Despite the popularity and commercial success of Jewish-authored entertainment, it faced considerable opposition from various quarters. The most vocal faction consisted of self-proclaimed upholders of traditional social, political, and cultural values – a coalition that ranged from morality campaigners aligned with the Protestant and Catholic churches to the extreme proponents of *völkisch* thought. All of these groups expressed, to a greater or lesser degree, antisemitic prejudices in their attacks on the new forms of commercial and mass culture. They not only excoriated but also exaggerated Jewish influence (even though Jews did indeed play a disproportionately large role in popular entertainment). Reinhard Mumm, an outspoken conservative nationalist pastor and politician (as well as the son-in-law of Adolf Stöcker, arguably the most prominent antisemite of the Wilhelmine era), adopted an approach that exemplifies this attitude. Film censorship was abolished at the end of 1918, but Mumm led the effort to have it reinstated with antisemitic arguments: "From the beginning up to the present, the new business has been [...] essentially in Jewish hands. And with the first emergence of cinemas, all discerning friends of the *Volk* began to air complaints about the moral and artistic corruption of the *Volk* brought about by cinema" (Mumm 1920, 3). The dichotomy between Jews and the Gentile *Volk* was a mantra repeatedly proclaimed by racist nationalists; and as we have seen, scholars such as Mosse believed that such a cultural split actually existed (although, of course, not for racist-essentialist reasons). One can, however, read the evidence in another way: the commercial success of "Jewish" popular entertainment proved that its enthusiastic espousal of novelty and modernity appealed to many sectors of the actual *Volk* (the populace at large, in a statistical rather than ideological sense). That is precisely what horrified Mumm and other conservatives and rightists, whose harping on Jewish corruption of the cultural sphere interfaced seamlessly with National Socialist rhetoric. It culminated in infamous books like *Film-"Kunst" Film-Kohn Film-Korruption*, which pretended to unmask the "almost complete Jewification" of the film industry before 1933: this placed "a propaganda instrument of unimagined reach and a significant area of cultural activity" into the hands of a "clique alien to the *Volk*" (Neumann, Belling and Betz 1937, 40). Most conservative and *völkisch* commentators aimed their criticism mainly at film, which they regarded as the most dangerous (because it was influential and successful) mass medium, but they launched similar attacks against other forms of popular and mass culture: revues, cabarets, operettas, and popular songs.

A diametrically opposite quarter simultaneously leveled criticism at "Jewish" popular arts and mass media. Zionists opposed the assimilationist implications of films, revues, and other genres that encouraged all viewers – whether Gentiles or Jews – to embrace the inclusive culture of modernity, which touted individual success and happiness. Viewing such self-fulfillment as a break from traditional mores, Jews (whether Zionist or not) who took their faith seriously and disapproved of its dilution also attacked the new forms of popular entertainment. In *Das alte Gesetz*, before he goes onstage during Yom Kippur, Baruch recites Kol Nidre in his dressing room. The scene suggests that Jewish faith can be retained while bending it to secular demands; but traditionalists might well counter that little meaning would remain for the holiest of days. Such scenes imply that individuals should be free to select or reject parts of their religious heritage as they fashion their identities and pursue their careers in the modern world; but cafeteria-line Judaism (or Catholicism, or Protestantism) is the perennial bane of people with more traditional faith.

Not only Zionists and Jewish traditionalists but also more assimilated German-Jewish *Bildungsbürger* challenged the popular arts. The Central Association of German Citizens of Jewish Faith (*Centralverein deutscher Staatsbürger jüdischen Glaubens*), the major anti-defamation league, kept a watchful eye on entertainers who represented Jewish characters on stage and screen (Jelavich 2012, 33–39). On the one hand, they believed that self-deprecatory jokes about Jews or stock figures such as "little Moritz" and the Jew-as-trickster hindered all of their efforts at constructing an image of Jewish respectability, measured according to the social, cultural, and ethical standards of the Gentile bourgeoisie. On the other hand, they feared that Jewish entertainers who portrayed themselves as somewhat dishonest or philandering characters – even though in a humorous and sympathetic manner – played into antisemitic stereotypes. Emil Faktor, the editor-in-chief of a major liberal newspaper (and a classic Jewish *Bildungsbürger*, with a doctorate in law), opined that Jews' portrayal of questionable characters allowed the antisemites to declare: "That's the way they are, and they even brag about it!" (*Berliner Börsen-Courier*, 23 April 1926).

Jewish entertainers repeatedly tried to fend off these accusations. Responding defensively in an interview in 1916 (the year that *Schuhpalast Pinkus* was released), Lubitsch claimed that "films set in a Jewish milieu" were "offensive" only if they lacked a feel for "the essence of Jewish humor" or engaged in "boundless exaggeration." Obviously, he considered that his films did not suffer from those faults but rather embodied the following traits: "Wherever it appears, Jewish humor is sympathetic and artistic, and it plays such a great role everywhere that it would be silly to forgo it on the screen" (*Der Kinematograph*, 30 August 1916). Lubitsch certainly believed that the characters he portrayed were "sympathetic," and we can assume that most of his audience did so as well.

As antisemitism increased during and after the war, so did sensitivity toward Jewish self-deprecatory humor. The issue came to a head on 22 April 1926, when the Centralverein hosted two large public assemblies, whose combined attendance was well over a thousand, to protest the telling of Jewish jokes in public. In the subsequent issue of the Centralverein newspaper, the editors expressed particular dismay at the popular comic type that Lubitsch had portrayed a decade earlier: "When in school 'Little Moritz' turns out to be a loud-mouthed, unchildlike, totally unconstrained and morally deficient young Jewish man; when the essence of this humor resides in having a Jewish smart aleck contradict all notions of children's moral constraint, decency, and naiveté, then this is no longer humor, wit, or comedy, but rather a crude distortion of Jewish types that exist neither in Eastern Europe nor here with us" (*CV-Zeitung*, 30 April 1926). The statement voiced arguably serious concerns, but the "here with us" (in contrast to "Eastern Europe") was also telling: it was the voice of the assimilated German-Jewish *Bildungsbürgertum*.

That brings us back, in conclusion, to the thesis of this essay. Although the two issues were often conflated, we must analytically distinguish between opposition to overtly Jewish entertainment and *bildungsbürgerlich* hostility to popular and mass culture in general. Many conservative and all *völkisch* rightwing Gentiles conflated mass culture with "Jewishness," which they equated with all the perceived evils of the modern world. By contrast, and for opposite reasons, Jewish self-defense associations objected specifically to the portrayal of less-than-reputable Jewish characters on stage and screen; they did not code modernity itself as Jewish. This cultural "Jewish question" was, however, separate from a broader attack on mass culture that had nothing to do with perceived Jewish engagement in the popular arts; rather, it was based on the social, cultural, and ethical values of the *Bildungsbürger*, which prized aesthetic high-mindedness and moral and intellectual uplift – values that were shredded by mass entertainment. Indeed, precisely that attitude, I suspect, blinded scholars for so many decades to Jewish contributions to popular and mass culture. Not only educated and cultured émigrés such as Mosse, but professors in general belong, by definition, to the *Bildungsbürgertum*, and their professional and social habitus steers them toward the cultural and intellectual attitudes of their historical counterparts. Whether consciously or not, a *bildungsbürgerlich* inattention to (if not disdain of) popular and mass culture, perhaps combined with queasiness over the self-deprecatory self-characterization of Jewish entertainers, might well have excluded the topic from research agendas. If so, then the concerns of the Centralverein enjoyed a long afterlife.

I propose moving beyond that attitude, but I certainly do not suggest turning the tables and excluding German-Jewish *Bildungsbürger* from the annals of history: on the contrary, that area still requires considerable research. We should, however, consider a different narrative of German-Jewish cultural history that builds upon a more recent basis of scholarship, whose prospects are at least as promising. This new narrative might read some something like this: For German Jews, popular and mass culture in late imperial and Weimar Germany played a role similar to that of the Enlightenment and classicism in the eighteenth century. The Enlightenment empowered Jews to break with their traditional values and lifestyle and to enter into an alliance with a Gentile *Bürgertum* that was asserting its worth vis-à-vis the dominant aristocratic elites. A century later – long after the *Bildungsbürger* had succeeded in securing their social status and cultural authority – nascent forms of commercial entertainment and mass culture enabled new generations of Jews from middling social strata to break free from their traditional roots and to join the ranks of socially comparable Gentiles. This modern popular culture, which appealed to a much wider swath of the population – both Jewish and Gentile – challenged traditional bourgeois values by promoting greater individual autonomy and diversity (which had been the original promise of *Bildung*, although realized only for very few). Indeed, Jews played a much more active role in this later development than in the earlier one. If this thesis is valid, then we should turn the scholarly page and start writing exciting new chapters in the history of German-Jewish culture.

Bibliography

Aschheim, Steven. *Culture and Catastrophe: German and Jewish Confrontations with National Socialism and Other Crises*. New York: New York University Press, 1996.

Ashkenazi, Ofer. *Weimar Film and Modern Jewish Identity*. New York: Palgrave Macmillan, 2012.

Büschenthal, L.M. *Sammlung witziger Einfälle von Juden, als Beyträge zur Charakteristik der jüdischen Nation*. Elberfeld: H. Büschler, 1812.

Döblin, Alfred. "Erlebnis zweier Kräfte" [1922]. Alfred Döblin, *Schriften zu Leben und Werk*. Olten: Walter-Verlag, 1986. 40–45.

Jelavich, Peter. *Berlin Cabaret*. Cambridge, MA: Harvard University Press, 1993.

Jelavich, Peter. "'Am I Allowed to Amuse Myself Here?': The German Bourgeoisie Confronts Early Film." *Germany at the Fin de Siècle: Culture, Politics, and Ideas*. Ed. Suzanne Marchand and David Lindenfeld. Baton Rouge: Louisiana State University Press, 2004. 227–249.

Jelavich, Peter. *Berlin Alexanderplatz: Radio, Film, und the Death of Weimar Culture*. Berkeley. University of California Press, 2006.

Jelavich, Peter. "When Are Jewish Jokes No Longer Funny? Ethnic Humour in Imperial and Republican Berlin." *The Politics of Humour: Laughter, Inclusion, and Exclusion in the Twentieth Century*. Ed. Matina Kessel and Patrick Merziger. Toronto: University of Toronto Press, 2012. 22–51.

Mosse, George. *German Jews beyond Judaism*. Bloomington: Indiana University Press, 1985.

Mumm, Reinhard. *Die Lichtbühne. Ein Lichtblick aus den Verhandlungen der Deutschen verfassunggebenden Nationalversammlung*. Berlin: Deutschnationale Schriftenbetriebsstelle, 1920.

Neumann, Carl, Curt Belling and Hans-Walther Betz. *Film-"Kunst" Film-Kohn Film-Korruption*. Berlin: Verlag Hermann Scherping, 1937.

Otte, Marline. *Jewish Identities in German Popular Entertainment, 1890–1933*. Cambridge, UK: Cambridge University Press, 2006.

Prawer, S.S. *Between Two Worlds: The Jewish Presence in German and Austrian Film, 1910–1933*. New York: Berghahn Books, 2005.

Richarz, Monika. "Occupational Distribution and Social Structure." *German-Jewish History in Modern Times*. Ed. Michael A. Mayer. New York: Columbia University Press, 1997. 3: 35–67.

Schlüpmann, Heide. *Unheimlichkeit des Blicks: Das Drama des frühen deutschen Kinos*. Basel: Stroemfeld/Roter Stern, 1990.

Stratenwerth, Irene, and Hermann Simon, eds. *Pioniere in Celluloid: Juden in der frühen Filmwelt*. Berlin: Henschel Verlag, 2004.

Volkov, Shulamit. "The Ambivalence of *Bildung*: Jews and Other Germans." *The German-Jewish Dialogue Reconsidered*. Ed. Klaus Berghahn. New York: Peter Lang, 1996. 81–97.

Emily J. Levine
Aby Warburg and Weimar Jewish Culture: Navigating Normative Narratives, Counternarratives, and Historical Context

According to Gershom Scholem, Aby Warburg's *Kulturwissenschaftliche Biblio-thek Warburg* – both in scholarship and in personnel – kept its distance from Judaism. "For about twenty-five years [Warburg's library] consisted almost entirely of Jews whose Jewish intensity ranged from moderate sympathies to the zero point and even below. I used to define the three groups around the Warburg library, Max Horkheimer's *Institut für Sozialforschung*, and the metaphysical magicians around Oskar Goldberg as the three most remarkable 'Jewish sects' that German Jewry produced. Not all of them liked to hear this" (Scholem 1988).

To a certain degree, Scholem was correct. Born in Hamburg in 1866, Warburg trained in the field of the "new cultural history" promoted by such figures as Karl Lamprecht and Jacob Burckhardt, an approach that aimed to integrate the *Schatten,* or dark aspects of the classical heritage, into modernity. By 1912, he innovated the methodological approach he called iconology, which tracked the development of images over time. Drawing on disciplines as diverse as anthropology, numerology, and the occult, Warburg sought to understand how gestures in images reflected deep societal tensions between primitivism and modernization. His *Kulturwissenschaftliche Bibliothek Warburg* (literally, the Warburg Library of Cultural Science, hereafter, the Warburg Library), a library with 60,000 volumes at its peak, was devoted to revealing precisely these contradictory impulses that he called the *Nachleben der Antike,* or the afterlife of antiquity.[1] Although Warburg did not leave a prolific body of published works, his library, rich with symbolism, became an inspiration for the fields of memory, film, and visual studies and offered an open book for German Jewish history.

The second generation of Warburg scholars, who are largely responsible for introducing Warburg and his library to the English-speaking world, affirmed Scholem's judgment. Sir Ernst Gombrich, who served from 1959 until 1976 as the director of the London Warburg Institute (the postwar iteration of Hamburg's Warburg library, which was incorporated into the University of London in 1944), towered over the image of Warburg. He created the Warburg many of us initially

---

1 The development of this library and a portrait of its most active scholars, Ernst Cassirer and Erwin Panofsky, is the subject of Levine, *Dreamland of Humanists: Warburg, Cassirer, Panofsky, and the Hamburg School* (2013a).

encountered – the Warburg whose tensions were smoothed over and shadows turned into the heroic artistic creativity of Dürer's great works. Gombrich white-washed not only Warburg's scholarship and depression but also his Judaism. What the Austrian diplomat and historian Emil Brix called Gombrich's "restrained fury" at the notion of a separate "Jewish culture" in fin de siècle Vienna applied to his treatment of Warburg, whose Jewishness, we are told, disappeared with his rejection of Jewish law (Brix 1997).

Peter Gay's assessment of the Warburg circle similarly reflects the sensibil-ity of this generation of émigré scholars. Preoccupied with his own "non-Jew-ish Jewishness" and eager to preserve the legacy of Enlightenment rationality, Gay assessed the Warburg library as "Weimar at its best;" ultimately, however, he argued that it conducted its work in what he called "peaceful obscurity" and "serene isolation" (Gay 1981, 33–34). This judgment reflects a bias that we have inherited about Weimar Jewish culture that is both geographical and intellectual. For Gay and subsequent scholars, Weimar culture denotes Berlin and intensify-ing romanticism. Insofar as Warburg and his friends were tethered to the Renais-sance and the Enlightenment – that is, a broad-based liberal humanism – their contributions are irrelevant to Weimar's political and cultural trajectory and, as implied by Gay, George Mosse, and other scholars – this intellectual sensibility made them culturally and politically naïve.

The current image of Warburg has swung in the opposite direction. He is no longer an Enlightenment figure but "toujours Nietzschenne." He talks to butter-flies; he imagines a visit to the serpent ritual dance on the Hopi Indian reserva-tion; and he studies astrology and numerology.[2] Interestingly, we lack a rounded understanding of his relationship to Judaism. For some scholars, it is critical that this new Warburg obsessively kept tabs on antisemitic incidents on the Eastern front, scribbling down aphorisms and thoughts on scraps of paper and storing them in *Zettelkasten* that are now searchable. Others regard Warburg's iconol-ogy as useful for understanding Nazism (Didi-Huberman 2008). Other than his watchdog attitude towards antisemitism, however, Warburg was not, according to this reading, really a Jew.[3] Although I am not seeking to rehabilitate Warburg as a Jew, I contend that we obtain a skewed portrait not only of Warburg but also of Weimar Jewish culture by overlooking the Jewish and Republican features of his life and work.

---

2 Examples of this "newer" Warburg can be found in works by Didi-Hubermann (2002); Michaud (2004); and Steinberg (1995).
3 Charlotte Schoell-Glass (1998, esp. 53) argues that antisemitism is the primary explanatory principle in Warburg's art-historical scholarship.

Just as the "old Warburg" told us more about the émigré generation than about Warburg himself, this "new Warburg" reveals 1970s Parisian post-structuralist approaches and the 1990s effort by art historians in Hamburg to rebuild that field (Papapetros 2003, esp. 171–174). Yet these portraits do not tell us about Warburg "wie es eigentlich gewesen" (how it essentially was), to borrow Ranke's dictum about the past. They contribute to narratives – about the Enlightenment, totalitarianism, or Jewish identity – in which Warburg is a mere pawn. Although such narratives are not unique to Weimar Jewish history, the field certainly lends itself to such transference. Steven Aschheim (2007, 93) has explored this phenomenon in his work *Beyond the Border*; the question of the vicissitudes of Weimar German Jews as icons in competing narratives informs my reconstructive treatment of Warburg and his milieu. Indeed, many of our portraits of Weimar Jews such as Warburg seem to be inventions of necessity in service to claims about the fate of European Jewish culture as a whole.

This essay moves beyond both the normative and counternarratives of German Jewish history to situate Warburg's life and career in the time and place in which his work was formed.[4] While acknowledging that we historians inevitably invest personally in our subjects, in my examination of Warburg, I intend to use historical context to ameliorate the effects of that transference.[5] Warburg's own scholarly approach can be a helpful guide here. In a series of articles about the early Renaissance, he articulated his greatest scholarly innovation – that social context was critical for understanding art. Just as one cannot, according to Warburg, comprehend the work of Botticelli or Ghirlandaio without situating their painting in the broader milieu, so too, one should treat Warburg's own context as an organizing principle rather than as mere atmospheric "setting."[6] As an alternative to these competing Warburgs, this essay draws on three interrelated contexts as interpretive frameworks – the urban, financial, and the political. Such attention to context does not imply a reductive explanation of ideas by their context. Rather, this account of Warburg as embedded in various institutional contexts enriches our understanding of the Warburg circle and suggests a

---

4 Whereas Peter Jelavich's contribution in this volume attempts radically to supplant the Gay-Mosse narrative with one that focuses on popular culture, my revision seeks to refocus the narrative of Jewish intellectuals in a way that revises the political and cultural implications of their work.

5 In this respect, this essay dovetails with a theme latent in the contributions from Shulamit S. Magnus and Matthias Morgenstern in this volume – locality's effect on the prospects and realities of distinct Jewish communities.

6 While intellectually probing, Sylvia Ferretti's study (1989) is typical in its disembodied account of Warburg. Even Gombrich lacked the necessary urban context, according to Felix Gilbert (1972, 381).

model for reintegrating the plurality of paths taken by Jewish intellectuals in the Weimar Republic.

Warburg reportedly said he was a "Hamburger at heart, Jew by blood, [and] Florentine in spirit" (Bing 1960, 113). It is worth emphasizing the first of these elements because this multifaceted identity seems to converge in his *Vaterstadt*, the city of Hamburg, which is the key to enriching our portrait of Weimar Jewish culture. Hamburg has long confounded German historians, challenging generalizations of Germany as autocratic, aristocratic, and insular. As an imperial "free city," a legal status awarded by Emperor Frederick I in the twelfth century, Hamburg enjoyed republican self-rule by a local senate whose members came from merchant families and whose politics balanced local and international interests. For this reason, Warburg came to believe that Hamburg's fate was tied to that of the Weimar Republic, which also straddled the European and the German, the national and cosmopolitan.

Money mattered in Hamburg. As the socialist Willi Bredel explained of Hamburg's free-city status: "The Hamburg burghers bought their freedom" (Bredel 1960, 16). Even if this was normative for the establishment of a free city in the Holy Roman Empire, this strong urban identity persisted in the nineteenth century, as it did in other regions outside Prussia, despite political centralization.[7] Hamburg's urban mercantile identity revealed itself in a number of ways, including its support – more for trade-related reasons than out of nationalism – for Germany's annexation of its neighboring territory, Schleswig-Holstein. Hamburg's merchants also successfully lobbied against Germany's protectionist policy in 1878 to ensure continuation of the city's trade without disruption by German tariffs.[8] Because of a political structure based on *Honoratioren* – volunteers from the "notable" class rather than a professional civil service – political decisions were based mainly on economic concerns, including those of shipbuilders, property owners, and industrialists. Mary Lindemann (2006, 26–28, 46) has shown how such urban concerns as crime were often articulated in financial narratives. In Hamburg, being a good merchant meant being a good citizen.

Though mercantile cities are not necessarily more tolerant than other places, as Francesca Trivellato argues with respect to Livorno, Hamburg's "we'll-do-busi-

---

7 Regionalism as the source of cultural creativity had great purchase, for example, in Saxony, which had long lost the political luster of its "Augustan" Golden Age but maintained a vibrant cultural identity in the nineteenth century. See Zwahr (2000).

8 Maiken Umbach (2005, 666) argues that the inherently contentious relationship between city and nation-state and center and periphery is particularly evident – here, in architectural choices – in the case of "second cities."

ness-with-anyone" mentality undoubtedly benefitted Jews.[9] Warburg attended the Johanneum Gymnasium, which as early as 1802 admitted Jews, including Jacob Bernays, the son of Hamburg's chief rabbi, who went on to become a respected philologist.[10] After the loosening of state restrictions in 1868, Hamburg's Jews enjoyed many rights not yet granted in other German states. They could live wherever they desired, join previously exclusive trade guilds, and marry gentiles. The Warburgs benefited from this openness. Referred to by locals as the "King of Hamburg," Aby's younger brother Max served in Hamburg's Citizen's Assembly and Chamber of Commerce. Reflecting the Jews' central role in Hamburg industry, Max and the city's most powerful shipping magnate, German Jew Albert Ballin, were termed *Kaiserjude*. Of the one third of Hamburg's population that was active in commerce, Jews represented over 17 percent, or nearly five thousand individuals.[11]

Hamburg's inclusiveness had its limits. According to Lamar Cecil's classic biography of Ballin, outside of their business interactions, Jews and Gentiles did not mix at the stock market, and the two groups occupied separate tables at the central social location, the Alster Pavilion (Cecil 1967, 37). Moritz M. Warburg believed that such segregation reflected the inevitability of the Warburgs' exclusion as Jews. When the thirty-year-old Max considered running for a seat in Hamburg's elite Senate, Warburg senior advised, "That is not for us; you will not be seen as a coequal" ("Aby Warburg Anecdotes." WIA).[12] In short, the Warburgs were accepted – almost.

In the Weimar Republic, these contradictions became more acute. In that politically tumultuous era, the Senate welcomed Jews and appointed a Jewish mayor, a remarkable feat; yet antisemitism, especially among young students at the newly founded university, festered. Nearly two thirds of upper and upper middle class voters supported the National Socialists at the peak of its national

---

9 Francesca Trivellato (2009) challenges this position in *The Familiarity of Strangers: The Sephardic Diaspora, Livorno, and Cross-Cultural Trade in the Early Modern Period*.

10 Germans introduced compulsory education between 1816 and 1870, although most Jews tried to open their own schools rather than attend Christian ones. More commonly, "most Christian parents took their children out of school when Jews began to attend around 1800" in Trier (Kaplan 2005, 121, quote on 123). On Jacob Bernays, see Momigliano (1994, esp. 154).

11 This regional difference may have been connected to the process of bureaucratization in general. Hamburg instituted civil registration for marriage in 1866, for example, whereas in Prussia that process did not occur until 1874. On the development of Jewish life in Hamburg, see Krohn (1974, 71).

12 Indeed, unconverted Jews did not become senators until after the revolution of 1918 (Lippmann 1964, 103).

popularity.[13] When conducting business with Jews was no longer an option in 1938, Hamburgers' tolerant spirit burned less brightly. As Frank Bajohr (2002, 80) has shown, regional economic concerns rather than genuine sympathy motivated Hamburg's local authorities in the Third Reich to implement an anti-Jewish policy towards Warburg & Co. in a way that preserved the bank's autonomy and protected its interests.

As this inconsistent treatment of Jews reveals, Hamburg was not a "special case" for Jews – to evoke the line by Hamburg-born historian Percy Schramm. Progressive and reactionary, affluent and a hotbed for socialism, Hamburg most likely acquired these characteristics as a typical consequence of the development of the nineteenth-century city, which bred such tensions as a result of rapid and uneven industrialisation.[14] These tensions infused Warburg's work. As the Hamburg-trained British art historian Edgar Wind later reflected, Warburg was motivated by the "things in between" (Wind 1931). Warburg believed that through analyzing a moment of historical transition and tension such as the Early Renaissance, one could gain insight into perennial human dilemmas. Such interstitial *topoi* as the merchant, the widow, and the bourgeois family recur in Warburg's early essays and serve this wider sociological purpose. These essays thus often seem to reflect Warburg's "working out" of his experience as the scion of a German Jewish banking family.

We should be wary, however, of mapping an idealized "spirit of a city" – be it Florence or Hamburg – onto Warburg's ideas.[15] Cities are manmade. Insofar as they have "auras," these are fashioned by individuals through civic institutions. These urban conditions, in turn, had real institutional implications for the development of ideas. First, Hamburg's cultural world grew from the ground up; it was not imposed from the state down. In such a world, merchant families such as the Warburgs exerted considerable control over culture. Understanding this, Warburg took his model not so much from Renaissance Florence as from the American Jewish philanthropists he met in 1895 in New York. When he returned to Hamburg, he reflected not only on the cultural meaning of primitive rituals he had witnessed in the American West, but he also contemplated the significance

---

13 According to Peter Pulzer (2003, 274), Hamburg's Mayor Petersen illustrates that outside Berlin, Jews could hold positions of prominence. Interestingly, the other prominent Jewish mayor in Germany in the Weimar period was Ludwig Landmann in Hamburg's sister city Frankfurt. On student radicalism in Hamburg, see Giles (1980). On voting patterns in 1932, see Hamilton (1982, 122).

14 Richard J. Evans's study of Hamburg (1987) examines the consequences of these developments through the case study of the Cholera Affair.

15 The personification of the city has become a recent trend among social scientists. See, for example, Bell and de-Shalit (2011).

of institutional innovation in the East. Inspired by the American example, he ultimately used his money to create a new kind of privately funded research institute.

Such scholarly institutions were important because they enabled Jews such
as Warburg to promote their burgeoning fields at a time when their identity and
iconoclastic ideas shut them out of traditional institutions. Warburg followed a
pattern similar to the sociological model that Shulamit Volkov sketched of chem-
ists in this period: he utilized the experience of periphery – urban and ethnic – to
cultivate a holistic and interdisciplinary approach to the study of images over
time, one that only later was reincorporated back into the university.[16] Though he
sometimes craved the legitimacy that further incorporation of his institute into
the university would have brought, Warburg never gave up the autonomy afforded
by his family's private financing of his intellectual endeavors. The simultaneous
freedom and demotion of this extra-university space is essential to understanding the full impact of Warburg's intellectual contribution. This predicament represents a strand in Jewish and intellectual life that became increasingly common
in the interwar period but has not been thoroughly integrated into either of the
reigning narratives.

The lives of Warburg, his family, and the community of scholars that gathered
around the new university that the Warburgs helped found in May 1919 reveal
the full implications of the intrinsic contradictions in Hamburg's urban identity.
Evolving out of a protracted dispute between scholars and bankers, the University of Hamburg was the focus of scholars' aims and anxieties in a city that had
never been known for its intellectual life.[17] One third of the monetary donations
for the university came from Jews, intensifying concerns about the new kinds of
scholars that private money bought.[18] An incident in 1928 known as the "Cassirer
Affair" illuminates the cultural and political nature of Warburg's goals for both
institutions – the university and his library – and illustrates how the various contexts discussed above can provide analytic tools for assessing Weimar Jewish life.

The incident's central protagonist was the philosopher Ernst Cassirer, whose
life intersected with Warburg's in the summer of 1919, when the new University of
Hamburg offered him, at the age of forty-five, his first position. It was a time, as
Fritz Saxl later remarked, when "hope was in the air," although as we have seen,
Hamburg was by no means immune to antisemitism. Cassirer got the job "despite

---

16 Shulamit Volkov (1994, 55) argues that the Kaiser-Wilhelm-Institut became a haven for Jewish professors who had been barred from entering the university. Interestingly, women scholars
also happily discovered that the institutes were not governed by the same legal restrictions that
limited their advancement in the university system (Vogt 2010, 161–179).
17 For a short history of the founding of the University of Hamburg, see Nicolaysen (2007).
18 On the reactionary strand in Hamburg, see Grolle (1997, 99–122).

[his] Jewish faith," as one faculty member explained ("Gutachten..." 1919). His appointment surprised even the Jewish psychologist William Stern, who had lived and worked in Hamburg since the pre-university days and was named to the university's first chair in psychology. Stern commented privately to another Jewish student, "Despite the revolution, one cannot expect *two* Jews as representatives of [the] philosophy [faculty in Hamburg]."[19] Stern had cause for concern because the summer before Cassirer began teaching, antisemitic students boycotted his university lectures (Cassirer Papers; "Antisemitische Stroemungen..." 1987, 1115).

Cassirer's decade in Hamburg was his most productive period. Before 1925, he published a number of works, including the first two volumes of his *Philosophy of Symbolic Forms*, in which he expanded his neo-Kantian framework to formulate a broad philosophy of culture. The synergy between Warburg's library and Cassirer's philosophy made that work possible. Even while Warburg was recovering from a postwar nervous breakdown in a sanitarium in Switzerland, he and Cassirer had already begun to build a strong intellectual and personal relationship mediated by Saxl (1958, 49–50) and the library. By the time Warburg returned to Hamburg in 1926 for the official library opening, Cassirer was a self-professed regular of the *Arbeitsgemeinschaft* of the library, as Cassirer called it in his dedication to Warburg in *Individual and the Cosmos in Renaissance Philosophy*.

Cassirer's presence vindicated Warburg's life's work – his library – especially because Warburg's depression prevented him from producing a substantial published legacy. When Warburg learned in June 1928 that the philosopher had received a job offer from the rival University of Frankfurt, his reaction was nothing short of hysterical.[20] During the month before Cassirer reached a decision, Warburg held long conversations with him and agonized with his brother Max and with his assistants Gertrud Bing and Saxl over what to do (A. Warburg 1928a and 1928b). He privately negotiated with Frankfurt's rector; he drafted a public statement for a special issue of the local newspaper; and he convinced Hamburg's mayor and one of the senators to solicit Cassirer personally (Cassirer Papers BRBML).

Depending on the context, Warburg attributed various meanings to this potential loss. His exchanges with *non-Jews* and his *public statement* on this affair

---

19 Emphasis my own (Stern 1919).
20 WIA, III.29.2.6. *Stuttgarter Neues Tagblatt*, 24 June 1928, Newspaper clippings sent from Max Goldschmidt to A. Warburg. WIA, III.29.2.6. *Essener Allgemeine Zeitung* (Essen) 22 June 1928; *Neue Badische Landeszeitung* (Mannheim) 23 June 1928; *Breslauer Zeitung* (Breslau) 23 June 1928; *Ostdeutsche Morgenpost* (Beuthen) 24 June 1928; *Der Tag* (Berlin) 24 June 1928; and *Koelnische Zeitung* (Koeln) 23 June 1928 are among the newspapers from which Goldschmit sent Warburg clippings.

reveal his anxiety about Hamburg's precarious intellectual world.[21] He invoked sympathy for the "provinces," contrasting it to the "Prussian university system" with what he termed its "established tradition, its greater abundance of power, and its understanding trustees."[22] In an article that he distributed to influential citizens, "Why Hamburg Should Not Be Permitted to Lose Cassirer," Warburg again warned that Hamburg's identity as an intellectual city depended on Cassirer, and he appealed to local pride in the "Hanseatic" city and the competition with its Prussian rival.[23]

Cassirer decided to stay, thanks in part to Warburg's tireless efforts. He also received an invitation to deliver a high-profile university address, a raise, and a hint that he could become the university's next rector. Warburg succeeded, as he had on a number of other occasions, in refuting notions of Hamburg's "intellectual wasteland." Warburg's private correspondence from this period indicates, however, that something else was at stake: namely, Hamburg's German-Jewish tradition. In confidence to his brother Max, Aby shared his fear that the true meaning of Cassirer's departure meant a loss to the German-Jewish community. "If Cassirer goes to Frankfurt, [Cassirer's star pupil Walter Solmitz] surely would follow him and that holds symbolic meaning for the individual: the organic potential for growth and the capacity of the bearer of the inherited German-Jewish constitution [*des alten Erbgutes in deutsch-jüdischer Hand*] would suffer an incurable blow."[24] Warburg echoed this sentiment in the diary of the Warburg library that he kept together with his assistants. This domino effect was dangerous, Warburg warned, because Solmitz was supposed to be "a representative of the next gen-

---

21 Claudia Naber's (1991) article draws on these sources in her tribute to the German Jews of Hamburg but she does not distinguish between privately and publicly shaped identities.

22 "Denn dem Universitaetsystem Preussens gegenueber, mit seiner bewiesenen Tradition, groesseren Machtfuelle und verstaendnisvollen Kuratoren, waere die Anziehungskraft Hamburgs nie ausreichend, um seine Lebensbahn wieder in die 'Provinz' abzulenken" (Cassirer Papers-Addition. Box 3).

23 "Wenn Professor Cassirer gehen wuerde, weil er eben glauben mueste, in Frankfurt eine breitere und verstaendnisvollere Umwelt zu finden, so wird ihm dies sein Kollege vom Ideendienst persoenlich verargen, wohl aber Umschau halten, ob Hamburg unserem Professor glaubwuerdig dartun kann, dass auch die hanseatische Universitaet ihn als lebenswichtiges und fuehrendes Organ bracht, dessen persoenliche Entfaltung zugleich eine unschaetzbare Staerkung des Universitaetsgedantens an sich bedeutten wuerde" ("Warum Hamburg den Philosophen Cassirer nicht verlieren darf" WIA. 29.2.4).

24 "Er [walter Solmitz] wuerde, wenn Cassirer nach Frankfurt geht, diesem sicher folgen und das bedeutet im Symbol des einzelnen Menschen gesehen, dass die organische Wachstumsfaehigkeit und Tragfaehigkeit des Mittraegers *des alten Erbgutes in deutsch-juedischer Hand* einen unheilbaren Naehrschaden erleiden Wuerde (italics my own)" (A. Warburg 1928).

eration [who] would carry on the torch of the German-Jewish spirit."[25] Warburg worried that if Cassirer left, he would take Hamburg's German-Jewish present and future with him.

Warburg's utterances to his Jewish inner circle – Bing and Saxl were also Jewish – do more to complicate rather than clarify Warburg's Jewish identity. To be sure, the Warburg Library was certainly not a library of *Jewish* scholarship; nor did it resemble a library of what is now called Jewish Studies. Scholars like Peter Freimark (1991) have remarked that book collecting is a Jewish activity. This incident does not, however, invite a reductive Jewish reading of Warburg's book collecting any more than it does of his scholarship. For as much as he "packed and unpacked" his library, Warburg never achieved the spiritual satisfaction Walter Benjamin evokes in his famous essay. While not completely "performa-tive," as some scholars describe the nature of identity, Warburg's Jewish identity is nonetheless far from essentialist.[26] As this incident reveals, the formation and articulation of Warburg's Jewish identity was embedded in its historical contexts. Moreover, Warburg clearly spoke with different emphases depending on those contexts.

Warburg's positioning of his identity is evident in the calculating way he crafted the image of his library. He denied access to such Jewish movements as the Wissenschaft des Judentums that he thought would tarnish the library's secular reputation. Conversely, Warburg welcomed attention in the nationalist and even in the antisemitic press. The drama of the "Cassirer Affair" reveals the difficulty in pinpointing Warburg's Jewishness: For Warburg, Cassirer's success in the secular realm reflected pride on the Jewish community. This idea is challenging for a historian to prove because of the often opaque aspects of Jewishness in this circle of secular German Jewish intellectuals. The role of the city of Frankfurt as a foil in Warburg's self-fashioning helps clarify the relationship of this incident to Warburg's Jewish identity.

As a free city with its own "Weimar-era" university, Frankfurt had a long pedigree as competitor to both Hamburg citizens and the Warburg family (Meyer 1988, 446). It also presented a foil to Warburg's intellectual vision and, seemingly, his cultural mission. Whereas Isaac Deutscher later characterized "non-Jewish Jews" as unaffiliated Jews who nonetheless were still tied to a Jewish identity, Warburg

---

25 "Der Beweiß, daß er und die KBW zusammen funktionieren müssen, läge in einer Gestalt wie [Walter] Solmitz; er, als Vertreter der nächsten Generation würde die Fackel deutsch-jüdischer Geistigkeit weiter tragen und würde eben durch die idealistische Sendung von Cassirer und der KBW in lebendigem Atmen gehalten" (Schoell-Glass and Karen Michels 2001, 263).
26 According to Roberts (2002, 234), for example, both the "new woman" and the "Jew" "perform" their identity.

treated certain identifiable Jews with overt Jewish interests as "Jewish Jews."[27] Warburg did not aspire to resemble Deutscher's non-Jewish Jews or Frankfurt's Jewish Jews; instead, he viewed the German-Jewish tradition embodied in Cassirer and the Warburg Library as uniquely possible in Hamburg.

Home to the German-Jewish "Jewish" philosophers of the Freies Jüdisches Lehrhaus, Frankfurt was, in the 1920s, reputed to be *the* place to study Jewish texts. The city with "the most famous of all Jewish communities in Germany" welcomed the revitalization of modern Judaism. In fact, Frankfurt was so receptive to the Jewish community that, in the early Zionist debates, one activist proposed it as a solution to the Jewish problem (Scholem 1988, 131–132). The city's university also reflected this Jewish spirit. Like Hamburg's university, the University of Frankfurt was privately funded, and in Frankfurt, these private donors consisted disproportionately of Jewish families. Because of its association with "Jewish money," however, the University of Frankfurt earned the noxious label "Jew University" and during the Nazi period faced the threat of closure. Although they had raised nearly two-thirds of the money for Hamburg's university, the Warburgs disapprovingly observed that Frankfurt's parallel development had been "anxious and Jewish" (*ängstlich-jüdisch*) (Lustiger 1988, 74; Fritz Warburg 1913). Warburg was determined that the University of Hamburg not become Frankfurt.

The same could be said of his library, for which he claimed a *universal* mission. Associating Scholem with the Frankfurt Lehrhaus, Warburg refused Scholem's request to publish his work, even though, as Saxl pointed out, his perspective was highly relevant to the library's scholarly goals (Lorenz 1996).[28] Warburg regarded the purpose of the Lehrhaus and its affiliates as avowedly Jewish and devoted to adult Jewish education.[29] He kept "Jewish Jews" at arm's length.[30] When Solmitz reported that Toni Cassirer had expressed interest in moving to

---

27 It is worth noting that by "Jewish Jews," Warburg did not mean the religiously observant but those who promoted a public project of reconciling Judaism with the demands of Western philosophy and the modern world, such as Scholem, Buber, and Rosenzweig, and therefore threatened Warburg's model of distinct and separate-spheres for the secular and religious worlds. Isaac Deutscher (1968, 25) coined the term in 1958 at a lecture during Jewish Book Week to the World Jewish Congress.

28 Scholem (1928) remarked that Cassirer's work was of tremendous interest to a kabbalist.

29 Michael Brenner (1966, 69–70) argues that such learning represented one way that modern Jews expressed their Jewishness.

30 In his personal life, too, Warburg expressed a similar disdain for such "Jewish Jews." As a student at the university in Bonn, Warburg repeatedly complained in letters to his mother about the Jews who spoke Yiddish and possessed the bad table manners common to Jews (A. Warburg 1886).

Frankfurt, Warburg snidely commented that she sought "ghetto warmth" (*Ghetto-Wärme*) (Grolle 1994, 12; TKBW, 278).

An offer from Frankfurt's university, of course, was difficult to turn down. In addition to offering a competitive package of teaching responsibilities, salary, and pension, the University of Frankfurt would give Cassirer an opportunity to work in a city with a rich intellectual history. To Warburg's dismay, Hamburg's citizens still celebrated their home primarily as a port city, not as a place for serious scholarship. Acknowledging the harbor as the heart of the city, the university held all of its major academic celebrations on ships (Staatliche Pressestelle 1928). The harbor – not Hamburg's internationally acclaimed intellectual life – earned Bismarck's adoration for Hamburg and its nickname "Gateway to the World." Frankfurt's commercial reputation, in contrast, did not come at the expense of its intellectual status. Cassirer's friend Ernst Hoffmann, a Heidelberg professor, echoed this sentiment and cautioned Cassirer: "Do not forget that Hamburg is the city of the Hamburg America Line and Frankfurt the home of Goethe" (Toni Cassirer 1981, 169). Given Goethe's supreme importance for Cassirer, Hoffman's appeal was enticing.

For Warburg, the "Cassirer Affair" exposed the dual precariousness of Hamburg's intellectual and Jewish identities. The moment when these identities are threatened provides a window into their self-fashioning. The outcome was significant not only for Warburg but also for the Weimar Republic. Warburg's cultural and political positioning in the Cassirer Affair reveal the essence of the academic and social politics in Germany's new democratic republic, perhaps in any democratic society.[31] In the shifting priorities of particularity and universality, Warburg's negotiations offer an example of Jews' perception of their relationship to different audiences. In the wider urban context, Cassirer, renowned as the best Kant scholar, was essential to Hamburg's intellectual reputation. In the particular Jewish one, Warburg *kvelled*, considering that Cassirer's success in the wider world of secular scholarship made him the bearer of the true "torch of the German-Jewish tradition." Warburg linked this formulation of "private Jews, public Germans" to the unique possibilities of Hamburg.

Second, the focus on the city changes our understanding of both Warburg's Jewishness and Weimar Jewish history. In this respect, it is telling that in the "Cassirer Affair," Frankfurt emerges as the urban competition to Cassirer's tenure in Hamburg. On one hand, as Steven Aschheim has suggested, Hamburg's Warburg Library and the Frankfurt Institute for Social Research share much in common both institutionally and intellectually: both groups cultivated intellectual life

---

31 The role of German Jews in the long history of minority and majority societies is the subject of Till van Rahden's contribution to this volume.

in spaces that were privately funded, largely by Jews, and used those spaces to promote bodies of scholarship that were liberal rather than radical, interdisciplinary, and generally counternarratives to the traditional histories of Western thought (Aschheim 2015). No doubt, this similarity represented part of the threat to Warburg and his cultural aspirations for Hamburg. For although both cities were essentially commercial, only Hamburg's cultural reputation had suffered as a result. Moreover, there is reason to believe that Warburg saw evidence of a backlash against Frankfurt's Jews. His interest in avoiding a similar "perception problem" in Hamburg motivated his strict private-public division of Jewishness. In light of this urban comparison, Hamburg's mayor's decision not to publicize the overwhelming contribution of Jews to the university seems justified. Indeed, the comparison highlights Warburg's remarkably similar yet distinctly different private Jewish and urban identity.

In both cases – the emergence of "private" Jewishness and the consequences of locality – institutions create the conditions for our understanding of Jewish life. In this way, the "Republican moment" that develops around the Warburg circle in interwar Hamburg parallels the "Jewish Republicanism" in late nineteenth-century France discussed by Philip Nord.[32] In Hamburg, a constellation of institutions created the possibility for an inclusive culture of secular Republicanism. Not unlike in the French case, hitching one's fate to the Republic had negative consequences. Nord's observation about French Jews could apply as easily for Germany in 1933 as it did for the Dreyfus Affair: "To the extent that the Jews tied their destiny to that of the republic, they suffered when the regime suffered" (Nord 1995, 89).[33] Moreover, despite Warburg's careful positioning, one of the tragedies of this tale is that antisemites also viewed Cassirer's success in the secular realm as Jewish. This should not, however, detract from the centrality of this paradox for understanding the Weimar Republic and its legacy.

Examining Warburg's life and work through the prism of his many contexts provides a more nuanced portrait of the humanist Jewish intellectual in the Weimar Republic than either the normative or the counternarratives permit.

---

32 According to Philip Nord (1995, 64–65), the university provided one of many institutional settings in which civil society was nested, where Jews, Liberal Protestants, and Freemasons promoted Republicanism. Thanks to Till van Rahden, who alerted me to the similarities between my work and Nord's. Nord cites Aron Rodrique's essay (1990, 196) as his inspiration for this term. Cassirer's "cosmopolitan nationalism" in his scholarship and university leadership, which connected the fates of the Weimar Republic, intellectual history, and Hamburg make this parallel more meaningful. See Levine (2013b).

33 The French parallel extends to the self-fashioning and theatricality at work in the Dreyfus Affair. Mary Louise Roberts (2002) poses a similar question as to the difference between rhetoric and reality, essentialism and performativity in identity construction.

Whereas the Gay-Mosse reading might have dismissed Aby's musings to Max about Cassirer as either nostalgia or irrelevant, my exposition emphasizes the difference between Warburg's private and public utterances in order to restore his agency in his historical moment. Moreover, the context-based approach realigns Warburg's investment in the Jewish and Republican causes. Warburg, ultimately, is not punished for "betting on the wrong horse"; instead, he becomes a savvy institutional *Wissenschaftsmanager* who tried to control the reception of his intellectual community and projects. One of those receptions was, of course, that of his Jewish identity, which varies depending on one's perspective. Based solely on Warburg's public utterances or conversations with non-Jews, Warburg seemed to be a non-Jewish Jew. Given the unique place for Hamburg's Jews that Warburg clearly crafted in the institutions he shaped, however, any narrative of Weimar Jewish culture must feature not only Scholem's explicit revival of Jewish culture but also Warburg's affirmative, civic-motivated Jewish identity.

The French sociologist Pierre Bourdieu (1990, ix) remarked that Scholem emphasized different aspects of his identity depending on his audience, be it American or European, Jewish or Gentile. In this respect, Scholem resembled Warburg more than, perhaps, either of them would have liked to admit. Such an understanding of Warburg's Jewishness, or of Jewishness in general, requires relinquishing the need to pinpoint an "essential" Judaism, a suggestion that historians often make but rarely follow. A perusal of Warburg's own words – especially the private utterances – reveals a complicated Jewishness, ever in negotiation. The danger in abandoning essentialism is that any argument for Jewish selfhood is reduced to performativity. Insofar as we are historians, however, and not philosophers, then we cannot ignore what Bourdieu called *habitus*, a scholar's professional, institutional, and socio-economic predicament.[34] Only an explanatory principle that encompasses both the internal development of ideas and the external conditions of a scholar's surroundings captures the duality at the heart of a cultural and intellectual identity as slippery as Jewishness.

Inevitably, our own lives motivate the stories we tell about our subjects. Jürgen Habermas once observed that if the German Jewish intellectual did not exist, we would have to invent him.[35] German Jewish studies have played a key role in European, American, and Israeli Jewish identity in the last fifty years. Such tense debates over, for example, where Kafka's papers belong – Israel, Europe, or

---

34 The symbiosis between Bourdieu and the Warburg circle is evident in the fact that Bourdieu used the concept of *habitus* for the first time on the occasion of the French edition of Panofsky's *Architecture gothique et pensée scolatique* (Bourdieu 1970).

35 "If there were not extant a German-Jewish tradition, we would have to discover one for our own sakes" (Habermas 1958, 42).

America – are much more than merely academic. As historians, we have an additional obligation to be self-critical about that process and to begin historicizing the stories bequeathed by previous generations. This essay intervenes in these wider conversations by suggesting that we can ground this discussion of Jewishness by focusing on place. Aby Warburg constructed an identity – both Jewish and scholarly – that was rooted in the city of Hamburg, in which its sister city Frankfurt often served as a foil. An appreciation for the places in which we stage our own conversations – Berlin, Jerusalem, or New York, to name a few – might also help to expose the stakes in our own historical questions and the subjects that we choose.

Bibliography

Abbreviations used in this essay:
BRBML. Beinecke Rare Book and Manuscript Library, Yale University.
StA HH. Staatsarchiv Hamburg.
TKBW. Aby Warburg, Gertrud Bing, and Fritz Saxl. *Tagebuch der Kulturwissenschaftichen Bibliotek Warburg*. Ed. Karen Michels and Charlotte Schoell-Glass. In *Gesammelte Schriften: Studienausgabe*. Ed. Horst Bredekamp, Michael Diers, Kurt W. Forster, Nicholas Mann, Salvatore Settis, and Martin Warnke. Berlin: Akademie Verlag, 2001.
WIA, FC, GC. Warburg Institute Archive, Family Correspondence, General Correspondence.

"Aby Warburg Anecdotes." WIA, III.134.1.6.
"Antisemitische Stroemungen in der Hamburger Studentenschaft." July/August 1919. *Hamburger Echo*. Excerpted in Lorenz, Ina Susanne. *Die Juden in Hamburg zur Zeit der Weimarer Republik: eine Dokumentation*, Hamburger Beiträge zur Geschichte der Deutschen Juden, Bd. 13. Hamburg: H. Christians, 1987.
Aschheim, Steven E. *Beyond the Border: The German Jewish Legacy Abroad*. Princeton, NJ: Princeton University Press, 2007.
Aschheim, Steven E. "The Weimar Kaleidoscope – and Incidentally Frankfurt's not Insignificant Role in It." *100 Years of Frankfurt University: German and German-Jewish Scholars*. Göttingen: Wallstein Verlag: 2015.
Bajohr, Frank. *"Aryanization" in Hamburg: The Economic Exclusion of Jews and the Confiscation of Their Property in Nazi Germany*, Monographs in German History 7. New York: Berghahn Books, 2002.
Bell, Daniel A. and Avner de-Shalit. *The Spirit of Cities: Why the Identity of a City Matters in a Global Age*. Princeton: Princeton University Press, 2011.
Bing, Gertrud. *Rivista storica italiana* 71 (1960): 100–113.
Bourdieu, Pierre. "Postface." *Architecture gothique et pensée scolastique*. Ed. E. Panofsky. Trans. P. Bourdieu. Paris: Minuit, [1967], 2nd rev edn. 1970. 133–167.
Bourdieu, Pierre. "Preface." *In Other Words: Essays Toward a Reflexive Sociology*. Trans. Matthew Adamson. Stanford: Stanford University Press, 1990. ix.

Bredel, Willi. *Unter Türmen und Masten: Geschichte einer Stadt in Geschichten*. Schwerin: Petermänken-Verlag, 1960.

Brenner, Michael. *The Renaissance of Jewish Culture in Weimar Germany*. New Haven: Yale University Press, 1996.

Brix, Emil. *The Visual Arts in Vienna c. 1900: Reflections on the Jewish Catastrophe*, 1. Two texts based on lectures given on the occasion of the seminar "Fin-de-siècle Vienna and its Jewish Cultural Influences," 17 November 1996, with a Preface by Emil Brix, 40 pp. London: Austrian Cultural Institute (Occasions, 1), 1997.

Cassirer, Toni. *Mein Leben mit Ernst Cassirer*. Hildesheim: Gerstenberg, 1981.

Cassirer, Ernst. Papers-Addition. GC, BRBML, Box 3, Folders 78a and 78b.

Cassirer, Ernst. Papers-Addition. GC, BRBML, Box 2, Folder 44.

Cecil, Lamar. *Albert Ballin: Business and Politics in Imperial Germany, 1888–1918*. Princeton, NJ: Princeton University Press, 1967.

Deutscher, Isaac. "The Non-Jewish Jew." *The Non-Jewish Jew and Other Essays*. London: Oxford University Press, 1968.

Didi-Hubermann, Georges. *L'image survivante: Histoire de l'art et temps des fantômes selon Aby Warburg*. Paris: Editions de Minuit, 2002.

Didi-Hubermann, Georges. *Images in Spite of All: Four Photographs from Auschwitz*. Chicago: University of Chicago Press, 2008.

Evans, Richard. J. *Death in Hamburg: Society and Politics in the Cholera Years, 1830–1910*. London: Penguin Books, 1987.

Ferretti, Sylvia. *Cassirer, Panofsky, and Warburg: Symbol, Art, and History*. Trans. Richard Pierce. New Haven: Yale University Press, 1989.

Freimark, Peter. "Jüdische Bibliotheken und Hebraica-Bestände in Hamburg." *Tel Aviver Jahrbuch für Deutsche Geschichte* 20 (1991): 459–467.

Gay, Peter. *Weimar Culture: The Outsider as Insider*. Westport, CT: Greenwood Press, 1981.

Gilbert, Felix. "From Art History to History of Civilization: Gombrich Biography of Aby Warburg." *The Journal of Modern History* 44 (1972): 381–391.

Giles, Geoffrey J. "The Academic Ethos in the Face of National Socialism." *Minerva* 18 (Spring 1980): 171–179.

Grolle, Joist. *Bericht von einem schwierigen Leben, Walter Solmitz, 1905–1962: Schüler von Aby Warburg und Ernst Cassirer*. Hamburger Beiträge zur Wissenschaftsgeschichte 13. Berlin: Dietrich Reimer, 1994.

Grolle, Joist. "Blick zurück im Zorn: Das Revolutionstrauma des Ernst Baasch." *Hamburg und seine Historiker*. Ed. Joist Grolle. Hamburg: Verlag Verein für Hamburgische Geschichte, 1997.

"Gutachten für die philosophische Professur." Hochschulwesen II 361–5 II A I 3:8, 6 June 1919. StA HH.

Habermas, Jürgen. "The German Idealism of the Jewish Philosophers." *Philosophical Profiles*. Trans. Frederick G. Lawrence. Cambridge, MA: MIT Press, 1985. 21–43.

Hamilton, Richard. *Who Voted for Hitler?* Princeton, NJ: Princeton University Press, 1982.

Kaplan, Marion A., ed. *Jewish Daily Life in Germany, 1618–1945*. New York: Oxford University Press, 2005.

Krohn, Helga. *Die Juden in Hamburg: Die politische, soziale, und kulturelle Entwicklung einer jüdischen Großstadtgemeinde nach der Emanzipation 1848–1918*. Hamburger Beiträge zur Geschichte der deutschen Juden 4. Hamburg: Hans Christians, 1974.

Levine, Emily J. *Dreamland of Humanists: Warburg, Cassirer, Panofsky, and the Hamburg School*. Chicago: University of Chicago Press, 2013a.

Levine, Emily J. "The Other Weimar: The Warburg Circle as Hamburg School." *Journal of the History of Ideas*, 74 (2013b): 307–330.

Lindemann, Mary. *Liaisons Dangereuses: Sex, Law, and Diplomacy in the Age of Frederick the Great*. Baltimore: Johns Hopkins University Press, 2006.

Lippmann, Leo. *Mein Leben und Meine amtliche Tätigkeit: Erinnerungen und ein Beitrag zur Finanzgeschichte Hamburgs*. Hamburg: Hans Christians, 1964.

Lorenz, Ina. "Das 'Hamburger System' als Organisationsmodell einer jüdischen Grossgemeinde: Konzeption und Wirklichkeit." *Jüdische Gemeinden und Organisationsformen von der Antike bis zur Gegenwart*. Ed. Robert Jütte and Abraham P. Kustermann. Vienna: Böhlau, 1996. 221–255.

Lustiger, Arno, ed. *Jüdische Stiftungen in Frankfurt am Main*. Frankfurt on the Main: Jan Thorbecke Verlag Sigmaringen, 1988.

Meyer, Anne Marie. "Warburg in His Early Correspondence." *The American Scholar* 57.3 (Summer 1988): 445–452.

Michaud, Philippe-Alain. *Aby Warburg and the Image in Motion*. Trans. Sophie Hawkes. New York: Zone Books, 2004.

Momigliano, Arnaldo. "Jacob Bernays." *Essays on Ancient and Modern Judaism*. Ed. Silvia Berti. Trans. Maura Masella-Gayley. Chicago: University of Chicago Press, 1994. 148–170.

Naber, Claudia. "'Die Fackel deutsch-jüdischer Geistigkeit weitertragen': Der Hamburger Kreis um Ernst Cassirer und Aby Warburg." *Die Juden in Hamburg 1590 bis 1990: Wissenschaftliche Beiträge der Universität Hamburg zur Ausstellung "Vierhundert Jahre Juden in Hamburg."* Ed. Arno Herzig and Saskia Rohde, vol. 2. Hamburg: Dölling und Galitz Verlag, 1991. 393–406.

Nicolaysen, Rainer *"Frei soll die Lehre sein und Frei das Lernen": Zur Geschichte der Universität Hamburg*. Hamburg: DOBU Verlag, 2007.

Nord, Philip. *The Republican Moment: Struggles for Democracy in Nineteenth-Century France*. Cambridge, MA: Harvard University Press, 1995.

Papapetros, Spyros. "The Eternal Seesaw: Oscillations in Warburg's Revival," review of Georges Didi-Huberman's *L'image survivante: Histoire de l'art et temps des fantomes selon Aby Warburg* (2002). *Oxford Art Journal* 26 (2003): 169–174.

Pulzer, Peter. *Jews and the German State: The Political History of a Minority, 1848–1933*. Detroit: Wayne State University Press, 2003.

Roberts, Mary Louise. *Disruptive Acts: The New Woman in Fin-de-Siècle France*. Chicago: University of Chicago Press, 2002.

Rodrique, Aron. "L'exportation du paradigme révolutionnaire, son influence sur le judaïsme sépharade et oriental." *Histoire politique des juifs de France: entre universalisme et particularisme*. Ed. Pierre Birnbaum and Michel Abitbol. Paris: Presses de la Fondation nationale des sciences politiques, 1990.

Saxl, Fritz. "Ernst Cassirer." *The Philosophy of Ernst Cassirer*. Ed. Paul A. Schilpp. New York: Tudor Publishing Company, 1958.

Schoell-Glass, Charlotte. *Aby Warburg und der Antisemitismus: Kulturwissenschaft als Geistespolitik*. Frankfurt on the Main: Fischer, 1998.

Schoell-Glass, Charlotte and Karen Michels, eds. *Aby Warburg: Tagebuch der Kulturwissenschaftlichen Bibliothek Warburg*. Berlin: Akademie-Verlag, 2001.

Scholem, Gershom. Gershom Scholem to Fritz Saxl. 11 October 1928. WIA, GC.

Scholem, Gershom. *From Berlin to Jerusalem: Memories of My Youth*. Ed. and trans. Harry Zohn. New York: Schocken Books, 1988.

Staatliche Pressestelle I–IV 135-I 5396, 17 June 1928. StA HH.

Stern, William to Jonas Cohn, 7 May 1919. Quoted in *Der Briefwechsel zwischen William Stern und Jonas Cohn: Dokumente einer Freundschaft zwischen zwei Wissenschaftlern*. Frankfurt on the Main: Peter Lang, 1994.

Trivellato, Francesca. *The Familiarity of Strangers: The Sephardic Diaspora, Livorno, and Cross-Cultural Trade in the Early Modern Period*. New Haven: Yale University Press, 2009.

Umbach, Maiken. "A Tale of Second Cities: Autonomy, Culture, and the Law in Hamburg and Barcelona in the Late Nineteenth Century." *American Historical Review* 110 (June 2005): 662–666.

Vogt, Annette. "Barrieren und Karriere – am Beispiel der Wissenschaftlerinn." *Frauen in der Wissenschaft – Frauen an der TU Dresden: Tagung aus Anlass der Zulassung von Frauen zum Studium in Dresden vor 100 Jahren*. Ed. Hildegard Küllchen. Leipzig: Leipziger Universitätsverlag, 2010.

Volkov, Shulamit. "Die Juden in Deutschland 1780–1918." *Enzyklopädie Deutscher Geschichte*. Munich: R. Oldenbourg Verlag, 1994.

Warburg, A. to Charlotte Warburg ("Mama"). 25 October 1886. WIA FC.

Warburg, A. "Warum Hamburg den Philosophen Cassirer nicht verlieren darf." WIA, 29.2.2.

Warburg, A. A. Warburg, record of his own thoughts, 3 June 1928a. WIA, (GC); WBI, III.29.2.7.

Warburg, A. A. Warburg to Max M. Warburg, 13 June 1928b WBI, FC.

Steinberg, Michael P. and Aby Warburg. *Images from the Region of the Pueblo Indians of North America*. Ithaca, NY: Cornell University Press, 1995.

Warburg, Fritz to A. Warburg, 28 November 1913, WIA, FC.

Wind, Edgar. "Warburgs Begriff der Kulturwissenschaft und seine Bedeutung für die Ästhetik." *Zeitschrift für Ästhetik und Allgemeine Kunstwissenschaft* 25 (1931): 163–179.

Zwahr, Hartmut. Foreword to *Saxony in German History: Culture, Society, and Politics 1830–1933*. Ed. James Retallack. Ann Arbor: The University of Michigan Press, 2000.

Ofer Ashkenazi
The Jewish Places of Weimar Cinema: Reconsidering Karl Grune's *The Street*

Jewish immigrants to Germany, mainly, from Eastern Europe, and their children played a decisive role in the formation of the so-called German national cinema in the period preceding Hitler's rise to power. Until recently, this well-documented phenomenon had a surprisingly minor impact on the study of the social, cultural and political aspects of Weimar film.[1] A close look at the productions of the German studios of the 1920s, however, reveals that the particular experiences of the Jewish filmmakers vitally affected their shape. In various genres – from adventure and horror films to melodramas and domestic comedies – Germany's post-World War I films repeatedly addressed the experiences, hopes, and fear that characterized immigrant Jews' encounter with the urban bourgeoisie. Instead of embodying German national sentiments and memories, the popular genres of Berlin films often adopted the perspective of outsiders who wished to assimilate into the bourgeoisie and obliterate the differences between them and their middle-class peers. This essay illustrates this widespread trend through an analysis of the acclaimed, genre-defining film, *Die Straße* (The Street, Dir. Karl Grune, 1923). A close reading of this film will demonstrate the ways in which the self-reflections on Jewish experience in modern Germany constituted the ideological and aesthetic sensibilities normally identified with Weimar cinema. I shall focus my analysis on the spatial symbolism in Grune's influential film. His use of place in his discussion of identity formation links some of the most enduring motifs in Weimar film with some key concepts in the pre-1933 discussion of Jewish acculturation.

1 Weimar film and German-Jewish identities

And how much of this poison was produced and distributed! [...] It was appalling, and could not be overlooked, that the Jew was chosen in so great a number for this disgraceful vocation (Hitler 1933, 62).

Traditional readings of Weimar film associate it with various "German" tendencies that allegedly distinguished the nation on the eve of Hitler's rise to power. This tra-

---

1 The few exception to the general post-1945 scholars' disregard for Jewish immigrants' role in Weimar film include Feld (1982, 337–368); Arnheim (1962, 220–241).

dition echoes a prevalent tendency in the discussion of film in Germany throughout the twentieth century. Ever since the inception of German cinema, critics,
filmmakers, and politicians have repeatedly invoked the cinema's unmatched
ability to display and shape the national "spirit."[2] Germany's political and military
leaders, aware of the powerful relationship between the nation, its objectives, and
its cinema, mobilized the local film industry for the national war efforts during
World War I (Kreimeier 1999, 38–47). Throughout the Weimar era, numerous filmmakers, reviewers, and newspaper advertisements habitually linked the "unique
qualities" of German films to the particularities of the national inclinations and
aspirations.[3] Post-1945 scholars of the German cinema conventionally replicated
this perception, while emphasizing the alleged correlations between the cinematic imagery of the Weimar Republic and the (almost inevitable) rise of Nazism
Brilliantly canonized in the works of Siegfried Kracauer (1947) and Lotte Eisner
(2008 [1952]), this reading of Weimar films portrayed them as manifestations of the
extraordinary encounter of the "German psyche" with modernity and its crises.

Kracauer and Eisner placed film within a comparatively simplistic trajectory of German national history, in which a shared cultural heritage and experiences reflected and instigated a shared destiny. Contemporary historians and film
scholars are suspicious of this premise. In contrast to the aforementioned teleo-
logical analyses, recent studies tend to emphasize the multiple readings embedded in Weimar cinema and point to the variety of contexts that gave meaning
to these films (Scheunemann 2006; Elsaesser 2000; Rogowski 2011). The disso-
ciation of Weimar films from the national grand narrative – i.e., the rise and fall
of the Weimar Republic – has enabled scholars to link these films to a diverse
set of experiences, emotions, and memories, such as combat experience, urban
women's sensitivities, left-wing politics, and mass escapism. Scholars' reading of
Weimar film as a heterogeneous body of works representing various views and
feelings was accompanied by a growing awareness of the ways transnational col-
laborations in production and distribution influenced local cinematic imagery
(Saunders 1994; Kreimeier 1999, 146–172). With a few exceptions, however,
studies continue to contextualize Weimar cinema within the German national
framework of *German* experiences, politics, and culture (e.g., German postwar
political turmoil; German artistic trends; the German soldier in war and defeat;
modernization of the German women; or the German *Heimat* in times of crisis)

---

2 See surveys of such discussions in Hake (1993, 3–104); Kaes (1978); and Elsaesser and Wedel
(1996).
3 Such understanding was common among writers of various political convictions, for instance,
Kalbus (1922); Balázs (1928); Olimsky (1930, 114–117). See survey in Hake (1993, 107–129); Ashkenazi (2010, 11–42).

(Petro 1989; Hake 1992; Kaes 2009; Murray 1990; Kester 2003; Lüdecke 1973; Hales 2007; McCormick 2001).

The significance of recent approaches to Weimar film scholarship notwithstanding, they still tend to overlook a fundamental set of experiences and social sensibilities that was shared by a large group of filmmakers. Memorable directors, producers, cameramen, and scriptwriters such as Joe May, Fritz Lang, Karl Grune, Carl Mayer, Robert Wiene, Erich Pommer, Henrik Galeen, Ernst Lubitsch, Richard Oswald, Leontine Sagan, Hanns Schwarz, Wilhelm Thiele, Karl Freund, Helmar Lerski, Paul Leni, Willy Haas, Billy Wilder, Robert Siodmak, and Béla Balázs – to name but a few – belonged to a first or second generation of Jewish immigrants to Germany's urban centers. The hundreds of Jewish employees of the Weimar film industry included the filmmakers responsible for many of the most successful films of the era (Wedel 2004, 27–35; Stern 2003, 203–225) and, more importantly, the ones responsible for the films that are normally remembered, studied, and taught as representative of the pre-1933 German cinema.

Noah Isenberg's recently published *Weimar Cinema: An Essential Guide to Classic Films of the Era* is a case in point. This collection of essays provides state-of-the-art, sophisticated analyses of the "most significant, most widely taught, and most widely available films of the period" (Isenberg 2009, 9). Although all the films discussed in this framework had a Jewish director, producer, or scriptwriter (in many cases, more than one of the above), the collection, on the whole, ignored this extraordinary fact and its implications. Isenberg's inattention (or indifference) to the filmmakers' background replicates an aspect of the post-1945 discussion of Weimar film. Kracauer and Eisner, themselves German-Jewish émigrés, failed to acknowledge the Jewish origins of many of the director and writers who shaped the films they linked to "German" characteristics. Indeed, Eisner and Kracauer merely followed the common practice of the film reviewers of the 1920s – many of them of Jewish ancestry – who rarely noted the Jewish (and immigrant) background of the directors, scriptwriters, producers, and camera operators under discussion.[4]

Weimar film was neither "a Jewish domination" (as some post-1933 Jewish commentators termed it [Myerson and Isaac Goldberg 1933, 158]), nor did it expose inherently Jewish traits (as Hitler, for instance, imagined). As Siegbert S. Prawer recently noted, the remarkable Jewish presence in Weimar cinema merely testifies that Jews integrated well into this industry and found effective (and lucrative) ways of collaborating with non-Jewish filmmakers (Prawer 2005). Nevertheless, in the cultural context of the Weimar Republic, film became an unparalleled arena

---

4 See discussion in Ashkenazi (2012, 3–5).

for contemplaing Jewish experience and Jewish identity. By and large, Weimar Jewish filmmakers belonged to a segment of Central and Eastern European Jewry that greatly benefited from bourgeois acculturation in an age where biologically defined antisemitism increasingly undermined the possibility of acculturation and assimilation (Niewyk 1980, 43–81; Verhey 1996, 85–96; Benz et al. 1998; and van Rahden 2007). The films they made mediated the fears and hopes of this segment of European Jewry and they often promoted the idea of a multicultural, liberal community that would accept the notion of multilayered identity.

Thus, whereas few characters of Weimar films were identified as Jews, stand-in figures – acculturated bourgeois outsiders – appeared frequently on the German screens of the 1920s. Numerous popular German films portrayed a protagonist who desperately strives to integrate into urban middle-class society, despite her or his inherent, immutable "difference." Weimar viewers encountered various types of sympathetic "others" who sought to avoid exclusion by concealing their differences, including their sexual orientation (in Magnus Hirschfeld and Oswald's *Different from the Others*), their gender (in Lubitsch's *I Do not Want to Be a Man*), their undesirable genetic heritage (Galeen's *Alraune*), or their foreign ethnicity (in May's *Mistress of the World*).[5] In all of the above-mentioned films, as in many others, the protagonists' attempts to conceal their "true" selves do not end with the obliteration of their differences. In portraying the protagonists' efforts to blend into German middle-class society, these films touch upon the prospects of acculturation and provide a vision of a tolerant society, in which "Others" – such as Jews – could be different, but equal.

As Steven Aschheim (2010, 21–38) convincingly argued in a different context, the recurrent emphasis on acting out and mimicry as an assimilation strategy associated such protagonists with the stereotypical Jew, who endeavors to emulate the appearance, gestures, and taste of the *Bildungsbürgertum*. This stereotype had played a key role in the pre-1933 German-Jewish identity discourse and in German antisemitic literature (Shahar 2007; Bayerdörfer 2009, 153–174). In antisemitic circles, the alleged Jewish mastery of visual deception and constant role-playing had become a symbol of an inauthentic entity, against which authenticity could be measured.[6] German-Jewish commentators also addressed the Jewish "talent" for acting and simulation. Instead of exploring the Jewish "nature" or "fate," however, they emphasize specific historical experiences of Jews in the age of urbanization and mass culture. Some, such as Hannah Arendt, echoing the opinion of antisem-

---

5 Richard Oswald, *Different from the Others* (Anders als die Andern, 1919); Ernst Lubitsch, *I Don't Want to Be a Man* (Ich möchte kein Mann sein, 1918); Henrik Galeen, *Alraune* (1927); Joe May, *Mistress of the World* (Die Herrin der Welt, 1919/1920).
6 For instance, Panizza (1980, 63–79); Blüher (1921, 19–20).

ites, scoffed at the efforts to "ape the gentile" (Arendt 1944, 99–100); others, such as Arnold Zweig and Robert Weltsch, portrayed this endeavor as a means of maintaining a distinctive position vis-à-vis their social surrounding while embracing the ideology and daily practices of the liberal (Prussian) bourgeoisie. In their account, the urban bourgeoisie demanded constant acting, and the Jewish "talent" situated "the Jew" at the forefront of modern society (Zweig 1928, 23, 25; Weltsch 1913, 158).[7] The objectives, needs, and conduct of the protagonists depicted in Weimar movie theaters suggest that German Jewish filmmakers were closer to Zweig's optimistic assessment of Jewish behavior than to Arendt's contempt of it.

A stereotypically "Jewish" use of mimicry in order to assimilate into an exclusive social circle is one of the most common motifs in the comedies, adventure, and horror films made by Jewish filmmakers during the Weimar years. As the following analysis of Grune's *The Street* demonstrates, Jewish filmmakers also emphasized two other elements of the contemporary Jewish identity discourse, which are usually cast in terms of place and displacement. The first relates to the portrayal of the bourgeois protagonist as rooted in a place to which he does not, and cannot, belong. As a stranger, he is innately displaced in his natural urban habitat. This dual relation to the urban landscape complements another stereotypically Jewish duality that appears in numerous films of the era, namely, the expression of different identities in private and public spheres. The spatial encoding of identity enabled Jewish filmmakers to envisage an intricate sense of personal and collective identity, in which different elements, different strata, are reconciled in a way that resembles – or, at least, could be imagined as – the coexistence of different urban spheres.

As I shall demonstrate, Grune's film also highlights Jewish filmmakers' genius for double encoding. Similar to many other heroes of the 1920s German-Jewish cinema, Grune's protagonist is simultaneously a stereotypical Jew and a typical, confused urbanite in an era of rapidly changing urban landscapes and social practices.[8] This double encoding, initially perfected in Lubitsch's early comedies, made the film relevant for a wide audience of middle-class urbanites (Ashkenazi 2010b); at the same time it incorporated the Jewish identity discourse and Jewish experience into German mainstream culture.

---

7 Walther Rathenau (1995 [1867], 267–268) made a similar, though different point in favor of Jewish emulation.

8 Henry Bial (2005) utilizes the notion of "double encoding" in his analysis of the way 'Jewishness' is encoded on the stage and screen in the U.S. German-Jewish filmmakers in the 1920s possessed a similar ability to produce imagery that expressed different meanings for Jewish and non-Jewish audiences and to hint simultaneously at the (stereotypically) "Jewish" and the (typically) "bourgeois" aspects of the characters.

2 Jewish places in the urban jungle: Karl Grune's *The Street*

> The stranger is fixed within a certain spatial area – or one whose delimitation is analogous to being spatially limited – but the position of the stranger is thereby essentially determined by not belonging in it from the outset [...] (Simmel 2009 [1908], 601–602).

Karl Grune's early film *The Street* (Die Straße, 1923) is perhaps the most lucid example of the spatial encoding of the bourgeois Jewish condition in Weimar film. The simplistic plot features a nameless bourgeois male protagonist who lives comfortably in his apartment but craves to escape it and explore the mysterious nocturnal city streets. When he finally sneaks out, his (apparently irresistible) longing for new experiences is exploited by the "typical" denizens of the street, the fraudulent felons. Seeking to sample the unfamiliar pleasures of the city, he roams around its commercial center, then, together with another, equally amorous suitor, follows an attractive woman to a nightclub and to her apartment. There, in the petit-bourgeois residence, the protagonist finally discovers that he was courting a prostitute, who collaborated with a criminal in an attempt to rob the naïve suitors. The scheme ends with the killing of the other suitor, while the protagonist is wrongly arrested by the police as the suspected murderer. At the end of the film, deceived, manipulated, and on the brink of committing suicide, the protagonist is released and returns to his dimly lit apartment to find security and solace.

This duality of urban spheres, at home and in the street, echoes a long cultural tradition of modern literature and it lies at the basis of Jewish assimilatory aspirations. As several commentators have noted, in various realms of modern bourgeois culture, the private sphere was designed to perform a dialectical role: as a realm that enabled individual particularism (through the promise of intimacy and control over the arrangement of the space, which distinguished it from the transitory city surfaces), and a realm in which to express and affirm one's belonging to bourgeois society (through demonstrating "adequate" taste and developing mechanisms of self-monitoring) (Bird 1999, 34–42; McCann 2004, 184–186; Shklar 1989, 24; Adorno 1966, 80–81).[9] Perceiving the private sphere as a bourgeois realm that legitimizes otherness without leading to exclusion was a fundamental aspect of the post-Enlightenment Jewish endeavor toward acculturation. The famous duality suggested by Judah Leib Gordon in his 1863 poem "Hakiza

9 See also Jonsson (2004, 49–53); Assmann (1999, 158–162, 299–300); Rice (2007, 9–36); Bachelard (1964, xxxiii). See also Koshar (1998, 1–7); Benjamin (1978, 155); Foucault (1977, 278 and 1983, 211–212); and Bourdieu (1984 and 1990).

Ami" – to "be a man in the street and a Jew at home"[10] – presupposes this notion in order to formulate the hybrid identity of the Jewish individual. An acculturated Jew can be a "brother to [his] countrymen" and still maintain his otherness, because modern social reality allows the expression of otherness in a specific sphere (and, equally important, because Jewish otherness *can* be expressed in the limited private domain).

As Marion Kaplan has shown, the formation of the Jewish middle class in Germany to a large extent depended upon Gordon's duality. Jewish embourgeoisement was made possible when middle-class Jews "displayed their Germanness [in the street] while they privatized their Jewishness" (Kaplan 1991, 11).[11] Ideally, therefore, the bourgeois notion of the private sphere functioned as an essential vehicle for Jewish acculturation because it enabled Jews to direct their struggle toward acceptance as equal members of the educated middle class despite their "difference" instead of striving to "amalgamate and disappear," that is, to erase their differences within the German nation.[12] The role of the private sphere in urban Jewish experience, however, can also be seen as indicative of the failure of the German Jewish "symbiosis." As Wolfgang Benz asserted, whereas Jews and non-Jewish Germans constantly interacted in the public domain, these relationships "rarely extended to the private sphere." According to this characterization, as a reaction to the Jews' social exclusion, the Jewish private sphere became a place of isolated consolation, a refuge from "the humiliation of daily existence" (Benz 1992, 97).

The Street demonstrates the brilliant ability of Weimar Jewish filmmakers to portray protagonists with desires and fears that are both stereotypically Jewish and typical of the white-collar urbanites of the post-World War I era. The plot follows – indeed, caricatures – the traditional discussion of urban individualism in modern literature; at the same time, the emphasis on distinctively different notions of belonging at home and in the street and the utter difference between the protagonist and the "ordinary" city dwellers situates the narrative within a specific Jewish identity discourse. Within this framework, Grune's melancholic allegory is particularly interesting because it adds complexity to Judah Leib Gordon's duality of "home" and "street." Here, as the protagonist's behavior indicates, the longing to be "in the street" – and to be different there than "at home" – is an indispensable part of being "at home." When the journey "outside" ends in colossal failure, the private sphere regains its status as a location provid-

---

10 Literally, "be a Jew in your dwelling and a man when you walk out" (Gordon 195, 17).
11 See also Brenner (1996, 166); Gilerman (2009, 17–52).
12 On the replacement of "amalgamation" by "assimilation" (where the different components retain their identities), see Niewyk (1980, 96–100).

ing shelter and consolation, albeit a dull, meaningless, and sad form of consolation. Like the city Jews depicted by Benz who could never thoroughly integrate into their environment, the husband returns home at dawn to find comfort in the family, its traditions, and routines.[13]

With its encoding of identity through spatial duality (private and public urban spheres), its emphasis on the irresistible emotional drive to "walk-out," and its claim to be an "authentic" representation of urban life, *The Street* is a genre-defining work.[14] Unsurprisingly, the "street film" genre attracted – and was dominated by – ethnically Jewish filmmakers, such as Leo Mittler, Joe May, Paul Czinner, and Grune (Prawer 2005, 92). *The Street* itself was the product of cooperation between a number of Jewish artists and entrepreneurs. Born Berthold Grünwald into a Jewish family in 1890 Vienna, Karl Grune, similar to Henrik Galeen, Richard Oswald, and several other 1920s filmmakers of Jewish background, began his show business career as a moderately successful stage actor. A veteran of World War I who fought and was wounded on the Eastern front, Grune arrived in Berlin in 1918, where he acted in the Deutsches Theater and the Residenz-Theater. Thanks to the efforts of his brother-in-law, the Jewish critic Max Schach, Grune obtained his first job as a scriptwriter and director in the studio of the Jewish producer Friedrich Zelnik. *The Street*, his fifteenth film, was the third feature he directed for Stern Film, a production company owned by Grune and Max Schach (who was also the executive producer of the film) (Lode 2004, 293–295). The Jewish scriptwriter Carl Mayer (whose vital contribution to Weimar cinema includes some of the most recognizable films of the era, such as *The Cabinet of Dr. Caligari*, *The Last Laugh*, and *Berlin, Symphony of a Great City*) developed the idea and the guidelines for *The Street*'s narrative.[15] The Jewish Expressionist artist Ludwig Meidner designed the set of *The Street* in a way that uncannily combined surface realism with the apocalyptic anxiety that characterizes his paintings of city landscapes.[16]

Despite the Jewish background of Grune and of many of his collaborators on *The Street*, studies of the film have never linked it to a specifically Jewish experience or aspiration (Kaes 2005; Vogt 2001; Murray 1990 and 1993; Hales 1996;

---

13 In an early review, Siegfried Kracauer (1924) pointed to this homecoming scene as a key moment in the film.
14 Willy Haas's (1925) reference to this film and to Grune's "intensive mimetic vision" is representative of its reception. See also Murray (1990, 80–82).
15 *The Cabinet of Dr. Caligari* (Dir. Robert Wiene, *Das Cabinet des Dr. Caligari*, 1920); *The Last Laugh* (Dir. Friedrich Wilhelm Murnau, *Der letzte Mann*, 1924); *Berlin, Symphony of a Great City* (Dir. Walther Ruttmann, *Berlin, Sinfonie der Grosstadt*, 1927). For a discussion of Mayer's career, see Ashkenazi (2012, 71–74).
16 In works such as *Apocalyptic Landscape* (1913) and *The Burning City* (1913), (Eliel 1989).

Cowan 2013; Murphy 2010, 2–10; and Hake 2002). Writing in 1947, Siegfried Kracauer even described Grune's film as a prominent manifestation of the "German psyche" in the German cinema. According to Kracauer, *The Street*'s protagonist personifies the pathological German leaning toward "authoritarian behavior" that underlies a psychological "development from rebellion to submission" (Kracauer 1947, 119, 157).

In an early review penned in 1924, however, Kracauer suggested a different motivation for *The Street*'s protagonist, which echoes the aforementioned role of "home" and "the street" in Weimar Jewish identity discourse. "At the beginning," according to Kracauer, "the husband [...] lies down on the sofa in a bourgeois apartment, which should be [his] *Heimat*, but cannot be such a place [...]; he gazes onto the street [...]" (Kracauer 1924). According to this interpretation, the film depicts unfulfilled yearnings for a *Heimat* within a reality that lacks the traditional spheres of the *Heimat*, namely, the rural landscape beyond the city. A popular trope in modern German culture, *Heimat* symbolized authentic relations between the landscape and the national community that granted the individual a sense of true belonging as well as a genuine means of expression (Confino 1997; Waldenfels 1990). Allegedly a remnant of pre-modern sentiments and ways of life, the *Heimat* served as a temporary refuge or an alternative mindset within the modernization of urban spheres, providing a sense of authenticity and consolation to those who felt ill at ease with modernity yet did not wish to reject it altogether.[17] As Kracauer implies, this type of national landscape beyond the city fails to offer a solution to the tormented, *Heimatlos* protagonist of *The Street*. His flight to the street is therefore neither an empty "rebellion" nor a mere surrender to his passions – as Kracauer maintained in 1947 – but a desperate quest for his authentic identity, a search for the place in which he can feel "at home." Because the film portrays solely (middle-class) urban spaces, it associates the search for a *Heimat* with the struggle to envisage a new *bourgeois* identity, perhaps even as a substitute for national identity and its alleged manifestation in nature.[18]

Grune's protagonist, however, cannot find an alternative *Heimat* in the city landscapes from which he frantically flees to return home. The first scene, before the protagonist walks out of his apartment, allows the viewers two different glimpses of the city. In the first shot emphasized by Kracauer, the protagonist lies on his sofa and gloomily gazes at the ceiling, on which the nocturnal urban

---

[17] Different aspects of the interrelationship between *Heimat* imagery and urban modernity are explored in Applegate (1990); Williams (2007); and Lekan (2004).

[18] Hans Kohn depicted in a similar manner the urban – stereotypically Jewish – protagonist of Gustav Hermann's *Dr. Herzfeld*: "the big city, the absolute opposite of *Heimat*, becomes his *Heimat*" (Kohn 1922, 33).

lights – apparently emanating from passing cars and flashing commercial bill-
boards – cast a threatening yet fascinating series of shadows. From the apartment
interior, the outside world exists merely as an unintelligible silhouette; yet the
mesmerized protagonist is unable to ignore its alluring presence. The shadows'
simulation of outside reality implies the deceptive and irrational nature of the
protagonist's perception of the city. The city's silhouette on the inner walls of
the apartment recalls the style of the so-called expressionist films of the early
Weimar years, which frequently employed conspicuously artificial sources of
light to underscore the twisted, strange, shadowy reality perceived or shaped by
irrational minds.[19]

The following sequence enhances this perception. The protagonist gazes out
the window, looking at the city itself but failing to see it. As the camera adopts
the protagonist's point of view, the spectators realize that the protagonist is not
tempted to escape from the apartment to the actual street, but rather into a fantasy
world that exists "outside," beyond the boundaries of his world. The identification of the film's point of view with the protagonist's longing gaze launches a
montage comprising quick cuts between, and juxtaposition of, "stereotypical"
images of the great city: cars rushing diagonally across the frame; hordes of
people roaming the streets in seemingly arbitrary motion; a city fairground seen
from a speeding rollercoaster; careless "new women" inside a nightclub; a frantically laughing clown, and so forth.[20]

This hallucinatory vision appears just before the protagonist walks out onto
the city streets. As he enters that strange realm, he resembles numerous other protagonists on their way out the door as depicted by Weimar Jewish filmmakers. *The
Street*'s protagonist similarly longs to be "invisible" – and to feel "at home" – in
a sphere to which he does not "normally" belong (i.e., a sphere he hitherto experienced only in dreams or hallucinations). Such protagonists, however, normally
set off for places that inherently would dispose the individual to alienation: they
included, for instance, European urbanites going to China, Africa, and the Ameri-
cas (May's *Mistress of the World*); a German soldier in wartime France (Oswald's
Dr. Bessels Verwandlung, 1927); a bourgeois resident of Berlin who went to climb
the Alps (Lubitsch's *Meyer aus Berlin*, 1919). Unlike them, Grune's protagonist
goes out to "his" street, to the public places of "his" city, namely, places with
which he should have been familiar. Yet, they are strange and alluring for him
just as foreign lands are for the protagonists mentioned above. Although he has
the appearance of an ordinary "man in the street," his gestures betray anxiety
and strangeness. He is an inhabitant of the city and supposedly belongs there no

---

19 As noted by Eisner (2008, 129–137).
20 Impressed reviewer repeatedly mentioned this scene. (Wesse 1928, 229–232).

less than he does inside, at home, but he behaves as if the street is a foreign territory: strange, perilous, and alluring.

This city dweller's improbable detachment from "the street," his lack of knowledge about it, and his perception of the street as an exotic, distant realm underscore the disparity between residing and belonging. Indeed, the protagonist of *The Street* seems to personify Georg Simmel's portrayal of "the stranger" (Der Fremde), a concept commonly identified with modern Jewish urbanites: "a member of the group" within which he resides, who is "at the same time an externality and opposition" (Simmel 2009, 602).[21] Indeed, when the protagonist rushes outside, away from his apartment, he fails miserably to be just like everyone else; he lives in the city as an outsider. Consequently, the police identify the protagonist – almost by default – as a criminal. His ultimate failure to be "a man in the street" – his exclusion from society by the policemen who wrongly arrest him for murder – further underscores the difference between the emulation of accepted bourgeois norms in the private sphere and the ability to go unnoticed in the bourgeois public sphere.

As the Jewish critic Béla Balázs noted, the protagonist represents something more than a foreigner in the street. As he runs through the "irrational succession of images" that portray the city landscape, his individuality is reduced to an abstraction; instead of the hybrid identity of "the stranger," he exhibits an utter loss of subjectivity (Balázs 1924). According to this interpretation, he will never be able to assimilate in the street, because – like the street itself, which turns into a "psychologically-visionary realm" (as Anton Kaes [1996, 27] phrased it) – the protagonist becomes a "ghostly impression" of reality.[22] In his 1947 reading of this film, Siegfried Kracauer, in fact, similarly portrays the street as a sphere that (implicitly) renders acculturation impossible or meaningless: fundamentally, he maintains, the street discards culture and civilization; it is a barbaric "jungle swept by unaccountable instincts" (Kracauer 1947, 121). The streets, the public spheres into which the protagonist seeks to integrate, are either an extension of his fantasy or a reference to a social environment that denies his belonging from the outset.

Read as an allegory on assimilation, *The Street*'s depiction of the city appears to be a visual embodiment of the frequently quoted definition of the Jews' relationship with Germany as an "unrequited love affair."[23] Advocates of Jewish

---

21 On the identification of "the stranger" with the urban Jewish merchant, see, for instance, Mendes-Flohr (1999, 21–22).

22 Balázs (1924) indicated that the street, the focal point of the film, is a "ghostly impression" of reality.

23 For the use of this phrase, see Arendt (1970, 184–185); Myers (2003, 163); and Albanis (2003).

nationalism or dissimilation, however, coined and emphasized the expression "unrequited love" in pre-1933 Germany, whereas Grune viewed the problem from the viewpoint of an urban liberal supporter (and beneficiary) of acculturation. His film, therefore, is indifferent to the notion of national identity and instead examines the integration of outsiders into the urban middle class. First and foremost, *The Street* focuses on the city rather than the state as the sphere that dictates the content and boundaries of modern (Jewish) identity discourse. The film does not portray alternative spheres beyond the residential and leisure areas of the urban middle class (including its petit-bourgeois criminal elements). Consequently, the people "in the street" have no common ground on a national basis; their collectivity is strictly one of shared *habitus* and morality.[24] Grune's film is, therefore, an examination of the boundaries of bourgeois collective identity, which views the inability of the stranger to integrate into a middle-class community as a devastating tragedy.

Indeed, Grune seems to be interested primarily in characterizing the changing bourgeois society of the post–World War I cities. Not so much "a jungle swept by unaccountable instincts," the street is a sphere in which the norms of the emerging mass consumption culture reign. The street is, initially, the place where commodities overwhelmingly dominate visible reality. Celebrated as a triumphant demonstration of Grune's extraordinary sense of realism – or, as one critic asserted, Grune's affinity "for the truth" (Harbach 1925; "Brüder Schellenberg" 1926) – the film's urban public sphere contains mostly display windows, which appear in almost every street scene. Like many of his urban contemporaries, Grune envisages urban mass consumption as a social phenomenon that initiated a fundamental transformation of bourgeois culture and society.[25] In this hour of social transition, facing the emergence of mass consumption culture, the Jewish love affair with modern urban culture is metaphorically personified by the protagonist's impulsive attraction to the appealing woman he meets in the street, the prostitute. His desire to be with this creature of the street, to possess her for a limited time – only so long as he remains outside of his apartment – leads him to follow her through the night. The protagonist's attraction to the prostitute thus

---

24 For the discussion of *Habitus* in this context, see Lässig (2004 and 2001). The filmmakers' decision to situate it in Paris, rather than in a German city, undermines further the national aspect of identity formation in the film. Notably, "Paris" here is also devoid of particular landmarks; it is a metaphorical big city rather than a real place.

25 On the emergence of mass consumption culture in Weimar cities and its reception as a vital break with the bourgeois past, see Koshar and Confino (2001, 136); McElligott (2001, 7); Coyner (1977); and Nolan (1994, esp. 109–120). As some scholars have noted, despite the abundant references to rupture and crisis, mass consumption culture was a rather limited phenomenon in Weimar (Mason 1976, 77–79).

discloses aspirations for belonging and for social mobility as much as it exhibits suppressed sexual desires.[26] Similar aspirations are apparent, for instance, in Lubitsch's comedy *Meyer from Berlin*, where Meyer, the (stereotypically Jewish) city dweller, courts a female mountaineer during his pitiful attempt to climb the Alps. *The Street*, however, is a tragedy, and the night ends neither with sexual intimacy nor with a Lubitsch style friendship and collaboration. At the end of the night, the protagonist is excluded from society, finding himself in jail (where he considers suicide, an even more radical form of exclusion).

Notably, this conclusion is not the result of the protagonist's escape to the street but is a direct outcome of his attempt to venture into the private sphere of the people of the street, namely, the apartment of the prostitute and her scheming husband. The protagonist deserts the street for the first time as he follows the woman into the nightclub. His entrance to the club launches a sequence of hallucinations that resembles those he experienced before leaving his apartment, now projected on the wall at which he – and the viewers – gaze. The club is one of the two spheres in the film that actually fit Kracauer's allusion to the "jungle swept by instincts": no policeman is visible in this place where scoundrels easily trap their victims. Illusion, deception, and reality intermingle here to confuse the helpless outsider and emphasize his otherness. Weimar films conventionally portrayed the nightclub as the total antithesis to the bourgeois apartment: blatant adultery, hallucination (often drug or alcohol related), and indifference to the "real" identity of a person (behind her costumes)[27] replace monogamy, reason, and authenticity. Exploiting the expectations aroused by this spatial convention, Grune pinpoints the nightclub as a crucial location in the protagonist's transformation from awestruck but-invisible *flâneur* to victim of modern culture. Indeed, the villains quickly read his paralysis at the entrance to the club as a sign of his "otherness" and of his ensuing vulnerability.

In *The Street*, however, the climactic end to the bourgeois journey into the night does not take place in the club. The next stop in the nocturnal adventure is the second "jungle," the prostitute's apartment. The venture into the private sphere of other city dwellers ends with a murder and with the protagonist's ultimate realization that his freedom to roam the street is patently restricted. As the law enforcement officers' default assumption points to him as the murderer, his otherness – and status as victim – becomes evident: not only do the criminals

---

26 And, as in Lubitsch's comedies, this urge is realized in a realm saturated with commodities, in a way that alludes to the similarities between sexual drives and consumers' instincts (compare with Hake's description of Lubitsch's "commodity fetishism" in *The Oyster Princess* [Hake, 1992, 91–92]).

27 Lubitsch's *I Don't Want to Be a Man* and Schünzel's *Heaven on Earth, Crisis, Phantom*.

easily detect this but also the modern legal system instantly acknowledges it. The "happy ending," the protagonist's last-minute salvation once the real murderer is fortuitously revealed, seems somewhat arbitrary; the protagonist himself has no faith in the law enforcement authorities' efficiency and sense of justice. He therefore chooses not to stay in the street any longer, and returns home. In contrast to the definitive exclusion of the prison – or death – the isolation of the private apartment is partial and mainly psychological in nature (as the first scene suggests). The refuge of the private sphere provides the consolation that enables outsiders to exist in the urban environment despite their inability to assimilate.

The Street presents a gloomy portrayal of a person consumed by the desire to "be a man in the street" and by the belief that he could integrate but who learns that his assimilation is restricted to certain spheres and practices. His attempt to transcend these barriers results in his conclusive designation as the "other" (by the authorities). This narrative framework traces the general outlines of modern bourgeois Jewish experience but its comparatively pessimistic ambiance may be related to specific historical events that threatened to undermine the achievements of Jewish acculturation, most notably the assassination of Walther Rathenau. Appointed by Chancellor Joseph Wirth as Germany's foreign minister in January 1922, Rathenau was an advocate and an emblem of Jewish "amalgamation" (and, in his later years, assimilation) (Niewyk 1980, 96–97). One of the most prominent leaders of German industry, Rathenau urged his fellow Jews to break free of their "half voluntary, invisible ghetto" and to adopt the customs, habits, and behavior of the state that had granted them citizenship (Rathenau 1867; Mendes-Flohr 1995, 267–268). To many of his contemporaries, he personified the recent success of both Jewish assimilation and the liberal bourgeoisie (and the association of these groups with the young German democracy).[28] His murderers acted in the name of both antisemitism and anti-liberalism, in order to free Germany of the alleged antinational scheme of the Elders of Zion and of bourgeois politics (Barnow 1988, 44–45). Writing in 1928, Rathenau's friend and biographer Graf Harry Kessler observed that Rathenau's fate was similar to that "of his world" (Kessler 1930, 93).

The Street was the first script that Grune had written in two years and the first film script that he wrote after Rathenau's murder.[29] The film, which was produced a few months after the assassination in the summer of 1922, appears to share Kessler's distrust of the ability of Rathenau's world to face up to its rivals. Grune, however, envisages a cheerless status quo rather than an apocalyptic demise. The

---

28 As asserted by Maximilian Harden, cited in Young (1959, 249–251).
29 His previous script was written for the love triangle film *Mann über Bord* (1921). Grune directed two other films in between, but he did not write another script until *The Street*.

end of the film reassures viewers that – as long as he accepts the limited participation permitted to him in middle-class society – the protagonist's presence in the city is tolerated and secure.

3 Conclusion

The attempts to reconcile different aspects of modern experience, different identity perceptions – and their symbolic envisioning in the different spaces of the modern city – were not an essentially or exclusively "Jewish" phenomenon. The symbolism of *The Street* and of several other films that reiterated its basic structure was surely rooted in critical reflections on modern experience and its "crisis" in the post-World War I German city.[30] Nonetheless, the spatial encoding of identity in these films was also particularly embedded within the modern Jewish identity discourse in Central Europe, in which the duality of spaces was a recurring metaphor. For the filmmakers discussed here – middle-class Jews who had recently immigrated to Berlin – acculturation was a defining biographical experience. Their utilization of the spatial-duality cliché – and, in particular, the endeavor to formulate a notion of individuality that would transcend the dichotomy of "at home" and "in the street" – was simultaneously a commentary on the cultural discourse of assimilation and an insertion of this Jewish discourse into German mainstream culture.

Similar to many German films of the mid-1920s, *The Street* portrays the city as a place – or a set of places – with a unique capacity to embody the particularities of modern Jewish experience. The city projected on the Weimar screen thus becomes a "Jewish place" in two ways: it is the landscape in which Jewish acculturation takes place because of its toleration of a dual expression of identity "at home" and "in the street"; and it is an effective metaphorical sphere that explicates the multifaceted perception of identity upon which acculturation depends. While its narrative structure and visual symbolism resemble many German-Jewish productions of the 1920s, Grune's film displays an almost unparalleled pessimism. His protagonist's effort to be a "man in the street" falls short of concealing his "otherness" in public; his desire for intimacy in the private sphere of "ordinary" urbanites ends in a tragedy. After he is forcefully excluded from

---

30 Ever since the early days of the Weimar Republic, scholars have related various aspects of its culture to the experience of crisis. Todd Herzog (2009, 6), for instance, recently asserted that Weimar was "a *culture of crisis*, a society that [...] continually defined itself through its perceived crisis." See also Herbert Kraus (1932); Föllmer and Graf (2005); Peukert 1993; and Kniesche and Brockmann (1994).

society – put in prison – he paradoxically concludes that in order to be integrated into society, he must return to his solitude at home. Only in private, he is not (visibly) different from the others. This gloomy ending suggests another meaning for a "Jewish space" that points to the limited spaces in which successful acculturation took place.

Acknowledgment

This research was supported by "Daat Hamakom" I-Core Center at the Hebrew University of Jerusalem (Grant No. 1798/12).

Bibliography

Adorno, Theodor W. *Kierkegaard: Konstruktion des Ästhetischen*. Berlin: Suhrkamp, 1966.
Albanis, Elizabeth. "A 'West-östlicher Divan' from the Front: Moritz Goldstein beyond the *Kunstwart* Debate." *Towards Normality?: Acculturation and Modern German Jewry*. Ed. Rainer Liedtke and David Rechter. Tübingen: Mohr Siebeck, 2003. 217–236.
Applegate, Celia. *A Nation of Provincials: The German Idea of Heimat*. Berkeley: University of California Press, 1990.
Arendt, Hannah. "The Jew as Pariah: A Hidden Tradition." *Jewish Social Studies* 6:2 (1944): 99–122.
Arendt, Hannah. *Men in Dark Times*. Orlando: Houghton Mifflin Harcourt, 1970.
Arnheim, Rudolf. "Film." *Juden im deutschen Kulturbereich*. Ed. Siegmund Kaznelson. Berlin: Max Lichtwitz, 1962. 220–241.
Aschheim, Steven E. "Reflections on Theatricality, Identity and the Modern Jewish Experience." *Jews and the Making of Modern German Theatre*. Ed. Jeanette R. Malkin and Freddie Rokem. Iowa City: University of Iowa Press, 2010.
Ashkenazi, Ofer. *The Walk into the Night: Reason and Subjectivity in Weimar Film*. Tel Aviv: Am Oved, 2010a.
Ashkenazi, Ofer. "Rethinking the Role of Film in German History." *Rethinking History* 14.1 (Fall 2010b): 569–586.
Ashkenazi, Ofer. *Weimar Film and Modern Jewish Identity*. New York: Palgrave-MacMillan, 2012.
Assmann, Aleida. *Erinnerungsräume: Formen und Wandlungen des kulturellen Gedächtnisses*. Munich: C.H. Beck, 1999.
Bachelard, Gaston. *The Poetics of Space*. Phoenix: Orion Press, 1964. xxxiii.
Balázs, Béla. "Der Film arbeitet für Uns!" *Film und Volk* 1. 2–3 (1928): 7–8.
Balázs, Béla. *"Die Straße," Der Tag*, 18 March 1924.
Barnow, Dagmar. *Weimar Intellectuals and the Threat of Modernity*. Bloomington: Indiana University Press, 1988.

Bayerdörfer, Hans-Peter. "Jewish Self-Presentation and the 'Jewish Question' on the German Stage from 1900 to 1930." *Jewish Theater: A Global View*. Ed. Edna Nahshon. Boston and Leiden: Brill, 2009.

Benjamin, Walter. "Paris, Capital of the Nineteenth Century." *Reflections: Essays, Aphorisms, Autobiographical Writings*. Ed. Peter Demetz. New York: Shocken, 1978.

Benz, Wolfgang. "The Legend of German-Jewish Symbiosis." *Leo Baeck Institute Yearbook* 37 (1992): 95–102.

Benz, Wolfgang, Arnold Paucker, and Peter G. J. Pulzer, eds. *Jüdisches Leben in Der Weimarer Republik / Jews in the Weimar Republic*. London: Leo Baeck Institute, 1998.

Bial, Henry. *Acting Jewish*. Ann Arbor: University of Michigan Press, 2005.

Bird, Colin. *The Myth of Liberal Individualism*, Cambridge: Cambridge University Press, 1999.

Blüher, Hans. *Secessio Judaica. Philosophische Grundlegung der historischen Situation des Judentumes und der antisemitischen Bewegungen*. Berlin: Der Weisse Ritter, 1921.

Bourdieu, Pierre. *Distinction: A Social Critique of the Judgment of Taste*. New York: Routledge, 1984.

Bourdieu, Pierre. *The Logic of Practice*. Stanford: Stanford University Press, 1990.

Brenner, Michael. *The Renaissance of Jewish Culture in Weimar Germany*. New Haven: Yale University Press, 1996.

"Brüder Schellenberg." *Berliner Lokal Anzeiger*. 24 March 1926.

Confino, Alon. *The Nation as a Local Metaphor: Württemberg, Imperial Germany and National Memory, 1871–1918*. Chapel Hill: University of North Carolina Press, 1997.

Cowan, Michael. "Taking it to the street: screening the advertising film in the Weimar Republic." *Screen* 54. 4 (Winter 2013): 463–479.

Coyner, Sandra J. "Class Consciousness and Consumption: The New Middle Class during the Weimar Republic." *Journal of Social History* 10 (1977): 310–331.

Eisner, Lotte H. *The Haunted Screen: Expressionism in the German Cinema and the Influence of Max Reinhardt*. Berkeley: University of California Press, 1952.

Eliel, Carol S. *The Apocalyptic Landscapes of Ludwig Meidner*. Los Angeles: Los Angeles County Museum of Arts, 1989.

Elsaesser, Thomas. *Weimar Cinema and After*. New York: Routledge, 2000.

Elsaesser, Thomas and Michael Wedel, eds. *A Second Life: German Cinema's First Decades*. Amsterdam: Amsterdam University Press, 1996.

Feld, Hans. "Jews in the Development of the German Film Industry: Note from the Recollections of a Berlin Film Critic." *LBI Year Book* 28 (1982): 337–368.

Föllmer, Moritz and Rüdiger Graf. *Die Krise der Weimarer Republik*. Frankfurt on the Main: Campus Verlag, 2005.

Foucault, Michel. *Discipline and Punish: The Birth of the Prison*. New York: Vintage Books, 1977.

Foucault, Michel. "The Subject and Power." *Michel Foucault: Beyond Structuralism and Hermeneutics*. Ed. Hubert L. Dreyfus and Paul Rabinow. Chicago: University of Chicago Press, 1983.

Gilerman, Sharon. *Germans into Jews: Remaking the Jewish Social Body in the Weimar Republic*. Stanford: Stanford University Press, 2009.

Gordon, Judah Leib. "Hakiza Ami" [Awake, my people] (1863). *Kitvei Yehuda Leib Gordon: Shira*. Tel Aviv: Dvir, 1959.

Haas, Willy. "Zusammenarbeit mit Karl Grune." *Film-Kurier*, 16 September 1925.

Hake, Sabine. *Passion and Deception: The Early Films of Ernst Lubitsch*. Princeton: Princeton University Press, 1992.

Hake, Sabine. *The Cinema's Third Machine: Writing on Film in Germany, 1907–1933*. Lincoln: University of Nebraska Press, 1993. 3–104.

Hake, Sabine. *German National Cinema*. New York: Routledge, 2002.

Hales, Barbara. "Woman as Sexual Criminal: Weimar Constructions of the Criminal Femme Fatale." *Women in German Yearbook* 12 (1996): 101–121.

Hales, Barbara. "Projecting Trauma: The Femme-Fatale in Weimar and Hollywood Film-Noir." *Women in German Yearbook* 23 (2007): 224–243.

Harbach, Franz. "Der Regissuer Karl Grune," publicity material handed to viewers of Grune's 1925 film, *Brüder Schellenberg* (The Schellenberg Brothers), Deutsche Kinemathek Archiv, Berlin (SDK-SGA), folder 2794.

Herzog, Todd. *Crime Stories: Criminalistic Fantasies and the Culture of Crisis in Weimar Germany*. New York: Berghahn, 2009.

Hitler, Adolf. *Mein Kampf*. Munich: Franz Eher Nachfolger, 1933.

Isenberg, Noah W. *Weimar Cinema: An Essential Guide to Classic Films of the Era*. New York: Columbia University Press, 2009.

Jonsson, Stefan. *Subject without Nation: Robert Musil and the History of Modern Identity*. Durham: Duke University Press, 2004.

Kaes, Anton. ed. *Kino-Debatte. Texte zum Verhältnis von Literatur und Film 1909–1929*. Tübingen: Tage-Buch Verlag, 1978.

Kaes, Anton. "Schauplätze des Verlangens. Zum Straßenfilm in der Weimarer Republik." *Filmarchitektur. Von Metropolis bis Blade Runner*. Ed. Dietrich Neumann. Munich: Prestel, 1996. 26–32.

Kaes, Anton. "Urban Vision and Surveillance: Notes on a Moment in Karl Grune's *Die Straße*." *German Politics & Society* 23.1 (2005): 80–87.

Kaes, Anton. *Shell Shock Cinema*. Princeton: Princeton University Press, 2009.

Kalbus, Oskar. *Der Deutsche Lehrfilm in der Wissenschaft und im Unterricht*. Berlin: Carl Heymann, 1922.

Kaplan, Marion A. *The Making of the Jewish Middle-Class*. Oxford: Oxford University Press, 1991.

Kessler, Harry. *Walther Rathenau: His Life and His Work*. New York: Harcourt, Brace and Co., 1930 [1928].

Kester, Bernadette. *Film Front Weimar: Representation of the First World War in German Films of the Weimar Period (1919–1933)*. Amsterdam: Amsterdam University Press, 2003.

Kniesche, Thomas W. and Stephen Brockmann, eds. *Dancing on the Volcano. Essays on the Culture of the Weimar Republic*. New York: Columbia University Press, 1994.

Kohn, Hans. "Der Roman des Entwurzelten. Georg Hermann: Die Nacht des Dr. Herzfeld." *Juden in der Deutschen Literatur*. Ed. Gustav Krojanker. Berlin: Welt-Verlag, 1922. 27–40.

Koshar, Rudy. *Germany's Transient Past: Preservation and National Memory in the Twentieth Century*. Chapel Hill: University of North Carolina Press, 1998.

Koshar, Rudy and Alon Confino. "Regimes of Consumer Culture: New Narratives in Twentieth Century German History." *German History* 19:2 (2001): 135–161.

Kracauer, Siegfried. "*Die Straße*." *Frankfurter Zeitung* (Stadt-Blatt). 3 February 1924.

Kracauer, Siegfried. *From Caligari to Hitler: A Psychological History of the German Film*. Princeton: Princeton University Press, 1947.

Kraus, Herbert. *The Crisis of German Democracy: A Study of the Spirit of the Constitution of Weimar*. Princeton: Princeton University Press, 1932 [1919].

Kreimeier, Klaus. *The Ufa Story: A History of Germany's Greatest Film Company, 1918–1945*. Berkeley: University of California Press, 1999.

Lässig, Simone. "Bildung als *kulturelles* Kapital? Jüdische Schulprojekte in der Frühphase der Emanzipation." *Juden—Bürger—Deutsche*. Ed. Andreas Gotzmann. Tübingen: Mohr Siebeck, 2001. 263–298.

Lässig, Simone. *Jüdische Wege ins Bürgertum. Kulturelles Kapital und sozialer Aufstieg im 19. Jahrhundert*. Göttingen: Vandenhoek & Ruprecht, 2004.

Lekan, Thomas. *Imagining the Nation in Nature: Landscape, Preservation and German Identity, 1885–1945*. Cambridge, MA: Harvard University Press, 2004.

Lode, David. "Der filmische Filmer." *Pioniere in Celluloid: Juden in der frühen Filmwelt*. Ed. Irene Stratenwerth and Hermann Simon. Berlin: Henschel Verlag, 2004.

Lüdecke, Willi. *Der Film in Agitation und Propaganda der revolutionären deutschen Arbeiterbewegung (1919–1933)*. Berlin: Oberbaum, 1973.

Mason, Timothy W. "Women in Germany, 1925–1940: Family, Welfare and Work: Conclusion." *History Workshop* 2 (1976): 77–79.

McCann, Charles R. *Individualism and the Social Order: The Social Element in Liberal Thought*. New York: Routledge, 2004.

McCormick, Richard W. *Gender and Sexuality in Weimar Modernity: Film, Literature, and 'New Objectivity.'* New York: Macmillan, 2001.

McElligott, Anthony. *The German Urban Experience 1900–1945: Modernity and Crisis*. London: Routledge, 2001.

Mendes-Flohr, Paul. "The Berlin Jew as Cosmopolitan." *Berlin Metropolis: Jews and the New Culture, 1890–1918*. Ed. Emily D. Bilsky. Berkeley: University of California Press, 1999. 14–21.

Mendes-Flohr, Paul and Jehuda Reinharz, eds. *The Jew in the Modern World*. New York: Oxford University Press US. 1995.

Murphy, Richard. "Modernist Film and Gender: Expressionism and the Fantastic in Karl Grune's *The Street*." *Expressionism and Gender*. Ed. Frank Krause. Göttingen: V&R unipress, 2010.

Murray, Bruce A. *Film and the German Left in the Weimar Republic: From Caligari to Kuhle Wampe*. Austin: University of Texas Press, 1990.

Murray, Bruce A. "The Role of the Vamp in Weimar Cinema: An Analysis of Karl Grune's *The Street (Die Straße)*." *Gender and German Cinema: German Film History*. Ed. Sandra G. Frieden et al. Oxford: Berg, 1993. 33–41.

Myers, David N. *Resisting History: Historicism and its Discontents in German-Jewish Thought*. Princeton: Princeton University Press, 2003.

Myerson, Abraham and Isaac Goldberg. *The German Jew: His Share in Modern Culture*. New York: A. A. Knopf, 1933.

Niewyk, Donald L. *The Jews in Weimar Germany*. Baton Rouge: Louisiana State University Press, 1980.

Nolan, Mary. *Visions of Modernity: American Business and the Modernization of Germany*. Oxford: Oxford University Press, 1994.

Olimsky, Fritz. "Zehn Jahre Film." *75 Jahre Berliner-Börsen-Zeitung*. Ed. Arnold Killisch von Horn. Berlin: Berlin-Börsen-Zeitung, 1930. 114–117.

Panizza, Oskar. "The Operated Jew." Trans. Jack Zipes. *New German Critique* 21 (Autumn 1980): 63–79.

Petro, Patrice. *Joyless Streets: Women and Melodramatic Representation in Weimar Germany*. Princeton: Princeton University Press, 1989.

Peukert, Detlev. *The Weimar Republic: The Crisis of Classical Modernity*. New York: Hill and Wang, 1993.

Prawer, Siegbert S. *Between Two Worlds: The Jewish Presence in German and Austrian Film, 1910–1933*. New York: Berghahn, 2005.

Rahden, Till van. *Jews and Other Germans: Civil Society, Religious Diversity, and Urban Politics in Breslau, 1860–1925*. Madison: University of Wisconsin Press, 2007.

Rathenau, Walther [Hartenau]. "Höre, Israel!" *Zukunft*, 16 March 1867, 454–462.

Rogowski, Christian. *The Many Faces of Weimar Cinema*. Rochester: Camden House, 2011.

Rice, Charles. *The Emergence of the Interior: Architecture, Modernity, Domesticity*. New York: Taylor & Francis, 2007.

Saunders, Thomas J. *Hollywood in Berlin: American Cinema and Weimar Germany*. Berkeley: University of California Press, 1994.

Scheunemann, Dietrich. *Expressionist film*. Rochester: Camden House, 2006.

Shahar, Galili. *Theatrum judaicum*. Bielofeld: Aicthocic, 2007.

Shklar, Judith N. "The Liberalism of Fear." *Liberalism and the Moral Life*. Ed. Nancy L. Rosenblum. Cambridge, UK: Harvard University Press, 1989. 21–38.

Simmel, Georg. "Excursus on the Stranger." *Sociology: Inquiries into the Construction of Social Forms*. Leiden: Brill, 2009 [1908]. 1: 601–620.

Stern, Frank. "The Two way Ticket to Hollywood and the Master Image of 20th Century Modernism." *Placeless Topographies: Jewish Perspectives on the Literature of Exile*. Ed. Bernhard Greiner. Tübingen: Niemeyer, 2003.

Verhey, Jeffrey. "Der Mythos des 'Geistes von 1914' in der Weimarer Republik." *Die Weimarer Republik zwischen Metropole und Provinz: Intellektuellendiskurse zur politischen Kultur*. Ed. Wolfgang Bialas and Burkhardt Stenzel. Cologne: Böhlau, 1996.

Vogt, Guntram and Philipp Sanke. *Die Stadt im Kino: Deutsche Spielfilme 1900–2000*. Marburg: Schüren, 2001. 103–113.

Waldenfels, Bernhard. "Heimat in der Fremde." *Heimat: Analysen, Themen, Perspektiven*. Ed. Will Cremer and Anger Klein. Bonn: Bundeszenrale für Politische Bildung, 1990. 109–121.

Wedel, Michael. "Haltung und Unterhaltung." *Pioniere in Celluloid: Juden in der frühen Filmwelt*. Ed. Irene Stratenwerth and Hermann Simon. Berlin: Henschel Verlag, 2004.

Robert Weltsch. "Theodor Herzl und wir." *Vom Judentum. Ein Sammelbuch*. Eds. Hans Kohn et al. Leipzig: Kurt Wolf Verlag, 1913. 155–164.

Wesse, Curt. *Grossmacht Film. Das Geschöpf von Kunst und Technik*. Berlin: Deutsche Buch-Gemeinschaft, 1928.

Williams, John A. *Turning to Nature in Germany: Hiking, Nudism and Conservation, 1900–1940*. Stanford: Stanford University Press, 2007.

Young, Harry F. *Maximilian Harden, Censor Germaniae: The Critic in Opposition from Bismarck to the Rise of Nazism*. Hague: M. Nijhoff, 1959.

Zweig, Arnold. *Juden auf der deutschen Bühne*. Berlin: Welt-Verlag, 1928.

Jens Hacke

Jewish Liberalism in the Weimar Republic? Reconsidering a Key Element of Political Culture in the Interwar Era

Common belief holds that a Jewish component strongly influenced political liberalism and the liberal aspects of political culture in the Weimar Republic. The most important liberal newspapers such as the *Frankfurter Zeitung*, the *Vossische Zeitung*, and the *Berliner Tageblatt*, or the big publishing houses S. Fischer and Ullstein come to mind. Undoubtedly, many of the icons of the intellectual, academic, and artistic life were Jewish or stemmed from a Jewish background. Given the inextricable connection between the common perception of the Golden Twenties and the Jewish German personalities who exerted an inestimable influence on the cultural, scientific, and political realm, one need not enumerate all the familiar names. Countless books have dealt with the reason for this phenomenon – but we still lack a clear definition of the key elements of Jewish liberalism. Without attempting to provide an exhaustive answer in this essay, I shall present a perspective of political theory that tries to be sensitive to historical contexts, that is, in other words, a part of *the history of political ideas*. I would like to shed some light on the tangled relationship between a struggling, worldly, i.e., secular Jewishness and liberalism in times of crisis. The interwar era serves, of course, as a dramatic historical stage for this liaison.

The connection between different forms of Jewishness and liberalism is complex.[1] Indeed, there are enough examples of Jewish anti-liberalism, too. Steven Aschheim (2007, 2012) has shown in his writings how a specific branch of Jewish intellectuals – mostly philosophers who criticized liberalism, pluralism, mass modernity, and democracy – belonged to Weimar culture. They needed the framework of an open society, but at the same time, they kept their distance from liberal democracy. They looked for alternatives, whether Zionism, Marxism, elite-conservatism, or a revitalization of Jewish tradition. I leave aside many interesting groups such as the famous students of Heidegger (Hannah Arendt, Karl Löwith, Hans Jonas, and Herbert Marcuse), the Frankfurt School, or solitary thinkers such as Leo Strauss, Walter Benjamin, Franz Rosenzweig, et cetera.[2] Needless to say, all of them, for example, Hannah Arendt, Karl Löwith, and Max Horkheimer,

---

1 On the experience of difference, see Salecker (1999).
2 On the Jewish students of Heidegger, see Wolin (2001). Other aspects of the Jewish intellectual landscape in Weimar are treated in Schivelbusch (1985); Wiggershaus (1994); and Brenner (1996).

stood up against totalitarianism and reconsidered their former distance from parliamentary democracy. As Aschheim has pointed out, their intellectual brilliance, their radiant spirit, and their often enigmatic ideas, which keep legions of interpreters busy, still engage us, whereas the content of their political thinking is interesting mostly for its exotic strangeness (Aschheim 2007, 81ff.). Hannah Arendt might be an inspiring philosopher (although some question whether she ever followed a consistent methodology), but one can hardly call her a relevant thinker for a modern liberal democracy that rests on representation, institutions, and rule of law. Her importance lies in her ability to make us reconsider the foundations of our political convictions, to expand our horizon beyond the order of the day, and to stimulate our imagination.[3]

The theorists I shall discuss represent a different approach to politics and, significantly, they were concerned about the stability of democracy. Today, when their reasoning appears to make sense, it is not clear why recognition of them has faded. Perhaps, the academic world values originality more than common sense and prudence. The reasonable is often dismissed as boring. One should keep in mind, however, that in certain historical circumstances, it took more courage to opt for the rational, for moderation, for compromise, for plurality, for freedom, and for legal procedures than in others. The interesting question is: What made some intellectuals cling to liberal convictions in turbulent times when liberal democracy was not fashionable, when it was, in fact, regarded as an outmoded nineteenth century model?[4] A partial explanation is that a certain feeling of Jewishness, of *Bildungsbürgertum*, and of secular modernization enabled some thinkers to adhere to ideals that others threw overboard.

In discussing three very different thinkers of the interwar era who represent diverse types of Jewish experience, I shall examine them from a universalist angle. Although Jewish, they were concerned with matters of democratic politics in general; they did not restrict themselves to the fate of the Jew in modern society. I shall present the varieties of liberal thinking found in the work of three individuals: the economist and political scientist Moritz Julius Bonn (1873–1965), the jurist Hermann Heller (1891–1933), and the jurist, philosopher, journalist, and librarian Felix Weltsch (1884–1964). They stood for three different ways of combining Jewishness with a liberal understanding of politics and society. I hope to explain how a concept of liberal democracy that adapts itself to the challenges of

---

3 On Arendt, see Young-Bruehl (1976); Benhabib (1996).
4 The contemporary notion of the crisis facing liberal democracy was widespread. See, for example, the grand narrative of Liberalism that Fawcett (2014, 198ff) recently presented. See also Müller (2011, 7–48).

modernity can serve as a common denominator linking a liberal economist and political adviser, a social democrat and law professor, and a Zionist from Prague.

Although these three thinkers address political issues from different angles, they share common notions of personal freedom, equality of civil rights, protection of minorities, and parliamentary democracy. All three published important essays in S. Fischer's *Neue Rundschau*; they all were shaped by their family bonds to Austria or the German culture in the Habsburg monarchy, which gave them a strong affinity for diversity and pluralism and awareness of the danger of nationalism.[5] In the following essay, I would like to examine the influence of their Jewish consciousness on their worldview.

1 Moritz Julius Bonn – the ideal modernist liberal

Moritz Julius Bonn stemmed from a banking family in Frankfurt with international ties, especially to England, where some of his cousins lived. Bonn married an Englishwoman, Therese Cubitt, with whom he travelled extensively (Africa, America), uniting a curiosity for the world with research interests on imperial politics. Born in 1873, the world of the Kaiserreich thus exerted a major influence on his formative years, and his intellectual attitude fits the profile of an assimilated cosmopolitan Jewish liberal.[6] He studied with Lujo Brentano, one of the most important left-wing liberal economists who opposed the Historische Schule and was open to English New Liberalism and modern social politics. Bonn's career is remarkable in many ways: Not restricting himself to German topics, he worked in the field of international commercial relations and monetary policies. One of the first specialists on colonial matters, he was very critical of colonial enterprises, which he viewed not only as morally problematic but also as economically disastrous. Instead, he advocated the emancipation of the African and Asian peoples, who should learn to govern themselves.

---

5 Moritz Julius Bonn's mother was Austrian. Bonn and his wife purchased a house close to Salzburg in the mid-1920s, where they frequently spent time (Bonn 1949, 349ff.). Hermann Heller was born in Teschen, a Silesian town, studied in Graz, Vienna and Innsbruck and volunteered for the Austro-Hungarian Army in 1914. Felix Weltsch was born in Prague and lived there as a member of the German speaking minority, until he immigrated to Palestine in 1938.

6 On Bonn's life, see his intellectually stimulating and very entertaining autobiography: Bonn (1949). On a small scale, Bonn's role as a political thinker, economist, intellectual, and critic of the imperial age has recently been rediscovered by Clavin (2003); Hacke (2010, 2014b); and Gordon (2013).

On first sight, Bonn's Jewish identity seemed to bear all the signs of a secular, emancipated, and modern scholar who left religion and traditions behind to make his way into a "bürgerliche Gesellschaft." Bonn clearly suffered from the open and covert antisemitism of his times. Max Weber, with whom he was well acquainted and who held Bonn's academic work in high esteem, confessed to a colleague that it was impossible to nominate Bonn for a professorship because he was a Jew.[7] Bonn, therefore, opted for a career at the newly founded schools of commerce (Handelshochschulen) and served as a director from 1910 on in Munich and as a successor of Hugo Preuß in Berlin (1931–33). He earned his reputation in various fields not only as an academic but also as a political advisor and public intellectual, reaching his peak in the Weimar years. Had right wing antisemitic propaganda searched for the personification of all the features that were part of its world scheme, Moritz Julius Bonn could have served as an example of the liberal, well-educated cosmopolitan who was the target of their contempt. Carl Schmitt, who more than once benefited from his friend Bonn (he twice found him a job at the Handelshochschule in Munich and Berlin), shows this psychotic pattern: Schmitt oscillated between admiration and antisemitic malice towards Bonn, whom he met almost daily as colleague and friend, as his diary entries indicate. One time he found Bonn "charming" and "likable"; another time, he confessed "disgust and aversion to a world in which one has to endure such Jews [as Bonn]" (Schmitt 2010, 24, 147). Even after Bonn had left Nazi Germany for his London exile, Schmitt kept on having anxious dreams about him (Schmitt 2010, 291). Bonn represented – if one ignores the antisemitic prejudices – the true ideal type of a liberal whose identification with western democracy, expertise on the U.S., and struggle for reason were exceptionally modern.

Unfortunately, Bonn did not write a classic book or a series of works that belong to a canon of any kind. He dispersed his wisdom in many writings – books, essays, articles – that he hastily wrote for the order of the day. Nevertheless, his six books on America,[8] his large essay on *The Crisis of Democracy* (written in 1925 and simultaneously published in the US, UK, and Germany, 1927 in Spain), together with numerous articles in most of the best journals and newspapers of the time give an impression of his restless and enlightened spirit.

In *Crisis of Democracy*, Bonn defends parliamentary rule against the new totalitarian forces (and provides an early defense for the liberal theory of

---

7 Weber (1990, 295) wrote approvingly: "In München ist Bonn – Jude! – einer der allergescheidtesten [sic!] Leute unter dem Nachwuchs, sein Buch über Irland ist schriftstellerisch und inhaltlich vorzüglich."
8 See Bonn (1917, 1918, 1925b, 1927, 1930, 1931a). See also the following translations: Bonn (1931b, 1932, 1933).

totalitarianism).[9] The book, which contains the main elements of Bonn's liberal agenda, can be seen as a response to Carl Schmitt's famous deconstruction of liberalism, *Die geistesgeschichtlichs Lage des heutigen Parlamentarismus* (1923). It was no coincidence that Bonn became the most cited contemporary author in Schmitt's second edition of the book (Schmitt 1996, 9, 16, 21, 29). Bonn questioned Schmitt's plea for democratic leadership without parliamentary legitimation and opposed his Rousseauian vision of homogenous masses that would merely acclaim "yes" or "no."[10] Bonn's key terms were rule of law, a claim for "social pluralism" (in the English edition he used the term "cultural pluralism" instead), tolerance, protection of minorities, division of power, a social refining of capitalism. Was Bonn a liberal who accidently happened to be a Jew, or did his traditional background (Bonn described himself as a non-believer) shape his liberalism? Tentatively, we can say that Bonn's liberalism strove for the universal and at the same time drew its substance from his Jewish experience. In his memoirs, he credited his Jewish origin as providing a catalyst to the education of a liberal. Bonn (1949, 24) wrote:

> To belong to a small, not highly thought-of religious community is undoubtedly a social disadvantage. Yet the consciousness of being somewhat different from most of one's fellow citizens makes up for it; it gives one the vantage point of detachment. It may prevent one from being swamped by a craving for oneness with a more or less amorphous crowd; it contributes to a kind of personal integrity. It makes it easy to break away from hoary traditions; one has not to pay for personal freedom by being subjected to social excommunication, which might be strong enough to paralyze one's efforts. One becomes free without having to wear a martyr's crown.

In a climate of widely shared antisemitic stereotypes (which he noted in the United States as well), Bonn was careful, however, to evade the Jewish Question, especially in his autobiography, whose title ironically alluded to the figure of the "wandering Jew." It is not clear whether Bonn reflected upon this reference, although he mockingly speculated about "the legacy of the forty years in the wilderness which I inherited from my early forefathers" (Bonn 1949, 3). Despite these occasional hints at his Jewish heritage, Bonn gave the impression of a man who was not primarily concerned about his religious identity. This behavior might be a common feature of assimilated Jewishness. With regard to Nazi crimes, Bonn stuck to the tacit rules of the unsayable, avoiding any discussion of the persecution and destruction of European Jewry in the English edition of his memoirs.

---

9 Bonn's early interpretation of fascism and his implicit theory of totalitarianism are discussed in Hacke (2014, 65–67).

10 On the relationship between Bonn and Schmitt, see Hacke (2010, 31f., 39–46).

Only four years later, he mentions the "brutalities," "the murder of Jews," and the "bestialities" in the revised German translation, clearly intending to remind his ex-compatriots of their responsibility and guilt (Bonn 1953, 405). Even as Bonn commented on Nazi crimes, however, he generally did not draw a line to his and his family's fate as Jews. The only exception was a remark about his cousin Emma Bonn, a writer, who "was deported with other victims of Nazi brutality and died two weeks later in Theresienstadt" (Bonn 1949, 347).

Aside from that, Bonn favored a brighter view of his life, not wanting it clouded by his belonging to the victimized populace of European Jewry. He considered the issue important enough to respond (at the age of 81) to a review of his memoirs in the *Times Literary Supplement*, which, in his opinion, overrated his role as a victim of his times:

> I was a German Professor, and I was taught to deal with the world as it was, not as it ought to be – which may be pedestrian, but is not exclusively Jewish. [...] Your reviewer, I am afraid, is presenting me as an almost tragic figure who, striking the balance of his life, is faced by a deficit, and whose personal loss typifies the tragedy of German-Jewish relations. I may have misled him by a few melancholic asides. It would be base ingratitude on my part were I to accept his interpretation of the story of a rich life, which gave me far more than I deserved. The mantle of the Prophet, to whom his people would not listen, is too heavy for my shoulders.[11]

He treated antisemitism in a manner typical of his ironic approach. Notably, he did not marginalize antisemitism as a political factor, but he ridiculed it as being an atavism and the creed of simplistic populism. His references to Heinrich Heine reflect his own use of mockery and irony to deal with the matter. As a rational liberal, he was aware of the social psychology of antisemitism, whose widespread appeal depended on economic crisis and the decline of moral standards. I am not sure, as Patricia Clavin (2003, 32) suggests, whether Bonn "like so many others, failed to appreciate the centrality of antisemitism" to the National Socialist agenda. In fact, he wrote about antisemitism in a number of articles, analyzing the role of the Jew as a scapegoat in times of hardship (Bonn 1931c). Although Bonn stressed the relationship between an economic downswing and the National Socialists' political success, he knew the Nazi movement could not be explained exclusively by business cycles. Hitler and his party played on collective feelings, fears, and hopes; they promoted a "socialism for the dumb;" "this kind of socialism rages but does not expropriate" (Bonn 1931c, 5). Facing political irrationalism, Bonn sensed more a crisis of sentiments *[Empfindungskrise]*

---

11 A reader's letter by M.J. Bonn, published in the *Times Literary supplement* in October 1954 (exact date unknown). Newspaper clip found in Bonn's papers, Bundesarchiv Koblenz NL 1082/16.

than a crisis of thought [*Gedankenkrise*]. This circumstance caused incalculable danger, "for thoughts can be fought with thoughts, whereas sentiments can only be fought with changed facts" (Bonn 1931d, 153).

Bonn considered the only realistic way to overcome the consequences of the Big Crash lay in responsible measures to cope with economic problems. The politicians in charge needed to remain clear-headed and to operate within the framework of the constitution. Simultaneously, Bonn advised his readers to lower their expectations regarding the capability of politics to regulate social life and solve all problems. He regarded the attitude of holding the state responsible for its citizens' happiness as a sign of an ideology-fueled age. He preferred a civic culture, namely, methods of civic government [*Methoden bürgerlichen Regierens*] that would facilitate parliamentary rule. He upheld the liberal approach of convincing the people that they themselves as individuals were responsible for the functioning of democracy because governments cannot perform wonders; they can only reflect the desires and capacities of those they govern.

"They who would improve the system," Bonn (1928, 97) concluded, "must first improve themselves, not by standing by in arrogant pride but by doing their part to make the parliamentary system successful as a practical instrument, and at the same time abandoning their belief that governments of any kind are able to endow mankind with felicity on earth."

Similar to many of his fellow republicans (not few of them of Jewish descent), he later advocated a "militant democracy," to use Karl Loewenstein's famous phrase.[12] In his essay *Limits and Limitations of democracy*, Bonn (1938, 246) resolved: "No political system can endure whose members have not an ardent faith in its superiority to other systems. [...] The truth must be faced, however unpleasant it may be. Democracy cannot get over its limitations by merely asking for toleration of its mild creed from those who flatly deny the creed, and the need for toleration."

The totalitarian systems – whose origins Bonn traced back to the politics of violence and terror in the 1920s – that reached full force in National Socialism and Stalinism turned Bonn into a decisive opponent of appeasement politics in the 1930s. He learned that the liberal ideal of government by discussion and peaceful international commerce was inadequate when it came to dealing with ideological regimes that would not accept liberal premises. Unsurprisingly, Bonn retained his seasoned liberal approach in face of the challenging confrontation between the blocs after 1945. The continuity of his political thinking revealed the formula for Cold War liberalism.

---

12 Karl Loewenstein (1937) was credited with the invention of the term "militant democracy," but the idea was widespread at the time. On the concept of "militant democracy," see Müller (2012).

2 Hermann Heller – a social democrat of liberal conviction

Better known than Moritz Julius Bonn, but still not attracting the attention he deserves, Hermann Heller represents another way of transforming a Jewish background into a liberal notion of politics. For lack of a more adequate term, we can mark him as a liberal socialist. Heller combined the worldview of socialist revisionism in the tradition of Eduard Bernstein with an unconditional defense of parliamentary democracy grounded in the principles of representation, civic rights, personal freedom, and the separation of powers. Heller, incidentally, appreciated and cited Bonn (Heller 1926, 149). They eventually established contact, as the diary of the journalist Ernst Feder (*Berliner Tageblatt*) confirms (Feder 1971, 297). At least they were well informed about each other's work and both served as lecturers at the democratic "Deutsche Hochschule für Politik" in Berlin.[13]

Heller can be regarded as a liberal, not according to the political understanding of his times, but on the basis of the normative content of his political theory. First, and this makes Heller's case more difficult than Bonn's and Weltsch's, we have to acknowledge that Heller does not reflect upon his Jewishness anywhere in his works. Only when attacked for his closeness to the Hofgeismarkreis (a group of young socialists who wanted to overcome the socialist rejection of nation and state) and accused of being anti-Jewish, did he confess publicly that he was a Jew himself.[14] (In the same year, 1925, he left the Jewish "Kultusgemeinde.") Being Jewish and an acknowledged socialist did not help in obtaining a professorship. His late appointment as a professor of public law in Frankfurt in 1932 lasted not even a year; he was dismissed by the Nazi government and replaced by Ernst Forsthoff. Surprisingly, the extensive research on his work has so far omitted assessing the role and significance of his Jewish identity.[15]

It is not too far-fetched to view Heller's attitude towards the nation-state, the working class, and towards a relatively homogenous society in social and cultural terms from the angle of his Jewish experience. As a social democrat and Jew, he was used to his role as an outsider struggling for recognition and equal rights. Heller's conviction that one has to abandon the ideas of revolution and fundamental opposition to the state set him apart from his leftwing socialist com-

---

13 For further details, see Erich Nickel (2004).

14 Heller (1925, 561) defended himself during the discussion of his lecture on "Staat, Nation und Sozialdemokratie": "Weil ich positiv mich zur Frage der Nation geäußert habe, soll ich so ziemlich ein Verräter sein! Und der Vorwurf des Antisemitismus fällt zusammen, wenn ich euch sage, daß ich selber Jude bin."

15 See, for example, Schluchter (1968), Müller/Staff (1985), Llanque (2010), and Henkel (2011).

rades. Heller valued the Weimar Constitution as a suitable basis for implementing the "sozialen Rechtsstaat," best understood as a welfare state grounded in the rule of law (Heller 1929). Although Heller's rhetoric of the 1920s constantly employs socialist phraseology and demands the end of capitalism, his writings do not reveal a consistent economic theory. By the early 1930s, his vocabulary changed considerably and mellowed towards a more liberal tone. For Heller, who never cultivated a materialist Marxist approach to politics, the Social Democrats were the last heirs of liberal values. He considered that the bourgeois class [*Bürgertum*], especially the ideologists of the new political right, had betrayed the principles of liberal democracy that a liberal Bürgertum once stood for; it was a fight against their own formative ideas (Heller 1932). Heller believed that the Social Democrats ought to carry the torch of liberal reason rather than cling to shortsighted economic interests. For him, the most important antinomy was "Rechtsstaat" versus dictatorship, not socialist versus capitalist society. Heller obviously opposed socialist theories of fascism (Heller 1931). Rather than viewing fascism as an inevitable consequence of industrial capitalism or as the typical form of capitalist dictatorship, he compared fascism to bolshevism, describing them as "twin brothers of the same political spirit" (Heller 1929b, 437). Heller's answers to the serious crisis of democracy did not differ very much from those of liberals such as Bonn – an early form of a theory of totalitarianism combined with the idea of a "militant democracy," He turned down the idea of a Rätesystem and became an ardent advocate of representative parliament. Heller exemplified in practice a convinced republican. It is worth quoting the conclusion of his speech on the tenth anniversary of the Weimar Constitution, which he delivered in 1929 to the German Student Union:

> We promise to defend the Weimar constitution against all attacks from ideologies of violence. Whenever these aggressors ironically speak of voting paper democracy, we want to give them a very clear response: We are well aware of the fact that one cannot protect a state by voting paper alone, and we will practically prove this knowledge in the same moment as they try to launch a violent attack. On this occasion, we will defend the Weimar Constitution, if necessary with weapon at hand[16] (Heller 1929c, 377).

---

16 This is my English translation; the original text reads as follows: "Wir geloben, die Weimarer Verfassung gegen alle Angriffe von Gewaltideologen zu verteidigen. Wenn diese Angreifer immer wieder ironisch von Wahlzetteldemokratie sprechen, so wollen wir ihnen eines ganz deutlich sagen: Wir wissen sehr genau, daß man einen Staat nicht allein mit Wahlzetteln sichert, und wir werden ihnen dieses Wissen in dem Augenblick praktisch beweisen, wo sie einen Gewaltangriff versuchen sollten. Dann werden wir die Weimarer Verfassung verteidigen, wenn es sein muss mit der Waffe in der Hand."

As a Jew and as a Social Democrat, Heller wanted to fight his way into German society. In appealing for a homogeneous society, he was articulating the need for social balance, cultural understanding based on shared values, and a nation-state that recognizes its citizens of all religious and ethnic backgrounds as equals. Heller states:

> Social homogeneity can never neutralize the necessarily antagonistic structure of society. [...] [It] is always a social-psychological state in which the ever-present antagonisms and struggles of interests seem bound by a "we-consciousness" and "we-feeling," by a renewing community will. Such relative adjustment of social consciousness can deal with enormous tense contrasts, can digest enormous religious, political, economic and other antagonisms[17] (Heller 1928, 428).

One can understand Heller's political thinking in the context of his strong belief in the integrative powers of a "political democracy" that strives for social justice while maintaining a pluralistic society. Presumably, Heller's longing for integration reflected his feeling of being a social outsider, both as a Jew and a socialist. In keeping with this attitude, he volunteered for the Austrian army in 1914. Believing in the cohesive capacity of the nation-state, he did not support socialist internationalism. He himself suffered from exclusive racial nationalism; Heller was expelled from the Nazi-Volksgemeinschaft. He died in exile in Madrid as a later consequence of his war injuries.

Not surprisingly, Heller avoided singling out the case of antisemitism and the role of German or Austrian Jews; tragically, he wasted a fair amount of polemical energy on his rival Hans Kelsen, born in Prague and raised in the declining Habsburg Monarchy, also a liberal Social Democrat, and also Jewish. Kelsen did not share Heller's normative and sociological approach; instead, he upheld relativism, positivism and rationality as basic values of the democratic "Rechtsstaat". Kelsen would have been another worthy example of Jewish liberalism, closer to Bonn's rational realism. Instead, Hans Kelsen can serve as a bridge to the third and last protagonist I would like to present.

---

17 Again, my translation, the original text reads as follows: "Soziale Homogenität kann aber niemals Aufhebung der notwendig antagonistischen Gesellschaftsstruktur bedeuten. [...] [Sie] ist immer ein sozial-psychologischer Zustand, in welchem die stets vorhandenen Gegensätzlichkeiten und Interessenkämpfe gebunden erscheinen durch ein Wirbewußtsein und –gefühl, durch einen sich aktualisierenden Gemeinschaftswillen. Solche relative Angeglichenheit des gesellschaftlichen Bewußtseins kann ungeheure Spannungsgegensätze in sich verarbeiten, ungeheure religiöse, politische, ökonomische und sonstige Antagonismen verdauen."

3 Felix Weltsch – liberal Zionism, moderation and the audacity of the center

Primarily known for his affiliation with the circle of Franz Kafka and Max Brod or for being the cousin of Robert Weltsch, the editor of *Jüdische Rundschau* in Berlin, Felix Weltsch, born in Prague like Kelsen, a learned jurist and philosopher, was a thinker in his own right.[18] Compared to Bonn's skeptical liberalism and Heller's social realism, Weltsch's political views contain more idealistic and abstract elements. In his theoretical writings, however, he went far beyond the more or less limited (though liberal) Zionistic approach that defined his daily work as the editor of the Prague journal *Selbstwehr*. From early on, for example in an essay for Fischer's *Neue Rundschau* in April 1918 about "Organic Democracy" (Weltsch 1918), he set out to restore the principles of liberal democracy, promoting the creativity of compromise and the advantages of deliberative politics.

The community of exiled democrats recognized the significance of his work *Das Wagnis der Mitte* (Weltsch 1935). Klaus Mann (1993, 224f.) praised the book in his review as a strong voice of reason; in an anthology on German liberalism put together for Artemis/Zurich in 1944, the editor Federico Federici (1946, 431–442) included a chapter of Weltsch's book, which he valued as a major contribution to contemporary political theory. Indeed, Weltsch made a strong case for the defense of democracy; had he bothered to coin a phrase, his view could have outlasted Karl Loewenstein's theoretically weaker plea for "militant democracy" because his conception was more thoroughly developed. Affirming that liberalism and democracy were systematically intertwined, Weltsch maintained that democracy had to rely on the liberally defined freedom of the individual. Democracy, in his view, included not only a method of governing but also depended on education. Similar to many others, Weltsch worried about modern man as part of a depersonalized mass. He hoped to counter this development by strengthening educational efforts and thereby establishing a "Kultur der Demokratie" resting on critique, discussion, reason, and peace.

Taking issue with Hans Kelsen's *Wesen und Wert der Demokratie* (2006, 1–33), he argued that democracy had to violate its own principles when it comes to fighting its enemies. For Weltsch, it was a matter of higher morality [*höhere Sittlichkeit*] to isolate the opponents of the democratic constitution from the political discourse in order to save democracy. In Weltsch's view, "the history of recent years

---

18 Schmidt (2010) is short on Weltsch's thinking but rich in biographical detail. Kelsen (1926, 32) acknowledged Weltsch's work but criticized his synthetic and idealistic view on compromise in a parliamentary democracy.

has demonstrated in grotesque form that democracy, in democratically treating those who deny her principles, causes her own ruin." He admitted the moral and practical danger of a revolution against democracy. He did not, however, regard this as "an argument against democracy" but rather as the "boundary of democracy"; in other words, democracy had to set certain limits (Weltsch 1935, 87f.). The rule of law should serve to defend liberal rights "against evil," according to Weltsch (1935, 91). He envisioned an approach that Dolf Sterrnberger, one of the leading political theorists of the early Federal Republic, dramatically stated as a principle for a "Herrschaft der Freiheit" right after the war in 1946: "No freedom for the enemies of freedom! No compromise with the enemies of compromise! No equal right for the enemies of equal right!"[19]

Weltsch combined the spirit of self defence – it should be noted that the Zionist journal he edited in Prague was called *Selbstwehr* – with a certain dose of idealistic faith (which he freely admitted): "Democracy maintains that there is no majority for evil among responsible deliberating individuals. Surely, one person can be evil and bring misery to the world. Nevertheless we cannot and must not and do not want to assume that the majority, not the mass, but free and responsible human beings of a group or a people would want evil" (Weltsch 1935, 78).[20]

Weltsch's plea for a reevaluation of the center, his claim for a creative center [*schöpferische Mitte*] is remarkable in more ways than one. First, he used the model of the center as a combination of compromise, third way, and Aristotelian ethics. He made it clear that there was no meeting in the middle between two extremes but that the center had its own morality, a sort of common sense (a word he did not use, but this shortcoming is a common feature of German philosophy). Second, it is interesting that a German-Czech Jew, a devoted Zionist – an outsider in many ways – put the "audacity of the center" on the agenda. Possibly, his sensitivity about belonging to a minority and a longing for recognition and equal rights had some impact on his political thinking. Weltsch outlined an ethical understanding of the center, which contrasted with the behavior of "hysterical middle classes" that he witnessed in his time. Part of the "extremism of the center" was antisemitism exploited by calculating politicians as an outlet for the aggression of the masses. Antisemitism or the "pogrom outlet" [Pogrom-Ventil],

---

19 "Keine Freiheit für die Feinde der Freiheit! Kein Kompromiß mit den Feinden des Kompromisses! Kein gleiches Recht für die Feinde des gleichen Rechts!" (Sternberger 1947, 42f.).
20 My translation – the original reads as follows: "Die Demokratie ist der Ansicht, daß es unter verantwortlich wählenden Individuen keine Majorität des Bösen in der Welt gibt. Wohl kann der Einzelne böse sein und unendliches Unglück über die Menschheit bringen. Aber wir können und dürfen und wollen nicht annehmen, daß die Mehrheit, nicht etwa der Masse, wohl aber frei und verantwortlich sich entscheidender Menschen einer Gruppe und eines Volkes das Böse will."

Weltsch (1935, 32) ironically wrote, was "a gift of favor from above to the politicians of the whole world and to the rulers in the history of mankind; it is relatively safe for the ruling classes, convincing for the great majority, a cheap weapon and it has never failed."[21]

To my knowledge, Weltsch ceased to write on political theory after he arrived in Palestine in 1938. A humble and shy man of letters, Weltsch worked as a librarian at the Hebrew University of Jerusalem and focused on his writings about Kafka (Weltsch 1957). Israel's intellectual elite valued his liberal thought and his modesty.

4 Conclusion

Without aiming to define something as diverse as Jewish liberalism, I strove to provide a few examples of the many ways in which Jewishness and liberalism could interact. The assimilated liberal economist Moritz Julius Bonn and the Social Democrat Hermann Heller exemplify liberal political thinkers whose Jewish heritage may have had a decisive impact upon their advocacy of pluralism and individual rights. In the case of the Zionist Felix Weltsch, it is particularly surprising that his theoretical writings do not hint at his Jewish identity.

Jewish intellectuals, of course, belonged to every ideological camp, most prominently the socialist one. The special disposition for a sound and democratic liberalism among Jews of different backgrounds, however, is striking. Bonn, Heller, and Weltsch wanted to establish and protect liberal values and representative democracy because they believed that a liberal constitution with republican features was the only way to integrate modern pluralistic societies. They went beyond classic liberal notions in recognizing and promoting a new, more active role for the state. Bonn wanted the state to create a framework for economic enterprise while simultaneously guarding minority rights. His ideal of social and cultural pluralism pictured the coexistence of ethnic and religious groups based on equal rights and citizenship. Bonn also considered that modern governance was responsible for social harmony and a balanced *Sozialpolitik*. Heller, more so than Bonn, clung to the entity of the nation-state, but in a very different way from Carl Schmitt; his sense of homogeneity did not want to exclude but to promote

---

21 The German original reads as follows: "Es [das Pogrom-Ventil/der Antisemitismus] ist ein Gnadengeschenk der Vorsehung an die Politiker der ganzen Welt und an die Machthaber der großen Menschheitsgeschichte; es ist für die Herrschenden ungefährlich, für die überwiegende Mehrheit plausibel, ein billiges Mittel und hat noch nie versagt."

a relative adjustment of a set of liberal and social values. Felix Weltsch shared with Heller (in spite of his strong sense of Jewish community) an uncompromising appreciation of the individual and his rights. Democracy could survive only as long as it remained committed to liberal principles. As liberals, these men all elaborated concepts of modern society and were skeptical of *Gemeinschaft*. The experiences of Fascism and National Socialism shattered their faith in liberal progress, leading them to develop notions of militant democracy. In conclusion, it is sufficient to paraphrase Steven Aschheim (2012, 1f.): Bonn, Heller, and Weltsch did not theorize at the edges of liberalism; their Jewishness led them right to the center of liberal-democratic thought.

Bibliography

Aschheim, Steven. *Beyond the Border: The German-Jewish Legacy Abroad*. Princeton: Princeton University Press, 2007.

Aschheim, Steven. *At the Edges of Liberalism. Junctions of European, German, and Jewish History*. New York: Palgrave MacMillan, 2012.

Benhabib, Seyla. *The Reluctant Modernism of Hannah Arendt*. Thousand Oaks, CA: Sage, 1996.

Bonn, Moritz Julius. *Nationale Kolonialpolitik* (Schriften des Socialwissenschaftlichen Vereins der Universität München 5). Munich: Riegersche Universitäts-Buchhandlung, 1910.

Bonn, Moritz Julius. "Der moderne Imperialismus." *Grundfragen der englischen Volkswirtschaft* (Veröffentlichungen der Handelshochschule München 1). Munich/Leipzig: Duncker & Humblot, 1913. 127–156.

Bonn, Moritz Julius. *Amerika als Feind*. Munich: Müller, 1917.

Bonn, Moritz Julius. *Was will Wilson?* Munich: Müller, n.d. [1918].

Bonn, Moritz Julius. *The Crisis of European Democracy*. New Haven: Yale University Press, 1925a.

Bonn, Moritz Julius. *Amerika und sein Problem*. Munich: Meyer & Jessen, 1925b.

Bonn, Moritz Julius. *Geld und Geist. Vom Wesen und Werden der amerikanischen Welt*. Berlin: Fischer, 1927.

Bonn, Moritz Julius. "The Crisis of the Parliamentary System." *The Development of the Representative System in our Times. Five Answers to an Inquiry Instituted by the Inter-Parliamentary Union*. Ed. Inter-Parliamentary Union. Lausanne: Payot, 1928. 87–97.

Bonn, Moritz Julius. *Die Kultur der Vereinigten Staaten von Amerika*. Berlin: Wegweiser, 1930.

Bonn, Moritz Julius. *Prosperity: Wunderglaube und Wirklichkeit im amerikanischen Wirtschaftsleben*. Berlin: Fischer, 1931a.

Bonn, Moritz Julius. *Prosperity. Myth and Reality in American Economic Life*. London: Hopkinson, 1931b.

Bonn, Moritz Julius. "Die Psychologie des Nationalsozialismus. Seine Wurzeln und sein Weg (I and II)." *Neue Freie Presse* (Wien). 5 April, 5–6; 12 April, 1931c: 3–4.

Bonn, Moritz Julius. "Sinn und Bedeutung der amerikanischen Krise." *Neue Rundschau* 42.1 (1931d): 145–159.

Bonn, Moritz Julius. *The Crisis of Capitalism in America*. New York: Day, 1932.

Bonn, Moritz Julius. *The American Experiment. A Study of Bourgeois Civilisation.* London: Allen & Unwin, 1933.

Bonn, Moritz Julius. "Limits and Limitations of Democracy." *Constructive Democracy.* Ed. Ernest Simon et al. London: G. Allen & Unwin, 1938. 215–247.

Bonn, Moritz Julius. *Wandering Scholar.* London: Cohen & West, 1949.

Bonn, Moritz Julius. *So macht man Geschichte? Bilanz eines Lebens.* Munich: List, 1953.

Brenner, Michael. *The Renaissance of Jewish Culture in Weimar Germany.* New Haven/London: Yale University Press, 1996.

Clavin, Patricia. "A 'Wandering Scholar' in Britain and the USA 1933–1945: The Life and Work of Moritz Bonn." *Refugees from the Third Reich in Britain.* Ed. Anthony Grenville. Amsterdam/New York: Editions Rodopi, 2003. 27–42.

Fawcett, Edmund. *Liberalism. The Life of an Idea.* Princeton/Oxford: Princeton University Press, 2014.

Feder, Ernst. *Heute sprach ich mit. Tagebücher eines Berliner Publizisten 1926–1932.* Stuttgart: DVA, 1971.

Federici, Federico. *Der deutsche Liberalismus. Die Entwicklung einer politischen Idee von Immanuel Kant bis Thomas Mann.* Zurich: Artemis, 1946.

Gordon, Rob. "Moritz Bonn, Southern Africa and the Critique of Colonialism." *African Historical Review* 45.2 (2013): 1–30.

Hacke, Jens. "Moritz Julius Bonn – ein vergessener Verteidiger der Vernunft: Zum Liberalismus in der Krise der Zwischenkriegszeit. *Mittelweg 36* 17.6 (2010): 26–59.

Hacke, Jens. "'Volksgemeinschaft der Gleichgesinnten'. Liberale Faschismusanalysen in den 1920er Jahren und die Wurzeln der Totalitarismustheorie." *Mittelweg 36* 23.4 (2014a): 53–73.

Hacke, Jens. "Liberale Alternativen für die Krise der Demokratie. Der Nationalökonom Moritz Julius Bonn als politischer Denker im Zeitalter der Weltkriege." *Jahrbuch für Liberalismus-Forschung* 26 (2014b): 295–318.

Heller, Hermann. "Staat, Nation und Sozialdemokratie" (1925). *Gesammelte Schriften.* Tübingen: Mohr, 1992. 1: 527–563.

Heller, Hermann. *Die politischen Ideenkreise der Gegenwart.* Breslau: Hirt, 1926.

Heller, Hermann. "Politische Demokratie und soziale Homogenität" (1928). *Gesammelte Schriften.* Tübingen: Mohr, 1992. 2: 421–433.

Heller, Hermann. "Rechtsstaat oder Diktatur." *Neue Rundschau* 40.12 (1929a): 721–735.

Heller, Hermann. "Was bringt uns eine Diktatur? Faschismus und Wirklichkeit" (1929b). *Gesammelte Schriften.* Tübingen: Mohr, 1992. 2: 435–442.

Heller, Hermann. "Freiheit und Form in der Verfassung" (1929c). *Gesammelte Schriften.* Tübingen: Mohr, 1992. 2: 371–377.

Heller, Hermann. "Europa und der Faschismus" (1931). *Gesammelte Schriften.* Tübingen: Mohr, 1992. 2: 463–609.

Heller, Hermann. "Bürger und Bourgeois." *Neue Rundschau* 43.6 (1932): 721–736.

Henkel, Michael. *Hermann Hellers Theorie der Politik und des Staates. Die Geburt der Politik-wissenschaft aus dem Geiste der Soziologie.* Tübingen: Mohr, 2011.

Kelsen, Hans. *Die Verteidigung der Demokratie. Abhandlungen zur Demokratietheorie.* Ed. Matthias Jestaedt and Oliver Lepsius. Tübingen: Mohr, 2006.

Kelsen, Hans. *Das Problem des Parlamentarismus.* Vienna/Leipzig: Braumüller, 1926.

Llanque, Marcus. Ed. *Souveräne Demokratie und soziale Homogenität. Das politische Denken Hermann Hellers.* Baden-Baden: Nomos, 2010.

Loewenstein, Karl. "Militant Democracy and Fundamental Rights (I + II)." *American Political Science Review* 31 (1937): 417–432, 638–658.

Mann, Klaus. *Das Wunder von Madrid. Aufsätze, Reden, Kritiken 1936–1938*. Reinbek: Rowohlt, 1993.

Müller, Christoph and Ilse Staff. eds. *Staatslehre in der Weimarer Republik. Hermann Heller zu ehren*. Frankfurt on the Main: Suhrkamp, 1985.

Müller, Jan-Werner. *Contesting Democracy. Political Ideas in Twentieth Century Europe*. New Haven/London: Yale University Press, 2011.

Müller, Jan-Werner. "Militant Democracy." *The Oxford Handbook of Comparative Constitutional Law*. Ed. Michel Rosenfeld and Andras Sajo. Oxford: Oxford University Press, 2012. 1253–1269.

Nickel, Erich. *Politik und Politikwissenschaft in der Weimarer Republik*. Berlin: Rotschild, 2004.

Salecker, Hans-Joachim. *Der Liberalismus und die Erfahrung der Differenz. Über die Bedingungen der Integration der Juden in Deutschland*. Berlin/Bodenheim: Philos, 1999

Schivelbusch, Wolfgang. *Intellektuellendämmerung. Zur Lage der Frankfurter Intelligenz in den zwanziger Jahren*. Frankfurt on the Main: Suhrkamp, 1985.

Schluchter, Wolfgang. *Entscheidung für den sozialen Rechtsstaat. Hermann Heller und die staatstheoretische Diskussion in der Weimarer Republik*. Cologne/Berlin: Kiepenheuer, 1968.

Schmidt, Carsten. *Kafkas unbekannter Freund. Leben und Werk von Felix Weltsch. Zionist, Journalist und Philosoph*. Würzburg: Könighausen & Neumann, 2010.

Schmitt, Carl. *Die geistesgeschichtliche Lage des heutigen Parlamentarismus*. Nachdruck der 1926 erschienenen 2. Aufl. Berlin: Duncker & Humblot, 1996.

Schmitt, Carl. *Tagebücher 1930 bis 1934*. Ed. Wolfgang Schuller. Berlin: Akademie, 2010.

Sternberger, Dolf. *Dreizehn politische Radio-Reden*. Heidelberg: Lambert Schneider, 1947.

Weber, Max. *Briefe 1906–1908* (MWG II/5). Tübingen: Mohr, 1990.

Weltsch, Felix. "Organische Demokratie." *Neue Rundschau* 29.4 (1918): 433–454.

Weltsch, Felix. *Das Wagnis der Mitte. Ein Beitrag zur Ethik und Politik der Zeit*. Ostrau: Kittls, 1935.

Weltsch, Felix. *Religion und Humor im Leben und Werk Franz Kafkas*. Munich: Herbig, 1957.

Wiggershaus, Rolf. *The Frankfurt School. Its History, Theories, and Political Significance*. Cambridge, MA: MIT Press, 1994.

Wolin, Richard. *Heidegger's Children. Hannah Arendt, Karl Löwith, Hans Jonas, and Herbert Marcuse*. Princeton: Princeton University Press, 2001.

Young-Bruehl, Elizabeth. *Hannah Arendt. For love of the world*. New Haven: Yale University Press, 1976.

Till van Rahden
History in the House of the Hangman: How Postwar Germany Became a Key Site for the Study of Jewish History

For Marion Kaplan

1

Over the past fifty years, Germany has emerged as a key site for the study of Jewish history. In a country where the community of 120,000 Jews is barely larger than that of Montreal, there are state-funded research centers for Jewish history in Hamburg and Duisburg, Potsdam and Leipzig; three chairs in Jewish history in Potsdam, Düsseldorf and Munich; and two chairs in Jewish history at the Heidelberg "Hochschule für Jüdische Studien," sponsored by the Central Council of the Jews in Germany. Between them, these institutions employ about fifty scholars who work in the field of Jewish history. Jewish studies, in particular, continues to be a growth industry. In 2012 alone, the federal government granted generous funds to a consortium of universities in Berlin and Brandenburg to establish the "Zentrum Jüdische Studien" and to the University of Potsdam to set up the School of Jewish Theology.[1]

In conjunction with three generously funded Jewish museums in Berlin, Frankfurt, and Munich, these centers and chairs play an important role in the

---

1 The federal government accorded 7.9 million Euro for the Centre for Jewish Studies and 2.4 million Euro to the School of Jewish Theology (http://www.bmbf.de/de/18635.php; last accessed on March 26, 2015). This essay is an expanded and revised version of a talk I first presented at the University of California, San Diego, where Deborah Hertz graciously hosted me in March 2009. Since then I have presented versions of the paper at the Leo Baeck Institute's The Robert Liberles International Summer Research Workshop in July 2013; at the Zelikovitz Centre for Jewish Studies, Carleton University; The Borns Jewish Studies Program, Indiana University at Bloomington; Centrum für Jüdische Studien, Universität Graz. On each occasion I received stimulating criticism. I should like to thank especially Eliza Slavet, Mark Roseman, James Casteel, Klaus Hödl and Petra Ernst, Sharon Gordon and Guy Miron, as well as Eszter Gantner and Stefanie Fischer for their comments. A fellowship of the Cluster of Excellence "The Formation of Normative Orders" at the University of Frankfurt provided the means for a fruitful stay at the Institute for Advanced Studies in the Humanities, Bad Homburg, where I completed the essay. Research for this paper was made possible by the generous support of the Canada Research Chair Program.

culture and politics of memory in contemporary Germany. They train and fund graduate students and postdocs, organize international conferences, workshops, and lecture series, and each center edits its own publishing series in Jewish history in conjunction with major publishing houses, such as C.H. Beck, Mohr Siebeck, Vandenhoeck & Ruprecht, Böhlau, de Gruyter Oldenbourg, or Wallstein.[2] Although there is no formal branch of the Leo Baeck Institute for the Study of the History and Culture of German-speaking Jewry in Germany, a working committee, the so-called "Wissenschaftliche Arbeitsgemeinschaft des Leo Baeck Institut in der Bundesrepublik Deutschland," founded in December 1989, now has more than seventy members (Schüler-Springorum 2005; Ritter 2008).[3]

Perhaps less visible, but no less significant, history departments at major German universities regularly offer courses in Jewish history both at the undergraduate and graduate level. Participation in such classes has sparked a more sustained interest in the field in some cases. As one of its most remarkable activities, starting in 1991, the "working committee" of the Leo Baeck Institute in Germany has organized an annual workshop for twenty graduate students in Jewish history. According to Reinhard Rürup, the long-time head of the *Wissenschaftliche Arbeitsgemeinschaft* and organizer of the graduate workshops, more than 130 graduate students in Jewish history had participated in these events by 1999, and this number probably will be close to 300 by the end of this year (Rürup 1996). Former participants include Simone Lässig and Ulrich Sieg, who both received the German Historical Association's prestigious prize for the best "Habilitation," or second monograph; Michael Brenner, who holds the Chair in Jewish History in Munich; Stefanie Schüler-Springorum, head of the Centre for the Study of Antisemitism in Berlin; Miriam Rürup, director of the Hamburg Institute for the History of German Jews; Raphael Gross, director of both the London

---

2 Among several major works, C.H. Beck has published the four-volume *Deutsch-jüdische Geschichte in der Neuzeit* (2001–2007) along with the successor volume, *Geschichte der Juden in Deutschland. Von 1945 bis zur Gegenwart* (2012), and the *Geschichte des jüdischen Alltags in Deutschland: Vom 17. Jahrhundert bis 1945* (2003); since 1959, Mohr Siebeck has published the 84 volumes in the Schriftenreihe wissenschaftlicher Abhandlungen des Leo-Baeck-Instituts; Vandenhoeck & Ruprecht publishes the Schriften des Simon-Dubnow-Instituts since 2001 and Jüdische Religion, Geschichte und Kultur since 2005 (in each series, 23 volumes have appeared to date) as well as Toldot: Essays zur jüdischen Geschichte und Kultur (12 volumes to date); Wallstein publishes Hamburger Beiträge zur Geschichte der deutschen Juden (46 volumes to date); de Gruyter Oldenbourg publishes Europäisch-jüdische Studien since 2001 (23 volumes to date) and New Perspectives on Modern Jewish History since 2012 (6 volumes to date), and since 2001, Böhlau publishes "Lebenswelten osteuropäischer Juden" (16 volumes to date).
3 Tobias Unger, Technical University, Berlin, was kind enough to provide me with recent membership numbers. On the larger field of Jewish/Judaic Studies, see Brenner and Rohrbacher (2000).

Leo Baeck Institute and the Jewish Museum in Frankfurt and the future director of the Simon Dubnow Institute in Leipzig, and many scholars who hold positions in Jewish history in North America and in Great Britain, such as Nils Roemer, Anthony Kauders, and Benjamin Baader, Tobias Brinkmann, François Guesnet, and Mirjam Zadoff.

2

Such matter-of-fact observations cannot convey, of course, that the substantial and ever-increasing scholarly interest in Jewish history in Germany is in and of itself a remarkable, perhaps even odd phenomenon. In most countries that are home to important institutions in this area of research, mainly, if not exclusively, Jews write Jewish history. In Israel, the United States, and Canada, the study of Jewish history is closely linked to a dense network of Jewish communal institutions. In these countries, therefore, Jewish history consists predominantly of scholarship written by Jews, about Jews, and for Jews. As such, it is intimately connected to questions of Jewish communal survival and of Jewish identity, be they secular or religious, Zionist or diasporic (Funkenstein 1993; Raz-Krakotzkin 2002; Baron 1950; Gartner 1988; Biale 1996; Myers 1996). In today's Germany, however, primarily non-Jews write Jewish history.

By itself, this is not unusual. Just as you don't have to be an Orientalist to write a history of Orientalism or an aristocrat to study Alexis de Tocqueville, and just as you don't have to be Catholic to study "Apparitions of the Virgin Mary," or German to study Weimar culture, there is no need to be Jewish to work on Rahel Varnhagen or Abraham Geiger, Franz Rosenzweig, or Hannah Arendt. You don't have to be a triangle to teach geometry, Bertrand Russell allegedly said. Notwithstanding such a truism, the considerable presence of non-Jewish scholars remains exceptional in the field of Jewish history, an area of research that, as Jeremy Cohen, chair of Jewish History at Tel Aviv University, reminds us, "has always developed in relation to the experiences of the Jews: not only their past experiences [...] but also their present experiences, which determine the *manner* in which they study it – their motivations, their methods, and their perspectives" (Cohen 2009, 1). However else one may interpret this quotation, this cascade of possessive pronouns leaves no doubt to whom Jewish history belongs.

More importantly, the flourishing of Jewish history has occurred in a seemingly unlikely country for non-Jews to play such a prominent role in this area of research. Postwar Germany, after all, is literally the house of the hangman; it is a country in the shadow of genocide, total war, and unspeakable crimes. As

bystanders, millions of Germans watched while tens of thousands of German perpetrators, fervent antisemites as well as ordinary men and women, purposefully
and willingly initiated and participated in anti-Jewish discrimination, persecution, and ultimately the murder of six million Jews. Looking back on the world
of the camps and the destruction of European Jewry, the World Jewish Congress
in 1948 passed a resolution that emphasized, "the determination of the Jewish
people never again to settle on the bloodstained soil of Germany" (Resolutions
1948, 7, quoted in Geller 2005, 62).[4]

An awareness of moral failure, a sense of collective responsibility for these
horrendous crimes, and a collective feeling of shame has informed how many
Germans remember their genocidal past ever since the unconditional surrender
in May 1945. As early as 1952, the leading Catholic moral philosopher Romano
Guardini noted: "something monstrous had happened in our history of the past
twenty years." Events so terrible "that no one even had begun to come to terms
with [them]." It has been hard, perhaps even impossible for historians in postwar
Germany to view themselves as the guardians of past glory and as keepers of an
unblemished national history (Guardini 1952, 493).[5]

Ideas about past national splendor rarely resonate among a broader public in
the Federal Republic. It is hard to think of a German equivalent to "Blackadder,"
the brilliant historical sitcom that at once appeals to and subverts popular narratives about six centuries of a glorious British past. In today's Germany, the "Mystic
Chords of Memory" so central to American nationalism have been broken, and
the "sacred foundations" so important to a nostalgia for past grandeur in contemporary France have crumbled (Kammen 1991; Nora 1989, 11). One can, therefore,
best understand historical memory in postwar Germany as an ongoing attempt to
come to terms with a murderous past that will not go away. As Neil Mac Gregor,
curator of the bold exhibition "Germany: Memories of a Nation" at the British
Museum, notes, this is "a history so damaged that it cannot be repaired, but,
rather must be constantly revisited" (Mac Gregor 2014, xxxii; Confino 2006; Olick
2005; Fulda 2010; van Rahden 2011).

Many Jews, and not just those who had to justify why they would chose
to live their lives in the house of the hangman, viewed postwar Germany with
deeply ambivalent feelings. As many others, they were puzzled by the unlikely
emergence of postwar Germany as a stable, liberal democracy and the return of

---

4 In general, see Brenner (2012), especially Diner (2012); Kauders (2007); Stern (1991); Auslander
(2010); Lavi (2005); Rapaport (1997); and Varon (2014).
5 "Was ich ihnen sagen wollte: .[...] daß in der Geschichte unserer letzten zwanzig Jahre etwas
Ungeheuerliches steht, das noch vollkommen unaufgearbeitet ist." In general, see Meier (2010);
Assmann (2006); Bar-On (1989); Bohrer (2000); Jarausch and Sabrow (2002); and Geyer (2004).

Germany as a major player in world politics and the global economy. Yet, as the Israeli journalist Amos Elon noted in his fascinating travelogue, *Journey through a Haunted Land*, first published in 1966, the postwar German "prosperity" has been "dazzling." "Somehow as a foreigner and as a Jew," Elon went on, "you are imbued with a dark, inexplicable, rarely uttered feeling that the fortune bestowed on the West Germans is in some way indecent. Somehow you want to see Germans in hair shirts, barefoot, and covered with ashes" (Elon 1967, 108).

To complicate matters further, prior to 1933, German universities and research institutes had been even more hostile than similar institutions in England, France, or the United States to Jewish scholars' attempts to establish Jewish history as a respectable field of inquiry in the world of learning. The failure to establish Jewish history as a legitimate area of study at German universities in the late nineteenth and early twentieth centuries is especially surprising because German-speaking Central Europe was the birthplace and – until the Nazi rise to power – the center of the "Science of Judaism." The pioneers of modern Jewish historiography, Peter Beer and Leopold Zunz, Isaak Markus Jost and Heinrich Graetz, all wrote in German; yet, unable to find positions at universities, instead they taught at rabbinical seminaries, if they secured a position at all (Schorsch 1994; Brenner 2006). German universities embraced "Judenforschung" in the 1930s in order to facilitate justification of the discrimination, persecution, and murder of Jews. A number of leading postwar German historians such as Fritz Fischer and Hermann Kellenbenz began their careers at these antisemitic research clusters in the same way that postwar mandarins such as Werner Conze and Theodor Schieder laid the foundation for their careers in research conglomerates for "Ostforschung," where they advocated the "de-Judaization" of Poland (compare Hoffmann 1995, 678; Rupnow 2010 and 2011, Burleigh 1988, Große Kracht 2003, and Haar 2002 with Aschheim 2007).

After the Holocaust, the United States and Israel emerged as major centers for the study of Jewish history. Just as it was unthinkable that Germany would once again be home to a vibrant Jewish community, it seemed unlikely that German scholars would play a considerable role in the writing of Jewish history. It is, therefore, hardly surprising that, from its founding in 1955, the Leo Baeck Institute has been vexed by the question of the appropriate degree of contacts with scholars living and teaching in the house of the hangman. As early as January 1960, Robert Weltsch, director of the London branch, suggested that the Leo Baeck Institute should "actively" contact scholars in Germany no matter how "complicated" this might be (Schüler-Springorum 2005, 205). Indicatively. it took Weltsch, who also served as editor of the institute's now famous *Yearbook*, almost a decade to convince other members of the board that he might accept contributions by "non-Jews (Germans)" (Schüler-Springorum 2005, 205).[6]

The Leo Baeck Institute reached a consensus of sorts only in October 1964. Siegfried Moses, head of the Jerusalem branch, identified the need to "determine the types of themes we would encourage non-Jews to treat." This would require "careful consideration." According to Moses, "suitable tasks" for non-Jews would be the description of "objective facts," of "the conduct of non-Jews, non-Jewish groups, and non-Jewish organization vis-à-vis the Jews," whereas "the conduct of Jews" would "certainly be assigned to Jewish authors." When the institute wanted to expand its cooperation with scholars in Germany in the late 1960s, board members agreed not to invite "men who held any sort of office in the Nazi period" and instead actively to recruit "younger scholars," such as Reinhard Rürup, born in 1934, Ernst Schulin, born in 1929, or Monika Richarz, born in 1937. Although these relations became durable and close, it took another twenty years before they were formally institutionalized with the founding of the "Wissenschaftliche Arbeitsgemeinschaft des Leo Baeck Institut in der Bundesrepublik Deutschland" in 1989, and only during the 1990s was the dense network of research centers, institutes, and chairs in Jewish history established in Germany (Schüler-Springorum 2005, 207 and 211; Hoffmann 1995, 685).

The emergence of this lavishly founded institutional landscape coincided with a significant upswing of interest in the field of Jewish studies among graduate students and postdoctoral scholars. There are manifold reasons for this flourishing of the Jewish history field in Germany since the 1990s, and it is, perhaps, overly simplistic to view it as nothing more than a reflection of a collective sense of guilt, a shared feeling of shame, and a deeply ambivalent postwar German "philosemitism."

For one, after the seismic shift of 1989, questions of cultural and religious diversity seemed more relevant and, perhaps, urgent than during the Cold War. The rivalry between a capitalist West and a communist East had obscured national, ethnic, and religious conflicts, and it intensified at a time when Germany (just as other European countries) was more ethnically and culturally homogeneous than ever before, namely the 1950s and early 1960s. When modernization and secularization theory dominated the social sciences and the humanities, the triumph of nation-states seemed inevitable while memories of Europe's pluralist, perhaps even multicultural, past were fading fast.

---

6 The first article by a non-Jewish historian from Germany to appear in the *Yearbook of the Leo Baeck Institute* was Reinhard Rürup's (1969) now classic essay "Jewish Emancipation and Bourgeois Society."

When the Cold War ended, however, history returned. Ethnic, religious, and national conflicts served as a reminder that concepts of civil society have always had to negotiate the tension between the homogenizing force of the democratic nation-state and the reality of pluralism. When Germans faced up to the multicultural moment of the late twentieth century, some realized that they could ill afford to ignore their pluralist past and the rich repertoire of diverse languages that had characterized civil society in Europe since the Enlightenment.[7]

One element of such larger conversations about the history of diversity and difference, namely the rising interest in Jewish history, developed in tandem with a more widespread fascination with things Jewish that swept post-Cold-War Central Europe – even if I distinguish between non-Jews who study Jewish history and non-Jews who enact cultural and even religious traditions they believe to be authentically Jewish, such as Klezmer music, or who take on the persona of a Holocaust survivor.[8] "If West German consumerism was reflected in such things as the *Fresswelle*, literally the wave of gluttony, and the *Sexwelle*, which speaks for itself," Ian Buruma commented in the *New York Review of Books* as early as 1992, the German fashion of "*Betroffenheit* [that is, a vague sense of being personally concerned and involved] has resulted of late in a wave of interest in Jewish matters." Younger Germans, in particular, felt pain and even anger as they became aware to what extent the intellectual and cultural life of their country had been "maimed by the destruction of German Jews." "Postwar Germany," according to Buruma (1992), "feels like a person who has lost part of his brain, the part that Nazis hated most, the sparkling, witty, cosmopolitan part that lifted the German soul from its muddy soil."

The Berlin Jewish Museum, located at the heart of the city that conceived and administered the Holocaust, serves as a particularly intriguing example of a strange way of both commemorating and celebrating the importance of Jews for German history. The museum is by far the largest institution of its kind in Europe and, like the Memorial for the Murdered Jews of Europe, has become a global

---

7 Typical for the growing interest in diversity and difference are renowned and generously funded research institutes such as the Max Planck Institute for the Study of Religious and Ethnic Diversity in Göttingen, the Max Planck Institute for European Legal History's new research focus on "Multinormativity" and "Conflict Regulation," the Leibniz Institute for European History's recent umbrella theme "Negotiating Difference in Europe" (Umgang mit Differenz in Europa), the International Research Training Group "Religious Cultures in 19th and 20th-century Europe" at the Ludwig-Maximilians-Universität in Munich, or the Viadrina Center *B/Orders in Motion* in Frankfurt, Oder. In general, see Van Rahden (2005). For a guide to contemporary German controversies, see Heins (2013).

8 See Pinto (1996), Geyer and Hansen (1994), Gruber (2002), Richarz (1991), Stratton (2007), Zipes (1994), Weissberg (2004), Lehrer (2013), Eskin (2002), and Lappin (1999).

tourist attraction. As Edward Rothstein noted in *The New York Times* in May 2009, it is "a national museum devoted to exploring the history of a people this country was once intent on eradicating." The institution's enormous "symbolic importance" notwithstanding, according to the paper's chief music critic, it is "difficult to imagine" a Jewish museum that "could be as uninspiring and banal, particularly given its pedigree and promise" (Rothstein, 2009).[9] Such scathing criticism notwithstanding, the opening of the Berlin Jewish Museum in 2001, "was clearly one of the biggest official German events since reunification," as Amos Elon noted in the *New York Review of Books*:

> The gala opening on September 8 was, in effect, a state ceremony, fully timed to have a political effect. It was attended by 850 carefully chosen guests from among the German political elite, headed by President Johannes Rau and Chancellor Gerhard Schröder, ministers as well as foreign ambassadors, leading bankers and industrialists, prominent professors, artists, and other cultural figures, scions of ancient Prussian aristocratic families and powerful or super-rich foreign guests, mostly Jews and nearly all from the United States (Elon 2001).

Rarely has there been a starker contrast between an abundance of political symbolism attributed to a site of memory and the shortcomings of its permanent exhibition than in the case of the German capital's Jewish museum.

An event of comparable significance to the moral soul-searching in contemporary Germany was the inauguration of the monumental Memorial to the Murdered Jews of Europe in Berlin on 10 May 2005. Once again, the political and cultural elites from Germany, Europe, and across the globe assembled for the opening ceremony. Almost 60 years to the day after the defeat of Nazi Germany, a total of 1500 guests of honor, including all senior members of Germany's government, were exposed to "speeches, a short film and a medley of Yiddish and Hebrew songs, apparently intended to remind Berliners of the people and the rich Jewish-German culture that were destroyed" (Bernstein 2005).[10] No matter how valiantly German officials aimed to probe the limits of representation, however, such an endeavor necessarily remains aporetic, and prominent critics continue to raise painful questions. As Richard Brody notes in the *New Yorker*, the official title of the Memorial is so vague that it provokes the question whether the shorthand "Murdered Jews of Europe" includes "Claude Lanzmann's uncle, who was [...] killed in Paris by his jealous mistress." "The play of the imagination that the

---

9 Compare the thoughtful criticism of Steinberg (2007) and Herz (2005) with Bussenius (2014), published under the auspices of the Berlin Jewish Museum.
10 See also: Wefing (2005); Naumann (2005); Till (2005, 161–188); on the acrimonious controversies preceding the construction, see Jeismann (1999).

memorial provokes," the magazine's film critic argues, "is piously generic: something to do with death." "The mollifying solemnity of pseudo-universal abstractions," Brody (2012) concludes, "puts a gray sentiment in the place of actual memory."

In uncanny ways, the aesthetic courage, financial largesse, and commemorative monumentalism that helped build the Jewish Museum and the Memorial contrasts with the failure to build a site whose architecture met the challenge of adequately documenting the countless perpetrators and representing German crimes. When, in 1993, Peter Zumthor won the competition for the new building for the "Topographie des Terrors" to be built on the remnants of the former Gestapo Headquarters and the Reich Security Main Office, few anticipated that this bold decision would end in disaster. The Swiss architect understood better than others that he would have to build a "unique house for a unique place" that took seriously the preeminent place of the "Topographie" in a context of wounded nationalism. More than anything else, Zumthor wanted to undermine what he saw as a destructive "didacticism": "A building at a crime scene of memory must be calm and serene to allow for commemoration and empathy. It must transcend the didactically prepared phenomenon of the Holocaust, it must leave the media glamor behind" (Rauterberg 2001). Zumthor's building design preserved and integrated the ruins of the administrative center of the persecution and genocide of Jews in Nazi-occupied Europe. The architectural style aimed to let "the historical building" speak for itself, "to preserve and to show the few remnants of houses and structures used by the National Socialists." "Our concrete stick frame (Stabwerkgebäude)," Zumthor explained, "was not meant to symbolize anything. It was to have been itself, a transparent covering that concealed nothing. And as a result [...] it would have maintained an important building of the Nazi past that already had been half-buried and re-civilized" (Zumthor 2014, 59; Leoni 2014).[11]

Yet, a decade later, when the service towers were close to completion, the Berlin Republic decided to fire the Swiss architect and demolished the construction that he had designed. Zumthor, in turn, completed the Kolumba Museum in Cologne in 2007 and received the Pritzker Architecture Prize in 2009 "for work that is focused, uncompromising and exceptionally determined" (jury citation 2009). As the Berlin daily *Der Tagesspiegel* noted in retrospect: "At the central, authentic place of commemoration, no building will set an example that equals the outstanding architecture of the Holocaust Memorial and the Jewish

---

11 The original German: "Unser Stabwerkgebäude sollte nichts symbolisieren. Es sollte sich selber sein, eine transparente Hülle, nichts verbergend, und so [...] ein wichtiges Gebäude der nationalsozialistischen Geschichte, das schon mehr als halbwegs zugeschüttet und zivilisiert worden war, offen [...] halten."

Museum. [...] It is perhaps indicative of the unease about one's own past that Berlin and Germany are now making do with a dignified functional building" (Chp 2006).[12] The New Germany, then, embraced two national projects of cathartic redemption that invoke touching tales of Jewish suffering and uplifting stories of Jewish cultural creativity. In contrast, it hesitated to display similar courage and dedication when faced with the troublesome task of summoning up German perpetrators and crimes, a moral duty to remember that is as commendable as it is impossible.

In less monumental, but perhaps more effective and long-lasting ways, public schools have contributed greatly to a growing interest in Jewish history. Detailed and sophisticated teaching units on the Third Reich and the Holocaust have come to play an ever increasing role in German high school curricula over the past thirty years. True, there are good reasons not to confuse the study of antisemitism and the Holocaust with research on Jewish history. It is hardly surprising, however, that some students exposed to these curricula developed a lasting interest in those aspects of German and European history in which Jews were more than helpless victims of antisemitic ideology and Nazi persecution. Many students in senior high school who wrote term papers on the "Reichskristallnacht" in their hometown realized almost inadvertently what an important role Jews had played in the city's public life prior to 1933 (Liepach 2014; Pingel 1989; Hoffmann 1995, 684).

3

To summarize my argument so far, it is hard to ignore that there is something improbable and surprising, odd and, perhaps, uncanny about the flourishing of Jewish history as an area of inquiry in postwar Germany. It seems likely, although hard to demonstrate conclusively, that the complex and vexing challenges and dilemmas I have alluded to earlier inform contemporary German academic research in Jewish history. In order both to draw upon and engage such moral sensibilities, most scholars implicitly or explicitly take up the challenge of exploring Jewish history's place within larger narratives of German and European history, narratives against which Jewish experiences are often set up as a

---

12 The original German: "Neben der besonderen Architektur des Holocaust-Mahnmals und des Jüdischen Museums wird am zentralen, authentischen Ort der Erinnerung an die Täter kein Zeichen gesetzt. [...] Vielleicht entspricht es ja dem Unbehagen an der eigenen Geschichte, dass Berlin und Deutschland sich nun mit einem würdigen Zweckbau begnügen."

"counter-history" (Funkenstein 1993, 36; Biale 1999; Heschel 1998). This challenge, obviously, applies not only to scholarship in Germany; it speaks directly to larger debates about how to contextualize Jewish history within the mainstream of historical scholarship, a discussion that is familiar to anyone interested in the relationship between the universal and the particular in the writing of history, a question that I shall return to in my conclusion.

Ironically, the field of Jewish history in contemporary Germany benefited from what one might call an intellectual and scholarly "backwardness." What Alexander Gerschenkron famously described for economic developments may also hold true for the growth of an academic field; latecomers start as dilettantes only to experience unusually steep learning curves. As latecomers, German scholars encountered an already existing, rich body of scholarship in Jewish history that American and Israeli, as well as occasionally French and English scholars, had produced. As laggards, they quickly had to acquaint themselves with often acrimonious controversies that were comprehensible only against the background of academic contexts, political debates, and moral sensibilities that were very different from their own. Often this necessitated a work of translation and occasionally may have given rise to a sense of alienation – the first a practice, the latter a condition that do not exactly impede intellectual creativity.

In addition, the field of Jewish history, perhaps, particularly appeals to graduate students in Germany inclined to think outside the box of established interpretations of national history. Even German scholars in Jewish history focusing on Central Europe cannot ignore a rich body of scholarship in Russian and Polish-Jewish history, French, English, and American Jewish history. It encompasses traditions that each reflected distinct cultural and historiographical contexts and have developed specific concepts and conventions to analyze Judaism's encounter with modernity and the world at large (Steinberg 2007, 1). With the exception of narrowly construed Zionist narratives, various interpretations of Jewish history have always contained elements of cosmopolitan and post-national, diasporic, transnational, and transcultural stories. Long before labels such as entangled or connected, transnational or postcolonial history became fashionable among historians in general, specialists in Jewish history had viewed methodological nationalism with suspicion and had intuitively grasped the epistemological creativity of counter narratives. As the disenchantment with histories that focus on distinct nations spread, historians became increasingly sensitive to the permeability of what were often assumed to be closed 'cultural zones' and to the existence of vocabularies that cut across different religious and cultural traditions. Consequently, the focus of scholarly interest has shifted to phenomena of entanglement that Sanjay Subrahmanyam has so provocatively labeled "connected histories" (Subrahmanyam 1997, 748; idem 2012; Conrad and Randeria 2013).[13]

In his essay "Multiculturalism: A Liberal Perspective," the moral philosopher Joseph Raz suggested that we "should think of our societies as consisting not of a majority and minorities, but of a plurality of cultural groups" (Raz 1994, 174). By way of conclusion, I would like to draw on Raz's insight in order to argue that a key challenge for scholars in Jewish history, particularly those who work on the emancipation and post-emancipation period, is to step out of the long shadow of the minority history paradigm that corresponds directly with a nationalist narrative of majority history. The complex history of the Jewish Museum in Berlin illustrates this dilemma. Whereas the city originally planned to integrate its Jewish museum into the Berlin City Museum, museum planners eventually decided to house the Jewish museum in a separate building because Jewish history required its own story and its own history. "Yet," as Michael Steinberg has noted, "museologically and historically, the decision has its own complications, placing as it does the history of the Jews on a field separate from the history of other Germans. Here the museological quandary duplicates the historiographical one: giving the Jews 'their' history adopts a functionally nationalist paradigm for the organization of historical patterns and groups, which may do violence to the subject positions of precisely those whom the gesture seeks to redress" (Steinberg 2007, 180; Akcan 2010; Offe 1997).

The remarkable rise of Jewish history as one of the many variations of minority history that are being written these days comes at a price. One can read the growing specialization and fragmentation of history as a field of inquiry as a happy story about the Opening of the Canon. At the same time, the story of fragmentation is also an unhappy one. Over approximately the past 30 years, Kerwin Lee Klein has argued, historians have "abandoned much that was good in the older historical traditions. We have lost our willingness to tell the big story and to see history as literary and moral event." The rise of minority histories and subaltern studies led not only to the opening of the canon but also threatens to devolve into what Klein calls "subaltern one-upmanship: My hero is more subaltern than yours; my hero suffers two oppressions rather than one, or three oppressions rather than two; we have multiple, finite heroes and oppressions that can only be joined arithmetically" (Klein 1997, 11–12).[14]

---

13 It is remarkable how Subrahmanyam's work often addresses similar themes as S.D. Goitein; see Libson (1998). In general, see Rodgers (2014).

14 One should not confuse Klein's nuanced defense of a "big story" and of "history as literary and moral event" with current appeals for "big history" or a nostalgia for a manly history that provides muscular moral lessons for our contemporary predicament: see, especially, Simon et al.

The rise of a seemingly unlimited number of minority or subaltern histories has led to a fragmentation of understanding. This fragmentation may help us to understand why – despite its growth – Jewish history has had little impact on the mainstream historiography of modern Germany or Europe. In other words, although Jewish history has become a respectable area of specialization in modern European history, it has not had a remarkable impact on approaches to European history as such. Much of this has to do with the resilience of the majority–minority dichotomy. If Jews are a minority within European societies, their history can tell us little about the history of the majority. Within the context of Jewish history, Jews are agents; within the context of European history, Jews are victims, or, at least, objects of forces beyond their control.

One of the challenges specialists in modern Jewish history face today is to transcend the majority–minority dichotomy by questioning the 'given-ness' of a prior, normative European culture into which Jews (and other groups) were to be 'fitted.' Some leading scholars in the field have begun to suggest ways of rethinking the relationship between Jewish history and, for want of a better word, "general history." In 2007, Marci Shore identified an "emerging trend in Jewish historiography," namely, "the beginning of the end of an era in which Jewish history and European history were considered two discrete identities" (Shore 2007, 121).[15] Inviting readers to reconsider Jewish history in Renaissance Italy, David Biale, editor of the recently published *Cultures of the Jews*, argues that the contemporary model of assimilation as a linear process "is misleading when applied to the Jews in Renaissance Italy." In fact, Biale argues in his introduction to the volume:

> The Jews should not be seen as outsiders who borrowed from Italian culture but rather as full participants in the shaping of that culture, albeit with their own concerns and mores. The Jews were not so much 'influenced' by the Italians, as they were one organ in a larger cultural organism, a subculture that established its identity in a complex process of adaption and resistance. Jewish 'difference' was an integral part of a larger mosaic of Renaissance Italy. Expanding beyond Renaissance Italy to Jewish history as a whole, we may find it more productive to use this organic model of culture than to chase after who influenced whom (Biale 2002, xix).

Upon reflection, the convenient and seemingly self-evident juxtaposition of majority and minority history along with the "all but canonical boundary between

---

(2015) and Guldi and Armitage (2014). No matter whether one agrees with the moral certainties these "lessons of the past" promise to offer, such arguments are in danger of losing empirical richness and historiographical subtlety. If the past is a foreign country, attention to clues and peculiarities, elusive traces and hidden signs makes for safer travel. See Kracauer (1996 [1969]) and Ginzburg (1989 and 2012).

15 See also Aschheim (1998); Endelman (2013, 591).

Jewish and a presumptive 'general' history," are, perhaps, best understood, to quote Michael Stanislawski, as "a fictive artifact that obscures sound historical judgment" (Stanislawski 2004, 176).[16]

Once one turns to the chapters on Modern European Jewish history in *Cultures of the Jews*, however, one is in for a disappointment. Undoubtedly, all the contributions are erudite, carefully argued, and elegantly written. One is hardpressed, however, to identify the passages in the essays that address the challenge that David Biale's introduction identified, namely, integrating Jewish history into overall narratives of Modern European history in ways that would transcend the majority–minority dichotomy.

Scholars may start by exploring questions historians should have addressed long ago, namely, when, where, and why it became seemingly self-evident neatly to compartmentalize societies and their history into a majority and minorities. The dichotomy between majority and minority "is itself a product of a certain history" (Scott 2008, 1427). Rather than parroting this binary opposition, it might prove more fruitful to study its history. As a shorthand to describe relations between different ethnic or religious groups, the idea of a dichotomy between majority and minority is recent. In fact, it did not exist before 1919, when, in the wake of World War I and the collapse of the empires in continental Europe, the idea of democracy and the idea of the homogeneous nation-state triumphed simultaneously. Its increasing usage in the early twentieth century and the intense struggle over so-called "minority rights" during the "tribal twenties" coincided with the triumph of the ideal of the homogeneous nation-state. From the fifteenth century, the concept of minority referred to the state of being a minor, that is, a person under age. From the early eighteenth century, the term entered the sphere of parliamentary politics, referring to a party voting together against a majority in a deliberative assembly or electoral body. While both meanings are still familiar today, it has been forgotten that this terminology did not emerge as an innocent juxtaposition to the concept of majority or as an analytical description of a numerical relationship. The language of minor, of *minorité*, of *minoritas* and of *minorem* originally referred to "the condition of or fact of being smaller, inferior

---

16 Other scholars in Jewish and/or European history whose work exemplifies this trend are Leora Auslander, Elisheva Baumgarten, Natalie Zemon Davis, David Feldman, Anthony Grafton, Ruth HaCohen, Jonathan M. Hess, John Higham, Paula Hyman, Peter Jelavich, Marion A. Kaplan, Lisa M. Leff, George L. Mosse, Benjamin Nathans, David Nirenberg, Peter Pulzer, Monika Richarz, Reinhard Rürup, Ernst Schulin, or David Sorkin.

or subordinate," and as such, it drew on ideas of legal, political, intellectual, and moral deficiency (*Oxford English Dictionary* 2009).[17]

4

Perhaps, one way of avoiding the assumptions of moral deficiency and intellectual immaturity that underlie the dichotomy of majority–minority is by placing the relationship between the particular and the universal at the center of our understanding of nineteenth-and early twentieth-century European history. The universal, however, is neither the polar opposite of the particular nor is it a given; rather, it is an ever-changing arena that originates in the articulation of cultural differences. One challenge consists of fostering innovative scholarship on diversity that neither fetishizes differences as inherently valuable nor scandalizes them as a threat to liberal modernity. Perhaps it is best to conceptualize diversity not as the sudden emergence of the marginal "others" in the public realm but as an irreducible and omnipresent force in liberal societies.

Diversity, as George Kateb has noted, is the "inevitable," if not always "admirable, outcome of personal freedom" (Kateb 2006, 361–362; idem 1992). In any liberal polity, citizens bring (and have always brought) their specific identities, sensibilities, and fears into the public sphere. All citizens enter democratic polities as distinct individuals. It is a widespread, yet dangerous misunderstanding and ultimately a violent illusion to assume that, when citizens enter the realm of politics, they can check their particular moral passions and prejudices, fears and fantasies at the door. Without, perhaps, fully comprehending, citizens intuitively grasp the origin and content of their moral passions and the goal beyond the polity itself that they are pursuing.

In the face of such strong sentiments, it is obvious that a democratic polity is neither the starting point nor the ultimate destination of citizens. "In the political if not the geographic sense," David Novak has argued, all citizens are immigrants who bring their own "minority" culture into the public sphere (Novak 2005, xi). We would do well, therefore, to challenge the predominant tendency among scholars and the broader public to identify research on diversity with questions of marginality and migration. To move beyond the paradigm of minority studies

---

17 Not surprisingly, the first encyclopedia entries on the term date from the mid to late 1920s and often note that the concept is a neologism: Willms (1923); Kollenseher (1927); "Minderheiten, nationale" (1928); Grentrup (1929). See also the entries "Minor" and " Minority," "Major" and "Majority," *Oxford English Dictionary* (2009); Frank (2008) and Meijknecht (2010).

inherent in this equation, it might prove fruitful to start with the assumption that diversity – moral antagonisms, incommensurabilities, and struggles, in other words – originates within liberal polities. Conceptualizing it as a phenomenon caused by the immigration of foreigners or the emancipation of disenfranchised religious, ethnic, or racial groups may hinder understanding.

As a field of inquiry, Jewish history, in particular, offers a venue to question the validity of the binary oppositions that continue to shape scholarly and public controversies over diversity. We need to conceive the oppositions of minority and majority, of the religious and the secular, and of the particular and the universal as relative and fluid, rather than absolute and fixed in character, and to explore their mutual constitutiveness (*wechselseitige Verschränkung*). Reinhart Koselleck's reflections on the connectedness between experience and expectations shed light on the intimate relationship between these oppositions as well. To construct their relationship – analogous to concepts such as war and peace – as categories of a binary opposition that mutually exclude one another is to misrepresent their fundamental characteristics. The conceptual couples of the particular and the universal, of minority and majority, of the religious and the secular, like that of experience and expectations draw on a different logic. It is "redoubled upon itself; it presupposes no alternatives; the one is not to be had without the other" (Koselleck 2004, 257) With this in mind, scholars in the social sciences and the humanities might be well advised to resist the temptation unambiguously to classify specific ideas and practices as either particular or universal, as either secular or religious. Instead, it might prove more fruitful to uncover traces of the particular in languages of the universal and vestiges of the universal in ideas of the particular.

If some of the challenges I have identified in my conclusion resonate in conversations and debates among scholars in Jewish history in the United States or Israel, all the merrier. I do not believe that any scholar can eradicate her or his moral passions and convictions. We all have our own point of view, which may seem infuriating to some as it undermines our capacity to assume "The View from Nowhere" (Nagel 1986). Rather than negating our moral sensibilities and passions, we ought to transform them into what Siegfried Kracauer has identified as a key qualification for scholars in the humanities, namely "moral ingenuity." In "History: The Last Things before the Last," he argued that an adequate study of history "calls for the efforts of a self as rich in facets as the affairs reviewed" (Kracauer 1996 [1969], 62; Droysen 1977, 101, 106). If Kracauer is right, and I believe he is, we need carefully to harness our own fantasies, desires, and demons that emerge out of the moral dramas and moral incommensurabilities of our present rather than putting them aside. Whether a study is "good history," whether a historical interpretation is worth engaging, ultimately depends not so much on the scholar's place of residence or background as on his or her manner of advancing an argument and utilizing evidence. Moral ingenuity and analytical rigor, powers of imagination and literary skills will always take a particular form but are hardly the exclusive possession of one intellectual let alone one religious, ethnic, or national tradition.

Bibliography

Akcan, Esra. "Apology and Triumph: Memory Transference, Erasure, and a Rereading of the Berlin Jewish Museum." *New German Critique* 37.2 (2010): 153–179.

Aschheim, Steven E. "German History and German Jewry. Boundaries, Junctions, and Interdependence." *Year Book of the Leo Baeck Institute* 43 (1998): 315–322.

Aschheim, Steven E. "The Tensions of Historical Wissenschaft: The Émigré Historians and the Making of German Cultural History." Idem. *Beyond the Border: The German-Jewish Legacy Abroad*. Princeton: Princeton University Press, 2007. 45–80.

Assmann, Aleida. *Der lange Schatten der Vergangenheit: Erinnerungskultur und Geschichtspolitik*. Munich: C.H. Beck, 2006.

Auslander, Leora. "Archiving a Life: Post-Shoah Paradoxes of Memory Legacies." *Unsettling History. Archiving and Narrating in Historiography*. Ed. Sebastian Jobs. Frankfurt on the Main: Campus, 2010. 127–148.

Bar-On, Dan. *Legacy of Silence: Encounters with Children of the Third Reich*. Cambridge, MA: Harvard University Press, 1989.

Baron, Salo W. "American Jewish History: Problems and Methods." *Publications of the American Jewish Historical Society* 39.3 (1950): 207–266.

Bernstein, Richard. "Holocaust Memorial Opens in Berlin." *New York Times*, 11 May 2005.

Biale, David. "Between Polemics and Apologetics: Jewish Studies in the Age of Multiculturalism." *Jewish Studies Quarterly* 3 (1996): 173–184.

Biale, David. "Counter-History and Jewish Polemics against Christianity: The 'Sefer toldot yeshu' and the 'Sefer zerubavel.'" *Jewish Social Studies* 6.1 (1999): 130–145.

Biale, David, ed. "Preface: Toward a Cultural History of the Jews." *Cultures of the Jews: A New History*. New York: Schocken Books, 2002. xvii–xxxiii.

Bohrer, Karl-Heinz, ed. "Epilog: Schuldkultur oder Schamkultur. Der Verlust an historischem Gedächtnis." *Provinzialismus: Ein physiognomisches Panorama*. Munich: Hanser, 2000. 150–163.

Brenner, Michael and Stefan Rohrbacher, eds. *Wissenschaft vom Judentum: Annäherungen nach dem Holocaust*. Göttingen: Vandenhoeck & Ruprecht, 2000.

Brenner, Michael. *Propheten des Vergangenen. Jüdische Geschichtsschreibung im 19. und 20. Jahrhundert*. Munich: C.H. Beck, 2006.

Brenner, Michael, ed. *Geschichte der Juden in Deutschland von 1945 bis zur Gegenwart: Politik, Kultur und Gesellschaft*. Munich: C.H. Beck, 2012.

Brody, Richard. "The Inadequacy of Berlin's 'Memorial to the Murdered Jews of Europe.'" *The New Yorker*, 12 July 2012.

Burleigh, Michael. *Germany Turns Eastwards: A Study of 'Ostforschung' in the Third Reich*. Cambridge, UK: Cambridge University Press, 1988.

Buruma, Ian. "The Ways of Survival." *New York Review of Books* 39.13, 16 July 1992.

Bussenius, Daniel. *Von der Hauptstadtposse zur Erfolgsgeschichte: Die Entstehung des Jüdischen Museums Berlin 1971–2001*. Göttingen: Vandenhoeck & Ruprecht, 2014.

Chp. "Zeichen und Zweck." *Tagesspiegel*, 26 January 2006.

Cohen, Jeremy. "Introduction." *Rethinking European Jewish History*. Ed. Jeremy Cohen and Murray J. Rosman. Oxford: The Littman Library of Jewish Civilization, 2009. 1–12.

Confino, Alon. *Germany as a Culture of Remembrance. Promises and Limits of Writing History*. Chapel Hill: The University of North Carolina Press, 2006.

Conrad, Sebastian and Shalini Randeria, Eds. *Jenseits des Eurozentrismus: Postkoloniale Perspektiven in den Geschichts- und Kulturwissenschaften*. Frankfurt: Campus, 2013.

Diner, Dan. "Im Zeichen des Banns." *Geschichte der Juden in Deutschland von 1945 bis zur Gegenwart: Politik, Kultur und Gesellschaft*. Ed. Michael Brenner. Munich: C.H. Beck, 2012. 15–66.

Droysen, Gustav. "§5 Das Finden des Materials." and "§6 Die Heuristische Frage." *Historik. Historisch-kritische Ausgabe*. Ed. Peter Ley. Stuttgart: Frommann-Holzboog, 1977. 100–110.

Elon, Amos. *Journey through a Haunted Land: The New Germany*. New York: Holt, Rinehart and Winston, 1967.

Elon, Amos. "A German Requiem." *New York Review of Books*, 48. 18, 15 November 2001.

Endelman, Todd M. "New Turns in Jewish Historiography?" *The Jewish Quarterly Review* 103.4 (2013): 589–598.

Eskin, Blake. *A Life in Pieces: The Making and Unmaking of Binjamin Wilkomirski*. New York: Norton, 2002.

Frank, Manfred. "Minderheiten." *Handbuch der politischen Philosophie und Sozialphilosophie*. Ed. Stefan Gosepath et al. Berlin: De Gruyter, 2008. 1: 826–830.

Fulda, Daniel et al., eds. *Demokratie im Schatten der Gewalt: Geschichten des Privaten im deutschen Nachkrieg*. Göttingen: Wallstein, 2010.

Funkenstein, Amos. *Perceptions of Jewish History*. Berkeley: The University of California Press, 1993.

Gartner, Lloyd P. "Jewish Historiography in the United States and Britain." *Jewish History: Fs. Chimen Abramsky*. Ed. Ada Rapoport-Albert and Steven J. Zipperstein. London: Halban, 1988. 199–227.

Geller, Jay H. *Jews in Post-Holocaust Germany, 1945–1953*. Cambridge, UK: Cambridge University Press, 2005.

Geyer, Martin H. "Im Schatten der NS-Zeit: Zeitgeschichte als Paradigma einer (bundes-) republikanischen Geschichtswissenschaft." *Zeitgeschichte als Problem. Nationale Traditionen und Perspektiven der Forschung in Europa*. Ed. Alexander Nützenadel and Wolfgang Schieder. Göttingen: Vandenhoeck & Ruprecht, 2004. 25–53.

Geyer, Michael and Miriam Hansen. "German-Jewish Memory and National Consciousness." *Holocaust Remembrance: The Shapes of Memory*. Ed. Geoffrey Hartman. Oxford: Blackwell, 1994. 175–190.

Ginzburg, Carlo. *Clues, Myths, and the Historical Method*. Baltimore: Johns Hopkins University Press, 1989.

Ginzburg, Carlo. *Threads and Traces: True, False, Fictive*. Berkeley: University of California Press, 2012.

Grentrup, Theodor. "Minderheiten." *Staatslexikon*. 5th edition. Freiburg: Herder, 1929. 3: 1310–1320.

Große Kracht, Klaus. "Fritz Fischer und der deutsche Protestantismus." *Zeitschrift für neuere Theologiegeschichte* 10.2 (2003): 224–252.

Gruber, Ruth Ellen. *Virtually Jewish: Reinventing Jewish Culture in Europe.* Berkeley: The University of California Press, 2002.

Guardini, Romano. "Verantwortung: Gedanken zur jüdischen Frage. Eine Universitätsrede." *Hochland* 44 (1952): 481–493.

Guldi, Jo and David Armitage. *The History Manifesto.* Cambridge, UK: Cambridge University Press, 2014.

Haar, Ingo. *Historiker im Nationalsozialismus: Deutsche Geschichtswissenschaft und der 'Volkstumskampf' im Osten.* Göttingen: Vandenhoeck & Ruprecht, 2002.

Heins, Volker M. *Der Skandal der Vielfalt: Geschichte und Konzepte des Multikulturalismus.* Frankfurt on the Main: Campus, 2013.

Herz, Manuel. "Institutionalized Experiment: The Politics of 'Jewish Architecture' in Germany." *Jewish Social Studies* 11.3 (2005): 58–66.

Heschel, Susannah. "Jewish Studies as Counterhistory." *Insider/Outsider: American Jews and Multiculturalism.* Ed. David Biale et al. Berkeley: The University of California Press, 1998. 101–115.

Hoffmann, Christhard. "Juden und Judentum in der bundesdeutschen Geschichtswissenschaft." *Zeitschrift für Geschichtswissenschaft* 43 (1995): 677–686.

Jarausch Konrad H. and Martin Sabrow, eds. *Verletztes Gedächtnis. Erinnerungskultur und Zeitgeschichte im Konflikt.* Frankfurt on the Main: Campus, 2002.

Jeismann, Michael, ed. *Mahnmal Mitte: Eine Kontroverse.* Cologne: Dumont, 1999.

Jury citation. Pritzker Prize for Architecture. Laureate 2009. http://www.pritzkerprize.com/2009/jury (last accessed March 26, 2015).

Kammen, Michael. *The Mystic Chords of Memory. The Transformation of Tradition in American Culture.* New York: Knopf, 1991.

Kateb, George. *The Inner Ocean: Individualism and Democratic Culture.* Ithaca: Cornell University Press, 1992.

Kateb, George. "Can Cultures be Judged? Two Defenses of Cultural Pluralism in Isaiah Berlin's Work." *Patriotism and Other Mistakes.* New Haven: Yale University Press, 2006. 361–383.

Kauders, Anthony. *Unmögliche Heimat. Eine deutsch-jüdische Geschichte der Bundesrepublik.* Stuttgart: DVA, 2007.

Klein, Kerwin Lee. *Frontiers of Historical Imagination. Narrating the European Conquest of Native America.* Berkeley: The University of California Press, 1997.

Kollenseher, Max. "Minderheitsrechte, nationale, jüdische," *Jüdisches Lexikon.* vol. 4, part 1, Berlin: Jüdischer Verlag, 1927. 192–201.

Koselleck, Reinhart, ed. "'Space of Experience' and 'Horizon of Expectation': Two Historical Categories." *Futures Past: On the Semantics of Historical Time.* New York: Columbia University Press, 2004. 255–275.

Kracauer, Siegfried. *History: Last Things before the Last.* Oxford: Oxford University Press, 1969. (Reprinted, Princeton: Markus Wiener, 1995).

Lappin, Elena. "The Man with Two Heads." *Granta* 66 (1999): 7–65.

Lavi, Shai J. "'The Jews are Coming.' Vengeance and Revenge in Post-Nazi Europe." *Law, Culture and the Humanities* 1.3 (2005): 282–301.

Lehrer, Erica T. *Jewish Poland Revisited: Heritage Tourism in Unquiet Places.* Bloomington: Indiana University Press, 2013.

Leoni, Claudio. "Peter Zumthor's 'Topography of Terror.'" *Architectural Research Quarterly* 18.2 (2014): 110–122.

Libson, Gideon. "Hidden Worlds and Open Shutters: S.D. Goitein Between Judaism and Islam." *The Jewish Past Revisited. Reflections on Modern Jewish Historians*. Ed. David N. Myers and David B. Ruderman. New Haven: Yale University Press, 1998. 163–198.

Liepach, Martin, ed. *Jüdische Geschichte im Schulbuch: Eine Bestandsaufnahme anhand aktueller Lehrwerke*. Göttingen: V&R Unipress, 2014.

MacGregor, Neil. *Germany: Memories of a Nation*. London: Lane, 2014.

McCarthy, Margaret. Putting Stones in Place: Anne Duden and German Acts of Memory." *The German Quarterly* 77.2 (2004): 210–229.

Meier, Christian. *Das Gebot zu vergessen und die Unabweisbarkeit des Erinnerns: Vom öffentlichen Umgang mit schlimmer Vergangenheit*. Munich: Siedler, 2010.

Meijknecht, Anna. "Minority Protection System between World War I and World War II." *Max Planck Encyclopedia of Public International Law*, last updated: October 2010 (Oxford Public International Law; http://opil.ouplaw.com) (last accessed March 26, 2015).

"Minderheiten, nationale." *Meyers Lexikon*. 7th edition. Leipzig: Bibliographisches Institut, 1928. 498–499.

Myers, David N. *Re-Inventing the Jewish Past: European Jewish Intellectuals and the Zionist Return to History*. Oxford: Oxford University Press, 1996.

Nagel, Thomas. *The View from Nowhere*. New York, Oxford: Oxford University Press, 1986.

Naumann, Michael. "Ohne Antwort, ohne Trost: Das Holocaust-Mahnmal in Berlin ist ein rätselhaftes Monument." *Die Zeit: Wochenzeitung für Politik, Wirtschaft, Wissen und Kultur*, no. 19, 4 May 2005.

Nora, Pierre. "Between Memory and History: Les lieux de mémoire." *Representations* 26 (1989): 7–25.

Novak, David. *The Jewish Social Contract: An Essay in Political Theology*. Princeton: Princeton University Press, 2005.

Offe, Sabine. "Sites of Remembrance? Jewish Museums in Contemporary Germany." *Jewish Social Studies* 3.2 (1997): 77–89.

Olick, Jeffrey K. *In the House of the Hangman: The Agonies of German Defeat, 1943–1949*. Chicago: University of Chicago Press, 2005.

Oxford English Dictionary, Online edition (http://dictionary.oed.com) (last accessed on March 26, 2015); draft revisions March 2009.

Pingel, Falk. "Religionsgründer-verfolgte Minderheit-Fixpunkt im 'Krisenherd Nah-Ost': Juden und jüdische Geschichte in bundesdeutschen Geschichtsbüchern." *Internationale Schulbuchforschung* 11 (1989): 229–254.

Pinto, Diana. *A New Jewish Identity for Post-1989 Europe*. Policy paper / JPR 1996, no. 1. London: Institute for Jewish Policy Research, 1996.

Rahden, Till van. "Jews and the Ambivalences of Civil Society in Germany, 1800 to 1933." *Journal of Modern History* 77 (2005): 1024–1047.

Rahden, Till van. "Clumsy Democrats: Moral Passions in the Federal Republic." *German History* 29 (2011): 485–504.

Rapaport, Lynn. *Jews in Germany after the Holocaust. Memory, Identity, and Jewish-German Relations*. Cambridge, UK: Cambridge University Press, 1997.

Rauterberg, Hanno. "Schutzbauten des Widerstands: Ein Gespräch mit dem Schweizer Architekten Peter Zumthor." *Die Zeit: Wochenzeitung für Politik, Wirtschaft, Wissen und Kultur*, no. 45, 31 October 2001.

Raz-Krakotzkin, Amnon. "Geschichte, Nationalismus, Eingedenken." *Jüdische Geschichtsschreibung heute: Themen, Positionen, Kontroversen.* Ed. Michael Brenner and David N. Myers. Munich: C.H. Beck, 2002. 181–206.

Raz, Joseph, ed. "Multiculturalism: a Liberal Perspective." *Ethics in the Public Domain. Essays in the Morality of Law and Politics.* Oxford: Oxford University Press, 1994. 155–176.

Resolutions adopted by the Second Plenary Assembly of the World Jewish Congress, Montreux, Switzerland, June 27th–July 6th, 1948. s.l., s.a. (Montreux, 1948).

Richarz, Monika. "Luftaufnahme – oder die Schwierigkeiten der Heimatforscher mit der jüdischen Geschichte." *Babylon: Beiträge zur jüdischen Gegenwart* 8 (1991): 27–33.

Ritter, Gerhard A. "50 Jahre Leo Baeck Institut. Probleme und Tendenzen der Erforschung der deutsch-jüdischen Geschichte seit dem Zweiten Weltkrieg." *Geschichtswissenschaft und Zeiterkenntnis: Von der Aufklärung bis zur Gegenwart.* Ed. Klaus Hildebrand et al. Munich: Oldenbourg, 2008. 585–595.

Rodgers, Daniel T., ed. *Cultures in Motion.* Princeton: Princeton University Press, 2014.

Rothstein, Edward. "In Berlin, Teaching Germany's Jewish History." *New York Times,* 1 May 2009.

Rupnow, Dirk. "Brüche und Kontinuitäten. Von der NS-Judenforschung zur Nachkriegsjudaistik." *Geisteswissenschaften im Nationalsozialismus. Das Beispiel der Universität Wien.* Ed. Mitchell Ash et al. Göttingen: V&R Unipress, 2010. 79–110.

Rupnow, Dirk. *Judenforschung im Dritten Reich: Wissenschaft zwischen Politik, Propaganda und Ideologie.* Baden-Baden: Nomos, 2011.

Rürup, Reinhard. "Jewish Emancipation and Bourgeois Society." *Leo Baecck Institute Yearbook* 14 (1969): 67–91.

Rürup, Reinhard. "Die Faszination der deutsch-jüdischen Geschichte. Eine neue Generation von Historikerinnen und Historikern in der Bundesrepublik." *LBI Information* 5/6 (1996): 92–95.

Schorsch, Ismar. *From Text to Context: The Turn to History in Modern Judaism.* Hanover: Brandeis University Press, 1994.

Schüler-Springorum, Stefanie. "The 'German Question': The Leo Baeck Institute in Germany." *Preserving the Legacy of German Jewry: A History of the Leo Baeck Institute, 1955–2005.* Ed. Christhard Hoffmann. Tübingen: Mohr Siebeck, 2005. 201–237.

Scott, Joan W. "Unanswered Questions." *American Historical Review* 113 (2008): 1422–1430.

Shore, Marci. "Tevye's Daughters: Jews and European Modernity." *Contemporary European History* 16 (2007): 121–135.

Simon, Richard B. et al. *Teaching Big History.* Berkeley: University of California Press, 2015.

Stanislawski, Michael. *Autobiographical Jews: Essays in Jewish Self-Fashioning.* Seattle: University of Washington Press, 2004.

Steinberg, Michael P., ed. "Grounds Zero: History, Memory, and the New Sacredness in Berlin and Beyond." Idem. *Judaism Musical and Unmusical.* Chicago: University of Chicago Press, 2007. 177–220.

Stern, Frank. *The Whitewashing of the Yellow Badge: Antisemitism and Philosemitism in Postwar Germany.* Oxford: Pergamon, 1991.

Stratton, Jon. "Punk, Jews, and the Holocaust – The English Story." *Shofar* 25.4 (2007): 124–149.

Subrahmanyam, Sanjay. "Connected Histories: Notes on a Reconfiguration of Early Modern Eurasia." *Modern Asian Studies* 31 (1997): 735–762.

Subrahmanyam, Sanjay. *Courtly Encounters: Translating Courtliness and Violence in Early Modern Eurasia*. Cambridge, MA: Harvard University Press, 2012.

Till, Karen E. *The New Berlin: Memory, Politics, Place*. Minneapolis: University of Minnesota Press, 2005.

Varon, Jeremy. *The New Life: Jewish Students of Postwar Germany*. Detroit: Wayne State University Press, 2014.

Wefing, Heinrich. "Holocaust-Mahnmal: So ist es gemeint." *Frankfurter Allgemeine Zeitung*, 108, 11 May 2005, 37.

Weissberg, Liliane. "Reflecting on the Past, Envisioning the Future: Perspectives for German-Jewish Studies." *Bulletin of the German Historical Institute* 35 (2004): 11–32.

Willms, Hermann. "Minderheitenrechte." *Politisches Handwörterbuch*. Ed. Paul Herre. Leipzig: Köhler, 1923. 2: 121–123.

Wirsching, Andreas. "Die Deutschen und ihre Geschichte." Idem. *Abschied vom Provisorium: Geschichte der Bundesrepublik Deutschland 1982–1990. Geschichte der Bundesrepublik Deutschland*. Munich: Deutsche Verlags-Anstalt, 2006. 6: 466–491.

Zipes, Jack. "The Contemporary German Fascination for Things Jewish: Toward a Jewish Minor Culture." *Reemerging Jewish Culture in Germany: Life and Literature after 1989*. Ed. Sander Gilman and Karen Remmler. New York: NYU Press, 1994. 15–45.

Zumthor, Peter. "Topographie des Terrors." *Peter Zumthor. 1990–1997: Bauten und Projekte*. Ed. Thomas Durisch. 2. Zurich: Scheidegger & Spiess, 2014. 2: 57–79.

Stefanie Schüler-Springorum
Non-Jewish Perspectives on German-Jewish History. A Generational Project?

Vergangenheitsbewältigung is not only one of those untranslatable German words, but also a very German success story, it seems. Let us take one prominent example, the so-called *Stolpersteine*, i.e., Stumbling Stones. The *Stolpersteine*, as is well known, is a commemorative project that was launched in the mid-1990s by artist Gunter Demnig. It involves creating a small concrete block and brass plaque, which is then mounted flush with the pavement in front of the last residence of a specific Jewish victim of Nazism, listing his or her personal data. Although some important individuals, such as Charlotte Knobloch, head of the Jewish community in Munich, voiced criticism, the project initiated a wave of local commitment, even competition (Hamburg: 4000 Stones!, Berlin 5000 Stones!) in more than 900 German towns and cities. Thus far, it has been expanded to fifteen European countries and to other groups of victims, such as "gypsies, those persecuted for political reasons, homosexuals, Jehovah's witnesses, and victims of euthanasia," in sum, more than 40,000 stones by now.[1] At the same time, numerous newspaper articles, some academic analysis, a documentary, and a smartphone app deal with the subject; most importantly, primarily lay historians under supervision of a local history workshop group, academic institutions, and engaged historians are conducting an impressive amount of biographical research. In Hamburg, for example, several groups have published a total of sixteen volumes with extensive biographical data on each individual victim, grouped according to the respective section of the city.[2] The emotional drive behind this impressive personal engagement is obvious: In these memorials, as it is stated on the webpage of Hamburg Stumbling Blocks: "The victims appear in word and image before us, and thus are saved from being forgotten."[3] At a large gathering on the occasion of the presentation of the volumes on Hamburg residents murdered under Nazism, one of the speakers went a step further and proudly declared: "Their intention was to annihilate these persons, and in that they failed!"[4] Obviously, they did not.

This emotional outburst is, however, a telling example of a phenomenon that historian Norbert Frei so aptly called "Guilt Pride." One can easily conclude that

---

1 http://www.stolpersteine.eu/ (last accessed on 1 April 2014).
2 http://www.hamburg.de/stolpersteine/; http://www.stolpersteine-berlin.de/ (last accessed on 1 April 2014); see also Apel (2013); Schrader (2006, 173–181).
3 http://www.stolpersteine-hamburg.de (last accessed on 1 April 2014).
4 Personal experience of the author, Hamburg 2009.

the swelling wave of interest in the Holocaust in the last two decades is intimately linked to the psychological well-being of the non-Jewish majority living today in Germany, which, by means of remembering, is publicly distancing itself from the National Socialist past of its country and its families (Jureit and Schneider 2010). This, of course, is true of historians as well. On the one hand, they may look condescendingly at the unsophisticated "concerned laymen"; on the other hand, hiding behind the claim of "scientific objectivity," they themselves are not very keen on incisive (public) self-reflection about their own motives or the history-shaping context of their activity.

I would like to do the opposite and try to contextualize current interest in German-Jewish history. First, I shall look at the historical development of this interest, i.e., sketch a brief history of German-Jewish historiography in West Germany after 1945 and the role of the respective protagonists and their generational imprint.

Two things stand out in surveying the development of German-Jewish history *in* Germany after World War II and the Holocaust. First, the historiography of German Jews after 1945 retained a regional or local historical framework. A glance at the annual bibliography of the *Leo Baeck Yearbook* indicates that up to the present, this has been the central structural approach to German-Jewish history. This methodology contrasts starkly with that of Israeli, British, or American colleagues, for example, who, for the most part, pursue other perspectives and questions.

This German specificity, seemingly, derives from the period before 1933, namely to the long tradition of tracing the history of the Jewish communities, the *Gemeinden*, and of the *Landjudenschaften*, the territorial Jewish assemblies. Building on that very German historiographical tradition of *Landesgeschichte* – i.e., of Bavarian, Hessian, and Saxonian regional history, the scholarly German rabbis who in the nineteenth century began to write Jewish history placed it in a similar framework. They always wrote the history of their own *Gemeinde* or region. After 1945, when historians began, hesitantly and slowly, to reestablish German-Jewish history in the Federal Republic, they did so largely in the familiar institutional framework of the old regional history, soon to become somewhat old-fashioned (Buchholz 1998).

Second, it was mainly Jewish re-migrants in cooperation with a small number of engaged local intellectuals rather than professional university historians who launched these initial postwar initiatives in the 1950s and 60s. They then frequently linked up with the respective historical commissions and/or state archives in the area. Michael Brenner (2008, 207–223) has shown that in Bavaria, for example, Hans Lamm and Stefan Schwarz carried out valuable work on the history of the Jews in Bavaria and Munich, but they did not receive academic recognition for this in their lifetimes. Joseph Wulf similarly encountered difficulties while conducting research on National Socialism and attempting to establish a documentation center in the Wannsee Villa, the premises of the infamous conference. Distraught over the collapse of plans for such a center, he committed suicide in 1974. Several years ago, Nicolas Berg (2003) sketched Wulf's long, futile struggle for recognition from the guild of academic historians, and it took another decade until a biography of this pioneer of what was later to become *Täterforschung* was published (Kempter 2012). Shortly before his leap to death, Wulf wrote: "I have published eighteen books about the Third Reich, and they have had no effect. You can document everything to death for the Germans. There is a democratic regime in Bonn. Yet the mass murderers walk around free, live in their little houses, and grow flowers" (Kempter 2012, 384).

In Westphalia, by contrast, the development was more successful. After his remigration, Bernhard Brilling, the archivist of the former Breslau Jewish Community, in 1959 took over the direction of the Department for the History of German Jewry at the Protestant Institutum Delitzschianum at the University of Münster, under the direction of Karl Heinrich Rengstorff. There he was able to link up his own work with the established tradition of Westphalian regional history. We are indebted to him for salvaging extremely valuable archival materials and for his numerous early contributions to Jewish regional history of Westphalia, Silesia, and beyond (Honigmann 2004, 223–241). The documentary volume *Westfalia Judaica* (1967), which he edited with Helmut Richtering, was part of a trend in the early 1960s to document local or regional Jewish history in the institutional framework of ongoing local study groups and commissions. In this connection, researchers initially emphasized either the Middle Ages or the era of National Socialism, clearly equating Jewish history with the history of persecution.

Other newly-formed institutions included the Research Commission for the History of Frankfurt Jewry in 1961; the Historical Commission for the History of the Jews in Hessen in 1962; and in that same year, the Documentation Center for the Fate of Jews in Stuttgart. Only the ambitious exhibition "Monumenta Judaica," opened in 1963 in Cologne, aimed from its inception at presenting to an interested public "2000 Years of Jewish History and Culture of the Jews along the Rhine." In this case, too, only a few professional historians took part in preparing the extensive catalogue and handbook (Schilling 1963; Rohrbacher 2000, 164–176).

Whereas this project was very successful, most of the historical commissions and other institutes tended to exclude the public, in particular the first academic institution in the Federal Republic dealing exclusively with German-Jewish history, the Hamburg-based Institute for the History of German Jews. Here too, the initiative derived from re-migrants and local dignitaries with Jewish ancestry who had survived the "Third Reich" in mixed marriages. They campaigned vigorously at the end of the 1950s to have the former Hamburg Jewish Community Archive become the basis for a new research center. The orientation toward local history is a binding requirement in the Hamburg Institute's bylaws, even if its work now extends far beyond those local perimeters. Before the institute could be officially opened in 1966, however, it had to overcome its first scandal: The director designate, a theologian, was unable to take up his post because he turned out to have been a member of the SA and was still active in an organization that did missionary work among Jews. In order to avoid further problems, the Hamburg Senate in 1966 appointed a re-migrant from Israel as the institute's first director, Heinz Moshe Graupe, who had received a Ph. D. in philosophy in Berlin in 1932. In Hamburg, Graupe soon became embroiled in an ongoing dispute with his colleague at the neighboring institute, Werner Jochmann, director of the Research Center for the History of National Socialism in Hamburg.[5] Ostensibly about questions of content and probably also a matter of personal animosities, the controversy exposed a deeper issue lying below the surface, as the correspondence between Graupe and Jochmann reveals (Schüler-Springorum 2011). The sensitive question was: who had the authority for Jewish history in Germany? To whom did this history belong – the returning emigrants and survivors, who often dedicated themselves to this investigation as self-taught scholars – or the academically established, non-Jewish German professors such as Jochmann who were discovering this field via the history of antisemitism?

About the same time, in the mid-1960s, the Leo Baeck Institute (LBI) began establishing contacts in Germany in order to undertake its self-proclaimed task of writing a "Comprehensive History of German Jewry" (*Gesamtgeschichte des deutschen Judentums*). Forging such contacts were controversial debates at the Leo Back Institute at the time, and the initiative clearly came from the London branch of the LBI. Fearful of encountering those with a Nazi past, they carefully avoided the older generation and tried to set up cooperation with younger scholars instead. It is noteworthy that the London emigrants found it much easier to deal with non-Jewish German scholars than with Jews living on the soil of the perpetrators such as Lamm or Wulf. Another factor that doubtless played a role here was the respect among university-educated Jewish Germans for German academic qualifications, which most re-migrants lacked, or did not have to the same extent as their German colleagues. In Hamburg, the alignment was quite clear: the LBI used Jochmann as their contact while systematically excluding Graupe (Schüler-Springorum 2005).

---

5 Today: Research Center for Contemporary History – Forschungsstelle für Zeitgeschichte (FZH).

At the same time, the more senior German historians approached by the LBI did cooperate but clearly kept their distance. One of them, Werner Treue, described the reasons behind this reserved stance in a review:

> Questions pertaining to the Jews today [1952], whether political or historical, are for good reason taboo in Germany. Any attempt to deal with them stands in the shadow of the suffering that the Nazi regime inflicted on millions of Jews. And whoever, proceeding most cautiously, and with an ardor for reaching the truth, dares to look critically at some problem in Jewish history is constantly confronted by a dilemma: not only the looming prospect of being accused of adding a new antisemitism to the old one, but the danger of rendering a judgment where reserve and acceptance might seem a more proper response.[6]

You can also read these lines as a somewhat pretentious confession of the biographical bias of Treue, born in 1909. Indeed, there was need for a new generation – one ready to accept the Leo Baeck Institute's offer to cooperate and which then continued to conduct research on German-Jewish history. Among these researchers were the somewhat older Jochmann, Ernst Schulin (born 1929), Reinhard Rürup (born 1934), and Hermann Greive (born 1935). With the exception of Jochmann,[7] they belonged to a generation of historians who experienced Nazism as children or teenagers. They came to the university after World War II and then, in the words of Konrad Jarausch and Rüdiger Hohls, "were confronted with the catastrophic legacy of their parents and swore to do things better" (Jarausch and Hohls 2000, 37). Arriving at German-Jewish history via somewhat circuitous paths, they were united by a central question: *how was it possible, how could it happen*? In short, they basically were caught up in a confrontation with German society and its murderous facets. It is likewise no accident that the historians Reinhard Rürup and later Arno Herzig (born 1937) became involved in German-Jewish history through their engaged work in political education and a confrontation with contemporary antisemitism in the Federal Republic in the early 1960s.

They were most intrigued by the shipwreck of emancipation in the bourgeois era and the strength of antisemitism in the nineteenth century, that is, not so much the history of the Jews as such as the history of their civil equality or its lack, their deprivation of rights was foremost in their approach. On a personal level, they were also significantly influenced by the small number of re-migrants who had returned in the 1950s and 1960s to German universities and who, especially in Berlin, made a huge impression on the young students. In Berlin, a number of re-migrants active at the Free University Berlin were largely responsible for the establishment of the "Cultural History Section" within the Historical Commission

---

6 Quoted in Hoffmann (1995, 677).
7 For his biography, see: Schüler-Springorum (2004).

at the Friedrich Meinecke Institute. Despite its general title, the department dealt principally with Prussian and Berlin Jewish history.

One prominent figure in connection with German-Jewish history was Adolf Leschnitzer, formerly a high school teacher in Berlin and a staff worker at the *Reichsvertretung* under Nazism. In 1952, he began to journey every summer semester to Berlin as an honorary professor (he was thus not a re-migrant in the stricter sense). There, he had attracted a solid circle of some fifteen students, whom he deeply impressed with what one of them later described as his "dazzlingly fascinating" courses. Along with children of Jewish emigrants and survivors, such as Amos Funkenstein, Julius Schoeps, or Konrad Kwiet, non-Jewish Germans such as Monika Richarz and Stefi Jersch-Wenzel studied under him, doing their doctorates under his supervision.

Based on a unique mixture of academic learning, admiration, and awe for their respective life stories, Jewish emigrants and re-migrants exerted a considerable if not indispensable influence on this first small cohort of young, non-Jewish German scholars of German-Jewish History: They were looking, said Ernst Schulin, for "untainted paragons and concepts of value for a new orientation," and the remigrants, in their eyes, were "better, more trustworthy teachers" (Schüler-Springorum 2005, 214–215). Nevertheless, the influence of specific *German* historical traditions is noticeable in this first generation, too: almost all of them (with the exception of Monika Richarz [1974]) anchored their first studies on German-Jewish history in the framework of regional or *Landesgeschichte*. In 1964, for example, Stefi Jersch-Wenzel (1967 and 1978) submitted her dissertation on "Jewish Communal Administration in Prussian Cities in the First Half of the Nineteenth Century," followed by a habilitation thesis on the economic life of the Jewish and French minorities in pre-modern Berlin-Brandenburg. In 1966, Reinhard Rürup (1966) published an extensive study on the emancipation of the Jews in Baden, while Arno Herzig (1973) published his habilitation thesis in 1973 on Jewish emancipation in Westphalia.

The fact that almost half of those active in this early period were women testifies eloquently to the marginality for many years of this subfield of historiography in Germany. In the 1970s and 1980s, scholars did not deem Jewish history a specialty that was sufficiently 'serious' to advance a proper academic career. The women mentioned here (and to whom one should add the names of Ingrid Belke and Ursula Hüllbüsch) all began their academic trajectory outside the orbit of the universities, and they often remained stuck on the academic periphery, or they stayed on the margins for an extended period. They benefitted indirectly, however, from being able for many years to devote themselves exclusively to their 'favorite topics' in German-Jewish history. In contrast, their male colleagues, who in the 1970s received appointments as professors, necessarily dealt with German-

Jewish history as just one topic among many. The first chair for Jewish history and culture was established in Germany (by then 'united') only in 1997 in Munich. Consequently, in the 1970s and 1980s, the few interested professors devoted only a portion of their energy to German-Jewish historical research, especially to courses on such topics.

At the same time, the young historians, the cohort born in the mid-1930s, quite naturally absorbed the new stimulating approaches and postulates of social history, a current then developing in the Federal Republic, and modeled their own studies along the lines of this overarching 'new' paradigm. Nonetheless, given their topics, they actually remained a small marginal coterie within the guild of professional historians in the 1970s and early 1980s. In fact, it was social history, so long dominant in West Germany, which completely lost sight of German-Jewish history.

The cohorts of the 1940s and 50s, which we often group together somewhat clumsily under the rubric of the "generation of '68,'" are for all practical purposes absent from German-Jewish historiography, with one notable exception, Christhard Hoffmann, who, significantly, pursued his career in California and Norway. The 1968 generation focused on the working class and the revolution, structures and means of production, and class conflicts. National Socialism, yes – but interpreted as fascism. When in 1970, Joseph Wulf finally convinced the president of the Free University to establish his long-desired and fought for NS-documentation Center at the West Berlin University (after the Wannsee plans had failed), protests came from an unexpected direction: the students and the department for political research at the Free University: They objected to a center for this particular research interest, i.e., the persecution and genocide of the Jews, preferring a Center for Research on Fascism. In the face of this rebuff, the university canceled the project. Some years later, the head of the Jewish Community in Berlin, Heinz Galinski, with the support of Reinhard Rürup, then recently appointed professor at the Technical University in Berlin – took up the project again but with a tellingly different title. Finally opened in 1982 under the direction of another returning emigrant, Herbert A. Strauss, the institute was called the Center for Research on *Antisemitism*. Tragically, Joseph Wulf did not live to see this, nor did he witness the center developing into what had been *his* original intention, a center for Holocaust research, under Strauss' successor Wolfgang Benz (Bergmann, Hoffmann, and Rohrbaugh 2006).

Jewish history returned, albeit very slowly, to the flickering radar screen of historiography only in the late 1970s and early 1980s, when a new paradigm shift brought the everyday history of the 'people,' or the *Volk*, in terms of the parlance of that time, to the center of historical attention. In this context of *Alltagsgeschichte*, historians again began raising issues of identities and mentalities. They did so via the circuitous route of a familiar geographical-historical scale, namely local history (Heer and Ullrich 1989; Lüdtke 1989).

Detlef Siegfried has recently argued, underpinning his thesis with biographical evidence, that this turn among the younger generation of 1968 historians was also closely bound up with their shattered political dreams; it was specifically the ex-cadres of the diverse communist parties who now turned to concentrate locally on the history of the common man and woman (Siegfried 2008). The political left's need for a mooring, for being in a place, nourished the boom in local and dialect history in those years. Inspired by this political-moral impetus, an alternative *Heimatgeschichte*, local 'hometown and home region' history, generally spearheaded by local history workshops and by actively engaged teachers and archivists, started digging in situ where they were living. In the course of these local digs, the first excavated materials were, naturally, from the local Nazi past, right under their feet. Persecution and resistance, forced slave labor and concentration camps became the most frequent topics, seen through this highly local prism. In this context, interest also burgeoned in the earlier Jewish communities, the *Gemeinden*.

Here too, emphasis initially was clearly on the history of persecution. Attention turned to the Jewish community qua society usually only when it was necessary to describe the object of destruction, i.e., the former so-called "thriving Jewish community." Following the example of the small number of pioneers in German-Jewish historiography, early local and regional researchers, however, once again centered on the key epistemic question: "How could it happen?" The urge to gain an understanding of the mechanisms of the destruction of the Jews from the local perspective was salient. The historical microcosm became, as Monika Richarz (1991, 30) once put it, "the magic key for understanding the crime of destruction." Numerous studies reveal the importance of linking an interest in the local place – which nurtured a sense of identity – with an explicit pedagogical and political agenda that aimed at unearthing a repressed history. The goal was, by bringing this history to the surface, documenting it, and awakening public awareness of it, to prevent its potential re-occurrence: The associated slogans of this historiography were "never again" and "nip evil in the bud" – the old German dictum *"Wehret den Anfängen."*

From today's perspective, it seems easy to criticize or even ridicule many of these well-intentioned but hardly academically informed initiatives. It constituted, nevertheless, a formative period – which produced some of the leading teachers – that influenced and inspired a new generation of German researchers in German-Jewish history who were born roughly between 1960 and 1970. Not surprisingly, in light of the above-mentioned situation at the time, many of them framed their first approaches to German-Jewish history in the context of local history, which simultaneously, although not always, was the history of their hometowns.[8]

This venerable tradition notwithstanding, there are, in my eyes, potential pitfalls inherent in German-Jewish historiography *in* Germany that are exacerbated in connection with regional and local historical studies, where the *personal bonds* with a locality or region often still play a clear role in the choice of the topic. In such cases, a personal relationship to the object of investigation or sometimes linking it to and interweaving it with one's own family history reinforces the individual epistemic interest. This personal connection is even further intensified if, in twentieth century studies, direct contacts are established with Jewish survivors who can be interviewed and/or brought back to their old hometown in the framework of municipal programs to invite former Jewish residents back (often from abroad) for a visit (Nicou 2011).

The *moral-narcissistic surplus value* extracted from these encounters is often not perceived, let alone openly reflected upon. The local framework in this respect presents an especially slippery slope. Where else except before a local and familiar public can the public staging of one's own politically correct ego be so successful and have such a lasting impact on oneself? Throughout Germany, there are sufficient examples of these self-appointed local matadors, men and women, fighting against all resistance. Some are, no doubt, seriously deranged personalities and some come from non-academic fields outside the ranks of academic scholarship. My own generation's serious research, however, also badly needs this self-reflection because, as we all know, a "scientific scholarly approach" cannot protect you from the pitfalls of narcissism.

This surplus value has been *one* powerful motive for the engagement of this "middle" generation of non-Jewish historians of German-Jewish history. This became clear, for example, during a workshop on the problem of subject position organized a few years ago in the framework of the Graduate Collegium *Makom* at Potsdam University. A group of non-Jewish German colleagues there shared their very personal motives for their work (motives that were surprisingly similar). This group was quite small and relatively well acquainted with each other. Although the new cultural history has been vehemently advocating such self-reflection for years, in this subject area it remains a somewhat awkward, sensitive, perhaps even "unacademic" issue (Wierling 2003, 81–151). It was, therefore, probably not accidental that a colleague, the late Michael Zimmermann, who was working on the persecution of the Sinti and Roma during National Socialism rather than on German-Jewish history, confronted most impressively and honestly the role of a

---

8 For example (in the order of appearance): Schüler-Springorum (1996); Hopp (1997); Baumann (2000); van Rahden (2000).

German historian involved in oral history with survivors. No one from the field of German-Jewish history, or any other field, for that matter, has yet taken up his well-considered challenge (Zimmermann 1991).

In fact, this field has, however, clearly become more professionalized over the last thirty years within Germany as well. Again, the initial impulse came from the outside, i.e., from the London LBI that, together with Reinhard Rürup, established a German LBI network (*Wissenschaftliche Arbeitsgemeinschaft des Leo Baeck Instituts in der Bundesrepublik Deutschland* [WAG]) in 1989 with the explicit aim of promoting German-Jewish history in Germany. The above-mentioned generation, scattered all over Germany, welcomed the opportunity, from 1991 onwards, to discuss their dissertation projects in the regular *Doktorandencolloquia* that Rürup supervised together with various LBI members from abroad. We need not repeat here the oft-cited fame of these meetings – just read the acknowledgments in the dissertations written by this generation (Brenner 1999). It is worth mentioning certain points in order to understand subsequent changes. First, these colloquia offered then *young German scholars* of this "middle" generation their first encounter with the LBI and with Jewish studies abroad; it provided a personal and academic window to the world for these scholars, whose doctoral mentors, for the most part, were not specialists in Jewish history. Second, the group's rather small size enabled its protagonists to forge a specific group identity based on a certain structure of communication, professional networks, and sometimes personal friendships. Last but not least, a period of expansion in the 1990s, when various institutes or chairs in the field of Jewish studies were founded or enlarged (München, Leipzig, Potsdam, Frankfurt, Halle, Düsseldorf, to name just a few) facilitated their entry into institutions of higher learning.

Today, the expanded opportunities in Germany for study and training in the field of Jewish history assures the presence of an impressive number of younger German colleagues in the field who were able to acquire a solid education in Jewish studies. This generation, born in the second half of the 1970s and early 1980s, is far more cosmopolitan than its forerunners; they are equally at home in the American, Israeli, and German academic worlds, with most of them fluent at least in Hebrew and English.

Can we call this yet another German success story? I would like to offer two reasons why this is not quite so: the first has to do with the pitfalls of institutionalization in general and the second with the generational theme.

On the institutional level, we are paying a high price for the success of the enterprise, which could be called comfortable ghettoization or even self-ghettoization, in which Jewish studies has become an ever more specialized field. No one even thinks anymore about the old dream of the first generation – the Rürups and Richarz – of integrating it into general German history, of becoming ever more visible and more important *there* (Rürup 1990; Zimmermann 1990; Volkov 1996; The Future of German-Jewish Studies 2009). The phenomenon of segregation by specialization is, of course, not limited to Jewish studies. Gender studies is a case in point, and even in the sub-subfield of research on antisemitism, it is difficult to convince scholars from "general history" that this is not an exotic and highly specialized terrain but rather part and parcel of German (or Polish or American) history without which the latter cannot be properly understood.

Ultimately, the successful institutionalization has changed the generational profile: The younger generation experiences a certain feeling of saturation with regard to colloquia, exchanges, and networking *within* the field (not to be confused, to be sure, with better chances on the job market). At the same time, German-Jewish studies has become part of the establishment, highly appraised and acknowledged in both the academic and the public arenas. Unlike the situation in the 1980s and early 1990s, it, therefore, can no longer serve as a ground for generational conflict, for moral-political fights, or demonstrations. Future young rebels are more likely to be found in the newly established centers for Islamic studies in Germany, where they fight for the acceptance and integration of their field into the general departments of their respective universities. Engaging in Jewish studies *is* still a political issue in Eastern Europe, a kind of family issue, a demonstration of a certain moral standing; most obviously, some burning personal agendas lie behind the work of young colleagues from these countries. The consequences for our field in the long run remain to be seen. Certainly, this development has the potential to foster the break-up of national and identity frameworks, not only in German-Jewish studies, but also in a broader sense, as Till van Rahden argues in this volume.

At the same time, however, as professionals and as citizens, we should be careful not to lose the sense of belonging to a very specific academic field that was created in this country, Germany, by those whose family members and loved ones were murdered, and who themselves were forced to flee into exile. It was first and foremost *their* impetus and commitment that created institutions and networks and, only twenty years after the Holocaust, generously welcomed younger Germans to join them in discussions and research – an impetus that has born unpredictable rich fruits, whose flavor is certainly enriched by historiographical knowledge.

Bibliography

Apel, Linde. "Stumbling Blocks in Germany." *Rethinking History* 18.2 (2014): 181–194.
Baumann, Ulrich. *Zerstörte Nachbarschaften. Christen und Juden in badischen Landgemeinden, 1862–1940*. Hamburg: Dölling und Galitz Verlag, 2000.
Berg, Nicolas. *Der Holocaust und die westdeutsche Geschichtswissenschaft. Erforschung und Erinnerung*. Göttingen: Wallstein, 2003.
Bergmann, Werner and Christhard Hoffmann, Dennis E. Rohrbaugh, eds. *The Herbert A. Strauss Memorial Seminar at the Leo Baeck Institute*. March 29, 2006. Berlin: Metropol, 2006.
Brenner, Michael. "Perspektiven der Wissenschaftlichen Arbeitsgemeinschaft des Leo Baeck Instituts." *LBI Information* 8 (1999): 73–75.
Brenner, Michael. "Vergessene Historiker. Ein Kapitel deutsch-jüdischer Geschichtsschreibung der fünfziger und sechziger Jahre." *"Auch in Deutschland waren wir nicht wirklich zu Hause." Jüdische Remigration nach 1945*. Ed. Irmela von der Lühe, Axel Schildt, Stefanie Schüler-Springorum. Göttingen: Wallstein 2008.
Buchholz, Werner, ed. *Landesgeschichte in Deutschland. Bestandsaufnahme – Analyse – Perspektiven*. Paderborn: Schöningh, 1998.
"Discussion. The Future of German-Jewish Studies. " *Leo Baeck Institute Year Book* 54 (2009): 3–56.
Heer, Hannes and Volker Ullrich, eds. *Geschichtswerkstätten. Erfahrungen und Projekte der neuen Geschichtsbewegung*. Reinbek: Rowohlt, 1985.
Herzig, Arno. *Judentum und Emanzipation in Westfalen*. Münster: Aschendorff, 1973.
Hoffmann, Christhard. "Juden und Judentum in der bundesdeutschen Geschichtswissenschaft." *Zeitschrift für Geschichtswissenschaft* 43 (1995): 677–686.
Honigmann, Peter. "Das Projekt von Rabbiner Dr. Bernhard Brilling zur Errichtung eines jüdischen Zentralarchivs im Nachkriegsdeutschland." *Historisches Bewusstsein im jüdischen Kontext. Strategien – Aspekte – Diskurse*. Ed. Klaus Hödl. Innsbruck: Studien Verlag, 2004.
Hopp, Andrea. *Jüdisches Bürgertum in Frankfurt am Main im 19. Jahrhundert*. Stuttgart: Franz Steiner Verlag, 1997.
Jarausch, Konrad and Rüdiger Hohls. "Brechungen von Biographie und Wissenschaft, Interviews mit deutschen Historikern/innen der Nachkriegsgeneration." *Versäumte Fragen. Deutsche Historiker im Schatten des Nationalsozialismus*. Ed. idem. Stuttgart: Deutsche Verlags-Anstalt, 2000. 15–54.
Jersch-Wenzel, Stefi. *Jüdische Bürger und kommunale Selbstverwaltung in preußischen Städten 1808–1848*. Berlin: De Gruyter, 1967.
Jersch-Wenzel, Stefi. *Juden und "Franzosen" in der Wirtschaft des Raumes Berlin/Brandenburg zur Zeit des Merkantilismus*. Berlin: Colloquium-Verlag, 1978.
Jureit, Ulrike and Christian Schneider. *Gefühlte Opfer. Illusionen der Vergangenheitsbewältigung*. Stuttgart: Klett-Cotta, 2010.
Kempter, Klaus. *Joseph Wulf. Ein Historikerschicksal in Deutschland*. Göttingen: Vandenhoeck & Ruprecht, 2012.
Lüdtke, Alf, ed. *Alltagsgeschichte. Zur Rekonstruktion historischer Erfahrungen und Lebensweisen*. Frankfurt on the Main: Campus-Verlag, 1989.

Nicou, Lina. *Zwischen Imagepflege, moralischer Verpflichtung und Erinnerungen: das Besuchsprogramm für jüdische ehemalige Hamburger Bürgerinnen und Bürger.* Munich: Dölling und Galitz Verlag, 2011.

Rahden, Till van. *Juden und andere Breslauer. Die Beziehungen zwischen Juden, Protestanten und Katholiken in einer deutschen Großstadt von 1860 bis 1925.* Göttingen: Vandenhoeck & Ruprecht, 2000.

Richarz, Monika. *Der Eintritt der Juden in die akademischen Berufe. Jüdische Studenten und Akademiker in Deutschland 1678–1848.* Tübingen: Mohr Siebeck, 1974.

Richarz, Monika. "Luftaufnahme – Die Schwierigkeiten der Heimatforscher mit der jüdischen Geschichte." *Babylon* 8 (1991): 27–33.

Rohrbacher, Stefan. "Jüdische Geschichte." *Wissenschaft vom Judentum. Annäherungen nach dem Holocaust.* Ed. Michael Brenner. Göttingen: Vandenhoeck & Ruprecht, 2000. 164–176.

Rürup, Reinhard. "Die Judenemanzipation in Baden." *Zeitschrift für die Geschichte des Oberrheins* 114 (1966): 214–300.

Rürup, Reinhard. "An Appraisal of German-Jewish Historiography." *LBI Year Book* 35 (1990): 15–24.

Schilling, Konrad, ed. *Monumenta Judaica. 2000 Jahre Geschichte und Kultur der Juden am Rhein.* Cologne: Bachem, 1963.

Schrader, Ulrike. "Die 'Stolpersteine' oder Von der Leichtigkeit des Gedenkens." *Geschichte im Westen. Zeitschrift für Landes- und Zeitgeschichte* 21 (2006): 173–181.

Schüler-Springorum, Stefanie. *Die jüdische Minderheit in Königsberg/Pr. 1871–1945.* Göttingen: Vandenhoek & Ruprecht, 1996.

Schüler-Springorum, Stefanie. "Werner Jochmann und die deutsch-jüdische Geschichte." *Zeitgeschichte in Hamburg. Nachrichten aus der Forschungsstelle für Zeitgeschichte* 2 (2004): 14–20.

Schüler-Springorum, Stefanie. "The 'German Question'. The Leo Baeck Institute in Germany." *Preserving the Legacy of German Jewry. A History of the Leo Baeck Institute, 1955–2005.* Ed. Christhard Hoffmann. Tübingen: Mohr Siebeck, 2005. 201–235.

Schüler-Springorum, Stefanie. "Deutsch-jüdische Geschichte in Hamburg." *100 Jahre Geschichtswissenschaft in Hamburg.* Ed. Rainer Nicolaysen, Axel Schildt. Berlin: Dietrich Reimer Verlag, 2011. 253–269.

Siegfried, Detlef. "Die Rückkehr des Subjekts: Gesellschaftlicher Wandel und neue Geschichtsbewegung um 1980." *Geschichte und Geschichtsvermittlung: Festschrift für Karl Heinrich Pohl.* Ed. Olaf Hartung and Katja Köhr. Bielefeld: Verlag für Regionalgeschichte, 2008. 125–146.

Volkov, Shulamit. "Reflections on German Jewish History. A Dead End or a New Beginning?" *LBI Year Book* 41 (1996): 309–320.

Wierling, Dorothee. "Oral History." *Aufriss der Historischen Wissenschaft: Neue Themen und Methoden der Geschichtswissenschaft.* Ed. Michael Maurer. Stuttgart: Reclam, 2003. 81–151.

Zimmermann, Michael. "'Jetzt' und 'Damals' als imaginäre Einheit. Erfahrungen in einem lebensgeschichtlichen Projekt über die nationalsozialistische Verfolgung von Sinti und Roma." *Bios* 4 (1991): 225–242.

Zimmermann, Moshe. "Jewish History and Jewish Historiography. A Challenge to Contemporary German Historiography." *LBI Year Book* 35 (1990): 35–52.

Matthias Morgenstern
Rabbi S. R. Hirsch and his Perception of Germany and German Jewry

Samson Raphael Hirsch (1808–1888), the "champion of Orthodoxy" in nine-teenth-century Judaism in Germany, was, as Robert Liberles has noted, "a puzzle for his contemporaries and has remained so for later scholars seeking to unravel the complex components of his personality" (Liberles 1985, 113).[1] Contemporary and later scholarly literature paint an inconsistent picture of Hirsch and his work: One side portrays him as a radical's radical, an uncompromising and militant defender of Orthodox principles, and an advocate of Orthodox independence, hence segregation. This view, therefore, holds Hirsch responsible for the orga-nizational division of the Jews in Germany in the nineteenth century (Lichtheim 1951, 37). Another side calls him a reformer, a modernizer, and revolutionary, or, at least, "the most progressive leader of German Orthodoxy" (Liberles 1985, 113). His contemporaries and later researchers perceived underlying tensions in his character – in his life and work, acceptance of moderate reforms in synagogue service[2] coexisted with fierce opposition to reform in other spheres. Cultural openness under the motto of *Torah im derekh eretz* existed on the one side, and a grim battle in the arena of congregational politics – the Orthodox fight for orga-nizational independence from the larger Jewish community in Frankfurt, the famous *Frankfurt secession dispute* – prevailed on the other. He fought for civic and political rights during the 1848 revolution in Moravia, which seemed to make him a liberal on the one hand; in his dealings with religious affairs, he insisted on scrupulous observance of the norms of the *Shulhan Arukh* as he understood them on the other.[3] How then, does Hirsch's attitude toward Germany and his perception of German Jewry, including its task in history, fit into this contradict-ing picture?

The question of his relationship to Germany and German culture is part of the riddle. His "deeply felt attachment to German culture and his political loyalty to

---

1 I have discussed the diverse and contradictory features of Hirsch's image in Morgenstern (2002, 108–109).

2 Hirsch advocated a well-regulated synagogue service and pleaded in favor of sermons in the vernacular; during his time as Landesrabbiner in Oldenburg, he was also willing to leave out the Kol nidre prayer in the Yom Kippur service; cf. also Haberman (1998, 76).

3 Elsewhere, I have tried to show that the Hirschian separatist principle and Hirsch's cultural openness under the rubric of *Torah im derekh eretz* are not contradictory but part and parcel of one comprehensive strategy of Jewish self-assertiveness in the Frankfurt am Main context (Mor-genstern 2001, 14–28).

the German land" (Liberles 1985, 133) gives reason to regard him, from a Jewish point of view, as an assimilated middle-of-the-roader and accommodationist theologian who retooled Judaism as a "religion" in the Western European sense and did away with all Jewish nationalism, indeed all ethnic ties (Japhet 1948, 105–106).[4] At the same time, Hirsch consistently employed the language of Jewish nationhood, and he was either praised or criticized for his "latent nationalism" (Thieberger 1919/1920, 565) or even his "extreme religious nationalism" (Rosenbloom 1962, 238).[5]

In order to understand Hirsch´s perception of German Jewry, we must first compose a picture of Hirsch's perception of Germany and also of his understanding of himself as a Jewish leader working for his cause in the German-speaking countries. As Hirsch never addressed either of these topics openly and directly, we have to look for indirect indications in his oeuvre. His Biblical commentaries, a treasure trove full of – albeit never explicit – allusions to contemporary events can reward our search.[6]

1 Germany as "fatherland, birthplace and paternal home"

In his commentary on Genesis 12:1, published in 1867, Hirsch refers to God's telling the Patriarch Abraham to leave his country and go unto a land that He will show him. In his remarks on this text, the author – with reflections on the phonetic shape of the Hebrew words, a kind of etymology or pseudo-etymology typical of his style – surprisingly does not focus on the land that God promised to the Patriarch and later gave to the Israelites. Instead, he starts by mentioning the "land" that Abraham was leaving: "ארץ, מולדת and בית together form the soil

---

4 Cf. Gershom Scholem's remarks on Hirsch ("bourgeois accommodation of an orthodox kind," "ghastly accommodation theology") in his critique of Isaac Breuer's novel *Der Neue Kusari* (Scholem 1971, 328 and 329). (Originally in "Politik der Mystik," *Jüdische Rundschau*, 17 July 1934, 1–2).
5 Rosenbloom quotes Zvi Kurzweil. For Hirsch's emphasis on Jewish nationhood, see his Biblical commentary on Ex. 6:7 (S. R. Hirsch, The Pentateuch 2, 67): "... [I will] take you to be My people... a people, a Nation" (= Der Pentateuch 2, 53). Hirsch's delicate distinction between the German terms *Nation* and *Nationalität* are beyond the scope of this essay.
6 Scholarly literature on Hirsch uses his Biblical exegesis in order to decipher his attitude toward contemporary events and contemporary life. As he did not state his views directly, scholars deduce them from subtle remarks and allusions, which leads to often controversial results. Cf., for example, Liberles (1985, 194–195); Morgenstern (2002, 146); Tasch (2011) (cf. my review in: *Frankfurt Jewish Studies Bulletin* 37 (2011/12): 161–165). See also Ganzel (2010).

out of which the personality of people grows. אֶרֶץ, the country, the nationality, with all the special bodily, mental and moral characteristics which it gives, (אֶרֶץ, as our country, is אֶרֶס, to which our whole being is "married", עֶרֶשׂ, the cradle in which we grow to life... אֶרֶץ as the earth is our "cradle" and over it is שָׁמַיִם, our שָׁם, "there," our future (Hirsch 1973, 223).[7]

Although Hirsch only hints at the reason for this apparent shift of interest, it seems clear that his decision to emphasize the land where Abraham was born, and not the Promised Land, reflects the commentator's – and his readers' – relationship to the land where they were living, Germany:

> We have mentioned these thoughts innate in the Hebrew language to realise how deeply and intimately even our very language feels and values the worth of one's fatherland and birthplace. It is certainly not meant to be any belittleing of this factor if the planting of the first Jewish germ demanded forsaking fatherland, birth-place and paternal home. It is rather just the appreciation of these factors wherein lies the greatness of the isolation demanded there. This demand itself placed Abraham in the completest contrast to the ruling tendency of his age (Hirsch 1973, 224).[8]

This observation fits in with the widely held understanding of Hirsch and his writings as *typically German*. In fact, this perception applies not only to Hirsch himself and his oeuvre but also to his independent Orthodox congregation in Frankfurt am Main, the *Israelitische Religionsgesellschaft*. Similarly, the tendency has been to regard German-Jewish Neo-orthodoxy as a whole as the most typically Teutonic branch of modern Judaism.

Undeniably, Hirsch's life and work bore Germanic traits. Indeed, in the later decades of the nineteenth century, it was common to relate some characteristic features of his biography to central moments in contemporary German history.[9] He was born in Hamburg, the city in which, on 18 October 1818, the fifth anniversary of the Leipzig "Battle of the Nations," a modern synagogue service with a German-language sermon and an organ had been instituted. The young Hirsch witnessed his family's experiences in their fight against the local Reform movement (Liberles 1985, 115).

Forty-five years later, on 18 October 1868, on the fiftieth anniversary of the *Völkerschlacht*, when Hirsch was rabbi of the segregationist orthodox *Religions-*

---

7 The German original is in Hirsch (1867, 183[on Gen. 12: 1]); on Hirsch's relationship to the land of Israel, see Morgenstern (2014, 235–239).

8 The German original is in Hirsch (1867, 184); Hirsch's interpretation here differs considerably from that of his grandson Isaac Breuer who, in his novel *The New Kuzari* (1934), focuses on the departure and on the country that the Patriarch *is going* to; cf. Isaac Breuer (1934, 149–150).

9 I have dealt with this perception of Hirsch in my *From Frankfurt to Jerusalem* (2002, 141–147).

gesellschaft in Frankfurt, at a public appearance, he linked the German national fight for freedom with his own stance as an Orthodox rabbi facing the assaults of what he called "non-Judaism," i.e., the reformers within the Frankfurt Jewish community (Hirsch 1883/84, 41–56).[10] Hirsch's address, delivered in the synagogue of his Frankfurt congregation, was greeted as the best example of his German patriotism; its reception equaled that of his famous *Schillerrede*, delivered four years earlier on the hundredth university of the German poet Friedrich Schiller (1759–1805) (Hirsch 1912, 6: 308–321).[11] In the decades after the unification of imperial Germany in 1871, the Orthodox press in Germany emphasized a certain ideological closeness between the German-Jewish Orthodox movement led by Hirsch and Bismarck and his work.[12]

Typically German, albeit in another way, were his endeavors in the years before being appointed rabbi in Frankfurt. As *Landesrabbiner* of Moravia and Austrian Silesia (1847–1851), Hirsch lobbied for a reorganization of the Jewish congregational system. His deeply traditional Orthodox opponents there, who found his measures too radical, however, criticized as excessively bureaucratic his community-organizing endeavors, which were combined with demands for punctuality and strictness (Miller 2001, 390; Hildesheimer/Morgenstern 2013, 74–79).[13] The same typically German attribute applied to Hirsch's emphasis on studying the Hebrew Bible – the entire Hebrew Scriptures – rather than mainly or only the Talmud, which had been the usual practice among religious Jews until then.

---

10 Cf. p. 55: "Alles Göttliche läßt nicht mit sich spielen. Es verbrennen sich alle sicherlich die Finger die unter der Maske des Rechts die Gewalt, unter der Maske der Freiheit die Knechtung anstreben; eben so sicher aber auch die, die unter der Maske des Judenthums das Nichtjudenthum pflegen, die die Thora in den Arm nehmen und sie hochaufheben, und doch dabei im Herzen sprechen: Mit diesem alten Gesetz kommt man nicht hinein in die neue Zeit und nicht fort in derselben." (Divine things cannot be played with. All those will definitively have their fingers burnt who, under the mask of justice, seek violence, under the mask of freedom slavery; just like those who under the mask of Judaism cultivate Non-Judaism, who take the Torah into their arms and elevate it, but say in their hearts: With this old law one cannot enter the new era and one cannot make progress in it.) Hirsch continues, referring to "an admonishment for our human dignity (unsere Menschenwürde) and for our civil duties (unsere Bürgerpflichten), but also for our Jewish task, which is united to our human and civil duties in one consecration (unsere jüdische Aufgabe, die ja unsere Menschen- und Bürgerpflichten in Einer Weihe umfaßt)." For Hirsch's German patriotism, see Schiller (5749/1989, 21–25).
11 For the English translation of the *Schillerrede*, cf. Shapiro (2008/09, 174–185).
12 Cf. Morgenstern (2002, 144–147).
13 Miller (2011, 189) contrasts Hirsch´s interventionist approach regarding communal affairs to his political struggle. He refers to the difficulties Hirsch encountered in Nikolsburg that caused him considerable frustration and led to his surprising departure from his position in Moravia only four years after he had been greeted there and welcomed as a messiah.

His fight for secession within the Frankfurt community, which pitted him against the Würzburg Rabbi Seligmann Bär Bamberger in the 1870s, followed a similar pattern. The issue concerned the law requiring all Jews in the city of Frankfurt to belong to the local community and pay taxes to it. Referring to the obligation of Orthodox Jews in Frankfurt to contribute financially to institutions run by the larger community that did not operate according to the Halakhah, Hirsch maintained that this situation entailed "the harshest moral constraint [...] that has ever been perpetrated by the state against human conscience" (Hirsch 1912, 4: 244).[14] The rabbi welcomed the state's adoption in 1876 of the Prussian secession law, which permitted Jews from the Frankfurt liberal main Jewish community to secede without relinquishing their ties to Judaism altogether (Morgenstern 2002, 144–147). Beyond the German borders, this entire issue, which to this day touches upon the legal relationship between state and religion in Germany, was and continues to be hardly understandable.

Even more hard to grasp was the *Torah im derekh eretz* slogan that Hirsch had brought to particular prominence with his educational program and its realization in the Frankfurt *Realschule*. This motto, taken from Pirkei avot 2:2 ("excellent is the study of Torah together with a worldly occupation"), called for combining Torah and secular culture, placing "religious and secular studies on the same footing, giving them an equal role in the education of the child" (Haberman 1998, 77). This motto's strong association with Hirsch and his Frankfurt congregation meant that it was soon seen as reflecting a *typically German* issue. Particularly in Eastern Europe, this close association had a negative effect on its influence and propagation because Orthodox circles viewed German culture as a danger.[15] German "cultural orthodoxy" was far from uncontroversial. When twentieth century religious Zionists in the State of Israel utilized Hirsch's educational concepts, they did so with conspicuous embarrassment or avoided mentioning the original German context of these concepts (Mordechai Breuer 1996, 86).[16]

---

14 Cf. Morgenstern (2002, 141).

15 This perspective gained new acceptance among large segments of the East European Orthodox after World War II and the Holocaust. The historian Mordechai Breuer (1996, 85–86) recalls the first public address in Jerusalem given by Itche Meyer Lewin, then president of Agudat Israel in Poland, after his dramatic escape from German-occupied Poland to Palestine. Quoting a Biblical verse and referring to a talmudical passage, Lewin then said: "Now we must realize that all the achievements of German culture and civilization, which some of us thought were gifts of hesed [i.e., mercy], are nothing but sin and crime. Therefore, let us turn our backs on all non-Jewish culture. Nothing is left to us but the four cubits of Torah." For discussions on Hirsch's legacy in contemporary Orthodox Judaism, see http://haemtza.blogspot.co.il/2013/12/rabbi-samson-raphael-hirsch-ztzl.html#disqus_thread (last accessed 31 December 2013).

16 On the reception of *Torah im derekh eretz* in the State of Israel, see Stern (1987).

2 Hirsch's links to foreign countries

Hirsch's own *Germanness* and that of his oeuvre, however – at least insofar as his self-understanding is concerned – is a debatable question. First, it is worth noting that Hirsch had lived and worked outside of Germany, as Landesrabbiner of Moravia in Nikolsburg, before he came to the somewhat central city of Frankfurt in 1851. Although his stay in Moravia was short, his experience in the southeastern part of Europe was a decisive moment in his life. In the preceding years, from 1841 to 1847, he had officiated as *ostfriesischer Landesrabbiner* in Emden. That territory belonged to the Kingdom of Hannover, which until 1837, under the reigns of King George IV and King William IV, had been under British Regency. It is understandable that, during this time, Hirsch applied for the position of Chief Rabbi of the British Empire in London,[17] a position that was finally awarded to Rabbi Dr. Nathan Marcus Adler of Hannover. The journal *Der Orient* (no. 37, 10 September 1844, 282) reported that Hirsch was the only one among the four leading rabbinical candidates – all of whom were Germans: Nathan Adler (Hannover), Benjamin Hirsch Auerbach (Darmstadt), and Dr. Hirsch Hirschfeld (Wollstein) – to deliver his application in English (Hildesheimer/Morgenstern 2013, 61).[18] In nineteenth-century Germany, in this respect, Hirsch was an exception, and it was definitely not his lack of linguistic skills that hindered him from receiving the London position.

In 1860, only nine years after he had started to officiate as rabbi of the independent Orthodox *Israelitische Religionsgesellschaft* in Frankfurt, the congregation that later generations regard as his life's work, Hirsch surprisingly seems to have been willing again to leave Germany in order to accept a position as Chief Rabbi in Amsterdam. In the Dutch capital, the Jewish congregation was looking for a leader that, on the one hand, could enjoy the confidence of its Orthodox members ("enerzijds [...] vertrouwen genoot van de orthodoxie"), and on the other, would be able to deal with the representatives of the liberal bourgeoisie of the city ("anderzijds [...] voldoende gezag kan doen gelden ook op de ver van de kern afstaande intellectuelen en andere exponenten van het liberale burgerdom") (Meijer 1963, 60).[19] From his time as chief rabbi in neighboring Emden

---

17 Cf. Hildesheimer/Morgenstern (2013, 61).

18 This little detail may be emblematic of Hirsch's openness, which paved the way for his influence among Jews in the Anglo-Saxon world and even beyond the borders of Orthodoxy. For the impression Hirsch made on Kaufmann Kohler (1843–1926), who was Hirsch's student in his youth and after his emigration to North America became the president of the Hebrew Union College, see Haberman (1998, 73–102).

19 Cf. *Israelit*, no. 19, 11 October, 1860, 243; no. 22, 24 October, 1860, 263–264; cf. Hildesheimer/Morgenstern (2013, 114, 163, 168).

(1841–1847), Hirsch had been aware of the Jews' situation in the Netherlands, and he had previously traveled to Amsterdam. After an earlier visit to the Netherlands as a "wandering Jew," Hirsch delivered a literary report on his experiences, pointing out that part and parcel of any rabbinic endeavor in that country would be the Jewish leader's ability to deliver words of "תוכחה, מוסר und תורה" (rebuke, ethics, and Torah) in "gebildeter, ansprechender Nationalsprache" (Hirsch 1854/1855, 276), hence in Dutch.[20] Although Hirsch did not obtain the appointment as the "Opperrabbinaat" (Meijer 1963, 62), the community esteemed him sufficiently to make him an honorary member of the Amsterdam congregation (Brasz 2012, 80).[21] The Amsterdam rabbinate, however, was important enough for Hirsch to recommend his favorite son-in-law, Joseph Guggenheimer, husband of his daughter Sarah Hirsch (1834–1909), at that time rabbi in Stuhlweißenburg (Hungary), for this position (Meijer 1963, 62).

In all those years, Hirsch maintained his activities outside of Germany. It is noteworthy that his works were sufficiently relevant for Eastern European Jewish readers to be translated into Yiddish and Hebrew (Hildesheimer/Morgenstern 2013, 272–275).[22] Hirsch seemed very interested – because of his Moravian experience and his family ties with neighboring Hungary – in developments in the Austro-Hungarian Empire. His outreach to Hungarian Jews did not remain unnoticed. The reformer Leopold Löw (1811–1875), chief rabbi in Szegedin, polemicized against Hirsch in his Hungarian monthly and later weekly journal *Ben Chananja* (published in German). In his article under the title "Frankfurt und Ofen-Pest" (*Ben Chananja*, no. 17, 1867), he compared Hirsch to the Babylonian Rabbi Yehuda ben Bathira (and Hungarian Jewry to Jerusalem):

> Wie einst R. Jehuda b. Bathira, sein Netz über Jerusalem ausgebreitet hielt, wiewol er selbst in der am Eufrath liegenden Stadt Nisibis seinen Wohnsitz hatte', so hält die am Main resi-

---

20 See his article *Aus der Mappe eines wandernden Juden* (1854/1855), where he gives an account of his visit to Amsterdam one year before. It is, however, unlikely, that Hirsch himself spoke Dutch as most Dutch Jews spoke (or understood) German. My thanks to Chaya Brasz, Jerusalem, for her remarks on this topic and sharing her point of view.
21 According to Brasz (2012, 81), Hirsch was also invited to teach at the Orthodox Rabbinical Seminary (*Nederlandsch-Israëlitisch Seminarium*) in order to preserve it as an independent institution that would still be recognized by the Dutch Ministry of Education. It was not possible, however, to realize this offer, possibly because Hirsch (pace Brasz) had no doctorate. The entire affair seems to have embarrassed his Frankfurt followers, who maintained the strictest silence in this matter. Perhaps in the context of this offer, the first biography of Hirsch was published in the Netherlands by T. Tal (1893) (German translation: Samson Raphael Hirsch. Vortrag, in: Bibliothek des Jüdischen Volksfreundes, Teil 6. Der denkende Jude, Köln 1914).
22 Cf. *Die jüdische Presse*, no. 11, 1890, concerning the translation of Hirsch's *Nineteen Letters* and *Horeb* into Hebrew.

> dirende rabbinische Reaktion ihr Netz über das ungarische Israel ausgebreitet. Ja, sie ist
> eifrigst beflissen, ihr mesopotamisches Vorbild an Rührigkeit und Energie zu übertreffen
> (Hildesheimer/Morgenstern 2013, 159).[23]

The charge from "the left" that Hirsch was trying to manipulate Hungarian Jews received backing, paradoxically enough, "from the right." Akiva Yosef Schlesinger (1838–1922),[24] a disciple of the ultra-Orthodox Hungarian rabbis Samuel Benjamin Sofer (the *Ksav Sofer*) and Moshe Shik (the *Maharam Shik*), seems to have had Hirsch, among others, in mind when he warned his followers about emissaries that were sent from Germany "to Hungary in order to perform, in the mask of honest people, deeds of love, but (in reality only) for the purpose of destroying our country (Lengyel 2012, 39).[25]

In this context, it is remarkable that Hirsch's opponents "from the right" and "from the left" did not accuse him of some kind of German "imperialism" – promoting the German language and German-Jewish culture. On the contrary, they contended that he encouraged his Hungarian followers to study and use the language of their home. In the article "Hungarica," Löw ridiculed Hirsch's plea for the *Hungarian* language, combining attacks on Hirsch with mocking his col-

---

23 "As once Rabbi Yehuda ben Bathira spread out his net over Jerusalem, although his abode was in Nisibis on the Euphrates, so the rabbinic reaction domiciled in Frankfurt on the Main has spread its net over Hungarian Israel. Yes, the Frankfurters are enthusiastic and keen to overtake their Mesopotamian example in activity and energy." The quote was from the Babylonian Talmud (b. Pes 3b).

24 On Schlesinger cf. Elboim-Dror (2000).

25 Schlesinger did not mention the name of Hirsch, and the tone of his polemics ("von seinen Hauptquartieren sendet der Satan seine Gefolgsleute nach Ungarn" [from his headquarters, Satan sends his followers to Hungary]) is so furious and irreconcilable that it raises the question whether indeed, he really had Hirsch, after all, an Orthodox rabbi, in mind. However, in his work *Lev Haivri*, an edition of the Pressburg Rabbi Moshe Sofer's (1763–1839) last will glossed with his own commentary, Schlesinger clarifies the nature of the imminent danger. It was, as Leopold Löw remarked, forsaking the "pure" study of Torah in order to deal with grammar, a – so to speak – true *Hirschian* enterprise! In describing the evil he is trying to avert, Schlesinger used the imagery ("spreading out the net") that Löw was responding to (see above) – a Talmudic fable (b. Ber 61b) about a fox walking alongside a river seeing fish swarming from one place to another. "He said to them: 'From what are you fleeing?' They replied: 'From the nets cast for us by men.' He said to them: 'Would you like to come up on to the dry land so that you and I can live together in the way my ancestors lived with your ancestors?' They replied: 'Art thou the one that they call the cleverest of animals? Thou art not clever but foolish. If we are afraid in the element in which we live, how much more in the element in which we would die!' So it is with us. If such is our condition when we sit and study the Torah, of which it is written, for that is thy life and the length of thy days, if we go and neglect it, how much worse off we shall be." Cf. Löw (1867, 550) and Hildesheimer/Morgenstern (2013, 159–160).

league, Rabbi Esriel Hildesheimer (1820–1899) in the Hungarian town of Eisenstadt (Hungarian: Kismarton) and his yeshiva:

> Der Hr. Seminardirektor machte seine Zuhörer auf einen Aufsatz in dem Frankfurter Jeschurun aufmerksam, in welchem aus der Eigenthümlichkeit der hebr. Sprache, den Besitz nicht mit 'haben', sondern mit 'sein' (ל היה...) auszudrücken, ganz absonderliche apologetische Schlüsse gezogen werden.[26] Ein der ungarischen Sprache kundiger Seminarist erlaubte sich hierauf die Bemerkung, daß der Ungar eben so wenig das Zeitwort 'haben' kenne, als der Hebräer, und in vollkommener Uebereinstimmung mit letzterem das Zeitwort 'sein' dafür gebrauche. [...] Das hohe Rechtsgefühl, - fügte der ungarische Seminarist hinzu, – welches sich nach der Theorie des Hrn. Hirsch in dem hebr. Sprachgebrauche ausspricht, ist auch im Ung. nicht zu verkennen. [...] Diese Bemerkungen machten auf den Seminardirektor einen so tiefen Eindruck, daß er, wie ich aus dem mir vorliegenden Briefe ersehe, sogleich eine ungarische Grammatik und ein ungarisches Wörterbuch bestellte, und Herrn Hirsch in Frankfurt am Main brieflich aufforderte, sich die ungarische Sprache anzueignen, indem dieselbe ebenfalls im Jeschurun verherrlicht zu werden verdient. Wer hätte wol geahnt, daß den nationellen (!) Bestrebungen der ungarischen Juden von dieser Seite Sukkurs kommen werde? (Löw 1862).[27]

These remarks, polemical as they were, point to a characteristic feature of Hirsch's – and of his followers' – ideology of *Torah im derekh eretz* with regard to the local culture in each country where they tried to gain influence.[28] His remarks on the Biblical text Gen. 12:1 seem to downplay not only the importance of the Promised Land to which the Patriarch was told to go; he also insists that Abraham's ultimate goal was not merely a change of his geographical place. Abraham

---

26 Cf. Hirsch (1861, 118–121).

27 Translation: The director of the seminar drew the attention of his listeners to an essay in the Frankfurt Journal *Jeschurun* (edited by Hirsch; MM) apologetically deducing conclusions about certain characteristics of the Hebrew language that expresses possession not with 'to have' but with 'to be' (ל היה...). One of the seminarists who knew Hungarian allowed himself to remark that this language also does not have the auxiliary verb 'to have' but uses – like the Hebrews – 'to be.' The sublime juridical sentiment, which – according to the theory of Herr Hirsch – finds expression in the Hebrew use of language, should not be misjudged also in the Hungarian. These remarks made a deep impression on the director of the seminar, so that – as I learned from a letter that is in front of me – he immediately ordered a Hungarian grammar and dictionary and invited Herr Hirsch in Frankfurt in a letter to study the Hungarian language, which should be equally praised in Jeschurun. Who would have suspected that the national aspirations of the Hungarian Jews would gain support from this side?

28 The German neo-Orthodox advisors of the nascent Agudat Israel movement during World War I displayed a similar political approach. During the German occupation of Poland, opponents criticized, on the one hand, their anti-Zionist stance and on the other, their lack of enthusiasm for the German cause: they refused to propagate the Yiddish language as a "Germanizing" factor in the occupied lands. Instead, they pleaded for the use of the language of the country (hence Polish) also in intra-Jewish affairs (Morgenstern 2002, 72).

fled the land of Mesopotamia because it was a land of corruption; leaving it was a "mental movement towards the future" (Hirsch 1973, 230).[29] Ultimately, the Patriarch was striving not to reach another country (in physical-geographical terms) but to get closer to God. In this context, Hirsch emphasizes that "the achievement of 'nearness to God'" was "equally within the reach of the Lapp in Lapland as that of the Greek in Greece" and that "where Abraham lived [...] murderers can also live" (Hirsch 1973, 233).[30] In this regard, there is no difference between Lapland, a country at the periphery of Europe, and Greece – of course, the author has in mind classical Greece, which, in his nineteenth century context, he regarded as the highest example of cultural excellence. Hirsch insisted that it is God himself who "demands that every Jew find his personal well-being only in the context of the country" where he lives, and "in whichever land Jews shall live as citizens [ ] they shall honor and love the princes and government as their own [...] and contribute with every possible power to their good" (Hirsch 1992, 480–481).

What, then, does Hirsch's special and undeniable attachment to the German language and culture mean in this rather cosmopolitical context? In order to find an answer to this question, the following remarks will address Hirsch's understanding of *Bildung*, his interpretation of Christianity in Germany, and his understanding of Prussia's contribution to the historical development of the rights of the Jewish-Orthodox minority in Germany.

3 Hirsch's understanding of *Bildung*

Hirsch shows his appreciation of Germany and German culture most strongly through his admiration for the concept of *Bildung* (culture, education). His address at his school in Frankfurt on Friedrich Schiller's centenary (1859) represents the most famous expression of this attitude (Hirsch 1912, 6: 308–321).[31] In this address, he extolled the poet as a model for Jews, praising his ethical teachings and declaring that Jews and non-Jews could learn about the idea of freedom from him (Haberman 1998, 78).

Hirsch's Biblical commentary of 1867 reveals – albeit indirectly – how deeply his admiration of *Bildung* was rooted in his Jewish *Weltanschauung*. Only a few

---

29 Hirsch (1867, 190) ("eine geistige Hinbewegung, ein Hinstreben zu dem futuralen oder imperativen Begriffe").
30 Cf. Hirsch (1867, 191): "Das kann der Lappe in Lappland wie der Grieche in Griechenland erreichen" (on Gen 12:6–7).
31 This text, also printed separately, was translated by Marc Shapiro (2008/2009). For the importance of the Germanic notion of *Bildung* in Hirsch's oeuvre, see also Ellenson (1992, 11).

pages away from his remarks on Abraham, in his explanation of Genesis 10: 5 (נפרדו איי הגוים כארצתם מאלה): "from these the groups of nations separated out in their lands"), referring to the offspring of Noah's son Japhet, Hirsch writes about Ashkenas, comparing him to Javan (Greece). Pointing to the Hebrew root "parad," to separate out parts, he comments that Javan (Greece) and Ashkenas (Germany) are two peoples that provide examples of national splitting up and decentralization. In such decentralized states, he continues, "hat stets die Bildung die größte Pflege gefunden" (Hirsch 1867, 162).[32]

In this context, it is noteworthy that Hirsch's understanding of "Bildung" seems to parallel the etymological explanation in Grimm's *Dictionnary*, the second volume of which, with the letter "B," had appeared just a couple of years before (1860). The theologically interesting point in the explanation by the Grimm brothers was the linkage of the concept of *Bildung* to the Biblical notion of man's creation in the image ("Bild") of God (Grimm 1860, 2: 22).[33] In his commentary on the verse Gen. 1: 27 (ויברא אלהים את האדם בצלמו), Hirsch points out: "צלם means the outer covering, the bodily form." "If all the compassion and love, the truth and equity and holiness of the Divine Rule wished to appear cased in an exterior visible form, it would appear in the figure which the Creator gave man" (Hirsch 1973, 30–31).[34]

In an astonishing way, this exegesis seems to echo his etymological outline of the root "חנך" (whence the modern Hebrew noun חנוך, hinukh, [education], is derived from) later in his remarks on Gen. 14:14 וישמע אברם כי נשבה אחיו וירק את (חניכיו ילידי ביתו): "By חנך the young human being receives not a straitjacket, but a spiritual garment in which he is to move."[35] According to Hirsch, both Hebrew roots (חנך and צלם) relate, therefore, to outer clothing, a sort of "garment." Does the logic of the Hebrew language suggest this explanation, as Hirsch's etymological considerations want to make his readers believe or do we see here the influence of an etymologizing theology of *Bildung* in the wake of the Brothers Grimm?[36] Stretching his Hebrew etymology even farther, Hirsch adds, in his commentary

---

32 The English translation by Isaac Levy is: "Culture has always been accorded the greatest care in small states" (Hirsch, 1973, 198). Hirsch published his commentary on Genesis in 1867, four years before the unification of the German Reich (1871).

33 Cf. also Johann Gottfried Herder (1829, 137): "Das Göttliche in unserm Geschlecht ist also Bildung zur Humanität."

34 The German original is in Hirsch (1867, 27): צלם means "die äußere Hülle, die leibliche Gestalt [...]." Also: "in unserer Hülle, d.h. wenn alle die Barmherzigkeit und Milde, die Wahrheit und das Recht und die Heiligkeit der göttlichen Waltung in einer äußeren, sichtbaren Hülle auftreten wollte, so würde sie in der Gestalt erscheinen, die der Schöpfer dem Menschen erteilte."

35 Hirsch (1867, 212). My translation; this text is missing in Isaac Levy's translation into English.

36 See also Hirsch's remarks about the Hebrew root חנך in Num. 7: 10 and Dtn. 20: 5.

on Gen 7: 4, that *hinukh* deals with the forming of the "I" (anokhi): "חנך is the setting, the practicing, getting habituated in one's vocation" (Hirsch 1973, 149; Hirsch 1867, 123).[37]

To be sure, Hirsch based his explanations on – to say the least – dubious philological assumptions[38] concerning etymological affinities of Hebrew roots and on the idea that Hebrew was the original language of mankind, a language to be studied and understood without reference to other Semitic languages (cf. Haberman 1998, 85–86). In this context, it seems that Hirsch wanted – in a (from a scholarly point of view) forced and artificial manner – to refer to a concept that is better understood in terms of *German* etymology; by transposing it into his Biblical commentary, he clearly indicated his appreciation of German culture and *Bildung*. Although Hirsch conspicuously advocates an educational concept that views *hinukh* as a process bringing man into the "form" that the Creator had destined for him, he fails to connect it explicitly to the German etymology of *Bildung*. From a Jewish point of view, this means that he stopped short of essentializing it.[39] For Hirsch, finding the idea of Jewish education already in the Hebrew Bible signified conceptualizing and implementing a positive vision of traditional Judaism and the Jewish community in the intellectually open world of the Emancipation, a world that comprised the entire Western hemisphere. He considered that this idea – in his terms *Torah im derekh eretz* – had a strong affinity to German *Bildung*, but it was not identical with it.

4 Hirsch's perception of Christianity in Germany

Clearly, the religious identity of most of Hirsch's "fellow Germans" constituted an important element in his assessment of Germany. It is hard to find explicit references to the German attributes of Christianity in Hirsch's texts. Among the

---

37 Hirsch's theory, based on ideas by medieval Jewish grammarians and kabbalistic speculations on the Hebrew language, rests on the assumption that Hebrew words have two-letter roots (in this case, the "root" נך) while the additional letter is a "prefix" (in this case the guttural letters ח or א) that modifies the basic meaning of the "root." Thus he arrives at assimilating the concepts of "I" (אנכי) and "education" (חנוך).

38 Heinrich Leberecht Fleischer, in "Aus Briefen" (1862) is quoted as having characterized Hirsch's exegesis as driven by " phantastischer etymologischer Willkür" (fantastic etymological arbitrariness) (Haberman 1998, p. 84, n. 36). Cf. Mordechai Breuer (1995, 381–400).

39 Note the instances where Hirsch *did* use the German term *Bildung*, e.g., in his remarks on Gen. 2: 6 ("die ... Bildung des Menschen von der Erde") and his translation of Gen 5:1 ("bildete er ihn in die Ähnlichkeit Gottes").

most noteworthy in his biblical commentary is his statement (on Gen. 14: 13) that Abraham was "the first 'Protestant'" (Hirsch 1867, 211).[40] Traditional midrashic sources regard Esau [hence Edom, one of Abraham's grandsons] – at the same time brother and foe of Jacob-Israel – as the archetypical emblem of Christianity (Avemarie 1994; Langer 2009; Morgenstern 2011). In light of this interpretation, Hirsch, by antedating in his midrash-like explanation, so to speak, the "origins" of a "Christian" idea by two generations and attributing it to the first Patriarch, was, perhaps, attempting to secure a deeper theological grounding for this modern – and leading – form of Christianity in Germany at that time. Hirsch offers a theological framing of Abrahamic ecumenism avant la lettre.[41] One midrashic explanation, however, does not exclude another. In emphasizing the relevance of the surrounding non-Jewish culture, Hirsch thus also imparted new meaning to the traditional identification of Christianity with Edom by focusing on Germany and particularly German Protestantism. This perspective revises the old identification, transforming the relationship between Judaism and Christianity in Germany, in the age of emancipation, from conflict to partnership.

In Hirsch's midrashic explanation, the famous scene in Genesis 33 symbolizes the hopes of his era: Jacob returns from exile in Mesopotamia and meets his brother, bringing him presents. In his commentary on Gen. 33:4 ("Esau ran to meet him and embraced him, fell upon his neck and kissed him, and they wept"), we read the following:

> That here purely humane feelings overcame Esau is warranted for by the little word ויבכו, they wept. A kiss can be false but not tears that flow at such moments [...]. This kiss, and these tears show us that Esau was also a descendant of Abraham. In Esau there must have been something more than just the wild hunter. Otherwise how could he have had the ability to domineer [sic] the whole development of mankind (which the Romans actually did I.L.). The sword alone, simply raw force, is not able to do that (Hirsch 1973, 511).[42]

Changing to the present tense, Hirsch then describes his perception of the contemporary world. This European Christian world will, he hopes, continue to become more and more "humane" – a term that arouses thoughts of Friedrich

---

40 According to Hirsch, Abraham was "the Ebrew," "העברי" (Hirsch 1973, 255), "the one who stands on the other side, who stands in opposition to the whole world" (Hirsch 1973, 256), "(d)er Jenseits Stehende, der ganzen Welt Gegenüberstehende, der erste 'Protestant'" (Hirsch 1867, 211).
41 For Hirsch, this was, of course, at the same time an apologetic move: for one, he was affirming the hermeneutical superiority of the Jewish sources, demonstrating that they were capable of interpreting contemporary phenomena such as nineteenth-century Protestantism; for another, Hirsch was usurping the term "Protestant" for his own (Jewish) side.
42 Cf. Hirsch (1867, 420). The remark ("which the Romans actually did") was added by the translator.

Schiller and Herder[43] – and that will prove its "humaneness" with regard to its treatment of the Jewish minority, repenting from a past of pogroms and violence and abolishing legal and social discrimination.

Hirsch continues: Esau, too, gradually lays the sword aside more and more, turning gradually more and more towards humaneness. Precisely in his relationship to Jacob, Esau has the best opportunity to show the effect on him of the principle of humaneness. When the strong respect the rights of the strong it may well be wisdom. Only when the strong, in this case, Esau, fall round the necks of the weak and cast aside the sword, does it show that right and humaneness [*Menschlichkeit*] have made a conquest (Hirsch 1973, 511).[44]

These lines were published in 1867, some years before – with the outburst of the *Berliner Antisemitismusstreit* and the hate campaign of the Protestant Hofprediger Adolf Stöcker (1835–1909) – dark clouds appeared on the horizon, ushering in a new and more pessimistic period of Jewish-Christian relations in the Reich. Even in the 1870s, however, Hirsch persevered in his optimism, believing that, with the age of emancipation, a new era had irrevocably begun. His positive attitude towards Germany rested mainly on his perception of Prussia, the leading (and Protestant) factor in German politics, which in the 1860s had initiated a process leading to the establishment of the North German Federation, the annexation of Frankfurt to Prussia and, finally, in 1871, to the unification of Germany. His own community affairs in Frankfurt, his struggle with the liberal-dominated Board of the larger Jewish congregation, and the Orthodox fight for organizational independence now rested in Prussian hands. During the *Kulturkampf* unleashed by the anticlerical *May Laws* of the Prussian Minister of Culture, Education, and Church Affairs Adalbert Falk, Prussia became, in Hirsch's view, the guarantor of

---

43 Cf. Herder (1829, 137–138): "Humanität ist der *Charakter unseres Geschlechts*; er ist uns aber nur in Anlagen angeboren, und muß uns eigentlich angebildet werden. Wir bringen ihn nicht fertig auf die Welt mit; auf der Welt aber soll er das Ziel unsres Bestrebens, die Summe unsrer Uebungen, unser Werth seyn: denn eine *Angelität* im Menschen kennen wir nicht, und wenn der Dämon, der uns regiert, kein humaner Dämon ist, werden wir Plagegeister der Menschen [...]. Humanität ist der Schatz und die Ausbeute aller menschlichen Bemühungen, gleichsam die Kunst unsres Geschlechts. Die Bildung zu ihr ist ein Werk, das unablässig fortgesetzt werden muß;/ oder wir sinken [...] zur rohen Thierheit, zur Brutalität zurück." Herder's statement, which regards human beings as oscillating between the "angelic" and the "bestial" as they move towards the "humane" character of their existence, accords perfectly with Hirsch's presentation of the Biblical figure of Edom fighting with Jacob (Gen. 32–33). We know that Hirsch and his community read Herder's texts because Hirsch's monthly *Jeschurun* dealt with Herder : cf. Kohut (1868/69); Von der Krone (2010, 293).
44 Cf. Hirsch (1867, 420).

the freedom of religion and freedom of conscience (Morgenstern 2002, 144–147; 261–264; pace Liberles 1985, 189–195).

5 Hirsch's perception of Prussia as the leading ally of Orthodox Judaism in Germany

The association of Hirsch's cause with the Prussian *Kulturkampf* was an essential part of his and his followers' self-image (Morgenstern 1998). A facilitating factor was the fact that Jewish and non-Jewish reformers inspired by the ideas of the Enlightenment and the French Revolution were never interested in the issue of a religious (or nationalist) Jewish *collective*; the reformers and liberals fought only for the emancipation of *individual* Jews. Under these conditions, the conservative Berlin ministerial bureaucracy, whatever its motives were, assumed responsibility for the Jewish community in the Prussian lands, beginning with the Jewish law for the Grand Duchy of Posen (Poznań) of June 1 (1833) and the law for the rest of Prussia of July 23 (1847). The Jewish corporations created in Posen were subject to Prussian administrative law, but not to the law regulating religious communities. Implicitly, one could interpret this as meaning that the Jews were recognized as a separate ethnic (not religious!) group along with the Germans and Poles.

According to the Orthodox understanding that Hirsch shared, in passing these two laws, the Berlin authorities, for the first time, brought the Jewish communities under public corporative law, if only for the purpose of regulating certain internal affairs. Thus, after the annexation of Frankfurt to Prussia in 1866, Hirsch's Frankfurt Orthodox community was betting that the new administration would align its interests with those of traditional Judaism in their seemingly common fight against "vulgar liberalism" (Freund 1911, 120). The Orthodox perceived the momentum of events between 1866 and 1871 (the unification of Germany) as creating new realities that were destined to change the Jewish state of affairs. Hirsch welcomed the passing of the "Law on Secession from the Synagogue Community" of July 28, 1876, considering this law a logical extension of the events of 1871, of German unity. In his opinion, in both cases a new, free, and united society had been established and gained recognition. Rejecting the charge of "separatism," Hirsch and his followers claimed that, in fact, they really wanted a united Jewish community, but one based on Sinaitic law. "Germany's liberation from the bonds of the old feudal state also brought equality for the German Jews," an observer stated (Raphael Breuer 1930/31, 89–90). The political situation after 1871 and the new politico-religious stances (for instance, the first Vatican Council) made it important, as Isaac Breuer put it, to "permanently disable if not eliminate [...] interdenominational conflict" (Isaac Breuer 1913, 10). Bismarck had therefore decided "to extend the protective arm of the state over all citizens, priests and laymen both, and let there be no doubt that the modern concept of sovereignty would not tolerate within its territory a foreign power as its neighbor, never mind as its superior" (Isaac Breuer 1913, 10–11).

It was incompatible with the new situation to compel Jews to be members of synagogual institutions. The Prussian "secession law" of July 28, 1876 thus permitted all Jews to withdraw from their local communities on religious grounds without thereby leaving Judaism altogether. Its § 2 specified the procedure to be followed "with civil effect": "The person who is withdrawing [...] declares his withdrawal before the judge of his place of domicile, adding assurance that this withdrawal is based on religious reasons" (Morgenstern 2002, 263).

According to this interpretation, Prussian legislation laid the foundation for the organizational independence of Orthodox Judaism in Germany; this perspective invariably gave independent Orthodoxy an advantage in popular appeal over competing Orthodox Jewish groups, namely the *Gemeindeorthodoxie*, in the German-speaking countries. This historiosophy laid the foundation for the grand image of Hirsch's Frankfurt neo-Orthodox movement – its self-image as a "freedom and unity movement" parallel to the national-level events in Germany (Morgenstern 2002, 139–144). This led to the pro-Prussian and later pro-German alignment of independent neo-Orthodoxy in the last third of the nineteenth century and the first decades of the twentieth century. Hirsch's and his followers considered that the Prussian state made it possible to secede and thus guaranteed freedom of conscience for Orthodox Jews in Frankfurt and beyond.[45]

6 German Jews' historical mission according to Hirsch

German Jews' historical mission according to Hirsch – he assumed that he could address only observant Jews – had at least three dimensions corresponding to the

---

[45] As late as 1931/32, Hirsch's grandson Isaac Breuer wrote: "The Prussian state gives us more justice than Reform Judaism and the Orthodox community [...]. In Prussia, the congregations faithful to the Torah have gained full recognition [...]. When will the Zionists learn from the Prussian state to respect the Torah?" (Isaac Breuer 1931/32, 171–172). The tragic consequences of this approach in the 1930s, when large parts of Hirschian neo-Orthodoxy saw no reason to revise their positive view on developments in Prussia and in Germany are beyond the scope of this article; for the neo-Orthodox attempts to find a modus vivendi with the National Socialist rulers, see Morgenstern (2002, 282–284).

three assets of Germany and German culture: German Jews had to realize their ideal of *Torah im derekh eretz* in harmony with the concept of *Bildung*; they had to prepare themselves for their historical task of meeting *Edom* (Christianity); and they had to live up to the expectations aroused among the Orthodox as a result of the Prussian secession law [*Austrittsgesetz*] and parallel law in other German lands.

6.1 Torah im derekh eretz

Hirsch based his educational approach on the assumptions that God had revealed himself equally in nature, history and in the Torah and that the various modes of revelation were closely interconnected. He thus considered that the study of each of these modes of revelation leads to the perfection of Man, to his being formed "in the image of God." In his first work, *Nineteen Letters* (1836), he had tried to use this highly optimistic epistemological assumption in order to bring religious and secular knowledge into harmony. The final aim of this harmonization was a "Judaism that can understand itself" [*sich selbst verstehendes Judentum*] and "Man-Israel," the anthropological formulation of this idea. This ideal was meant to correspond to the unity of God´s revelation in the Torah, in history, and in nature, thus forming the cosmological counterpart to the educational challenge of *Torah im derekh eretz*. Suffice it here to give one of many examples of its meaning for him and his followers:

Part of this challenge entailed the study of languages and of grammar – for his Frankfurt followers, not Hungarian, of course (this obligation, according to Hirsch, existed only for Hungarian Jews), but German grammar and primarily, Hebrew grammar. Hirsch made the study of Biblical philology and Hebrew grammar a subject of Jewish learning. In doing so, he transgressed a formal ban (*issur*) by the famous Pressburg Orthodox Rabbi Moshe Sofer (the "Hatam Sofer") on spending one´s time on studying grammar. The "Hatam Sofer" called grammar, even Hebrew grammar, a subject for heretics (Hildesheimer/Morgenstern 2013, 160). The talmudic sentence ומנעו בניכם מן ההגיון in the Babylonian Talmud (tractate Berakhot 28b: "and keep your children from meditation") appears in the polemics that Hirsch undertook. Rashi understood this as "do not teach them too much in scriptures" (לא תרגילום במקרא יותר מדאי), meaning do not undertake too much reading of Scripture (Schatz 2009, 182–183). Living in a milieu where the Bible (albeit the Christian Bible) formed the basis of the surrounding non-Jewish culture, where Bible studies flourished and general literature abounded in biblical language, imagery and allusions, Hirsch was unwilling to renounce his right to the Jewish biblical heritage.[46] This was one of the reasons that he advocated the study of the Bible and wrote his famous commentaries.

6.2 "Israel" meets "Edom"

German Jews should utilize the favorable historical circumstances by preparing themselves for the task of "Jacob's" (Judaism's) meeting with "Edom" (Christianity). Hirsch´s understanding of Christianity's role in salvation history for the Jewish people is one of the most astonishing aspects of his writings. In debating their liberal opponents, the adversaries of Jewish emancipation in nineteenth century Germany contended that it was an undesirable illusion to expect the Jews to integrate into non-Jewish society because European society, in their view, bore an unalienable Christian character that would keep Jews apart. Hirsch did not regard this as a reason to oppose Jewish emancipation. For him, the Christian character of the surrounding society was no hindrance to the historic progress that he envisioned. The Holy Scriptures foresaw the Christian character of Europe. Orthodox Jews' integration into Western society would be possible provided that the Jews remained faithful to their destiny, that they abided by their Torah, and that, finally, "Edom" would rediscover its Abrahamic roots and learn true humaneness. "Edom" would than distance itself – as Hirsch's positive reference to Lessing's *Erziehung des Menschengeschlecht* indicates – from narrow confessionalism and enable Jewish emancipation. In his commentary on Gen. 27: 39f, Isaac's famous words of blessing to his firstborn son, Edom, Hirsch writes: "Your sword will be the means by which you will carve your history in the world. You will be the stronger, will conquer the world – to lay the conquered world at the feet of Jacob. 'Rome,' the power of the sword, conquers the world, only, ultimately, after discovering all its errors, to lay it at the feet of the ideals of Jacob-Israel (Hirsch 1973, 451)."[47]

In addition to this somewhat triumphalist feature (Edom laying the conquered world at the feet of the ideals of Jacob), Hirsch provides another positive meaning to the brothers' meeting: Jacob, too, has something to accomplish and to learn in this rendezvous. Jewish sources, according to Hirsch, suggest that not only the Gentile world but also the Jews "lack" something. Divine decree had deprived the

---

46 It is noteworthy that he wrote a commentary on the Psalms (1882) – for an Orthodox rabbi of the old tradition not really a subject of "learning"! Hirsch shared his predilection for this part of the Hebrew biblical canon with a liberal thinker such as the Jewish Neo-Kantian philosopher Hermann Cohen! Cf. Cohen (1966, 598 [index]); Dober/Morgenstern (2012, 253 [index]).
47 Cf. Hirsch (1867, 369).

Jews of a "normal" human existence in terms of a political entity with their own statehood. According to Hirsch's definition, the Jews' anthropological condition in the period before the coming of the Messiah was certainly inferior to that of the Gentiles; the Jews compensated for this "lack," to be sure, with their readiness to bear the yoke of heaven, to obey the revealed commandments of the Torah, which singled Israel out. In Hirsch's remarks on Gen. 32: 8 we read:

> As Jacob and Esau opposed each other here, so, right up to the present day, do Jacob and Esau stand one against the other. Jacob: a pater familias blessed with children, serving, working, filled with care. Esau a "finished made man." What Jacob had achieved after struggling for it for twenty toilsome years, in spite of the blessing he had received and the first-born right he had obtained, and which now he brought home as the great prize he had won, viz. to be able to be an independent father of a household, that others have as their natural expectation from the cradle, that Esau, "the finished made" man, had already had in full measure when Jacob left home; and while Jacob by the labor of his hands had succeeded in obtaining the happiness of being a father of a family, Esau had become in the meantime, a political personality, a leader of an army [...] Thus, the external contrast between the "holder-on to the heels" and the "made" man (Hirsch 1973, 498).[48]

In this picture, Edom (אדום), in Hirsch's etymology linked to Adam (אדם), man, is the "normal" man, who knows to defend himself as a political personality, and the leader of an army whereas Jacob's existence resembles the Jewish existence in the Diaspora. Israel/Jacob, according to Hirsch, is female, passive, deficient, whereas Edom, ruling states, kings, and enjoying political power, is male, active. Hirsch, however, regards Israel as more "human" than Edom, because Edom, with his emphasis on military power and strength, fails to show the true human feeling of compassion. His "masculinity" lacks the "feminine" side of humanity. Ultimately, Hirsch believed, and he assumed that these days were not far away, humanity's true destiny would be realized when "Jacob" and "Esau" meet again. "Edom" would then weep and acknowledge his brother, and "Jacob" would succeed in elevating him to true humaneness. In most of his texts, Hirsch preferred not to elaborate on these eschatological expectations, but in this context, he hoped that in the not so distant future "Jacob's" deficiency, his "female" and passive existence in exile, would come to an end.[49]

---

48 Hirsch's explanation rests, again, on his linguistic theory concerning the structure of the Hebrew language. "Edom," in this case, is closely linked to "Adam," "der fertig gemachte Mensch."
49 Cf. Hirsch (1873, 620) (on Lev 26: 43) where he says that when the Jews "in Galut" will have attained "the expiation of their guilt," they will be ripe "for the future permanent return to the land of their independence" (Hirsch 1973, 3: 807).

6.3 The challenge of the Secession Law

The third challenge of observant Jews in Germany was to live up to the expectations that the newly won freedom in the German lands offered. For Hirsch, this meant actively utilizing the legal conditions that the Prussian state was providing. With the famous *Austrittsgesetz*, the Berlin Landtag, according to Hirsch, had offered freedom of religion and freedom of conscience for the Orthodox minority. German-Jewish Orthodoxy was, as Josef Wohlgemuth put it, a Torah-true remnant of observant Jews that had maintained itself in the "center of world culture, in the country in which the philosophical, scientific, and historical theories that set themselves against the basic ideas of Judaism were born or at least found their principal development" (Wohlgemuth 1918, 164 165). The task of German Jews who had proudly survived in such a country should have been to build Jewish communities based solely on the foundation of Siniatic law and independent of the large Reform-dominated communities.

Hirsch was deeply disappointed that even the majority of the Orthodox Jews in Frankfurt, let alone Orthodox Jews all over Germany, did not heed his call and did not leave the main congregation. Although some of his followers tried to present a different picture, Hirsch himself seems to have realized that the challenge of his last years, his attempt to persuade the members of his own kehillah to use the possibilities of the Austrittsgesetz, was a failure (Liberles 1985, 210–226; Morgenstern 2002, 148–155). German Orthodox Jewry did not meet this challenge. Deeply discouraged by his community's unwillingness to follow him and his failure to win acceptance for the secession decision, in 1877, Hirsch resigned his position as school principal of the Frankfurt Orthodox Realschule in favor of his son Mendel Hirsch, obviously grooming him to be his successor as rabbi. After Hirsch's death in 1888, however, by a majority, the community rejected Mendel Hirsch as his father's successor to the rabbinate and elected Hirsch's son-in-law Salomon Breuer instead (Morgenstern 2002, 166).

It is, however – in light of subsequent twentieth-century history – Hirsch's German patriotism, not the above-mentioned failures, that lead to debate and embarrassment when contemporary modern Orthodox Jews contemplate Hirsch's life and work.[50] Scholars should try to understand and evaluate Hirsch's life and work on his own terms and refrain from assigning value judgments. It is useful, nevertheless, to realize that Hirsch based his understanding of Germany on deeply embedded nineteenth-century conceptions and presuppositions and, ultimately,

---

50 Cf. the discussion on the occasion of Hirsch's 125th yahrzeit in http://haemtza.blogspot. co.il/2013/12/ rabbi-samson-raphael-hirsch-ztzl.html#disqus_thread (last accessed 31 December 2013); my thanks to Chaya-Bathya Markovits for drawing my attention to this blog.

on his view of Germany's function for the course of Jewish history. Hirsch did not limit his cultural openness to Germany and German culture and – no matter how close he felt to Germany and how deeply he was influenced by concepts that originated in German culture (such as his understanding of *Bildung*) – he refrained from openly and explicitly identifying his Jewish ideas with German concepts. Partly for this reason, in the second part of the twentieth century, Hirsch's followers successfully acculturated throughout the countries of the German-Jewish Diaspora. Translated into English and Hebrew, primarily in North America and in the State of Israel, Hirsch's texts and ideas acquired new meaning in new contexts. Today, only a small group of scholars read Hirsch's texts in the German original. They remain a living legacy in translations.

Bibliography

"Aus Briefen," [Geiger, Abraham (?)]. *Jüdische Zeitschrift für Wissenschaft und Leben*, 2 (1872): 149–160.

Avemarie, Friedrich. Esaus Hände, Jakobs Stimme. "Edom als Sinnbild Roms in der frühen rabbinischen Literatur." *Die Heiden. Juden, Christen und das Problem des Fremden.* Ed. R. Feldmeier and U. Heckel. WUNT [Wissenschaftliche Untersuchungen zum Neuen Testament] 70. Tübingen: J.C.B. Mohr, 1994. 177–208.

Brasz, Chaya. "Dutch Jewry and its Undesired German Rabbinate." *Leo Baeck Institute Yearbook* (2012): 73–86.

Breuer, Isaac. *Die Preußische Austrittsgesetzgebung und das Judentum*. Frankfurt on the Main: Verlag des Israelit, 1913.

Breuer, Isaac. "Preußen und die jüdische Gemeinde." *Nahalath Zwi* (1931/32): 167–172.

Breuer, Isaac. *Der Neue Kusari*. Frankfurt on the Main: Verlag der Rabbiner Hirsch-Gesellschaft, 1934.

Breuer, Mordechai. "Il commento al Pentateucho di Samson Raphael Hirsch." *La lettura ebraica delle Scritture*. Ed. Sergio J. Sierra. Bologna: Edizioni Dehoniane, 1995. 381–400.

Breuer, Mordechai. "Orthodoxy in Germany and the East." *Leo Baeck Institute Yearbook* (1996): 75–86.

Breuer, Raphael. "Was hat Rabbiner Hirsch unserer Zeit zu sagen?" *Nahalath Zwi* (1930/31): 84–101.

Cohen, Hermann. *Religion der Vernunft aus den Quellen des Judentums*. Darmstadt: Wissenschaftliche Buchgesellschaft, 1966.

Dober, Hans Martin, Matthias Morgenstern. *Religion aus den Quellen der Vernunft. Hermann Cohen und das evangelische Christentum* (Religion in Philosophy and Theology 65). Tübingen: Mohr Siebeck, 2012.

Elboim-Dror, Rachel. "The Ultimate Ghetto: A Subversive Ultra-Orthodox Utopia." *JSQ* 7 (2000): 65–95.

Ellenson, David. "German Jewish Orthodoxy: Tradition in the Context of Culture." *The Uses of Tradition. Jewish Continuity in the Modern Era*. Ed. Jack Wertheimer. New York: Jewish Theological Seminary of America, 1992. 5–22.

Freund, Ismar. "Staat, Kirche und Judentum in Preußen." *Jahrbuch der jüdisch-literarischen Gesellschaft* 14 (1911): 109–138.

Ganzel, Tova. "Explicit and Implicit Polemic in Rabbi Samson Raphael Hirsch's Bible Commentary." *HUCA* 81 (2010): 171–191.

Grimm, Jacob and Wilhelm Grimm, eds. *Deutsches Wörterbuch*, vol. 2. Leipzig: Hirzel, 1860.

Haberman, Jacob. "Kaufmann Kohler and Samson Raphael Hirsch." *Leo Baeck Institute Yearbook* (1998): 73–102.

Herder, Johann Gottfried. *Briefe zur Beförderung der Humanität. Sämmtliche Werke zur Philosophie und Geschichte*. Stuttgart/Tübingen: Cotta, 1829.

Hildesheimer, Meir and Matthias Morgenstern. *Rabbiner Samson Raphael Hirsch in der deutschsprachigen jüdischen Presse*. Münster: LIT, 2013.

Hirsch, Samson Raphael. "Aus der Mappe eines wandernden Juden." *Jeschurun*, no. 5 (1854/55): 270–278.

Hirsch, Samson Raphael. "Jüdische Welt- und Lebensanschauungen. Allgemeine Begriffe: היה." *Jeschurun* (December 1861): 118–125.

Hirsch, Samson Raphael. "Worte, am 18. Oktober 1863 in der Synagoge der Israelitischen Religionsgesellschaft zu Frankfurt a. M. gesprochen." *Jeschurun* 10 (1863/64): 41–56.

Hirsch, Samson Raphael. *Der Pentateuch übersetzt und erläutert. Erster Teil: Die Genesis*. Frankfurt on the Main, 1867; *Dritter Teil: Leviticus*. Frankfurt on the Main: J. Kauffmann, 1873.

Hirsch, Samson Raphael. "Worte, bei der Schulfeier der Unterrichtsanstalt der Israelitischen Religionsgesellschaft zu Frankfurt a. M., den 9. Nov. 1859 am Vorabend der Schillerfeier gesprochen." *Samson Raphael Hirsch, Gesammelte Schriften*. Ed. Dr. Naphtali Hirsch. Frankfurt on the Main: Kauffmann, 1912. 6: 308–321.

Hirsch, Samson Raphael. *The Pentateuch translated and explained, rendered into English*. Trans. Isaac Levy, vols. 1–4, 2nd ed. Gateshead: Judaica Press, 1973.

Hirsch, Samson Raphael. *Chorew. Versuch über Jisraels Pflichten in der Zerstreuung*. Zurich/Basel: Morascha, 1992.

Japhet, Saemy. "The Secession from the Frankfurt Jewish Community under Samson Raphael Hirsch." *Histora Judaica* 10 (1948): 99–122.

Klugman, Eliyahu Meir. *Samson Raphael Hirsch. Architect of Torah Judaism for the Modern World*. New York: Mesorah Publications, 1996.

Kohut, Adolf. "Die Verdienste Herders um die Juden und die jüdische Wissenschaft." *Jeschurun* (1868/69): 155–167, 228–245.

Langer, Gerhard. *Esau. Bruder und Feind*. Göttingen: Vandenhoeck & Ruprecht, 2009.

Lengyel, Gábor. *Moderne Rabbinerausbildung in Deutschland und Ungarn. Ungarische Hörer an Bildungsinstitutionen des deutschen Judentums (1854–1938)*. Münster: LIT, 2012.

Liberles, Robert. *Religious Conflict in Social Context. The Resurgence of Orthodox Judaism in Frankfurt am Main, 1838–1877* (Contributions to the Study of Religion 13). Westport/London: Greenwood Press, 1985.

Lichtheim, Richard. *Toldot hatsiyonut begermaniyah* (The history of German Zionism). Jerusalem: Hotsaat hasifriyah hatsiyonit, 1951.

Löw, Leopold. "Frankfurt und Ofen-Pest." *Ben Chananja*, no. 17, (1867): 550.

Löw, Leopold. "Hungarica." *Ben Chananja*, no. 8, 19 February 1862: 63–64.

Meijer, Jaap. *Erfenis der Emancipatie. Het Nederlandse Jodendom in de eerste helft van de 19e eeuw.* Maarlem, 1963.

Miller, Michael. *Rabbis and Revolution. The Jews of Moravia in the Age of Emancipation.* Stanford: Stanford University Press, 2011.

Matthias Morgenstern. "Bildung als Prinzip jüdischer Selbstbehauptung. Thora im Derech Eretz: Das pädagogische Konzept S.R. Hirschs im Rahmen seiner nationaljüdischen Strategie." *Die Samson-Raphael-Hirsch-Schule in Frankfurt am Main. Dokumente – Erinnerungen – Analysen.* Ed. Kommission zur Erforschung der Geschichte der Frankfurter Juden. Frankfurt on the Main: Waldemar Kramer Verlag, 2001.

Matthias Morgenstern. *From Frankfurt to Jerusalem. Isaac Breuer and the History of the Secession Dispute in Modern Jewish Orthodoxy.* Leiden: Brill, 2002.

Matthias Morgenstern. "Book review: Roland Tasch, *Jüdische Erfahrungswelten im historischen Kontext.* Berlin, 2011." *Frankfurt Jewish Studies Bulletin* 37 (2011/12): 161–165.

Matthias Morgenstern. "Kulturkampf in Israel." *JSQ* 5, no. 3 (1998): 277–287.

Matthias Morgenstern. "Between the Noahide Laws and Israelite-Edomite Brotherhood: Paradigms of Humanity in Modern Jewish Orthodoxy." *The Quest for a Common Humanity.* Ed. K. Berthelot and M. Morgenstern (Numen Book Series 134). Leiden: Brill, 2011. 101–121.

Matthias Morgenstern. "Neo-Orthodoxie." *Enzyklopädie jüdischer Geschichte und Kultur.* Stuttgart/Weimar: JB Metzler Verlag, 4: 341–346.

Matthias Morgenstern. "Orthodoxie." *Enzyklopädie jüdischer Geschichte und Kultur.* Stuttgart/Weimar: JB Metzler Verlag, 4: 449–455.

Matthias Morgenstern. "The Embarrassment of Joshua: Strategies for Interpreting the Biblical Account of the Conquest of Canaan in German-Jewish Neo-Orthodoxy in the Late Nineteenth and Early Twentieth Centuries." *The Gift of the Land and the Fate of the Canaanites in Jewish Thought.* Ed. Katell Berthelot, Joseph David, and Marc Hirshman. Oxford: Oxford University Press, 2014. 230–250.

Rosenbloom, Noah H. "Religious and Secular Co-equality in S. R. Hirsch's Educational Theory." *JSS* no. 4 (1962): 223–247.

Schatz, Andrea. *Sprache in der Zerstreuung. Die Säkularisierung des Hebräischen im 18. Jahrhundert.* Göttingen: Vandenhoeck & Ruprecht, 2009.

Schiller, Mayer. "The Forgotten Humanism of Rabbi Samson Raphael Hirsch." *Jewish Action* (Shavuot, summer 5749) (1989): 21–25.

Scholem, Gershom. "Politik der Mystik." *Jüdische Rundschau*, 17 July 1934, 1–2.

Scholem, Gershom. "The Politics of Mysticism: Isaac Breuer's New Kuzari." *The Messianic Idea in Judaism and other Essays on Jewish Spirituality.* New York: Schocken, 1971. 325–334.

Shapiro, Marc. "Rabbi Samson Raphael Hirsch and Friedrich von Schiller." *The Torah u-Madda Journal* 15 (2008/2009): 174–185.

Silber, Michael. "The Emergence of Ultra-Orthodoxy: The Invention of a Tradition." *The Uses of Tradition. Jewish Continuity in the Modern Era.* Ed. Jack Wertheimer. New York: Jewish Theological Seminary of America, 1992. 23–84.

Stern, Eliezer. *Haideal hahinukhi shel Torah im derekh eretz* (The educational ideal of Torah im derekh-eretz). Ramat Gan: Bar-Ilan University, 1987.

Tal, Tobias. *Samson Raphael Hirsch. Een Levensschets.* Amsterdam, 1893.

Tasch, Roland. *Jüdische Erfahrungswelten im historischen Kontext.* Berlin: De Gruyter, 2011.

Thieberger, Friedrich. "Samson Raphael Hirsch." *Der Jude* (1919/1920): 556–566.

Krone, Kerstin von der. *Wissenschaft in Öffentlichkeit: Die Wissenschaft des Judentums und ihre Zeitschriften*. Berlin: De Gruyter, 2010.
Wohlgemuth, Josef. "Zionismus, Nationaljudentum und gesetzestreues Judentum." *Jeschurun* (1918): 1–31, 133–173, 257–288, 437–478.

Shulamit S. Magnus

Between East and West: Pauline Wengeroff and her Cultural History of the Jews of Russia

Pauline Wengeroff (1833–1916) was the author of an extraordinary, two-volume set of memoirs entitled, *Memoirs of a Grandmother: Scenes from the Cultural History of the Jews of Russia in the Nineteenth Century*. As their full title proclaims, Wengeroff couples her and her family's story with that of Russian Jewry in the era of its transformation from tradition to modernity. It was a most remarkable project coming from a woman born in 1833; we have nothing vaguely comparable in claim or scope from another woman in the history of Jewish literature.[1]

Wengeroff's work is remarkable in many other ways. It gives a rich portrayal of traditional Jewish society in Russia with a particular focus on women's religious practices and piety. It tells a dramatic tale of the dissolution of traditionalism in this society, then the world's largest Jewish community (over five million people at the time she wrote), from the perspective of women, marriage, and families. Wengeroff's writing is unprecedented, too, in treating men as subjects of inquiry: she does not simply and unconsciously consider them as generic Jews whose experience is universal and normative but as a specific case whose behavior differed from that of women – another focus of her work.[2] Wengeroff, of course, does not use the term, "gender," but her woman-centered narrative is profoundly gendered, asserting that women and men had very different experiences of modernity and that there was a power shift between them that led to the loss of Jewish tradition. According to this reading, not just the opening of outside cultures to Jews and Jewish receptivity to those cultures but dynamics between women and men led to the loss of Jewish tradition. Men, she claims, modernized rashly, thoughtlessly abandoning tradition. They also coerced women to do the same and took from them their traditional domestic control and mandate to transmit Jewish culture to the children, with catastrophic results. In short, hers is an argument for the cultural power of women (albeit, I argue, not from a feminist stance).

---

1 For a comparison of Wengeroff's *Memoirs* with the zikroynes of Glikl Hameln, see my Introduction to Pauline Wengeroff, *Memoirs of a Grandmother: Scenes from the Cultural History of the Jews of Russia in the Nineteenth Century* (2010).

2 To be clear: Wengeroff does treat men as "generic Jews," but she also considers them as specific and separate in observed behavior from women.

Memoirs is a carefully crafted and beautifully written narrative by a brilliant woman who "loved books" and was very well read in Jewish, German, Russian, and even English literature (the latter, in translation). From the beginning, Wengeroff intended her work to be published, that is, to have a public, not just a private readership. She achieved this during her lifetime, to wild acclaim in scores of reviews in the Jewish and non-Jewish press, which she preserved, some of which are published in her volumes, I believe at her prompting.[3] Her talent, ambition, and success are extraordinary.

Among the fascinating aspects of working on Wengeroff and her *Memoirs* is studying the many, even contradictory, readings and misreadings of her. As important as the complicated question of Wengeroff's intentions in her work is the question of her reception how others read her and used her work. *Memoirs of a Grandmother* went through three largely German-language editions (the work also has some Hebrew and Yiddish and a few Polish words) during Wengeroff's lifetime and two posthumously. Not long after publication of the first volume, in Berlin, in 1908, the Jewish Publication Society of America (JPS) came very close to publishing an English translation. No less a figure than Solomon Schechter, president of the Jewish Theological Seminary of America, championed an English edition, calling *Memoirs* "the greatest human document" he had ever read – and Schechter, one of the greatest scholars of Jewish literature of his time, had read a great deal. *Memoirs* had the warm endorsement of the scholars and communal leaders, Israel Friedlaender, and Cyrus Adler, and, initially at least, of the financier, Jacob Schiff and of Judge Mayer Sulzberg – in short, of the most prominent figures of U.S. Jewry at the turn of the twentieth century. Some members of the Publication Committee of JPS and others at that time read the work as an apologia for Orthodoxy; some still read it that way. Wengeroff's own son, Semyon (Simon) Vengerov, a noted Russian literary historian, leading Pushkin scholar, and intimate of Nabokov, – that is, a man familiar with literature and, presumably, his mother – characterized her as defending "Orthodoxy," a serious misreading, I argue.[4] A sufficient number of members of the Publication Committee of JPS (not including Schechter and Friedlaender), however, went from reading *Memoirs* as a testament to traditionalism to reading it as an apologia for assimilation and conversion so that, ultimately, despite great initial enthusiasm for the project, JPS rejected it for publication. How could the same work be read in contradictory ways? At JPS, *Memoirs* seemed to have functioned like a Rorschach test of anxious

---

3 On all these issues, see Magnus (2010, 2014) and my biography, *A Woman's Life: Pauline Wengeroff and Memoirs of a Grandmother*.

4 See Semjon Wengeroff's entry in *Wininger* (1925–1936, 6: 257), signed, "Ihr Sohn."

projections about Jewish communal prospects in the U.S, but that means that its meaning was somehow malleable. [5]

Indeed, Wengeroff's meaning is more difficult to parse than her seemingly innocuous (and, I argue, intentionally misleading) title – *Memoirs of a Grandmother* – would indicate. That goes for reading her Jewish ethnicity, too, my subject here. Wengeroff's subtitle – *Scenes from the Cultural History of the Jews of Russia in the Nineteenth Century* – would reasonably lead us to conclude that its author was an *Ostjudin*, as would the fact that she was born in Bobruisk and raised in Brest-Litovsk (which Jews called "Brisk"), in a region she and other Jews called *"lite"* (Lithuania). Wengeroff grew up in a very pious home. Her father studied in the *kollel* of the Volozhin yeshiva as a married man; her mother was a religious fanatic, phobic about European and secular culture – for males (she facilitated its study for Wengeroff and her other daughters under the double standard about this that prevailed in traditional Jewish culture. As was true for the vast majority of other Jews of the Pale in the nineteenth century, Wengeroff's mother tongue was Yiddish, as recalled conversations and letters that she records in *Memoirs* testify. She lived most of her life within the Russian Empire, if not always inside the Pale. All this would seem to qualify her solidly as an Ostjudin.

Wengeroff's work, however, comes to us as not as *zikhroynes fun a bubbe* but as *Memoiren einer Grossmutter: Bilder aus der Kuturgeschichte der Juden Russlands im 19ten Jahrhundert*, its two volumes published by the Poppelauer House in Berlin. Wengeroff's attachment to the German language and cultural things German began early and was profound. For all his piety, details of which punctuate descriptions in both her volumes, her father was positively disposed to the pedagogic reforms of the Haskalah (he opposed other parts of its agenda). He welcomed the visit of Max Lilienthal, the German *maskilic* rabbi deputized by Tsar Nicholas I's minister of public education to tour the Pale in 1840 and peddle the necessity and inevitability of cultural reform to its overwhelmingly traditional, resistant Jewish population. Remarkably, her father even took his sons-in-law, whom he was supporting to study Talmud, to see Lilienthal, who was reviled and even attacked physically in some Russian Jewish communities. As part of Wengeroff's engagement contract, her father made her fiancé commit to learning German because it was important in their region for "social reasons," about whose nature, unfortunately, she does not elaborate. Wengeroff, who learned German and Russian and other secular subjects through tutors, became her husband's German tutor after their marriage – that is, she was a central, if not the

---

5 On this, see my article, "Wengeroff in America: A Study in the Resonance of Conversion and Fear of Dissolution in Early Twentieth Century American Jewry," forthcoming in *Jewish Social Studies*, and my *A Woman's Life: Pauline Wengeroff and Memoirs of a Grandmother*.

sole, agent of his secularization, whose effects (but not her own role in them) she decries in *Memoirs*.

As an adolescent, Wengeroff was part of a circle of *maskilim* in Brisk that included women and met on Saturdays to read *maskilic* works. She herself made the works of Schiller available to the young men of the group, several of whom were members of her immediate family, who proceeded to place it (*Don Carlos*) within the folios of the Talmud they were supposed to be studying in the family's study room. To deceive Wengeroff's mother, they chanted it to the traditional singsong of sacred study (the deception failed; Wengeroff's mother was phobic about modernity and Haskalah, not stupid or deaf). As a newlywed at mid-century in her husband's Ukrainian hometown, Wengeroff "read through" not only Schiller but Heinrich Zscholdte, a German Protestant theologian who authored a wildly popular, eight-volume work of meditations that lauded "the home as a privileged space for moral self-improvement, the sanctification of motherhood and marriage, and the cultivation of personal virtue," middle class values that were distinctly Central- and West European.[6] In reading him, Wengeroff was participating in a German middle class cultural phenomenon.[7]

Wengeroff was anything but an obscurantist, a simple apologist for tradition. She evokes traditional culture and society with love and reverence but not uncritically. Much in her memoirs betrays her standing as a devotee of basic *maskilic* values.[8] Her terminology reveals this, too. Writing of Schiller, she says that his:

> [...] *poetry pierced the stifling, dank atmosphere of the ghetto like a breath of spring* [my italics] and the Jews marveled at all the magnificence and beauty which so suddenly appeared before them. Schiller played an important role in the lives as well as the literature of the Jews. When the Jewish youth first began to read foreign works, they began with Schiller, who enchanted them and through whom they perfected their knowledge of German. The men studied Schiller by heart; so did we young girls, and soon, knowing Schiller was an indispensable part of the curriculum of the cultured Jew: he studied Talmud, and Schiller – indeed, the latter with the same method as Talmud [...]. At that time, many translations into

---

6 See Wengeroff 2014, 85. Characterization is from Baader (2006, 114). Wengeroff does not specify which work she was reading; presumably, it was Zschokke's *Stunden der Andacht*.

7 Wengeroff also says that at this time, she was reading (August Friedrich Ferdinand von) "Kotzebue" (1769–1819), a German dramatist, as well as various Russian-language authors and one English-language author (in translation, although she does not state this; she did not know English). Wengeroff typically mentions authors by last name only, expecting her readers to recognize her reference – a significant indication of her expected audience. She mentions that she brought the German-language works from home (Brisk), picking up the Russian-language ones in her in-laws' home. On German middle-class values that the emerging Jewish middle class in Germany adopted and adapted, see Kaplan (1990). On the bourgeois behaviors that Wengeroff, and her husband, Chonon, adopted, and those he, in particular, did not, see Magnus (2015).

8 On this subject, see Magnus (2010, 2014).

Hebrew appeared, published by the best Jewish poets, who all tried their hand at Schiller. The reason for this popularity is the nature of Schiller's poetry, its intellectual character, and the gravity and pathos of his idealism, which viewed everything through the lens of the ethical (Wengeroff 2014, 2: 43–44).

For all her esteem for and attachment to traditional Jewish culture and learning, Wengeroff met an essential requirement for a *maskil,* a stance that separated modern Jews from those who created and joined ultra-Orthodoxy: she believed that traditional Jewish culture was not self-sufficient, that the best of European, but especially German enlightenment culture, conveyed noble ideals of which Jews were in need. It is safe to say that she shared the belief of many of her acculturating co-religionists in Germany that these ideals were fully compatible with and even helped realize, the values of Judaism.

I could readily quote other remarks by Wengeroff about the superiority of German Enlightenment culture and the "stifling, dank atmosphere of the ghetto." I shall cite one more, which comes in what I consider a signature expression of hers, one of several places in which she gives her gendered reading and indictment of Jewish modernity full voice:

In this transitional era, child rearing was entrusted to the mother, the natural teacher of her children, only for that period when the child required nothing but difficult sacrifice and arduous work. But as soon as the time for moral education arrived, the mother was brutally shoved aside and her authority over and care for the child ended. The woman, who still clung to tradition with every fiber of her being, wanted to impart it to her children, too: the ethics of Judaism, the traditions of its faith, the solemnity of the Sabbath and festivals, Hebrew, the teachings of the Bible – this book of books, this work for all times and peoples. She wanted to transmit this whole treasure to her children, in beautiful and exalted forms – together with the fruits of the Enlightenment, together with the new that West European culture had produced.

But to all pleas and protests, they received always the same answer from their husbands: "The children need no religion!" The young Jewish men of that time knew nothing of moderation and wanted to know nothing of it. *In their inexperience, they wanted to make the dangerous leap instantly from the lowest rung of culture straight to the highest* [my italics]. Many demanded of their wives not just assent but submission, demanding of them abolition of all that was holy but yesterday (Wengeroff 2: 110–111). (Note that Wengeroff extols the best that West – not East – European culture, had produced).

In these excerpts, we see Wengeroff's cultural taxonomy, which places enlightened West European culture at the apex and unenlightened, traditional Jewish culture well below it, in a stale, inferior sphere. This, from a woman who waxes poetic about Talmud and pointedly notes the benefits of its study even to secularizing Jewish men: Talmud – subject of a new tsarist phobia (joining older anti-Judaic phobias about Christ-killing) and of much *maskilic* criticism – the more telling her defense of it; this, from a woman who writes at length and with great sympathy about traditional women's ritual and spirituality.[9] Nevertheless, she regarded traditional Jews as living in a cultural ghetto that needed the piercing light of Schiller.

We have further evidence of Wengeroff's love of classical German literature from a vignette in the memoirs of Vladimir Medem (1879–1923), one of the founding leaders of the Russian-Jewish socialist party, the Bund. Medem recalls cultural evenings in his (converted) parents' home in Minsk (in the 1890s), in which participants declaimed "classic works of literature" (by which, he means German works) it was either Heine or Goethe, he recalls and he notes an elderly Wengeroff listening to them in rapture (Medem 1979, 21). Wengeroff twice cites Heine in *Memoirs*: his praise of "Schalet," and of the profound and ennobling rest of the traditional Jewish Sabbath, endorsements for which she could have found readily in traditional and East European sources.[10]

At the very least, Wengeroff is a complicated case, neither simply "East" nor "West." Of course, we know that these binaries are simplistic and distortive, but if further evidence were needed, Wengeroff certainly provides it.

The question of Wengeroff's chosen language for her *Memoirs* is an obvious, central one. Why German? Why not Yiddish? Or Russian? Let us first address why she did not use Hebrew. Wengeroff appears to have a good knowledge of traditional Hebrew – that is, of the weekday and holidays prayer books, the Passover Seder, and even a Biblical text, the chapter of Proverbs chanted on Friday nights to the female head of household. Wengeroff cites these texts meaningfully, moved by them: she understands them, albeit, likely with the help of Yiddish translations and/or commentary, written and oral. This is in contrast to her evocation of the *recitative* performance of the "Song of Songs" by her father and other male relatives at her childhood Passover Seders; in that case, she focuses on a powerful sensory experience she loved, rather than on the meaning of the words.[11] Her

---

9 On the emergence of a phobia about Talmud during the reign of Nicholas I (during Wengeroff's childhood), see Klier (2001).

10 Wengeroff references Heine without naming the specific source in his work (1: 208, see n. 290, 1: 331–332); the other reference to Heine (2: 112). Wengeroff also cites Disraeli, though not by this name, as well as Russian and traditional Yiddish writers and works, on which, see my introductions to volumes one and two.

11 Compare Wengeroff's writing about traditional Hebrew texts that she understood and the Seder chanting of the "Song of Songs" (1: 132, 161–162, 206).

Hebrew, however, like that of the vast majority of Jews, men and women, did not suffice for composition.[12]

Why not Yiddish? Wengeroff refers to it as *"jargon,"* which derogatory usage alone, employed by writers of the emerging Yiddish literature as well as the language's many detractors, may not indicate her contempt for it.[13] Yet, in describing what appear to her as primitive, simple Jews, women and men, she notes pointedly that they "spoke the purest *jargon*" – the language fit the type.[14] She, the highly literate daughter of two literate parents, from a wealthy, prominent home, was not this "type." Yiddish was the language of the "ghetto" (a term Wengeroff employs to refer to a cultural rather than physical space, walled-in ghettos of the Central European and Italian type not existing in Russia).[15] It was her mother tongue but not her language of self-presentation. Writing in Yiddish would also have consigned her work to the East, whereas Wengeroff was profoundly oriented westward; she expended considerable efforts to publish her work in the U.S and Germany and strove for publication in England, too.[16] Although there was a large and growing Yiddish-reading diaspora in the U.S. and England by the time Wengeroff published, clearly, neither this nor the Yiddish-reading masses in the Old Country were her desired audience: Wengeroff shared the prejudices of Western, Europeanized Jews about Ostjuden.[17] Her focus may have been Oriental, but her gaze was determinedly Occidental.

Wengeroff was fluent in Russian. She not only tells us in *Memoirs* that she studied it with tutors; she also left behind an archive of her correspondence, much of it in Russian, including with her husband and children. [18] Russian, then, was a language of intimacy for her and her family, not just an instrument necessitated by business contacts with Russian officialdom, essential to the work of her father, father-in-law, and husband, respectively, a building contractor for Nicho-

---

12 On women whose Hebrew sufficed for composition, see Cohen (2005) and Feiner (1998).

13 As Michael Stanislawski (1988, 48) notes, "jargon" was the standard term of the day for "the insipid dialect that Eastern European Jews persist in speaking to the disgust of all educated Jews" (here, paraphrasing a piece by the poet laureate of the East European Haskalah, Judah Leib Gordon).

14 For Wengeroff's associations of "jargon" with "common" and poor people and those with basic traditional, but not enlightened learning, see Wengeroff (2010, 1: 115, 117, 173, 178, 196).

15 On the gendered uses of Yiddish and Hebrew in East European Jewish society and the class and cultural connotations that went with this, see Parush (2004) and Seidman (1997).

16 On Wengeroff's authorial ambition and strenuous efforts on behalf of her own work, see Magnus (2015a, 2015b).

17 On Wengeroff's class prejudices, see Magnus (2010 and 2015a).

18 Other letters are in German; many include some Yiddish/ Hebrew words or phrases. Wengeroff's papers are preserved in the Pushkin Archive, cited henceforth in the text as PD, with archival number and, when available, date.

las I; holder of a government liquor concession; and head of a commercial bank. Intimate use of Russian by itself marks her as anything but a simple traditionalist: the vast majority of Jews under Russian rule born in the first half of the nineteenth century, or even in its in second half, lived in the Pale among Polish and Ukrainian-speaking populations and did not need Russian, even as an economic instrument. [19] The Haskalah would come to make Jewish acquisition of Russian a centerpiece of its program. This was a government priority from the beginning of tsarist rule over a substantial Jewish population, which met with increasing success in the second half of the nineteenth century, particularly among young, secularly educated, upwardly mobile segments of the Jewish population (such as Wengeroff's children). Wengeroff herself (2: 142) alludes to "government Russification of the Jews," beginning in the 1860s, with Russian introduced to replace German as the language of instruction in Jewish schools. The need for this encouragement is evident in the central emphasis placed on it by Russian Jewry's main representative organization, The Society for the Promotion of Culture among the Jews of Russia, founded in 1863.[20] Wengeroff and her family would have been exemplars of success in this area.

Indeed, I have discovered that Wengeroff did not compose *Memoiren einer Grossmutter* in German, and certainly not in the fluent, flawless German of the published work, but largely in Russian – with German, and some Yiddish and Hebrew and Polish phrases. Among Wengeroff's papers is a handwritten manuscript of some 250 pages in very poor physical condition. Smudged, its writing very hard to make out, it is, nonetheless, clearly a draft for the work that comes to us as *Memoiren einer Grossmutter* – and its predominant language is Russian (PD, archival number 949). Moreover, handwritten letters in German from Wengeroff to Solomon Schechter are full of spelling and grammatical errors.[21] Definitive evidence that Wengeroff received help putting the text into the polished, flawless German of the published work comes from her papers. There we find letters to her from Louise Flachs-Fockschaneanu, an accomplished translator from Russian to German and vice versa (Flachs-Fockschaneanu was a close friend of Wengeroff's

---

19 Jews in the Pale used local languages when necessary for their business dealings. See the statistics on Jews' language usage in Polonsky (2010, 2: 162–185). According to the tsarist census of 1897, a quarter of Jews in the Empire knew how to read and write Russian, but the qualifying criteria for determining this literacy were very minimal and the knowledge of most of these Jews did not exceed basics, even at this late date. Of 5,125,000 Jews in the Empire, 96.8 percent said Yiddish was their mother tongue; only 3 percent (162,610) listed other languages (Slutsky 1970, 35).
20 On acquisition of Russian by Jews of the Russian Empire, see Stanislawski (1983, 109–118 and 1988, 45–67); Nathans (2002); Horowitz (2008 and 2: 1771–1773); Rabinowich (2011, 378–379).
21 The correspondence with Solomon Schechter is in the Archives of the Jewish Theological Seminary of America, Solomon Schechter Collections, ARC 101, Correspondence Box 7.

daughter, Zinaida, herself a Symbolist author and prolific translator of European literature into Russian, and vice versa; this, I surmise, was the route for her connection to Wengeroff). Without stating the reason for her gratitude, Wengeroff acknowledges Flachs-Fockschaneanu warmly in *Memoirs*, saying, "I cannot send this little work, the intellectual child of an old woman, a 'child born in old age,' as the Jews say, into the world, without thanking my friend Louise Flachs-Fockschaneanu for her gracious encouragement" (Wengeroff 2010, 1: 95). Letters from Flachs-Fockschaneanu to Wengeroff, however, in which she refers to edited passages and encourages Wengeroff in her work, remove all doubt about her contribution.[22]

Given Wengeroff's fluent Russian, why did she labor, as we now know she did, to publish her life's work in German? Wengeroff, as we see from *Memoirs* as a whole and from the quoted excerpt about Schiller in particular, regarded Germany as *the* site of high culture, and the German language as its vehicle of expression, not only in Germany but also in the world she knew and above all, respected, especially in Russia. In his reminiscences of the German literature evenings in his parents' home, Vladimir Medem remarks: "there was something [...] characteristic in the fact that within this circle only German authors were read, and only in the German language." German served "as the vernacular" among "the genteel-intellectual environment" of Minsk (Medem 1979, 21), of which Wengeroff was an integral part during her many years in that city. In her comments about the substitution of Russian for German in Jewish schools in the 1860s (a policy change she ties, correctly, to the aftermath of the Polish rebellion of 1863–65), she links the weakening of (in her mind, already ineffective) Jewish instruction to this change. "Russification" to Wengeroff meant confinement to a specific culture, however much that culture presented itself as "general" (remarkably, these are her quotation marks).[23] German was the language of the universal but, simultaneously, so profoundly associated with things Jewish that a flourishing symbiosis was possible. Any weakness in Jewish education was the fault of teachers and school directors, not of the use of German. With the imposition of Russian, however, she laments, the Jewish curriculum was abbreviated, Hebrew instruction for girls even eliminated altogether, with the enthusiastic cooperation of "the Jewish teachers" (2: 142).

Given all this, attempting to define Wengeroff's Jewish ethnicity by language is a complicated and unrewarding venture. Her letters to her husband are

---

22 PD, archival number 1018.

23 See my comments about Wengeroff's use of quotation marks to challenge the notion that Russian culture was universal, a perception prompted, I argue, by her Jewish nationalism (2: 196, n. 5).

in German and Russian; to a sister and brother (when all are middle-aged and elderly), in German – as they are to Wengeroff's professional contacts, including Solomon Schechter, whose mother tongue was also Yiddish – two Ostjuden corresponding in German.

It is clear to me that Wengeroff eventually wished to leave Russia, a desire that apparently emerged after the pogroms of 1881–82, although she probably began trying to do so only after her husband's death, in 1892. As a widow, she spent significant time in Germany – she had two sisters in Heidelberg and composed at least part of *Memoirs* there; in a most poignant construction, she refers to the writing table her sister Helene had provided as her "homeland" (Wengeroff 2014, 2: 26). Letters she wrote to Theodor Herzl, in German, also emanate from Heidelberg (PD, archival number 975).[24] She spent three years in Vienna, from 1881–83, while her husband was still alive, and considerable time in Berlin, where her publisher was located. From letters she wrote to her sister, Kathy, who was extending financial support to her and appears to have wanted her to return to Minsk, however, we see that Wengeroff lingered in Berlin not just for business reasons but because she liked it there. In Berlin, she felt free from the terror of pogroms and the pervasive Jew-hatred that plagued her in Minsk and basked in respect and acceptance as a cultural figure.[25] Berlin, not Minsk, suited her.

When Wengeroff sought to publish *Memoirs*, she did not send it to any of the Jewish journals published in Russia, despite having published Russian-language excerpts from what would become *Memoirs* in the premier Russian-language Jewish journal, *Voskhod*, in 1902 and having close relatives involved in funding cultural projects of the Society for the Promotion of Culture among the Jews of Russia.[26] Instead, she sought serialization in the *Allgemeine Zeitung des Judentums*, German-speaking Jewry's premier organ, whose editor, Gustav Karpeles, was a pioneer of Jewish literary history. Recognizing the quality of what he read, Karpeles told her that it merited publication as a book – extraordinary encouragement at the turn of the twentieth-century from a culturally powerful man for a woman and her work. Several other prominent men assisted Wengeroff in her

---

24 See too, Letter from Wengeroff to Herzl, 27 Jan. 1904 (4 Shevat 5664), and Herzl to Wengeroff, dated 1 Feb. 1904, in the Central Zionist Archives, Jerusalem, file ZI/354, and in *Theodor Herzl Briefe* (1996, no. 5487, 6: 520 and 7: 520).

25 Undated, unfinished, Russian-language letter from Wengeroff to Kathy Sack (Zak, Ekaterina Julievna (hence the letter remained among Wengeroff's papers) (PD, archival number 957). Apparently, in connection with the financial concerns that are evident in this and other letters from this time (when *Memoirs* was first published), her sister was concerned about the cost of rented space for Wengeroff in Berlin, as opposed to Wengeroff's having her own housing in Minsk.

26 See Magnus (2010, 18, n 56, 244; and 2015a). On women, including Wengeroff, who published in *Voskhod*, see Balin (1998, 8–9).

aspirations to publish, including the Zionist writer and journalist, Alexander Tsederbaum, who suggested publishers in Berlin. Ultimately, she secured publication by Poppelauer, which published Karpeles' work.

We often hear of perceptions, mostly negative, by westernized Jews of Ostjuden at the end of the nineteenth century and the early decades of the twentieth, the era of mass emigration from Eastern Europe. *Ostjuden*, however, had perceptions and derogatory opinions of *Westjuden*, as well, which were articulated earlier than we might have expected, for which Wengeroff is a source. Among her many citations of folklore and folk songs from East European Jewish society, she brings the following in a section about children's amusement at Purim from the time of her childhood:

> The most amusing thing for us children was the so-called "Ballad of the She-Goat." An animal hide with a goat head on top was held up on two poles by a man hidden inside. The goat's neck was hung with all kinds of colored glass beads and corals, silver and brass coins, little bells and other sparkling, glimmering stuff. Two large bells fastened on both horns rang shrilly and blended with the other little tinkling trinkets to make a most peculiar sort of "music." The good man in the goat hide made all sorts of movements, dancing, leaping high and low. The leader of the She-Goat Ballad took charge of the singing with a merry, husky voice.

> The little ballad went as follows:
> On the high mountain, on the green grass,
> Stood a few modern Jews with long whips,
> Tall men are we,
> Modern garb do we wear,
> Our Father, Our King,
> Our hearts rejoice,
> Merry will we be,
> Wine shall we drink,
> We'll drink wine,
> We'll eat dumplings,
> And won't forget God (Wengeroff 2010, 115).

The above is my translation. Here is the original, as Wengeroff (1908, 1: 33) cites it – in transliterated Yiddish – (parenthetical translations into German are Wengeroff's):

> Afen hoichen Barg, afen grünem grus (gras)
> Stehn a por Deutschen mit die lange Beitshen.
> Hoiche manen seinen mir
> Kürze kleider gehen mir.
> Owinu Mielach (Unser Vater, König)
> Dus Harz is üns freilach (fröhlich)

Freilach wellen mir Wein.
Wein wellen mir trinken
Kreplach wellen mir essen
Un Gott wellen mir nit vergessen.

I would date Wengeroff's recollections of these childhood Purim celebrations to around 1840. We see here clearly the stereotyped image of *"Deutschen"* – "Germans" – which I translate as "modern Jews" because it meant the same thing for the children of her youth. They are tall (well fed, not like poor, East European Jews), wear short jackets, not caftans – and have long whips – not Talmud folios but symbols of power, mastery, cruelty. They are sacrilegious hedonists. It is clear that these Germans are Jews: they chant *avinu malkenu*. As Steven Aschheim (1982, 152) notes, "In Eastern Europe, the term *"daitsh"* – 'German' – was synonymous with the modern, beardless, heretical Jew."

This ditty, ridiculing assimilated, nihilistic, and hedonistic German Jews, is the East European Jewish counterpart to westernized Jews' contempt of their Eastern co-religionists and their culture; note the attributed hypocrisy of claiming not to forget God in the act of doing so. Examples of fulsome contempt are certainly to be found in East European Jewish writing, including *belles lettres*. In his *Dos Meserl* (Kiev, 1887), for example, Sholem Aleichem conveys traditional perceptions of a *"daitsh"* who came to a small Ukrainian town as "one of the wicked, for whom hell is too good," because he went "without a hat, without a beard, without sidelocks, and his *kapote* was half-cut."[27] Children in Brest-Litovsk (Brisk), however, sang the ditty Wengeroff cites well before mid-century, predating Sholem Aleichem's expression by nearly half a century. Ostjüdisch resentment of and contempt for (stereotyped) Westjuden attained expression earlier than we might have expected.[28]

Finally, to muddy the waters still further and to return, in conclusion, to Wengeroff herself, and how she was read: *Memoirs* was reviewed widely in the Jewish and non-Jewish press in Russia, Germany, Austria, even Holland; I saw about 40 such reviews. All were wildly enthusiastic, with one partial exception, in the *Israelitishce Monatsschritft* (Breslau), which, although positive, complained that she had echoed the caricature of the Talmudic "splitting of hairs." Surely, the most remarkable of the reviews appeared in the *Berliner Tageblatt*, a mass-circulation (ca. 250,000), liberal daily. Although the *Tageblatt* employed many Jews

---

27 Cited in Bartal (1985, 3–4).
28 Bartal (1985, 13) dates the emergence of negative expressions about "German" Jews ("goyishe yidn" – un- or non-Jewish Jews!) in the latter decades of the nineteenth century, but in Wengeroff, we have evidence of such expression decades earlier.

or people of Jewish origin, it was not a "Jewish" organ (except by definitions the Nazis would come to use), much less one that could possibly be construed as supporting the perpetuation or revival of any form of Jewish traditionalism.[29] After expressing relief that a book about life in Russia, let alone Jewish life, was not simply a "Jobiade," but was "radiant" with a "warm hearted piety," the reviewer ("J.E.P.") states that the reader:

> [...] listens to the old narrator as *if she were the little grandmother of us all* (als sei sie unser aller Grossmütterchen) telling us marvelous fairy tales in the [...] dark; fairy tales that we ourselves once beheld and experienced, when we were young [...]. One's heart celebrates memories in this reading and one's soul laments *all that we moderns have lost in the battle for bitter life* – all that was deep and heartfelt, which once made life a serious celebration. What a naïve, spirited book that has no other purpose but to hold up to us the mirror of *our own past...* [my italics].

In this extraordinary reading, a German reviewer looks beyond the Jewishness of Wengeroff's story and sees in it an evocation of the *temps perdu* that Germans, and indeed all 'moderns,' have undergone by dint of their modernity. This perception is the more remarkable because the experience she portrays was not just of Jews but of Ostjuden, objects of such scorn and hostility in fin de siècle Germany, and these Jews were undergoing transformation under the banner of Enlightenment emanating from Berlin.

Wengeroff herself, as I have argued here, represents an interesting case in this dialectic: On the one hand, by birth and place of residence for most of her life, she was an *Ostjudin*. On the other hand, she published her book in Berlin, in flawless, idiomatic German, giving the impression that this was her level of fluency and natural language of expression, a ploy that speaks even more forcefully for her attachment to the language. Her love for High German culture of the *Aufklärung* is evident from even a cursory reading of *Memoirs*. Wengeroff could thus pass for an extraordinary, dual spokeswoman of Jewish eastern "authenticity," and simultaneously, of Jewish, westernized modernity, a figure of East and West. Surely, this was one key to her success in the early twentieth century, by which time nostalgia for the Jewish past and idealization of *Ostjuden* were live currents in Jewish cultural life. Wengeroff was uniquely positioned to serve as translator of East to West, and West to East, even as a bridge between them: Other, yet familiar, sympathetic, accessible, and understandable. Her gaze was both Oriental and Occidental, of and about both.

---

29 On the *Berliner Tageblatt*, see Laqueur (1976).

In sum, Wengeroff's writing and the reactions to it suggest a far more variegated perception of self and Other in East – and West – European Jewry than stereotypes would imply, and leave much to ponder.

Bibliography

Aschheim, Steven E. *Brothers and Strangers: The East European Jew in German and German Jewish Consciousness, 1800–1923*. Madison: The University of Wisconsin Press, 1982.

Baader, Benjamin Maria. *Gender, Judaism, and Bourgeois Culture in Germany, 1800–1870*. Bloomington: Indiana University Press, 2006.

Balin, Carole B. "Jewish Women Writers in Tsarist Russia, 1869–1917." Ph. d. diss. Columbia University, 1998. 8–9.

Bartal, Israel. "The Image of Germany and German Jewry." *Danzig: Between East and West: Aspects of Modern Jewish History*. Ed. Isadore Twersky. Cambridge, MA: Harvard University Press, 1985. 1–18.

Cohen, Tova. "The Maskilot: Feminine or Feminist Writing?" *POLIN* 18 (2005): 57–86.

Feiner, Shmuel. "Haishah hayehudiyah hamodernit: Mikreh mivhan beyahasei hahaskalah vehamodernah" [The modern Jewish woman: a critical study in the relationship of the Haskalah and modernity]. *Eros, erussin, veissurin, miniyut umishpahah bahistoriyah*. Ed. Israel Bartal and Isaiah Gafni. Jerusalem: Merkaz Zalman Shazar, 1998. 253–303.

Herzl, Theodor. *Theodor Herzl Briefe, 1903–Juli 1904*. Berlin: Propyläen, 1996.

Horowitz, Brian. *Jewish Philanthropy in Late Tsarist Russia*. Seattle: University of Washington Press, 2008.

Horowitz, Brian. "Society for the Promotion of Culture among the Jews of Russia." *YIVO Encyclopedia*. New Haven: Yale University Press, 2008. 2: 1771–1773.

Kaplan, Marion. *The Making of the Jewish Middle Class: Women, Family, and Identity in Imperial Germany*. New York: Oxford University Press, 1990.

Klier, John. "State Policies and the Conversion of Jews in Imperial Russia." *Of Religion and Empire: Missions, Conversion, and Tolerance in Tsarist Russia*. Ed. Robert Geraci and Michael Khodarkovsky. Ithaca: Cornell University Press, 2001. 92–114.

Laqueur, Walter. *Weimar: A Cultural History*. New York: Capricorn, 1976.

Magnus, Shulamit S. Introductions to vol. 1 and 2 of Pauline Wengeroff, *Memoirs of a Grandmother: Scenes from the Cultural History of the Jews of Russia in the Nineteenth Century*. Ed. and trans. Shulamit S. Magnus. Stanford: Stanford University Press, 2010, 2014.

Magnus, Shulamit S. *A Woman's Life: Pauline Wengeroff and Memoirs of a Grandmother*. Oxford: The Littman Press, forthcoming, 2015a.

Magnus, Shulamit S. "Wengeroff in America: A Study in the Resonance of Conversion and Fear of Dissolution in Early Twentieth Century American Jewry." forthcoming in *Jewish Social Studies* 2015b.

Medem, Vladimir. *The Life and Soul of a Legendary Jewish Socialist*. Ed. and trans. Samuel A. Portnoy. New York: Ktav, 1979.

Nathans, Benjamin. *Beyond the Pale: the Jewish Encounter with Late Imperial Russia*. Berkeley: University of California Press, 2002.

Parush, Iris. *Reading Jewish Women: Marginality and Modernization in Nineteenth-Century Eastern European Jewish Society*. Waltham, MA: Brandeis University Press, 2004.

Polonsky, Antony. *The Jews in Poland and Russia, 1881–1914*. Oxford: The Littman Library, 2010. 2: 162–185.

Rabinowich, Osip Aronowich. "Russian Must Be Our Mother Tongue," and "Program" (Society for the Promotion of Culture among Jews). *The Jew in the Modern World. A Documentary History*. Ed. Paul Mendes-Flohr and Jehuda Reinharz, 3rd ed. New York: Oxford University Press, 2011.

Seidman, Naomi. *A Marriage Made in Heaven: The Sexual Politics of Hebrew and Yiddish*. Berkeley: University of California Press, 1997.

Slutsky, Yehuda. *Ha'itonut hayehudit-rusit bameah hatish'ah 'esreh* [The Jewish-Russian press in the nineteenth century]. Jerusalem: Mosad Bialik, 1970.

Stanislawski, Michael. *Tsar Nicholas I and the Jews: The Transformation of Jewish Society in Russia, 1825–1855*. Philadelphia: The Jewish Publication Society, 1983.

Stanislawski, Michael. *For Whom Do I Toil: Judah Leib Gordon and the Crisis of Russian Jewry*. New York: Oxford University Press, 1988.

Wengeroff, Pauline. Papers in Pushkin Archive, Archival Division, fond 39 (Pushkinskii Dom, Vengerova, Paulina Iulievna; P. Vengerova), St. Petersburg, Russia.

Wengeroff, Pauline. *Memoiren einer Grossmutter: Bilder aus der Kulturgeschichte der Juden Russlands im 19. Jahrhundert*. Berlin: Poppelauer House: 1908, 1910, 1913, 1919, 1922.

Wengeroff, Pauline. *Memoirs of a Grandmother: Scenes from the Cultural History of the Jews of Russia in the Nineteenth* Century. 2 vol. Ed. and trans. Shulamit S. Magnus. Stanford: Stanford University Press, 2010, 2014.

Winniger, Salomon. "Semjon Wengeroff." *Grosse jüdische National-Biographie*. Cernauti: Orient, 1925–36. 6: 257.

Shelly Zer-Zion

The Anti-Nazi Plays of Habimah during the 1930s and the Making of Eretz-Israel *Bildung*

> Professor Mannheim and Otto Frank are two Jewish figures that are no other than the reincarnation of the Jew Süss and Shylock, whose characters left modern imprints on the twentieth century, in a period when the world's fate hung in the balance, an era of sensual overdose and the horror of destruction, fighting with Don Quixotesque chivalry for Jewish rebirth and human freedom (Finkel 1971, 41).

Shimon Finkel thus recalls three of the leading roles he played in Habimah during the 1930s: the title role in *Jud Süss* staged by Zvi Friedland in 1933, the title role in *Professor Mannheim* staged by Leopold Lindtberg in 1934, and Shylock in *The Merchant of Venice* staged by Leopold Jessner in 1936.[1] These three roles constituted a turning point in Finkel's artistic career, turning him into one of Habimah's stars and identifying him as a classical actor. They were all also related – directly or indirectly – to the fate of German Jewry under Nazism.

The rise of Nazism directly affected Jewish culture in Mandatory Palestine. According to Zionist organization estimations, more than 68,000 Jewish refugees from central Europe arrived in the country between 1933 and the outbreak of World War II. The newcomers brought their professional and artistic culture to Palestine, participating in the local cultural scene both in urban cities – such as Jerusalem and Haifa – and the agricultural settlements (Gelber 1990).[2] As the Yishuv leadership was heavily involved in saving central European Jews and their property, a public discourse arose around its role in fighting Nazism (Wagman 1999). Focusing on the Eretz-Israel theater scene, this article will examine the artistic reaction of Habimah – regarded as a national theatrical institution – to the rise of Nazism.

According to theater historian Thomas Postlewait (2009), theater performance functions simultaneously on two parallel levels, constituting both a public event similar to any other that takes place in the public sphere and an artistic event – a theatrical metaphor for current reality. In light of this observation, I would like to engage in a close reading of the staging of the three Habimah

---

1 He also played the role of Otto Frank, Anne Frank's father, in *The Diary of Anne Frank* – a stage adaptation of the diary by Frances Goodrich and Albert Maurice Hackaett produced by Habimah in 1957.

2 For the cultural activity of German Jewish immigrants in Palestine, see, for example, Lewy (2005); Ziva Sternhell (2005); and Kenaan-Kedar (2005).

productions in which Finkel played a leading role: *Jud Süss*, *Professor Mannheim*, and *The Merchant of Venice*. Discussing the tension between the plays' functions as cultural and as artistic events, I shall also analyze the artistic formula they embodied in reference to the plight of German Jewry. At first glance, they merely broadened the concept of the "negation of the diaspora" that prevailed in contemporary discourse, stressing the decline of Jewish life in Europe as a negative counter image to the impending spiritual and physical revival stimulated by the return to the land. Further examination, however, reveals the company's passion for European *Bildung* and its method of incorporating this into its performative aesthetics.

1 Performance as political event

The play *Jud Süss* premiered in July 1933. Habimah had made Mandatory Palestine its permanent home only two and a half years earlier, following a temporary sojourn of a year and a half in Berlin. After arriving in Palestine, the troupe struggled to retain its international reputation and establish itself as an elite Hebrew troupe within the framework of the Yishuv: Eretz-Israel audiences and critics frequently criticized its repertory choices, which did not meet their aesthetic and ideological expectations.

During the late 1920s, the troupe had established an administrative secretariat centered in Berlin to manage its financial affairs. The secretariat, whose members were well versed in the local Berlin Jewish culture, recommended that the troupe put on a stage adaptation of *Jud Süss* – both because it regarded the character as especially appropriate for a Hebrew-Zionist troupe and because of the growing German-Jewish interest during the late Weimar republic in the historical figure (Protocol 1929). Joseph Süsskind Oppenheimer (1698–1738), a court Jew for Duke Karl Alexander of Württemberg, was executed on charges of sexual relations with Christian women following his patron's sudden death (Emberger and Ries 2006, 29–56). A legend in his own lifetime – the subject of numerous folk tales and poems, he became the archetype of the "wandering Jew" as a result of the flood of popular and scholarly literature that appeared after his death. He became a particularly popular object of artistic and scholarly attention in Weimar Germany, appealing especially to German-Jewish intellectuals, authors, and playwrights. Leon Feuchtwanger's *Jud Süss*, published in 1925, was merely one of a spate of scholarly, literary, and dramatic works on this theme during the period (Sheffi 2003). In my opinion, this interest reflects an intellectual tendency that Steven Aschheim calls "post-*Bildung*" – a critical reevaluation of the notions of acculturation, self-improvement, and a sense of European belonging (Aschheim 1996, 31–44). In this climate, the "Jew Süss" exemplified the Jews' yearning and failure to find a home in Germany.

When the play premiered in July 1933, the Nazis had just come to power in Germany. Tel Aviv theater critics of the time quickly noted that its staging directly reflected contemporary events in Germany:

> The play [...] affords considerable room for comparison with current events. Like the court Jew Süss in the eighteenth century, who – despite all the benefits and hard labor with which he loyally served the Duke of Württemberg – ended his life in agony and disgrace, so today, German Jews who have sanctified Germany's name and enriched its creativity, are hunted and given into the hands of brutal abusers ("Habimah" 1933).

In contrast to the other productions the company staged in the early 1930s, the Hebrew reception of Habimah's *Jud Süss* evoked a strong sense of Eretz-Israel "hereness" – or cultural association with the performance's immediate surroundings (Carlson 2013). Local theater critics pessimistically compared the story of the protagonist in *Jud Süss* to the plight of contemporary German Jewry, who, they argued, were doomed to the same fate as their court Jew precursor. This attitude mirrored the prevalent Yishuv ideology of "the negation of the diaspora," which had been formulated and expressed by such leaders and intellectuals as Berl Katzenelson, David Ben-Gurion, and others.[3] In the audience's eyes, the play was an omen predicting the destruction of German Jewry – even before the introduction of the Nüremberg laws in 1935 that institutionalized many of the racial theories prevalent in Nazi ideology.

A year after *Jud Süss*, *Habimah* staged Hans Scheier's *Professor Mannheim* in July 1934 – one of the most explicit anti-Nazi performances of the 1930s in Mandatory Palestine. The play's political impact rested primarily on the way in which it reached the stage. Its director, Leopold Lindtberg, was among the first from the German theater scene to flee Germany to Palestine after having attracted attention as a rising star in his home country. After the rise of Nazism, he accepted a job offer from Margot Klausner, Habimah's administrative director, who hoped that he would settle permanently in the country and become Habimah's artistic director (Klausner 1971, 180–215). Although he staged four plays while working with Habimah between 1934 and 1935, he also began working at the Schauspielhaus Zürich, where he remained over a long career (Lindtberg 1990).

The German play's path to the Hebrew Habimah was even more complicated. The original version of the play, *Professor Mannheim*, was published in German

---

3 See, for example, Frieling (2009) and Shapira (2009).

in 1935 under the title *Professor Mamlock*. It soon became clear that the author was, in fact, a renowned physician, playwright, and activist in the German Communist Party (KPD) named Friedrich Wolf. While active in the leftist German theater scene, Wolf also worked with such prominent figures as Erwin Piscator and Bertolt Brecht. He wrote the play as a documentary journalistic drama by an opposition activist describing the Nazification of the German public sphere. After completing it, in July 1933, Wolf sent it to the Theater Union in New York. The play premiered in January 1934 in Yiddish at the Kaminsky Theater in Warsaw under the title *Dos gelbe flek* (The yellow badge). The exiled German-Jewish actor Alexander Granach played the role of Mannheim.

Granach was a well-known figure in Jewish theater circles.[4] Raised in an impoverished Yiddish speaking family near Lemberg, he made his way to Berlin, where he obtained a job as a baker. When – against all the odds – his acting talent was discovered, he made an effort to transform himself. He cultivated a native pronunciation of High German, studied acting, and underwent a series of plastic surgery operations in order to acquire the conventional features of a leading German actor. Eventually, he became a star in the preeminent Berlin theaters of the time. After the rise of Nazism, he escaped to Poland and thence to the Soviet Union, where he returned to Yiddish performances after long years of acting exclusively in German (Jakobi 2005, 178–197).

The Yiddish performance of the play in Poland was essentially a Jewish event of anti-Nazi protest, depicting the miseries inflicted on the Jews under Nazi rule in both real life and on the stage – Granach's own life mirroring the play's plot.

The *Habimah* production was the second staging of the play worldwide. The Eretz-Israel theater critics were well aware of the playwright's identity. Critic Eli'ezer Lubrani noted: "The author Hans Scheier was forced to use a pseudonym this time because his friends and relatives are still endangered by the same events and people that served as the backdrop to the play" (Lubrani 1934). According to Yesha'ayahu Kalinov, no need existed for such subterfuge because it was well known that *Professor Mannheim* was identical to *The Yellow Badge*, which had recently been staged in Warsaw (Kalinov 1934). In discussing the production in a Habimah youth forum, critic Dov-Beer Malkin similarly remarked that Finkel's acting was far more restrained than Granach's.

Both actors and audience shared the view that the Habimah production constituted, first and foremost, a political act of solidarity with Jewish anti-Fascist and anti-Nazi resistance in Europe. As Na'ama Sheffi notes, before television, a documentary play making the swift rounds between Berlin, Warsaw, and Tel

---

4 Shimon Finkel (1968, 15–120) recalled that, as a child and theater lover in Grodno, he had heard of Granach and dreamt about following in his footsteps.

Aviv functioned as a "living newspaper" – firsthand, authentic testimony about events taking place in Germany (Sheffi 2006). As theater critic German learned during one of the rehearsals, the actors themselves were aware of serving as witnesses and prophets of doom:

> We returned to the stage not in the happiest mood. The curtain fell and rose again. The acting began. The state of the Jews in Germany [...] today in Germany, and where will it be tomorrow? Four Jewish destinies, three who believe in Germany, and only one who believes in Eretz-Israel. [...] Germany is beautiful, its language is poetic, its concerns became the worries of the Jews. [...] And here, into this peaceful serenity, bursts the heavy storm of Hitler.

The third play under discussion here – Shakespeare's *The Merchant of Venice* – opened on 14 May 1936 under the direction of Leopold Jessner. Its production, like that of the two other plays, clearly constituted an anti-Nazi protest. Rather than expressing concern over events in Germany (*Jud Süss*) or advocating support of European anti-Nazi resistance (*Professor Mannheim*), however, this performance served to convey the ambivalence felt in the country towards the flood of German Jewish immigrants.

In this case, too, the play's director, Leopold Jessner played a central role in creating the public event. Jessner was the most important theater artist to reach Palestine, Together with Erwin Piscator and Max Reinhardt, he was considered one of the three leading directors responsible for shaping Weimar's theatrical style. Arriving as a stateless refugee, he embodied the danger facing German Jewry. At the height of his career, he served as the general director of the Berlin State Theater, a prominent representative of the Weimar trend towards innovative political theater (Feinberg 2003, 2010). As Margot Klausner (1971, 210–212) recalls, "Jessner had always shown an interest in Habimah when it toured Germany. [...] He was a cautious man and no longer in his youth – he was older than 60 – but, like all great men I have met, he was modest and very friendly."

Leaving his position at the Berlin State Theater in 1928, Jessner worked as an independent director until 1933. In danger as a Jew, a socialist, and a proponent of political theater, he fled from Germany, working first as a theater director in the Netherlands and Great Britain and then making his way to Palestine (Feinberg 2010). Well aware of Jessner's reputation, the intellectual circle around Habimah greeted Jessner's arrival with great excitement.

In a series of events prior and subsequent to the staging of *The Merchant of Venice*, he articulated his vision regarding the mission of Hebrew theater. Believing in its ability to create a unified public sphere integrating the disparate cultures that Jewish immigrants were bringing to the country, he declared: "If a congress of these 'wandering Jews' who give their wealth to all kinds of homelands were to be convened and each required to give an account of his deeds, I could defend myself only by appealing to two facts: that I worked in a foreign land as a Jew in the spirit of Judaism, and that, moreover, I was privileged to work with Habimah" (Jessner 1936a, 1936b).

Herein, he gives poignant voice to his personal tragedy – the collapse of his lifetime achievement and its reduction to the Jewish element alone. His disappointment with German-Jewish *Bildung* also manifested itself in the choice of *The Merchant of Venice*. He had, in fact, been one of the most outstanding interpreters of Shakespeare in the German theater of the republic, focusing on allegorical presentations of the ethical and political aspects of plays such as *Richard the Third* and *Macbeth* using abstract staging (Kuhns 1997, 173–217; Hortman 1998, 44 111). Although Habimah's management had shown an interest in collaborating with Jessner in producing *The Merchant of Venice* during its sojourn in Berlin, he had never staged that particular play, which deals so blatantly with Jewish identity (Protocol of Habimah general assembly 1930; Bonnell 2008, 5–118; Fischer-Lichte 2010). As it had been one of the most frequently performed Shakespearean plays in Germany from the time of the nineteenth century, this omission was striking (Bonnell 2008, 5–118). Shylock's dark vindictiveness, moreover, evinced the complexity of post-*Bildung* Jewish identity; moreover, the play contrasted sharply with the softness of *Nathan the Wise*, the symbol of German enlightenment (Bayerdörfer 1993).

Whereas the public discourse surrounding the earlier productions revealed the Eretz-Israel view of events taking place in Germany, the reception given *The Merchant of Venice* exposed a fear that German Jews might seize control of the country – represented by their taking over the national theater company. The Hebrew theater critics in Mandatory Palestine expressed doubts whether the dark Shylock was an appropriate figure for an all-Jewish audience. Lea Goldberg, for example, approved of the production of classic European plays, but she thought *Hamlet* a better choice than *The Merchant of Venice* (Goldberg 1931). Yesha'ayahu Kalinov was even more strongly opposed to producing a work with such a long antisemitic tradition in the Hebrew city of Tel Aviv (Kalinov 1936).

Seeking to turn the issue into a cultural touchstone, Habimah and its circle of friends encouraged discussion of whether the play should be produced, even putting it on "public trial" at the Ohel Shem auditorium on 23 June 1936. The event served as a performative platform for a public debate regarding Shylock in the political context of Palestine and interpretative traditions relevant to this setting ("The Literary Trial" 1936). Poet Alexander Penn, one of two witnesses for the prosecution, attacked Jessner fiercely:

If, for the world, the performance of *The Merchant of Venice* should serve as an accusation, then domestically – for those of us who come here in order to effect a spiritual and economic transformation in our lives – this play should serve as a serious warning, a self-defense against the petty Shylocks, speculators, and profiteers who are infiltrating the land. I, therefore, maintain that director Jessner has not understood that the objectives and aspirations of the Yishuv stand in fundamental antithesis to his analysis of the figure of Shylock. In my opinion, his interpretation is anti-educational, anti-Zionist, and informed by the exile ("The Literary Trial" 1936, 28).

According to Penn, Shylock represented exilic Jewish pathology; he was the enemy of Zionism. Jessner's Shylock symbolized the fourth and fifth waves of immigration – petit-bourgeois Jews escaping antisemitism and economic hardship in central Europe and Poland whose degenerate nature posed an immediate threat to the Zionist ideal of self-transformation.

The "lawyer for the defense" was theater critic Dov-Beer Malkin. In his arguments, he emphasized that Hebrew culture should take its cue from the German-Jewish intellectual milieu, whose members regarded *The Merchant of Venice* as a masterpiece. Leaving the interpretation of Shylock in the Eretz-Israel context open in this way made it possible to adapt the play to local conditions independently of Jessner's views. Ultimately, Jessner suffered the most from the trial, returning to Europe after staging two plays (*The Merchant of Venice* and *Wilhelm Tell*) and then moving to the United States.[5]

These three performances – *Jud Süss*, *Professor Mannheim*, and *The Merchant of Venice* – all constituted public events that evoked the "hereness" of Mandatory Tel Aviv, representing the local Eretz-Israel Jewish view on the events taking place in Germany. Critics expected Habimah, as a "national" theater, to address issues of national importance and give theatrical expression to the Yishuv's ideologies. Indeed, it conveyed a spectrum of responses within Jewish Mandatory Palestine to the plight of German Jewry – ranging from concern and solidarity to hostility and rejection. In the following section, I shall examine the way in which Habimah's presentation of politically imbued theater influenced the development of its performative and artistic language. I shall argue that, despite Habimah's rejection of European politics, its theatrical language, acting style, and mise-en-scènes expressed a deep longing for German and European traditional bourgeois culture.

---

5 For the public trial of *The Merchant of Venice*, see Zer-Zion (2003) and Berger (2011).

2 The yearning for Europe

Based on Mordechai Avi-Shaul's dramatic adaptation of Leon Feuchtwanger's novel, *Jew Süss* afforded the earliest vehicle through which Habimah sought to articulate its anti-Nazi artistic ethos. Having first translated the novel into Hebrew in 1929, Avi-Shaul then undertook a stage adaptation (Feuchtwanger 1929; Sheffi 2003). Shimon Finkel (1971) hypothesized that this staging was influenced by Ashley Dukes' English adaptation; an analysis of the play's script, however, reveals the extent to which it also bears the imprint of Habimah's unique features.

As Avi-Shaul acknowledged, his Süss oscillates between two opposing poles, Rabbi Gabriel – representing Süss' spiritual side, on the one hand, and Landauer, the businessman, symbol of Süss' practical temperament, on the other:

> Süss is undeterred. He creates a duke for himself, turning his Golem into a ruler who will serve his Jewish genius. [...] One day, he sees that the duke cannot distinguish the will of his creator from the instincts of his own heart. The vessel gained control over the one who holds it. [...] Süss's grandiose plans – the lofty political and financial structure – are dependent upon the arbitrary will of the person into whom the Jew breathed life. The noble destroyer relentlessly demolishes everything in his path, turning the sublime structure into ashes. [...] [Eventually,] he collapses. Without Süss's creative power, he is nothing more than heartless clay. When he breaks down, however, so does his creator. He has invested too much in his creation (Avi-Shaul 1933).

The two figures that most influenced Avi-Shaul's adaptation are the gentile Faust and the Jewish Maharal of Prague. Although the Jew Süss sells his soul to the vain Christian world in order to achieve power and pleasure in this world, his Mephisto is not the devil but a reincarnation of the Golem – earthly body, physical desire, and material hedonism. Like the Golem, the duke rises against his creator and demolishes everything he encounters in a burst of desire – including the Jews themselves, whom Süss had sought to redeem via his intimate relationship with the ruler, and Süss' daughter. He thus destroys all that Süss treasured most.

The duke-Golem makes Süss appear as a secular Maharal – a superman who yearns to pull downs the ghetto walls, create and demolish worlds, and gain power and authority. Unlike the Maharal, however, Süss is not divinely inspired; his power and creativity focus solely on material gain. Only after his fall and the death of his daughter is Süss able to acknowledge his hubris, repent, and return to Judaism and the Jewish collective (Avi-Shaul File 221109).

Staged by Zvi Friedland, one of Habimah's two in-house directors during the 1930s, the play bore the characteristic marks of his style, combining stage technology with interpretative casting and intensive work with the leading actors (Yerushalmi 2013, 87–112). The casting was very significant, particularly because the actors' performances in previous roles added an enhanced performative depth to the characters they portrayed.[6]

Aharon Meskin, who had attained international fame for his role as the Golem, played the role of Karl Alexander. Meskin first appeared in Habimah's 1925 production of *The Golem* based on H. Leivik's play and directed by Boris Illich Vershilov (Finkel 1980, 5–27). The Eretz-Israel audience was very familiar with this play, which had been a stalwart of Habimah's repertoire for over thirty years (Citron 1980). Bringing this theatrical history to the role, Meskin imbued it with violence and lasciviousness.

Shimon Finkel's casting as Süss reflected his own biography rather than evoking the earlier roles he had played. Finkel joined Habimah in 1927, when the troupe was in its temporary home in Berlin. At the time his artistic ambitions focused not on the company's Muscovite heritage but on becoming an actor on the German stage. Having left his home town of Grodno for the German capital in order to study acting, he regarded German theater culture as the height of sublime art.[7] As a student at Max Reinhardt's acting school, he immersed himself in the *Bildung* canon of dramatic literature, also undergoing three elective surgeries on his nose and palate in order to improve the clarity and depth of his voice. Such a demanding process of self-improvement, he believed, would turn him into a professional actor capable of playing leading roles on the German stage.

Loneliness eventually drove him to join a Hebrew troupe working in Berlin, with which he immigrated to Palestine, returning to Berlin a mere two years later. Only after he had resigned himself to the impossibility of achieving success on the German stage, he considered joining the Hebrew Habimah. He settled in Palestine, together with the rest of the troupe, in 1931. Even in his new theatrical home, however, he continued to yearn for a theater in the spirit of *Bildung* and the canonical German and European repertoire (Zer-Zion 2010).

Finkel seemed a natural choice for the role of Süss, with his deep voice, rhetorical tendencies, and tragic pathos – an acting style theater scholar Bert O. States called the "self-expressive mode" (States 1995). No other actor was better fitted for conveying Süss' desire for the splendor of the German court beyond the boundaries of Jewish life. Finkel notes that, despite the demands the role imposed upon him, he was ultimately satisfied with his artistic achievements, feeling that

---

6 Theater scholars contend that theater is an embodied medium in which the actors' bodies convey the knowledge and cultural significance of the theatrical performance; their presence, physical abilities, artistic repertoire, and biographies thus turn into cultural texts: see, for example, Taylor (2003, 1–52); Carlson (2001).

7 Eastern European educated Jews held German culture in the highest esteem: see, for example, Aschheim (1982, 246–254) and Shulamith S. Magnus' essay in this volume.

he had captured the character and its nuances. The most unconvincing part of his performance was his relationship with his daughter because of his difficulty in mastering and projecting onto the stage intimacy with the Jewish world (Finkel 1971, 30–31).

Although theater critics differed in their reviews, they all applauded Finkel's role as Süss. For example, Avraham Shmuel Yuris sharply criticized the stage adaptation, viewing Süss as a desiccated Nietzschean superman – a "Mephisto-like Shylock burning with vengeance" – with no genuine association with Jewish tradition, but he was captivated by Finkel's acting:

> At the center of the play stood Finkel's Süss. It was not, nor could be, Feuchtwanger's Süss. However, Finkel perfectly embodied the role of Süss in the play – and at a very high level. It was a classic work of art. At the beginning, a proud, confident knight at the duke's court; in the middle, a powerful minister of finance; and at the end, a vindictive Mephisto-like Jew – an avenger and martyr. In each period, he adopted a new disguise, another tempo, different acting (Yuris 1933, 34).

Habimah staged *Jud Süss* before it produced any classical tragedies – *Hamlet* or *Oedipus Rex*, for example; it constituted a Hebrew variation of an eighteenth-century German bourgeois tragedy. Although, like Schiller's *Love and Intrigue* or *Don Carlos*, it dealt with national-civil themes, in this case the hero was a Jewish citizen and the plot dealt with his relationship with the German court.

At first glance, *Professor Mannheim* appears to be completely different in character from the *Jud Süss* – written as an anti-Nazi agitprop by a playwright associated with the German leftist theater school of Bertholt Brecht and Erwin Piscator (Jakobi 2005, 178–197). The German-Jewish physician Mannheim (Mamlock), head of the surgical unit in a Berlin hospital, is a World War I hero who holds nationalist-liberal views. After his Christian wife blames him *and his race* for being stubborn, his son becomes an activist in a socialist underground movement, his daughter is bitten at school, and he is expelled from his position at the hospital, he commits suicide, shooting himself with his service revolver.[8]

In direct contrast to the stylized expressivity that characterized the performative poetics of the Habimah actors, Lindtberg sought to create a realistic performance in the new objective style (Lewy 2010). As Finkel observed:

> It was a journalistic play rather than a literary one. It was thus of transient, momentary significance – although at that time, this kind of play fulfilled a highly important function. This was the way Lindtberg approached it – as a burning actuality that demanded

---

8 Hans Scheier, *Professor Mannheim*. The dramatic text is available at the Israeli Center for the Documentation of the Performing Arts, File 225059.

close attention to the immediate, without any pretensions to a long-term perspective. Even I. Luftglas's realistic scenery [...] recalled [...] the square newspaper page (Finkel 1971, 41).

Like other theatrical creations from the same school, *Professor Mannheim* rejected German (-Jewish) liberalism, perceiving socialism as the only political philosophy that would lead to genuine equality. Unlike Piscatorian and Brechtian theater, however, rather than challenging the poetic norms of bourgeois drama, *Professor Mannheim* – whose protagonist was a German citizen of the Jewish religion – was a proper bourgeois tragedy: the play lamented the fall of a citizen wholeheartedly committed to the Weimar republic's liberal and national values. It depicted the Jews as the epitome of German civil order, part of the *Bildungsburgertum* – a social class identified with the cultural and social elite of German Jewry. Their behavior exemplified Hegelian ethical models of civic altruism – Mannheim's bravery in the war and the Jewish hospital janitor Simon's donation of blood.

Such civic tragedy infuriated theater critic Yesha'ayahu Kalinov: "Do these 'Scheiers' know the heights Zionism has attained in Germany nowadays? How people carry the 'yellow badge' with genuine pride? And how it has affected and still affects the Jewish milieu?" (Kalinov 1934). German-Jewish civic tragedy was scarcely credible to a theater critic born in a Russia where deep-rooted antisemitism had strongly stimulated Jewish and Zionist self-awareness (Volkov 2006, 13–32). Many others in the Eretz-Israel audience similarly were unable to understand or identify with the German-Jewish sense of loss; they regarded Mannheim's suicide as a manifestation of his tragic flaw – trusting the German state (Sheffi 2006). As in *Jud Süss*, Shimon Finkel's performance helped them identify with the play and intensified the tragic effect. As critic Eliezer Lubrani noted: "Finkel grows older, more mature. The character of Prof. Mannheim was imbued with human dignity and an unbounded belief in democracy and the German homeland. He succeeded in giving wonderful expression to the collapsing world of a Jewish person clinging with all his heart and body to German soil" (Lubrani 1934).

Fundamental differences characterize Süss and Mannheim: whereas the former undergoes a process of Jewish self-discovery, finally choosing martyrdom, Mannheim's tragedy derives from his inability to relinquish the possibility of a German-Jewish symbiosis (Sheffi 2006). Lubrani's critique nonetheless indicates the affinities between – and even the merging of – the two characters.

The dramaturgical aspects of the plays indicate that Süss and Mannheim are both imposing figures who are victims of a tragic flaw – the belief that Jews can find a civic home in Germany. Their performative features reveal that both characters were primarily shaped by Shimon Finkel's presence, voice, and dramatic skills, his self-expressive acting mode imposing his charismatic presence and virtuosity upon the various roles he played (States 1995). As he himself acknowledged, Lindtberg encouraged him to sharpen his artistic tools in order to construct an authentic and natural stage figure imbued by his own body, voice, and desires (Finkel 1971, 27–47).

The aim of imbuing a character with the actor's charismatic presence was the antithesis of the German espousal of new objectivity. Both Piscator and Brecht dealt extensively with the issue of the gap between reality and its stage representation, examining in their theatrical works – albeit through divergent stage techniques – the ethics of representation and the performers' responsibility to the reality they were seeking to represent (Innes 1972, 66–131; and Auslander 1997, 28–38). In contrast, on the Habimah stage, Wolf's agitprop theater became a conservative tragedy whose hero was a bourgeois and enlightened German-Jew who yearned for Germany; Finkel endowed the role with a tragic aura and evoked an intense emotional impact.

Habimah's production of *The Merchant of Venice* consolidated its anti-Nazi poetics. Staging it in line with his political interpretation of Shakespeare, Leopold Jessner provided the platform for the crystallization of the company's performative formula. Jessner's fascination with Shakespeare can be understood as an expression of his theatrical variation on the "post-*Bildung*" theme – i.e., the staging of a critical reading of the dramatic texts that formed the canon of European and German *Bildung*.

Although *The Merchant of Venice* is traditionally classified as a comedy, Jessner interpreted it as a tragedy. Viewing it as a protest against antisemitism and Jewish persecution across history, he regarded Shylock as a particularly apt character for Eretz-Israel audiences, thus rejecting his portrayal as a passive victim of fate: "The legend of a passive Shylock who meets a tragic end is inappropriate for a Habimah performance guided by a new train of thought. [...] [The performance] thus presents a weighty Shylock – not a passive Shylock but rather Shylock the *warrior*. Although he is defeated by the schemes of his opponents and ends tragically, he is not a passive but a *tragic hero* [italics in the original]" (Jessner 1936a).

Seeking to present Shylock sympathetically and to subvert the antisemitic images associated with the figure, Jessner (1936a) gave his Shylock majesty and intensified the conflict between him and the opportunistic world of Venice and Belmont. This interpretative choice further canonized German-Jewish tragedy on the Hebrew stage. Whereas Habimah's *Jud Süss* and *Professor Mannheim* presented a local Eretz-Israel variant of the German-Jewish bourgeois tragedy, its *Merchant of Venice* rooted the German-Jewish tragedy in the canon of world dramatic literature and the German-Jewish *Bildung* tradition. It was, in fact, the first Shakespearean tragedy to be produced in the Hebrew theater.

Meskin and Finkel shared the role of Shylock. Although they created two distinct characters, both portrayed Shylock as a fanatical avenger, committed to taking his revenge on the Venetian world that had excluded and humiliated him, even at the expense of his own self-destruction. Yesha'ayahu Kalinov recalled the powerful impression Meskin's Shylock made: "Meskin Kalinov in the role of Shylock [...] what a strong robustness. [...] As if the entire essence of the vision is: I am better than you, and my image, my appearance alone, can testify to that" (Kalinov 1936).

Unlike Meskin's powerful, firm figure, Finkel's Shylock was softer and gentler: "Finkel, who performed at the second premiere, is good and consistent in the role of Shylock. Good and consistent – but different. He is softer. He is more of a father. More precisely, a Jewish father, as his entire role is generally more Jewish. Not only in acting but also in speaking. The speech – and the smile" (Kalinov 1936).

Despite the difference between the two actors and their portrayal of the role, the visual design unified the two Shylocks. Both spurned his depiction as a pitiful East European Jew just liberated from the ghetto, appearing in traditional garb that was nonetheless clean and neat, with a trimmed beard and elegant appearance. He thus more closely resembled a court Jew on the cusp of the enlightenment – the very image of Süss – than a ghetto Jew.

The cultural associations linked with Meskin's stage presence evoked the image of the new Jew – a Golem capable of revolutionizing Jewish lives. Meskin portrayed Shylock as a gigantic man, conveying the belief that the role assigned to him in the Diaspora was far narrower than his bodily dimensions and charismatic power. Finkel, on the other hand, regarded Shylock as merely an additional role in a series of performances related to German Jewry. For him, Süss, Mannheim, and Shylock comprised a single character that evolved through three different plays. He perceived Shylock, like Süss, as "obsessed with one thing – avenging the insult against himself and his people" (Finkel 1971, 27–47).

Although his construction of Shylock as a positive figure may suggest that Jessner sought to depict the world of Venice and Belmont as dark, in fact, he chose a quite different artistic direction, invoking the Christian world through an enchanted and beautiful renaissance setting; Moshe Mokadi's set design included humanistic architecture and the Venetians wore light-colored garments.[9] The musical motif of Venice was also harmonic, reminiscent of lively Italian song – the sounds turning into a jarring cacophony only when the Jewish element entered (Rathaus 1936).

---

9 Photos from *The Merchant of Venice*, Habimah 1936, are available at the Israeli Center for the Documentation of the Performing Arts, File 221827.

The most distinctive artistic tool Jessner employed in fashioning the Christian world as a target of desire was his casting of Hanna Rovina in the role of Portia. Rovina was the company's first lady – its greatest star and icon. Her performance was immensely powerful; associations evoked by her former roles added depth to her deep voice and mysterious, ceremonial, and somewhat remote presence. Her performances as Leah in S. Anski's *The Dybbuk*, the Messiah in H. Leivik's *The Golem*, and the Messiah's mother in David Pinski's *The Eternal Jew* had already turned her into a national symbol. Her acting thus projected national meaning beyond the immediate artistic context of the roles she played (Gai 1995, 201–214; and Yerushalmi 2007). Yaacov Fichman's impression reveals the effect of her performance:

> Whose was the hand that burdened Shylock the most? It is the worthiest of his enemies. He is defeated by the one who truly obtains something of Renaissance clarity: Portia (Rovina). Rovina succeeded in realizing on stage this graceful character that is informed by the lightness of the period, the yearning for happiness and joy, but not by the cheap eagerness of the entire group. [...] It is not comfortable for a Hebrew actress to shed grace on a world where everything that is to its advantage is to our disadvantage, and her ability to overcome this must undoubtedly be seen as an artistic triumph for Habimah (Fichman 1936, 10).

Rovina's portrayal of Portia colored Belmont and Venice as the target of desire; Shylock's tragedy derived from the insult of his being excluded from this earthly paradise. The casting of Rovina as Portia also completed the consolidation of the performative formula of the German-Jewish tragedy in Habimah. Her participation in the performance marked the canonization of the Eretz-Israel performative genre that developed as a local variation of the traditional Bildung-inspired bourgeois drama and its centrality within Habimah's repertoire in 1936.

3 Conclusion

The analysis of these three anti-Nazi performances reveals the unique cultural stratification of Hebrew theater in Mandatory Palestine. The productions created events that shaped the Eretz-Israel public attitude towards Nazism and the fate of German Jewry, embodying public concern regarding the political developments in Germany and solidarity with the anti-Nazi European resistance, while also expressing the fear that German Jewish refugees might dominate the shaping of local Hebrew and Zionist culture.

Artistically, by dealing with images of German Jewry, Habimah created a Hebrew variation of the bourgeois tragedy genre, adapting it to its performative language while appropriating it into the *Zeitgeist* of the Tel Aviv of the 1930s. Thematically, the fall of the German-Jewish educated bourgeois male who sought to tear down the barriers of Jewish existence and craved for European *Bildung* reaffirmed Zionism as the only alternative for Jewish auto-emancipation. Simultaneously, the three plays rooted the craving for Europe and *Bildung* culture within Habimah's artistic vocabulary, imprinting it upon the corporality of its leading actors. They thereby helped to establish Habimah's status on the local Eretz-Israel theater scene of Tel Aviv as an elite Hebrew troupe engaged in serious art informed by both the European and German universal artistic standards of *Bildung* and Jewish and Hebrew national values.

Bibliography

Aschheim, Steven E. *Brothers and Strangers.* Madison: University of Wisconsin Press, 1982.
Aschheim, Steven E. *Culture and Catastrophe: German and Jewish Confrontations with National Socialism and Other Crises.* London: Macmillan, 1996.
Auslander, Philip. *From Acting to Performance: Essays in Modernism and Postmodernism.* London: Routledge, 1997.
Avi-Shaul, Mordechai. "Dmut hayehudi Zis" (The figure of the Jew Süss). *Bamah* 1 (1933): 19.
Avi-Shaul, Mordechai. *Hayehudi Zis: A play after Feuchtwanger.* Israeli Center for the Documentation of the Performing Arts. File 221109.
Bayerdörfer, Hans-Peter. "Shylock in Berlin: Walter Mehring und das Judenportrait im Zeitstück der Weimarer Republik." *Conditio Judaice* 3 (1993): 307–323.
Berger, Lee Michael. "Mishpato shel Shylock bepalestinah: 'Et hanevalah asher telamduni – ota e'eseh'" (Shylock's trial in Palestine: 'The villainy you teach me, I shall execute'). *Zmanim* 113 (2011): 46–57.
Bonnell, Andrew G. *Shylock in Germany: Antisemitism and the German Theater from the Enlightenment to the Nazis.* London/New York: Tauris, 2008.
Carlson, Marvin. *The Haunted Stage: The Theater as a Memory Machine.* Ann Arbor: Michigan University Press, 2001.
Carlson, Marvin. "The Theater Ici." *Performance and the Politics of Space: Theater and Topology.* Ed. Benjamin Wihstutz and Erika Fischer-Lichte. New York: Routledge, 2013. 15–30.
Citron, Itay. "Habimah's *The Golem.*" *Drama Review* 24.3 (1980): 59–68.
Emberger, Gurdrun and Rotraud Ries. "Der Fall Joseph Süß Oppenheimer: Zum historische Kern und der Wurzeln seiner Medialisierung." *Jud Süß: Hofjude, literarische Figur, antisemitische Zerrbild.* Ed. Alexandra Przyrembel and Jörg Schönert. Frankfurt on the Main: Campus, 2006.
Feinberg, Anat. "Leopold Jessner: German Theater and Jewish Identity." *Leo Baeck Institute Year Book* 48 (2003): 111–113.
Feinberg, Anat. "The Unknown Leopold Jessner: German Theater and Jewish Identity." *Jews and the Making of Modern German Theater.* Ed. Jeanette R. Malkin and Freddie Rokem. Iowa City: Iowa University Press, 2010. 232–260.

Feuchtwanger, Leon. *Hayehudi Zis* (*The Jew Süss*). Trans. Mordechai Avi-Shaul. Tel Aviv: Shtibel, 1929.

Fichman, Yaacov. "Al hateatron haklasi" (On classical theater). *Bamah* 4 (1936): 10.

Finkel, Shimon. *Bamah ukla'im: Hayei sakhkan uma'avako le'atsmauto* (Stage and curtains: The life of an actor and his struggle for independence). Tel Aviv: Am Oved, 1968.

Finkel, Shimon. *Bemevokh tafkidai: Khavayot misadnat habamah*. Tel Aviv: Mifalei Tarbut vehinukh, 1971.

Finkel, Shimon. *Aharon meskin veagadat hagolem: Perakim lezikhro* (Aharon Meskin and the legend of the Golem: Chapters in his memory). Tel Aviv: Akad, 1980.

Fischer-Lichte, Erika. "Theater as Festive Play: Max Reinhardt's Productions of 'The Merchant of Venice.'" *Jews and the Making of Modern German Theater*. Ed. Jeanette R. Malkin and Freddie Rokem. Iowa City: Iowa University Press, 2010. 219–231.

Frieling, Tuvia. "Palestinotsentriyut? David Ben-Gurion vshlilat hagolah betekufat hashoah" (Palestinocentrism? David Ben Gurion and the negation of the Diaspora during the Holocaust). *Shoah mimerkhak tavo – Ishim beyishuv haerets-yisraeli veyakhasam lanatsism velashoah 1933–1948*. Ed. Dina Porat and Aviva Halamish. Jerusalem: Yad Ben-Zvi, 2009. 372–353.

Gai, Carmit. *Hamalkhah nas'ah vaotobus: Rovina vehabimah* (The queen rode on a bus: Rovina and Habimah). Tel Aviv: Am Oved, 1995.

Gelber, Yoav. *Moledet khadashah – Aliyat yehudey merkaz europa veklitatam* (A new homeland: the immigration and integration of central European Jews). Jerusalem: Yad Ben-Zvi/Leo Baeck, 1990.

German. "*Professor Mannheim* – Rishmei leil khazarah" (*Professor Mannheim*: Notes from a rehearsal." *Bamah* 4 (1934): 37.

Goldberg, Lea. "'Hasokher mivenetsia' behabimah" (Habimah's *The Merchant of Venice*). *Davar*, 15 May 1936.

"Habimah" (Hebrew). *Kolno'a*. 14 July 1933.

"Hamishpat hasifruti 'al Shylock" (The literary trial of Shylock). *Bamah* 4 (October 1936): 23–41.

Hortman, Wilhelm. *Shakespeare on the German Stage: The Twentieth Century*. Cambridge, UK: Cambridge University Press, 1998.

Innes, Christopher. *Erwin Piscator's Political Theater: The Development of Modern German Drama*. Cambridge, UK: Cambridge University Press, 1972.

Jakobi, Carsten. *Der kleine Sieg über den Antisemitismus: Darstellung und Deutung der nationalsozialistischen Judenverfolgung im deutschspachigen Zeitstück des Exils 1933–1945*. Tübingen: Max Niemeyer, 2005.

Jessner, Leopold. "'Al hateatron haerets yisraeli vete'udato" (Eretz-Israel theater and its documentation). *Bamah* 3 (May 1936a): 3–7.

Jessner, Leopold. "Hatsagat habekhora shel 'hasokher mivenetsiyah' behabimah" (The Habimah premiere of *The Merchant of Venice*). *Haaretz* 15 May 1936b.

Kalinov, Yesha'ayahu. "Habimah – *Professor Mannheim*" (Hebrew). *Haaretz*, 27 July 1934.

Kalinov, Yesha'ayahu. "Hasokher mivenetsiyah behabimah" (Habimah's *The Merchant of Venice*). *Haaretz*, 22 May 1936.

Kenaan-Kedar, Nurith. "Deutsche Einwanderer und die bildende Kunst in der israelischen Gesellschaft." *Zweimal Heimat: Die Jeckes zwischen Mitteleuropa und Nahost*. Ed. Moshe Zimmermann and Yotam Hotam. Frankfurt on the Main: Beeren, 2005. 243–254.

Klausner, Margot. *Yoman Habimah* (Habimah Diary). Tel Aviv: Mo'adim, 1971.

Körte, Mona. "Figur ohne Original: 'Jud Süß' und 'Ewiger Jude' als Metafiguren der Geschichte bei Lion Feuchtwanger." *Jud Süß: Hofjude, literarische Figur, antisemitische Zerrbild*. Ed. Alexandra Przyrembel and Jörg Schönert. Frankfurt on the Main: Campus, 2006. 175–188.

Kuhns, David. *German Expressionist Theater: The Actor and the Stage*. Cambridge, UK: Cambridge University Press, 1997. 173–217.

Lewy, Tom. "Exilanten, Flüchtlinge, Migranten und Einwanderer: Jeckes im palästinischen Theater." *Zweimal Heimat: Die Jeckes zwischen Mitteleuropa und Nahost*. Ed. Moshe Zimmermann and Yotam Hotam. Frankfurt on the Main: Beeren, 2005. 153–163.

Lewy, Tom. "Konfliktim al mahut vetafkido shel hateatron bein 'olei merkaz-eropa vehayishuv beerets-yisrael shel shnot hasheloshim" (Conflicts over the role of the theater between central European immigrants and the yishuv in the 1930s). *Motar* (2010): 75–80.

Lidtberg, Leopold. *Eine Nachlasspräsentation*. Berlin: Akademie der Künste, 1990.

Lubrani, Eli'ezer. "*Professor Mannhein* behabimah" (*Professor Mannheim* at Habimah). *Davar*, 3 August 1934.

Magnus, Shulamith S. "Between: East and West: Pauline Wengeroff and her Cultural History of the Jews of Russia." *The German Jewish Experience Revisited*. Ed. Vivian Liska and Steven E. Aschheim. Berlin: De Gruyter, 2015.

Malkin, Dov-Beer. "Me-shikhot khug habimah leno'ar: 'Al *Professor Mannheim*" (From the conversations of the Habimah youth circle: About *Professor Mannheim*). *Bamah* 5–6 (1934): 56–60.

Nuy, Sandra and Paul Kornfeld. *Jud Süss: Studie zu einer dramaturgische Bearbeitung des 'Jud Süss'-Stoffes*. Anuf/Salzburg: Ursula Müller-Speiser, 1995. 9–34.

Postlewait, Thomas. *The Cambridge Introduction to Theatre Historiography*. Cambridge, UK: Cambridge University Press, 2009. 89–222.

Protocol of Habimah general assembly meeting, 1 February 1930. Israeli Center for the Documentation of the Performing Arts. File 244073.

Protocol of Habimah's secretariat meeting, 16 October 1929. Israeli Center for the Documentation of the Performing Arts. File 235309.

Rathaus, Karol. "'Al hamusikah leShylock" (On the music for Shylock). *Bamah* 10 (1936): 17–18.

Shapira, Anita. "Berl, haantishemiyut vehashoah" (Berl, antisemitism, and the Holocaust). *Shoah mimerkhak tavo – Ishim beyishuv haerets-yisraeli veyakhasam lanatsism velashoah 1933–1948*. Ed. Dina Porat and Aviva Halamish. Jerusalem: Yad Ben-Zvi, 2009.

Sheffi, Na'ama. "Jews, Germans and the Representation of *Jud Süss* in Literature and Film." *Jewish Culture and History* 6.2 (2003): 25–42.

Sheffi, Na'ama. "'Ulefetah sivuv begalgal hahistoriyah': *Professor Mannheim* behabimah 1934" ('And suddenly a turn in the wheel of history': Habimah's *Professor Mannheim* 1934). *Israel* 9 (2006): 25–47.

States, Bert O. "The Actor's Presence: Three Phenomenal Modes." *Acting (Re)considered: Theories and Practices*. Ed. Phillip B. Zarrilli. London: Routledge, 1995. 22–42.

Sternhell, Ziva. "Zwischen den Bergen Jerusalems und den Stränden Tel Avivs: Die deutsche Kultur und die Ausformung der israelische Kunst." *Zweimal Heimat. Die Jeckes zwischen Mitteleuropa und Nahost*. Ed. Moshe Zimmermann and Yotam Hotam. Frankfurt am Main: Beeren, 2005. 147–152.

Volkov, Shulamit. *Germans, Jews and Antisemites: Trials in Emancipation*. Cambridge, UK: Cambridge University Press, 2006.

Yerushalmi, Dorit. "Betzilah shel Hanna Rovina" (In the shadow of Hanna Rovina). *Zemanim* 99 (2007): 26–37.

Yuris, A. S. "Hayehudi Zis behatsagat habimah" (Habimah staging of the Jew Süss). *Bamah* 2 (1933): 34.

Zer-Zion, Shelly. "Shylock 'oleh leerets yisrael: Hasokher mivenetsiyah le-Shakespeare bebumuyo shel Leopold Jessner bishenat 1936" (Shylock comes to Eretz Israel: Shakespeare's *The Merchant of Venice* staged by Leopold Jessner in 1936). *Kathedra* 110 (December 2003): 73–100.

Zer-Zion, Shelly. "The Shaping of the Ostjude: Alexander Granach and Shimon Finkel in Berlin." *Jews and the Making of Modern German Theater*. Ed. Jeanette R. Malkin and Freddie Rokem. Iowa: Iowa University Press, 2010. 174–196.

Amir Eshel and Na'ama Rokem
Berlin and Jerusalem:
Toward German-Hebrew Studies

This essay provides an initial mapping of the emerging field of German-Hebrew studies. The field encompasses the study of German-Jewish culture, literature, and thought; the cultural and intellectual history of Zionism; modern Hebrew literature; and contemporary Israeli culture. It also includes the broad sphere of intercultural exchange between contemporary Germany and Israel: the extensive work of Israeli artists in Germany; the nascent Hebrew culture in Germany; the extensive translation and reception of Hebrew literature in Germany; the role Israel plays in the German literary and cultural imagination and vice versa; and the role that Germany and its past play in contemporary Israeli cultural, literary, and political discourses. We should not envision German-Hebrew studies as the small area at the intersection of all of these fields, as if charted on a Venn diagram. A mapping of German-Hebrew studies as a field in its own right reveals that it represents more than the sum of these different fields or the sum of what they have in common.

The interlinguistic conversation between the two languages dates at least as far back as Moses Mendelssohn's bilingual authorship and translation work in the late eighteenth century. Mendelssohn's famous Bible translation – its Hochdeutsch written in Hebrew characters to make it accessible to the broad Jewish readership – can be seen not only as the start of the Jews' linguistic assimilation into a German-speaking sphere but also as an embodiment of the linguistic hybrids that are created in the encounter between the two languages. Ensuing works often followed Mendelssohn's example and contained both translation and language mixture. They provide us with a fascinating prism through which to refract Jewish cultural and literary history, tying together different moments and questions in new and often unexpected ways.

Mendelssohn's successors in the Jewish Enlightenment continued throughout the nineteenth century to inhabit a cultural space deeply informed by the two languages. In German, they promoted a new "Wissenschaft des Judentum," while Hebrew-language publications such as *Hameasef* (1784–1811) were harbingers of a Hebrew Republic of Letters that would for many decades be oriented toward the German-speaking world.

In the first half of the twentieth century, German-speaking cities such as Berlin, Heidelberg, and Vienna were home – for extended or briefer periods – to some of the most important Hebrew writers of the time, including M. Y. Berdyczewsky, S. Y. Agnon, H. N. Bialik, S. Tschernichowsky, Leah Goldberg, Avraham Ben-

Yitzhak, David Vogel, and Uri-Tsvi Grinberg. Some of them, such as Micha Josef Berdyczewsky, Avraham Ben-Yitzhak (Sonne), and David Vogel, even explored the possibility of writing in German or of translating their own work into German. Others, such as Agnon and Goldberg, found interwar Germany a fertile topic for their fiction.

This situation coincided with the rise of various forms of Hebraism that preoccupied German Jews and non-Jews alike. Important examples of this cultural turn were new translations from Hebrew, following in the footsteps of Mendelssohn's famous Bible translation. The most prominent example is the translation of the Bible by Franz Rosenzweig and Martin Buber. Rosenzweig also translated medieval Hebrew poetry and Hebrew liturgy. These projects all claimed to bring a Hebrew spirit into the German language. Other authors and artists showed an interest in Biblical figures and tropes, in the figure of the "Land of the Hebrews," and even in the shape of the Hebrew letters.

Charting the lively traffic at the intersection of German and Hebrew in these early decades of the twentieth century presents a challenge. In this brief essay, we contend that there are two complementary sides to the task of writing this cultural history and chronicling its continuation through the end of the twentieth century. The first is the challenge of the archives. The untapped archives of the German-Hebrew exchange need to be located, accounted for, documented, and used productively, which has occurred only very partially until now. The second is the ethical challenge of accounting for this history without ignoring its moments of crisis but not reducing everything to them. Upon first reflection, these may seem like two very different challenges. We propose, however, that they are intertwined and that a productive engagement with German-Hebrew studies takes this link into consideration.

The radical upheaval at the heart of the twentieth century casts a difficult shadow on any talk of German-Hebrew bilingualism and eclipses the perception of a fruitful engagement of Hebrew authors with the German cultural realm. In the wake of the Holocaust, German and Hebrew may intuitively seem to inhabit mutually repellent magnetic fields. The notion that the two could cohabit a cultural space, coexist in a single mind, or even speak simultaneously within one literary text may seem hard to fathom. Nevertheless, certain linguistic and literary hybrids that mix the two languages reflect the experiences of exile, displacement, and loss. Notable examples are Paul Celan's use of Hebrew in his poems or the German language and bilingual fragments and poetic experiments that exist in the archives of authors such as Ludwig Strauss and Yehuda Amichai. Even a text that presents itself as embodying a teleology from German to Hebrew – Gershom Scholem's memoir, *From Berlin to Jerusalem* – is belied by a writing and publication history that moves back and forth between German and Hebrew, as did

Scholem's career more broadly. Scholem's memoir was published in Germany in 1977 and in English translation in 1980. Toward the end of his life, he worked on a substantially expanded version in Hebrew, which shines a different light on his early engagement with the Kabbalah; it was published after his death in 1982 (Idel 2012).

Scholem and Amichai belong to a larger group of German-speaking Israeli authors and scholars, such as Dan Pagis, Natan Zach, Elazar Benyoëtz, Ruth Almog, Aharon Appelfeld, Baruch Kurzweil, and Gershon Shaked, who played constitutive roles in the formation of the Israeli public and cultural spheres. What role, however, does the German language play in these authors' real or metaphoric archives? It would be worthwhile to study their archives, which are located in Israel and abroad, and to analyze the forms of self-translation and language mixture documented there. In addition, it is important to consider other cases such as Scholem's twice-written memoir that constitutes a public archive of movements between German and Hebrew. The relationship between the work of these Hebrew authors and that of a group of postwar authors and scholars who lived in Israel but wrote in German offers another interesting field for study. The latter include Werner Kraft, Max Brod, Ilana Shmueli, Manfred Winkler, and Shalom Ben-Horin, to name a few. The picture becomes even richer with the addition of a third category of figures belonging to both of these groups, such as Ludwig Strauss, who wrote and published in both languages, and Tuvia Rübner, who began writing and publishing in German, made a transition to Hebrew in the 1950s, and has returned to German-language writing in the past decade. These examples challenge the oft-repeated truism that after the rise of Nazism and especially after the Holocaust, the German language was silenced in Israel and the German-Hebrew dialogue came to an end.

The field of Hebrew literary studies has recently enjoyed what might be labeled an "archival turn." Scholars such as Yfaat Weiss, Shachar Pinsker, Maya Barzilai, Gideon Ticotsky, Adriana X. Jacobs, and Lilach Nethanel are gaining exciting new insights into major Hebrew authors by turning to their archives. Some of this work is limited, however, by its monolingual Hebrew orientation, specifically its disregard for German materials in the archive. For example, in her fascinating and groundbreaking book on the archive of David Vogel, Nethanel provides a powerful conceptual and theoretical framework for this archival turn. A key example for her is the different versions of the opening paragraph of Vogel's posthumously published Viennese novel, which she discovered in the archive and brought to light. Nethanel compares them and uses Vogel's revisions in order to reflect on the nature of the writing process and the traces that it leaves in the archive (Nethanel 2012). The fact that this same paragraph exists in the archive in Vogel's own German translation, however, hardly receives a mention.

This example suggests that the archives of authors from the pre-State and State periods still hold much promise, specifically for scholars who are interested in the German-Hebrew connection.

At the close of the twentieth century and the beginning of the twenty-first, the current generation of Israeli artists, musicians, performers, students, and writers has been drawn once more to German cities, primarily Berlin. Israelis travel to Berlin not only because of the vibrant cultural scene and affordable rents but also, we believe, because of a productive horizon of creativity that emerges yet again at the intersection of German and Hebrew. A number of contemporary Hebrew literary works that mix the two languages or touch on Germany, Berlin, and the German Jewish past in different ways provide glimpses of this fruitful creativity. Yoel Hoffman's novels blur the borders between Hebrew and German and document the dialect of Jewish immigrants in Mandatory Palestine and in Israel. Some authors, such as Judy Tal or Almog Behar, revisit and reinvent their German-Jewish family histories. Their writing is not simply historical fiction about German Jews, but rather an investigation of the continuing relevance of these family roots to the lives of contemporary Israelis. Others, such as A. B. Yehoshua, Haim Be'er, and Dudu Bossi, describe Israeli protagonists who travel to Germany and find different forms of freedom there. For the protagonist of Yehoshua's eponymous novel, *Molcho*, Berlin symbolizes the possibility of breaking free from his late wife; the first-person narrator in Be'er's novel *Upon a Certain Place* travels to Germany to overcome his writer's block; Dudu Bossi's Ovadia, in the novel *The Noble Savage*, is an Arab Jew who chooses to settle down in Germany and engage in cultural and political provocation there as an act of defiance against the Zionist establishment.

Benny Tsiffer, the editor of *Haaretz*'s Culture and Literature section, draws a line connecting the section's German-Jewish editorial roots, which go back to founder Salman Schocken, and his current editorial policy which, as he describes it, "continues the secret love affair with German culture, which has long since lost its original form and become an abstract fantasy" (Tsiffer 2012). Acute observers have described this love affair with German culture and the challenging ethical and political questions it raises for young Israelis. Among them are Fania Oz-Salzberger (2001), Ofri Ilany (2010) (writing for the blog "Eretz haemori"), and the authors and editors of *Spitz*, the Hebrew-language magazine in Berlin, and of *Mikan ve'eylakh* (which carries the suggestive subtitle *Hebräisch-diasporische Zeitschrift aus Berlin*, the Hebrew-diasporic journal from Berlin). Authors such as Katharina Hacker, Katja Behrens, and Maxim Biller reciprocate with a form of German Hebraism in their works or at least a fascination with Israel. One can find numerous, high-quality translations into German of Hebrew novels. Although barely acknowledged by the German academy, Hebrew literature enjoys great popularity with German audiences, often making it to the bestseller lists. Meetings and encounters between German and Hebrew authors have been a frequent occurrence, at least since the 1980s, initiated by figures such as Anat Feinberg and Efrat Gal-Ed, who are important mediators of Israeli literature and culture in Germany. In the spring of 2012 alone, the Literaturwerkstatt in Berlin hosted an event titled "Wie man Verse schmuggelt," bringing together Hebrew and German poets, and the Heinrich-Böll-Stiftung sponsored a German-Israeli literary day featuring an impressive lineup of German and Hebrew novelists (Literaturwerkstatt Berlin program description 2012; "Deutsch-israelische Literaturtage 2012" program description 2012).

Increasingly, the German-Israeli encounter is triangulated with the Israeli-Palestinian dialogue in works of literature – such as short stories by Saviyon Liebrecht and Uri Tzaig – and of popular culture – such as Ethan Fox's film *Walk on Walter*. Theater productions of plays by Yehoshua Sobol and others, which are staged regularly in Germany and Austria, raise related questions. In many cases, such as Yael Ronen's play *Third Generation*, which deals with historical trauma, the plays are actually German-Israeli co-productions. In this instance, the Tel-Aviv–based Habimah Theater and Berlin's Schaubühne acted as co-producers (Handelzats 2012).

A vast, fascinating, and thus far widely understudied area is the work of Israeli artists such as Dani Karavan in the German-speaking world. This terrain includes such towering works as Karavan's 1982–1986 "Ma'alot" next to the Heinrich-Böll-Platz and the Museum Ludwig, Cologne; the 1988–1993 "Die Straße der Menschenrechte" (The street of human rights) at the Germanisches Nationalmuseum in Nuremberg; the 1996–1999 "Garten der Erinnerung" (Garden of memory) in Duisburg; and his 2012 "Mahnmal für die von den Nationalsozialisten ermordeten Roma und Sinti" (Memorial for the Nazi-murdered Roma and Sinti).[1] Such works literally transformed the topography of major German cities. Karavan is the best known in the dynamic space of art that stretches between Germany and Israel and includes artists such as Zvika Kantor and Yoram Merose, who live and work in both Germany and Israel, and the Berlin-based Israeli video artist Omer Fast. The work of these and other Israeli artists, such as Michah Ulman, often touch on the memory of World War II and the Holocaust and attract much critical and public interest.

---

[1] Karavan's work in Cologne also generated a performance act of the acclaimed Karavan ensemble (led by his daughter, Yael), which took place on the same site 25 years after the work's completion. Event information on Karavan Ensemble homepage. http://karavanensemble.com/shows/maalot/ (last accessed 8 September 2014).

Questions of translation and reception are undoubtedly central to an investigation of the field of German-Hebrew relations, as is evident from the earlier-mentioned point of origin, a Bible translation. Translation in the other direction, from German to Hebrew, was also of fundamental importance to the project of the Haskalah. It retains an important role in ventures ranging from the literary journal *Keshet*, which published many contemporary German authors such as Thomas Bernhard and Günther Grass in the 1960s and 1970s, to the current lists of the major publishing houses in Israel, which frequently publish classical and modern German literature.

Within this field of literary exchange and translation, the Hebrew translations of German-Jewish authors, ranging from Heinrich Heine through Paul Celan to Barbara Honigmann, are often seen as a special case of domestication or repatriation of lost voices. Indeed, from 2008 to 2012, the Israel National Library fought and ultimately won a legal battle to claim the German-language archives of Max Brod – including manuscripts by Franz Kafka – as Israeli cultural patrimony. Regardless of one's assessment of the merits of this case, the striking fact that Israel claims these German-language documents as national property further demonstrates that contemporary Israel remains attuned to Germany and the German-Jewish past.

New research is bound to introduce further nuances and complexity into our briefly outlined narrative of the field of German-Hebrew studies. This investigation takes its cue from an academic environment that increasingly rejects a concept of individual languages and literary traditions as discrete and isolated entities and is replacing it with a global perspective, encompassing world literature and translation studies. More and more German departments are hiring experts on German-Turkish culture and are teaching German-Turkish bilingual texts, for example; the field of Hebrew literature has arguably advanced considerably from the time when it was studied in isolation from Yiddish or Arabic literature. This larger context does not, however, account for many of the particularities of the German-Hebrew contact zone or the German-Hebrew dialogue and the challenges of opening up this intersection for a productive scholarly conversation. The need to enhance and expand the nascent field of German-Hebrew studies is especially evident in the German-speaking world, specifically in the German academic landscape. With the telling exception of the Hochschule für Jüdische Studien (HfJS) in Heidelberg, no professorship dedicated to the study of modern Hebrew literature and culture exists in today's Germany. The Austrian and Swiss academic landscapes similarly lack this and adjacent fields of study.[2]

---

2 Recently, the Fritz Bauer Institute in Frankfurt has announced an exciting new collaboration with the Hebrew University in Jerusalem and the Van Leer Institute in Jerusalem on the topic

Not only the configuration of academic fields, scholars' training, and the organization of research programs account for the slow development of studies at this intersection, even though, of course, that is a significant part of the story, and one that merits further discussion. A deeper problem remains the impossibility of dealing with the issue without facing the Holocaust and confronting the question of its aftermath in the ethical, political, and cultural sense. In other words, the very project of telling this history as a single, continuous narrative that connects the emergence of the Hebrew Enlightenment in Germany with the current boom in German-Israeli exchanges across the abyss of the Holocaust raises serious moral and historiosophical questions. This, of course, is also why it is worthwhile.

Bibliography

"Deutsch-israelische Literaturtage 2012" program description. Heinrich-Böll-Stiftung. http://www.boell.de/bildungkultur/kulturaustausch/kulturaustausch-deutsch-israelische-literaturtage-14301.html (last accessed 30 September 2013).

Handelzats, Michael. "German-Israeli Co-production is Greater than the Sum of its Parts." *Haaretz*, 26 December 2012. http://www.haaretz.com/news/features/german-israeli-co-production-is-greater-than-the-sum-of-its-parts.premium-1.490033 (last accessed 8 September 2014).

Idel, Moshe. Foreword to Gershom Scholem, *From Berlin to Jerusalem: Memories of My Youth*. Philadelphia: Paul Dry Books, 2012. xi–xiii.

Ilany, Ofri. "Zurückbleiben Bitte." *Eretz haemori*. Blog, 16 September 2010. http://haemori.wordpress.com/2010/09/16/zuruckbleiben-bitte/ (last accessed 30 September 2013).

Literaturwerkstatt Berlin program description for "Wie man Verse schmuggelt." http://www.literaturwerkstatt.org/de/literaturwerkstatt-berlin/veranstaltungen/aktuelle-verans-taltungen/matinee-wie-man-verse-schmuggelt-777 (last accessed 30 September 2013).

Nethanel, Lilach. *David Fogel's Writing Hand: A Reflection on the Writing Process*. Ramat-Gan: Bar Ilan University Press, 2012.

Oz-Salzberger, Fania. *Israelis in Berlin*. Frankfurt on the Main: Suhrkamp, 2001.

Tsiffer, Benny. "Kmo beit-kneset sheyahleku bo kavod latarbut" (Like a synagogue where respect would be paid to culture). *Haaretz*, 14 July 2012. http://www.haaretz.co.il/literature/safrut/print/1.1774881 (last accessed 30 September 2013).

"Die deutsch-israelischen Beziehungen in den Geisteswissenschaften zwischen 1970 und 2000. Studien zu Wissenschaft und Bilateralität," which is likely to have a substantial impact on the field we are charting here.

Steven E. Aschheim and Vivian Liska
Postscript

In this collection – revisiting the German-Jewish experience – the absences are, perhaps, the most revealing aspect. There is almost no direct discussion of the Holocaust (when it appears, it does so as a historiographical rather than a historical phenomenon); there is almost no elaboration of German Jewry's great intellectual achievements, little of the usual valorization of its radical figures; and, with one or two exceptions, one rarely encounters the former emphasis on existential and political tensions. Theology, which receives sparse attention, is definitively not of the messianic or apocalyptic variety that previous discourse and earlier scholarship found so fascinating. Few declarations pronounce the Jews to be the very essence of modernism or anti-modernism or, indeed, *the* postmodernists *avant la lettre*. Moreover, contrary to fashionable transformations of Jews into metaphors, etherealized exemplifications of the "non-identitarian" and the "deterritorialized," as symbols of "textuality," most contributions stress concrete and quotidian experience and the manifold varieties of cultural sensibility that accompanied it.

In this volume, perhaps as a reaction to much in previous scholarship, neither trauma nor political radicalism receive special attention. Instead, one finds renewed respect for the German-Jewish investment in liberalism and its subtle reformulations; nuanced reflections upon the desire for, and strategies to achieve, bourgeois security; and an emphasis not only upon vaunted elitist *Bildung* but also on the Jews' significant role as entrepreneurs, performers, and consumers of popular culture. If these ruminations seem to bear a resemblance to an outdated "contribution" history, the similarity is misleading. Rather, these themes serve as ciphers, pointing out multi-faceted attempts at integration.

Earlier polarizing debates about relations between German Jews and non-Jewish Germans have given way to more nuanced and differentiated analyses. In some cases – *pace* Gershom Scholem – the traffic is now conceived as reciprocal and mutually enmeshed, not solely as a one-way street. To some degree, then, older, provocative narratives of the German-Jewish experience as one characterized by craven assimilation and self-delusion have lost much of their resonance. Assumptions regarding a pre-existing, "essential," "authentic" identity – while at times implicitly still present – may be yielding to an emerging, more fluid narrative. This approach, which emphasizes a (qualified and still often ambivalent) degree of co-constitutionality, regards both "culture" and "identity" not as fixed and static entities but as interdependent, evolving processes, allowing for gradations and more open-ended – if often coded – conceptions and expressions of Jewishness. Even discussions of *Bildung* in its traditional, quintessentially German Enlightenment meaning view it as an active, gendered, transcultural East-West interaction, or, from the viewpoint of an emerging Jewish Orthodoxy, as itself derived from traditional *Jewish* sources.

For some contributors, the freight, or heavy weight, of a singular Jewish identity, is thus somehow lightened, opening the way to a kind of self-fashioning according to the imperatives of class, outsider status, and other factors, as much as to "Jewishness" as such. This view of identity resists homogeneity and does not shy away from conflict and contradictions.

The contributions matching this description rest upon assumptions inherent in liberal discourse, facilitating and affirming a private-public split, a bifurcation of identities, and roles that ideologies such as Marxism, Orthodoxy, and all extreme, committed nationalist and totalitarian ideologies regard as conceptually unacceptable and existentially and politically suspect. To some degree, this may be a generational predilection. Yet, these approaches co-exist with other pieces in the volume that, in some way, adhere to rather "essentialist" notions of "Jewishness" or imply some still regulatively operative "authentic" Judaism. They demonstrate the ongoing analytic power and validity of these older paradigms. At this transitional moment, the field reflects unsettled epistemological and generational differences. We do not know the ultimate outcome.

If, however, we are, indeed, witnessing a dilution in the force of older grand narratives, this may bring both losses and gains. One result is a certain lack of urgency, of political relevance, and existential stocktaking, which may appear to diminish the magnitude and exceptionality of the German-Jewish experience. Arguably, the contributions may thus avoid the far more serious dangers of exemplarity, whether of the negative or the positive variety, and of "presentism" – the temptation to appropriate selectively chosen aspects of the past for present purposes, without always sufficiently facing – and struggling with – the intrinsic otherness of the past. Another potential pitfall might be the dissolution of grand conceptual and political structures and discourses such as charged contestations around "assimilation" versus "symbiosis," the grand achievements of High Culture and its famed personalities, the inevitability of demise, and warnings about the inherent and lethal nature of antisemitism, and so forth. Rather, this volume offers a plethora of topics, approaches, methods, and *Fragestellungen*. Neglected liberals, immigrant filmmakers, middlebrow and popular culture share the spotlight with Goethe and Schiller, Mendelssohn, Scholem, and Buber and propositions about the decay and doomed nature of German-Jewish existence.

Many of the present contributions represent "Jewishness" obliquely. The same applies to some of their protagonists, who may or may not have explicitly identified with Judaism or their Jewishness. Often their identity appears in coded form: as outsiders, they seek integration into the larger whole through their activities and cultural productions; yet, they remain distinctly recognizable in some way. The nature of that distinctiveness, of course, remains both elusive and highly contested. Yet – this is an apparent danger and at the same time integral to the continuing fascination of the topic – these newer, more quotidian approaches may be a form of subtle Jewish reclamation, a mode of accumulating symbolic capital, positing in a new key the centrality and importance of the German-Jewish experience and its cultural significance in all its multiplicity.

The grand narratives may be less visible on the historiographical radar, but they have far from disappeared: this volume includes some persuasive essays that in (perhaps slightly revised, updated) fashion adhere to some of their major premises. At the same time, other contributions present challenging new paradigms and methods. One striking example is the shift from focusing on *Bildung* as a major, perhaps the most critical, factor in understanding both the intellectual and upper-bourgeois German-Jewish experience to directing attention to the bearers and consumers of popular culture that in many ways constituted a challenge to *Bildung*. This emphasis now encompasses the creators, entrepreneurs, and audiences of vaudeville, films, cabaret, etc., which gave voice to previously stifled modes of ethnic expression but which also functioned as a mode of integrating into like classes. Previously neglected and unseen possibilities of mutual interaction between Jews and non-Jews now come to the fore. We should beware, however, of a certain continuing irony: whatever the differences, the emphasis on "Culture" remains a fixture not only of their historical subjects but also of the scholars who study them. The only current difference may be that the notion of "culture" becomes broader, more expansive, and analyzed in its "downward," more intimate and relaxed forms.

Another paradigmatic suggestion lies in overcoming simplistic assimilation – dissimilation and majority – minority binaries. Many contributions raise the possibility of "mutual constitutiveness," or, in perhaps slightly softer tones, of "reciprocal entanglement," while at the same time retaining tensions, conflicts, and power-hierarchies that still pertain to the German-Jewish experience, both collectively and psychically. Scholars in this field will have to maintain their guard against a tempting "victim" discourse as well as the apologetic, even celebratory mode. Balancing these tensions remains an endemic challenge to those in the field.

To some degree, many of the present contributions apply the so-called "spatial turn" to the dynamics of German-Jewish life. Although, to be sure, they cannot and do not dismiss the temporal (and thus diachronic-historical) factor, they attribute a more decisive, prominent role to place and its shaping force. Location within a particular German city, it is claimed, will influence or guide the parameters of one's civic identity and the possibilities and limits of Jewish-ness therein. Even within a specific urban environment, the tensions and links between the public and the private, the street and the home, become formative influences. These newer, localized approaches share place with essays that introduce broader spatial categories such as exile and homelessness, nomadism and diaspora into more global and familiar meta-approaches.

We notice another slight but significant shift in these pages: movement toward an Israel-centered view. Examples of this include an examination of intercultural transfer – the importation of *Bildung* and its discontents within a new theatrical culture in Palestine – and the virtual creation of a new discipline that focuses upon Hebrew-German literary, cultural, and political relations and the multiple sites of an ongoing engagement filled with tensions and affinities. On the surface, these may appear to be reconciliatory moves; in effect, they also encompass the complexities and rough edges of that encounter. Clearly, a field of this kind may well have been a taboo not too many years ago.

No matter how far removed from the catastrophe that befell German-Jewry, and regardless of the manifold changes that this volume demonstrates, to some degree, the field will remain unavoidably charged and emotionally invested. Some of these essays reflexively point to certain inherent difficulties, as well as to the complexities of the historian's viewpoint itself and the ensuing political and, indeed, existential issues. At least a few of the contributions clearly highlight questions of biography, nationality, and generational placement. A praiseworthy self-consciousness characterizes those approaches and warns us as to the dangers of disciplinary ghettoization and scholarly narcissism, of apologetic celebration or visceral condemnation, of the moral sensitivities and epistemological uncertainties regarding "ownership" of this history and the authority to pronounce upon it.

On reflection, this volume itself should be regarded as a document in transition, a point at which varying approaches and possibilities still co-exist and in which, nevertheless, a sense of alternative understandings, a certain opening up is in process. Only the future will reveal this volume's ultimate place in the scholarship and discourse to come of the German-Jewish experience.

Notes on Contributors

Steven E. Aschheim is Emeritus Professor of History at the Hebrew University of Jerusalem, where he taught cultural and intellectual history starting in 1982 and held the Vigevani Chair of European Studies. He has been a visiting scholar and professor at numerous universities in the U.S., Canada, and Europe. In 2013–2014, he was a Fellow of the Straus Institute for the Advanced Study of Law & Justice at New York University School of Law. His more recent works include: *In Times of Crisis: Essays on European Culture, Germans and Jews* (2001); *Scholem, Arendt, Klemperer: Intimate Chronicles in Turbulent Times* (2001); and *Beyond the Border: The German-Jewish Legacy Abroad* (2007). He is the editor of the conference volume *Hannah Arendt in Jerusalem* (2001). His latest book, *At the Edges of Liberalism: Junctions of European, German and Jewish History* appeared in June 2012.

Ofer Ashkenazi is Senior Lecturer in History and the director of the Koebner-Minerva Center for German History at the Hebrew University of Jerusalem. He is the author of the books *Weimar Film and Modern Jewish Identity* (2012) and *A Walk into the Night: Reason and Subjectivity in Weimar Film* (2010, Hebrew). He has published articles on various topics in modern German and Jewish history, including Weimar and East German cinema; German-Jewish athletes in exile; German humor about the Nazi past; contemporary Israeli documentary films; and the European interwar peace movement.

Amir Eshel is Edward Clark Crossett Professor of Humanistic Studies, Professor of German Studies and the director of Stanford University's Department of Comparative Literature. His research focuses on contemporary literature and culture in a global dimension, with a special interest in twentieth and twenty-first century German culture, German-Jewish history and culture, and modern Hebrew literature. He is the author of *Das Ungesagte Schreiben: Israelische Prosa und das Problem der Palästinensischen Flucht und Vertreibung* (2006) and of essays on various literary figures. A recent work is *Futurity: Contemporary Literature and the Quest for the Past* (2013). With Ulrich Baer, he published a book of collected essays, *Hannah Arendt zwischen den Disziplinen* (2014). With Yfaat Weiss, he co-edited a book of essays on Barbara Honigmann, *Kurz hinter der Wahrheit und dicht neben der Lüge: Zum Werk Barbara Honigmanns* (2013). Eshel is a recipient of fellowships from the Alexander von Humboldt and the Friedrich Ebert foundations.

Sander L. Gilman is Distinguished Professor of the Liberal Arts and Sciences and Professor of Psychiatry at Emory University. A cultural and literary historian, he is the author or editor of over eighty books. His *Illness and Image: Case Studies in the Medical Humanities* appeared in 2015; his most recent edited volume, *Judaism, Christianity, and Islam: Collaboration and Conflict in the Age of Diaspora* was published in 2014. He is the author of the pioneering study of the visual stereotyping of the mentally ill, *Seeing the Insane* (1982, reprinted in 1996 and 2014) and the standard study of *Jewish Self-Hatred* (1986). A member of the humanities and medical faculties at Cornell University for twenty-five years, he held the Goldwin Smith Professorship of Humane Studies. Prior to that, he held professorships at the University of Chicago and the University of Illinois at Chicago. He has been a visiting professor or fellow at numerous universities in North America, South Africa, The United Kingdom, Germany, Israel, China, and New Zealand.

Jens Hacke is a political scientist and historian at the Hamburg Institute for Social Research and teaches Political Theory at Hamburg University. He received his Ph.D. at Berlin's Humboldt University in 2005. Among his publications are *Philosophie der Bürgerlichkeit. Die liberalkonservative Begründung der Bundesrepublik* (2006); *Die Bundesrepublik als politische Idee. Zur Legitimationsbedürftigkeit politischer Ordnung* (2009); and numerous articles on issues in Germany intellectual history in the twentieth century. His other research interests include the history of liberalism and the political theory of democracy.

Moshe Idel is Professor Emeritus in the Department of Jewish Thought at the Hebrew University of Jerusalem, senior researcher at the Hartman Institute, and incumbent of the Matanel Chair for the Study of Kabbalah at the Sefad College, a Member of the Israel Academy of Sciences and Humanities, and currently President of the World Union of Jewish Studies. He is the author of several studies on Kabbalah and Hasidism and of *Old World, New Mirrors* (2009).

Ofri Ilany is a postdoctoral research fellow at Humboldt University, Berlin. His book, *In Search of the Hebrew People: Bible Research in the German Enlightenment (1752–1813)* will be published in the "Gesharim" series of the Leo Baeck Institute and Zalman Shazar Center for Jewish History. The book discusses the ways in which German scholars portrayed the ancient people of Israel, and describes the use of the ancient Hebrew cultural and political ideal as a model for German nation-building. Ilany is also a journalist, essayist, and literary critic. He writes for the *Haaretz* daily newspaper and founded the web magazine "Land of the Emorite" (Eretz Haemori). He is a book reviewer for the *Yedioth Aharonoth* literary supplement.

Peter Jelavich is Professor of History at Johns Hopkins University, specializing in the cultural and intellectual history of Europe since the Enlightenment, with an emphasis on Germany. His areas of interest include the interaction of elite and popular culture; the history of mass culture and the media; and the application of cultural and social theories to historical study. He is the author of *Munich and Theatrical Modernism: Politics, Playwriting, and Performance, 1890–1914* (1985); *Berlin Cabaret* (1993); and *Berlin Alexanderplatz: Radio, Film, and the Death of Weimar Culture* (2006).

Emily J. Levine is Assistant Professor of Modern European History at the University of North Carolina at Greensboro. Her research focuses on German Jews, European culture, intellectual history, and the relationships between contexts and ideas. Her first book, *Dreamland of Humanists: Warburg, Cassirer, Panofsky, and the Hamburg School* was published in December 2013 and her articles have appeared in the *Journal of Modern History* and the *Journal of the History of Ideas*. In the academic year of 2012–2013, she was an Alexander von Humboldt fellow in Berlin. Her new project deals with the transatlantic history of higher education.

Vivian Liska is Professor of German Literature and the director of the Institute of Jewish Studies at the University of Antwerp. She is also permanent Distinguished Visiting Professor at the Hebrew University of Jerusalem and a member of the visiting staff of New York University. Her academic work focuses on German literature, literary theory, German-Jewish thought, and Modernist literature and poetry after 1945. She is the editor of the book series "Perspectives on Jewish Texts and Contexts" (De Gruyter, Berlin), the *Yearbook of the Society for European-Jewish Literature* (with A. Bodenheimer), and *Arcadia. International Journal of Literary Studies* (with V. Biti). Her most important recent books are *Giorgio Agambens leerer Messianismus* (2008); *When Kafka Says We. Uncommon Communities in German-Jewish Literature* (2009); and *Fremde Gemeinschaft. Deutsch-jüdische Literatur der Moderne* (2011).

Shulamit S. Magnus is Professor of Jewish Studies and History at Oberlin College. Her works include *Jewish Emancipation in a German City: Cologne, 1798–1871*; a two-volume critical edition of Pauline Wengeroff's *Memoirs of a Grandmother*, which won the National Jewish Book Award and the Hadassah-Brandeis Institute Translation Prize, respectively; and a forthcoming biography of Wengeroff and her writing: *A Woman's Life: Pauline Wengeroff and Memoirs of a Grandmother*.

Matthias Morgenstern is Associate Professor of Jewish Studies at Tübingen University (Germany). He is editor of the series "Texte und Studien zur Deutsch-Jüdischen Orthodoxie" (Münster: Lit). His publications include *From Frankfurt to Jerusalem – Isaac Breuer and the History of the Secession Dispute in Modern Jewish Orthodoxy* (2002), *Theater und zionistischer Mythos – Eine Studie zum zeitgenössischen hebräischen Drama* (2002), and *Judentum und Gender* (2014). He is currently preparing the publication of a history of Jewish Studies at Tübingen University in the twentieth century since Adolf Schlatter (including the works of supporters of the Nazis and open antisemites like Gerhard Kittel and Karl Georg Kuhn) and a critical edition of the main writings of Isaac Breuer (1883–1946).

Till van Rahden holds the Canada Research Chair in German and European Studies at the Université de Montréal. He specializes in European history since the Enlightenment and is interested in the tension between the elusive promise of democratic equality and the recurrent presence of diversity and moral conflicts. He co-edited *Juden, Bürger, Deutsche: Zur Geschichte von Vielfalt und Differenz 1800–1933* (2001), and *Demokratie im Schatten der Gewalt: Geschichten des Privaten im deutschen Nachkrieg* (2010). Recent publications include a monograph, *Jews and other Germans: Civil Society, Religious Diversity and Urban Politics in Breslau, 1860–1925* (2008) and the essays "Fatherhood, Rechristianization, and the Quest for Democracy in Postwar West Germany," *Raising Citizens in the "Century of the Child,"* Ed. D. Schumann (2010) and "Clumsy Democrats: Moral Passions in the Federal Republic," *German History* 29 (2011): 485–504.

Na'ama Rokem is Assistant Professor of Hebrew Literature at the University of Chicago. Her publications include: *Prosaic Conditions: Heinrich Heine and the Spaces of Zionist Literature* (2013); "German–Hebrew Encounters in the Poetry and Correspondence of Yehuda Amichai and Paul Celan," *Prooftexts* (2010); and "Mit dem Wechsel der Horizonte kommt die Erweiterung des Horizonts: Mehrsprachige Erzählweisen in M.Y. Berdyczewskis *Miriam*" (in *Am Rand: Grenzen und Peripherien in der europäisch-jüdischen Literatur*, Ed. Sylvia Jaworski and Vivian Liska, 2012). She is currently writing a book about the encounter between Yehuda Amichai and Paul Celan.

Stefanie Schüler-Springorum is the director of the Center for Research on Antisemitism, Berlin. She studied history, anthropology, and political science and received her Ph.D. in 1993 from Bochum University. Recent works include *La Legión Cóndor en la Guerra Civil Española, 1936–1939* (2014) and *Geschlecht und Differenz* (2014) in a series on Perspectives in German-Jewish history. With Irmela von der Lühe and Axel Schildt, she edited *"Auch in Deutschland waren wir nicht mehr wirklich zu Hause." Jüdische Remigration nach 1945* (2008). She was co-editor with A. Schaser of *Liberalismus und Emanzipation. In- und Exklusionsprozesse im Kaiserreich und in der Weimarer Republik* (2010).

Stefan Vogt is a *Wissenschaftlicher Mitarbeiter* at the Martin Buber Chair for Jewish Thought and Philosophy at Goethe University, Frankfurt am Main. He received his Ph.D. from the Free University of Berlin and held research and teaching positions at the University of Amsterdam, at New York University, and at Ben-Gurion University of the Negev. His research interests include German-Jewish history, the history of nationalism, and the history of colonialism. He is the author of *Nationaler Sozialismus und Soziale Demokratie* (2006) and is currently completing his second book on *Zionismus und Nationalismus in Deutschland, 1890–1933*.

Bernd Witte is Professor Emeritus of German Literature at the Heinrich Heine University in Düsseldorf. From 2002 to 2006, he served as Dean of the Division of Humanities. From 2000 until 2010, he was President of the International Walter Benjamin Society. In 2007, he was elected Chair of the Board of the Freundeskreis des Goethe Museums Düsseldorf. Professor Witte has published extensively on a wide range of literary and cultural topics, ranging from Gellert and Goethe (*Goethe Handbuch*, 1996/99; *Goethe: Das Individuum der Moderne schreiben*, 2007) to Benjamin (*Walter Benjamin: An Intellectual Biography*, 1991), Kafka, Celan and Bachmann. His latest book publication is *Jüdische Tradition und literarische Moderne. Heine, Buber, Kafka, Benjamin* (2007). Currently, together with Paul Mendes-Flohr, he is editing the collected works of Martin Buber (21 vols).

Shelly Zer-Zion is a lecturer at the Theater Department of Haifa University. Her research focuses on twentieth century Hebrew theater and its interconnections with Yiddish and German theater cultures. She has published numerous articles on topics in the field. Her book *Habima in Berlin: Institutionalization of a Zionist Theatre* will appear in Hebrew, and Finkverlag will publish a German edition.